A HISTORY OF THE CITY OF CAIRO, ILLINOIS

John M. Lansden

A History of the City of CAIRO Illinois

John M. Lansden

With a Foreword by Clyde C. Walton

With Maps and Illustrations

SOUTHERN ILLINOIS UNIVERSITY PRESS
Carbondale

Printed in the United States of America

12 11 10 09 4 3 2 1

The Library of Congress has cataloged the original issue of this book as follows:

Lansden, John McMurray
A history of the city of Cairo, Illinois.
Reprint of the 1910 ed. published by R.R. Donnelley, Chicago.
Includes index
1. Cairo, Ill.—History. I. Alexander-Pulaski W. S. Bicentennial Commission. II. Alexander Co., Ill. Board of County Commissioners. III. Lansden, Robert L. IV. Title.
F549.C2L29 1976
997.3'999 75-38699

ISBN 978-0-8093-2936-6
ISBN 0-8093-2936-0
ISBN 978-0-8093-0762-3
ISBN 0-8093-0762-6

The paper used in this publication meets the minimum requirements of American National Standard for Information Sciences—Permanence of Paper for Printed Library Materials, ANSI Z39.48-1992. ∞

This new edition of
A History of the City of Cairo, Illinois
is dedicated to
Effie A. Lansden (1872-1941)
(Miss Effie)
Library Clerk, 1895-1903, Assistant Librarian, 1903-1922, and
Librarian, 1922-1941, Cairo Public Library
(A. B. Safford Memorial Library)
and
David Van der Burgh Lansden (1905-1973)
Cairo Lawyer, 1933-1973

TABLE OF CONTENTS

LIST OF ILLUSTRATIONS

FOREWORD

By Clyde C. Walton

CAIRO is as far south as you can go and still be in the state of Illinois. The city is located at the far tip of Illinois, where the Ohio River joins the Mississippi on its unending flow into the distant Gulf of Mexico. Today Cairo lives secure behind the mighty levees that protect it from ravage by the two great rivers. But it was not always so. For although Cairo exists because of the two rivers, and generally owes whatever measure of prosperity it enjoys to the rivers, it has also suffered enormously because of them. Indeed, the city has a never ending love-hate relationship with the Ohio and Mississippi rivers.

The city of Cairo is in its history as in its physical location entirely unique. Far and away the most useful and the most detailed study of that unique history is the volume written by John M. Lansden, entitled *A History of the City of Cairo, Illinois.* It was published, with many maps and illustrations, by R. R. Donnelley & Sons Company of Chicago in 1910. The book has long been out of print, and is much sought after by libraries and by collectors. It is now republished in this bicentennial year as a service to all those concerned with nineteenth-century urban development.

The author, John M. Lansden, was born in New Berlin, Sangamon County, Illinois, in 1836. He attended, first, a pioneer Illinois institution of higher education, Illinois College in Jacksonville and, next, Cumberland University in Tennessee. He moved East to continue his studies, and was graduated from the Albany Law School in New York state in 1865. He cast about for a place to begin his career, and chose Cairo because he was much impressed by its potential for a great future. He arrived in the city in 1866 and entered into the practice of law with Louis Houck, but this association ended when Houck left Cairo for an extended career in business in Cape Girardeau, Missouri, in 1869. Lansden then founded his own firm and, indeed, it survives to this day. It is the oldest law firm in Illinois in continuous service in which there has always been a principal who is also a direct male descendant of the founder.

Lansden married the daughter of David A. Smith, a prominent Illinois attorney. The couple had six children—two boys and four girls. From the marriage of his elder son, a lawyer, too, came three children: David, John, and Robert. David and John both died in 1973, but today Robert continues the family law firm in Cairo. It is Robert L. Lansden who is in large part responsible for this republication of his grandfather's *A History of the City of Cairo, Illinois.*

John M. Lansden had a lifelong interest in the history of his city. He gathered materials about Cairo history from many sources and for many years. His daughter, Miss Effie A. Lansden, served the Cairo Public Library as chief librarian for a considerable period of time. It follows that the strength of the Cairo Public Library's history collection reflects John M. Lansden's influence. Lansden read and studied many original letters, documents, ledgers, and related documents whose location is now unknown and which now must be presumed to be lost. It is in part because he unearthed so much original material and made such careful use of it that the book continues to be such a storehouse of reliable historical information. Interestingly enough, he was 74 years old when the book was published.

The author used the best sources available to him for his review of American and Illinois history which preceded the founding of Cairo. But he is at his best when he is digesting, synthesizing original documents and rare pamphlet materials, when he is reporting on events that occurred after he arrived in Cairo in 1866, and when he is writing about people he had known personally. And frequently the reader is pleasantly surprised when he comes across a sentence or two, or perhaps a paragraph, that demonstrates Lansden's considerable literary skill. For example, see how he described the significance of the isolated outpost of Kaskaskia to those French who were able to make only infrequent visits:

> It was indeed a resting place, and the society and customs, the religion and amusements, they there found were to them like a return to their own beloved France. It was civilized existence again, darkly shaded, it may be, by the aboriginal life that everywhere breathed over the face of the vast country. But to those who dwelt there, and perhaps more to the sojourners for a time, the shadow of Indian life served only to brighten by contrast the short and narrow strip of country which there skirted the great river.

It appears that he made an effort to put the best construction possible upon the maneuverings and schemes of the early promoters of the city, upon the somewhat dubious activities of the later Trustees of Cairo City Property, and, above all, upon the role played by the Illinois Central Railroad. In his discussion of early levee problems he points out how the city government and the railroad worked closely together, saying of one mayor, "He did not own the City Council, but had he owned it, the unanimity could not have been more unanimous." And later in the same chapter, apparently believing he had perhaps said more than some would approve, he added:

> To much that I have said in this chapter objection will no doubt be made; but it must be remembered that I am writing a history of Cairo, and that large parts of it relate to the Trustees and the Illinois Central Railroad Company. It was their city by birth and should have been theirs for nurture and not for exploitation. I might have written a history of Cairo and filled it full of nice things about everybody, corporations, land-trusts and all; but it would not have been history. Cairo's history is a history of facts, hard facts, most of them and most of the time.

Please note, however, that when it became possible to consider this republication of Lansden's *History of the City of Cairo, Illinois,* both because of the pressures of time and because it was clear that the book could easily stand on its own merits, it was decided to reissue the book without correcting such minor errors as it contained and without bringing it up to date. And this is what has been done, with the exceptions of a few of the more elaborate illustrations, including the large, folding map which was tipped in between pages 30-31 (it presented impossible technical problems). But at the same time, please recognize that, for example, the language used in reporting the lynching of William James (November 11, 1909) is that of the first decade of the twentieth century and should be read in that context. It seems hardly necessary to point out that a historian reviewing this disgraceful incident would use language markedly different from that used in this book and would in fact present the lynching in a modern and different perspective.

With this caveat, I join with all those who now will find it possible to own a copy of this hitherto scarce and elusive history of a unique Illinois community. Lansden's *History of the City of Cairo, Illinois* is an important, early Illinois urban history, and it is particularly appropriate that it is republished in this bicentennial year.

Northern Illinois University
23 September 1975

PREFACE

I HAVE lived in Cairo forty years and during all that time have been engaged in the practice of the profession of the law. I ought, therefore, to be fairly well acquainted with what has taken place, during that time, in and concerning the city and which was worthy of record or of a place in its history. For many years I have preserved papers and documents relating to the city, not at first with a view to writing a history thereof, but just as any one would preserve papers or documents he regarded as of more than usual interest. These have so accumulated that I have felt I could in no other way do a better service for the people of Cairo than by using them and other materials in the preparation of a history of the city. Besides this, I have not known of any one who had in contemplation the undertaking here attempted.

In the year 1864, Mr. Moses B. Harrell, then long a resident of Cairo, wrote an excellent short history of the city, and the same became the first fifty pages of a city directory of that year.

The History of Alexander, Union, and Pulaski Counties, published in 1883, twenty-seven years ago, contains three several parts relating to Cairo. These parts were written by Mr. H. C. Bradsby, who had before that time resided in Cairo many years. The book is a large one and contains many biographical sketches of citizens of Cairo. There are quite a number of copies of this history in the city I suppose; but of Mr. Harrell's history, there are now only a very few copies.

This history must necessarily contain much that is found in the other two, just as the second contains much that is found in the first; but I have found a great deal which I have deemed worthy of permanent record, which is not embraced in either of the other two books; and further, many matters merely touched upon in them I have presented much more fully.

It will be seen that the book contains much historical information about that part of our country which embraces our city, county and state—information that might have been omitted without affecting the local history; but it is believed little of it will be found so foreign to the local history as to seem wholly out of place. Local history would be very local indeed, which did not here and there show the relation of the locality to much that was outside and pertained to the country at large. Then, too, I have desired to create, in some small degree at least, a desire in the younger people of our community to know more of this part of the Valley of the Mississippi—this Illinois Country, in some respects the richest part naturally of the United States.

I have not been able to devote much time or space to biographical sketches. Ordinarily, it is quite difficult enough to choose between what ought and ought not to go into a local history like this. The book should be a history of the city and not of individuals, excepting, of course, of those persons who have been so identified with its establishment and growth that a history of it with them left out would seem very incomplete.

J. M. L.

Cairo, Illinois, September, 1910.

A History of the

City of Cairo, Illinois

HISTORY OF CAIRO

CHAPTER I

SKETCH OF THE ILLINOIS COUNTRY

THE geographical position of this place, at the junction of the two rivers, requires, it seems to me, a somewhat full account of the attention given it before any attempt was made to establish a city here, which was in the year 1818. This account may, therefore, be called the introductory chapter.

The colonial grants to Virginia of May 23, 1609, and of March 12, 1612, were for territory extending *"from sea to sea, West* and *North-west,"* or from the Atlantic to the Pacific Ocean. It was not then known how far westward it was to the Pacific coast; and the uncertainty about the western boundary of the grants afforded grounds for the territorial disputes which subsequently arose.

The French had entered the country by way of the St. Lawrence quite as early as the English had entered it further southward; and the former, pushing westward and southward, crossed these so-called sea-to-sea grants, which to them had nothing more than a mere paper existence. They, also, not long afterward, came into the country on the south and by way of the Mississippi River. Their claims to the country were based on the right of discovery and on other grounds not necessary to be noticed here. They established posts here and there in their widely extended dominions. Differences now and then arose between the authorities in Canada and those at New Orleans. Both claimed jurisdiction over the Illinois country, which embraced the whole country between the Ohio and the Mississippi rivers and west of Canada. But these jealousies of each other never interfered with their hearty co-operation against the English. All told, their numbers in the whole country were less than one-tenth that of the English; but they went everywhere and easily obtained favor with the original occupants of the country. Religion, business and amusement went hand in hand; and soon it became apparent that New France was to extend from the Gulf to the Great Lakes and thence eastward to the Alleghanies, and that the English were to have nothing west of that mountain range. Nothing shows so clearly the character and extent of the French claim as the fact that it embraced the Ohio River country and reached to the present site of Pittsburg, where they established their Fort Du Quesne.

The English, seeing their sea-to-sea grants so wholly disregarded, began to assert their supposed superior rights. They saw that should the French acquire permanent lodgment in the Valley of the Mississippi as they had in the Valley of the St. Lawrence and along the Great Lakes, they would be shut in by the Alleghanies and confined to the Atlantic coast. These territorial disputes, to which we can only make the barest reference, extended over well-nigh a century and a half. A few years of peace now and then ensued; but on the whole, a well-established state of controversy existed all the time. The two great nations were the actual claimants, and often the controversy in the new world was but the counterpart of that in the old, between the same parties. The English saw plainly that if they were not to be shut in by that coast range of mountains, they must maintain their asserted territorial lines by force of arms.

The country was not uninhabited. The Indians were everywhere. Wherever one went in the great broad land, he found himself within the bounds of some one of its innumerable tribes. The contending parties took little account of these early occupants. Each enlisted their aid against the other. In the one case, the Indian was to help the Frenchman for the Frenchman's sake; in the other, the Englishman for the Englishman's sake; but all the while, the contest was for the land and country the Indian himself claimed.

It was long a state of war, interrupted now and then by stirring events elsewhere. Canada was now and then entered, held, and abandoned by the English. Finally, in the year 1755 what proved to be the final struggle came on; and after the lapse of about seven years, the French and Indian or the French and English wars came to an end with the fall of Quebec, and the Treaty of Paris in 1763. It was a great victory. It was a great treaty. It settled the dispute which had lasted one hundred and fifty years. It cleared every cloud off the English title and made way for a consolidated empire, which never could have existed with New France between the Alleghanies and the Mississippi.

How the fates of nations are decided! Often a single battle, a single mistake in diplomacy, a single failure to grasp the great situation—these sometimes turn nations upside down and turn the current of events the world over. The new world, or our part of it, was the prize between the Anglo-Saxon and the Latin. They were both seeking to establish great colonies—seeking to reproduce themselves upon the newest and most fertile continent the earth afforded.

"Thus terminated a war which originated in an attempt on the part of the French to surround the English colonists and chain them to a narrow strip of country along the coast of the Atlantic, and ended with their giving up the whole of what was their only valuable territory in North America." "She was utterly stripped of her American possessions, little more than a hamlet being left her in lower Louisiana." (Hinton's United States.)

The Illinois country, after thus passing from France to England, was placed under the care of Captain Sterling, who was succeeded by Major Farmer, who in turn was succeeded by Colonel Reed in 1765; in which year the country was annexed to Canada. Reed was succeeded by Colonel Wilkins, whose administration was far more satisfactory than those of his predecessors.

Few persons in America and still fewer in England supposed that this victorious peace of 1763 would soon be followed by war between the victors themselves, but it was. The lapse of thirteen years witnessed the opening of our war of the Revolution, and in 1783, just twenty years after the peace of 1763, England surrendered to her thirteen colonies on the Atlantic coast, well-nigh all she had claimed and fought for during almost two hundred years. The Canadians seemed to think they wanted no more war, or they felt less friendly toward their neighbors than toward their distant rulers. Be that as it may, the peace of 1783 took the whole Illinois country out of what had been, under the French, alternately a part of Canada and a part of Louisiana.

Bare reference can only be made to the campaign of General George Rogers Clark, whom Virginia in 1778 had sent into the Illinois country, and thereby laid the foundation for the claim she subsequently asserted, that the country was hers by conquest as well as by virtue of those sea-to-sea grants. She had by her act of December 17, 1778, organized the territory and called it the County of Illinois, for which reason it has been spoken of as the mother county of all the counties in Ohio, Indiana, Illinois, Michigan, and Wisconsin. In another part of the book, giving an account of "Fort Jefferson," we give a letter of General Clark to Governor Jefferson, written September 23, 1779.

The colonies no longer fearing the French or the English, turned their attention to the question of the ownership of the Illinois country; and now arose a territorial dispute between them which constitutes one of the most interesting parts of our country's history. It is treated of and dwelt upon in so many histories and other works, that even partial enumeration of them is quite out of the question.

Here, as in many other matters of those early days, Virginia was the chief actor and claimant. By the treaty of 1763, England had surrendered all of her claims to the territory west of the Mississippi. This gave a definite western boundary to those sea-to-sea grants under which Virginia claimed. But while she was willing that her southern boundary should be a straight east-and-west line, she desired her northern boundary to run northwestward after reaching the Ohio River. This gave her nearly the whole of the Illinois country. Those colonies without territorial possessions urged that the territories should be ceded to the General Government, because, they said, they had been won and secured by the common blood and treasure of all the colonies. Virginia, following New York, but not without saying New York had nothing to cede, ceded her Illinois country. She had long held out, insisting that if she ceded the northwest territory to the General Government, the latter should guarantee to her the territory she claimed south of the Ohio River—that is, Kentucky. This desire for such a guarantee seemed to cloud somewhat her claim or title to the territory north of the river. Her session was made March 1, 1784; and this was followed by the justly celebrated ordinance of July 13, 1787. The territory was divided by the act of May 7, 1800, and the western part called Indiana Territory. The eastern part, a little later on, namely, in 1802, was admitted into the Union as the State of Ohio. The Indiana Territory was divided by the act of January 11, 1805, and the northern part called Michigan. It was again divided by the act of February 3, 1809, and the western part of it called Illinois, and the seat of government fixed *"at Kaskaskia on the Mississippi River."*

We need not trace the history of the remainder of the northwest territory, which now embraces the State of Wisconsin and that part of Minnesota east of the Mississippi River.

We have thus passed rapidly over the history of the Illinois country. From the Virginia charter of May 23, 1609, to the act of Congress, February 3, 1809, organizing Illinois territory, we have the long period of two hundred years.

The same form of territorial government provided for by the ordinance of 1787 was extended in turn to the territories of Indiana, Michigan, and Illinois by those acts of Congress of 1800, 1805, and 1809. It provided for a Governor, a Secretary of the territory, and three Judges to hold the territorial court; and when the territory was found to contain five thousand free male inhabitants, they were to have a general assembly, to consist of the Governor, the legislative council of five members, and a house of representatives of one member for each five hundred free male inhabitants. It will thus be seen that there were two forms or grades of government provided for the territory. In the first form or grade, the Governor and the three Judges were, from time to time, to adopt, publish, and report to Congress such of the laws of the original states as they deemed suited to the condition of the territory, and these laws were to continue in force, unless disapproved of by Congress, until the organization of the general assembly; and this carried the territorial government into the second grade. The five members of the legislative council were to be selected by Congress out of the ten persons nominated by the territorial house of representatives. It is worthy of notice that this celebrated ordinance prescribed certain property qualifications for the holding of offices in the territory. The Governor was required to have a freehold estate in one thousand acres of land, the Secretary of the territory, the three Judges, and the members of the legislative council, in five hundred acres, and the members of the house of representatives were to be the owners in fee of two hundred acres of land within the territory; and an elector of a representative was required to have a freehold estate in fifty acres. The act of Congress of May 20, 1812, further modified the ordinance by requiring the members of the council to be elected by the people; and for this purpose the Governor was directed to divide the territory into five districts, in each of which one member was to be chosen. Voters were required to be taxpayers, not real estate owners. The act limited the number of representatives to not less than seven nor more than twelve, until there should be six thousand free male inhabitants above the age of twenty-one years in the territory, from which time the government was to proceed according to the original ordinance.

CHAPTER II

EARLY FRENCH EXPLORERS AND MISSIONARY PRIESTS

THOUGH so often told, and now getting to be somewhat of an old story, it seems somehow naturally to fall into line with every account of places and points on the Mississippi River; and hence we beg to be allowed to refer briefly to some of the old French explorers.

M. Louis Joliet and *Father Jacques Marquette,* commissioned to accompany him, left the Mission of St. Ignace, May 17, 1673, to find the Mississippi and especially to find into what body of water it flowed. They crossed the lake and entered Green Bay, ascended Fox River, made the portage to the Wisconsin, and passing down that river reached the Mississippi June 17, 1673. Some of the incidents of this voyage on the great river were, their friendly reception by the Indians; their passage of the mouth of the Missouri, whose rushing waters filled them with wonder and some of them with fear; their pause, about July 1st, at the mouth of the Ouabache (Ohio) to reflect that the river was long and came from the country of the Iroquois; their arrival at the mouth of the Arkansas, where they became satisfied the great stream did not flow into the Gulf of California, but into the Gulf of Mexico; their return, July 17th, up the river and their passage again of the mouth of the Ohio about August 1st; and their arrival at Kaskaskia on the Illinois the latter part of that month. *Joliet* was the leader, intent on discoveries, intent on finding things; *Marquette,* the chronicler, the observer, the missionary, writing much about the Indians and their superstitions.

Father Louis Hennepin has been doubted, from time to time, by a number of writers, some of whom have found themselves in error and acknowledged the same. It would be quite out of place to enter into a controversy here and show why we should omit what he claims to have seen or discovered. We give two or three short extracts:

"The next day, being the 10th of March, 1660, we came to a river within forty leagues of the Tamaroa; near which, as the Illinois inform us, there is a nation of savages called Ouadebache. We remained until the 14th, because one of our men killed a wild cow as she was swimming over the river, whose flesh we were obliged to dry with smoke to preserve it. Being thus provided with Indian corn and flesh, we left that place the 14th, and saw nothing worth observation. The banks of the river are so muddy and so full of rushes and reeds, that we had much to do to find a place to go ashore.

"They, the Indians, called Sicacha or Chickasas, offered to go and settle themselves upon the river Ouabache to be near Fort Crevecoeur in the country of Illinois, whither they are traveling. This famous river of the Ouabache is fully as large as Meschasipi. A great many other rivers run into it. The outlet where it discharges itself into the Meschasipi is two hundred leagues from the Akansa, according to M. de La Salle's computation. The truth is, it is not so far, across the country, but it may be as much in following the course of the river Meschasipi, which winds about very much. Start over land it is not above five good days' journey. They crossed the river Ouabache August 26, 1687, and found it full sixty leagues along the river Meschasipi to the mouth of the river Illinois."

We are told to beware of *Baron de La Hontan* quite as much if not more than of Father Hennepin; but we must give the little he says about the Ohio river:—

"After we had spent two days with them, we pursued our voyage to the River *Ouabache,* taking care to watch the Crocodiles very narrowly, of which they had told us incredible Stories. The next day we enter'd the Mouth of that River, and sounded it, to try the truth of what the Savages reported of its depth. In effect, we found three Fathoms and a half of Water; but the Savages of our Company alledg'd that 'twas more swell'd than usually. They all agreed that 'twas Navigable an hundred Leagues up, and I wish'd heartily that my time had allow'd me to run up to its Source; but that being unreasonable, I sail'd up against the Stream, till we came to the River of the *Illinese,* which we made on the 9th of *April* with some difficulty, for the Wind was against us the first two days, and the Currents was very rapid."

This was in 1689. (See Thwaites' La Hontan's Voyages, Vol. 1, p 205).

Cavelier de La Salle, who, it seems in 1669, four years earlier, had gone as far southward as the Ohio River at the falls, was more interested in the story of the journey of Joliet and Marquette than any one else. It seemed strange to him that they had stopped short of the gulf, but he was thankful for it, no doubt. The deterrent effect of the stories of Indians on the lower Mississippi aroused in him few and slight fears. It was an opportunity not to be lost, an opportunity furnished by others, who should have taken it themselves.

La Salle, with Tonti and Membre, left Fort Miami, near where St. Joseph, Michigan, now stands, December 21, 1681, crossed the lake to the Chicago River, and, loading their canoes and baggage on sleds they there made, worked their way on land and frozen rivers down to a point at or below Lake Peoria, and from thence proceeded by water, and on the 6th of February, 1682, they rowed out upon the Mississippi. They were detained at the mouth of the Missouri by the floating ice until February 15th, when they proceeded on their journey. They reached the mouth of the Ohio about February 20th, the bluffs north of Memphis the 24th, and the Gulf April 9, 1682. There they erected the standards of Louis XIV and of the Church, and proclaimed the whole country of the great valley part of the dominions of the great French king.

Joutel, writing after the death of La Salle, speaks as follows of the Ohio:—

"The 19th of August (1687), we came to the mouth of the river, called Houabache, said to come from the country of the Iroquois toward New England. That is a very fine river. Its waters are extraordinary clear and the current of it gentle. Our Indians offered up to it, by way of sacrifice, some tobacco and beefstakes, which they fixed on forks and left them on the bank, to be disposed of as the river saw fit."

Father Jean François de St. Cosme, a Canadian Seminarian Priest, writing to the Bishop of Quebec, speaks of this place as follows:—

"We left Cape St. Antoine (Grand Tower) on the 14th of December (1699), and on the 15th, we halted for the night one league below the Wabache (Ohio), a large and beautiful river, which is on the left of the Mississippi and comes from towards the north, and is, they say, five hundred leagues long, and rises near the Sonontuans (Senecas). They go by this river to the Chananous (Shawnees) who traded with the English. On the 16th we started from the Wabache and nothing special befell us nor did we find anything remarkable until we reached the Acansias (Arkansas)."

Father Jacques Gravier left Michilimackinac September 8, 1700. His journey was by the Illinois and the Mississippi, and with his canoes and companions he reached the mouth of the Ohio about October 15, 1700. Here they were detained by the illness of one or two of their number until October 16th, when they resumed their voyage to the Gulf. While here Father Gravier was chiefly concerned about the illness of his companions, who seemed to have been taken with what the Father called the *tertian fever,* a fever coming on every third day, and for this severe disease he relates how he discovered a most excellent remedy. He says little about the two rivers or their junction, but like the few others who had preceded him, he looked forward anxiously to what was still to be found ahead of him. One point is reached only to arouse concern as to what is to be seen or met with further on. His account should be read, first to see his care for the Indians, who were then leaving their loved home on the Illinois for their new one on the Mississippi, where they established the second Kaskaskia, and, second, for the description of the wild game they saw and some of which they killed here and there. He speaks of the bears, and says those along the Mississippi were lean and those of and from the Ohio were fat, and that all of them seemed to be moving from the south to the north. The day they reached here they saw fifty of them, only four of which they killed—all they needed. It is interesting to read the whole account, found in Vol. LXV, Jesuit Relations, pp. 105-111. Of his remedy for the *tertian* fever, he says: "I found an excellent remedy for curing our French of their fever. A small piece of Father François Regis' hat, which one of our servants gave me, is the most infallible remedy that I know of for all kinds of fever." He speaks also of the fine weather. It was about the middle of the month of October, 1700. October is, perhaps, the finest month of our year.

Sieur Charles Juchereau de St. Denis, of France, and afterwards of Canada, obtained a concession from his government, and came hither with thirty other Frenchmen, in about the year 1702, and built a fort and a tannery here or within a few miles of the junction of the rivers. Pontchartrain had sought the establishment of a fort and post at this point. The French on the lower Mississippi claimed jurisdiction over everything adjoining that river on the east, throughout its entire length. Juchereau was, in modern phrase, a business Frenchman and prosecuted trade in this region with diligence and enterprise. The Canadian French were not friendly to his pursuits in this latitude. They wanted everything in the Illinois country made tributary to their St. Lawrence course of trade and traffic. The country here must have been swarming with buffaloes; for in the course of a year or two, Juchereau and his thirty Frenchmen had killed and skinned thirteen thousand of them and had their skins in store and ready for shipment. What a time they must have had hunting in this region! The country abounded in game of all kinds besides buffaloes. Think of the bears, the deer, the turkeys, the geese and ducks, and many other kinds of game. *Father Gravier,* in 1700, said the bears on the Mississippi were lean, but those on the Ohio were fat and well favored. Juchereau no doubt came down this far to be on the Wabash (Ohio) as well as on the Mississippi. They hunted in all three of these states, over in Ballard County (Ky.), Mississippi County (Mo.), and in our own Alexander County, and much further and in all directions. There were no game laws. No licenses were required nor descriptions of the hunters, and all seasons were hunting seasons. They were probably located on the little river north of us, and it is altogether probable they gave it the name of Cache. This name, *Cache River,* appears on an old map of 1755, but it no doubt bore that name long before it obtained a place on any one's map. The Indians did not give the river one of their names. The French named it, and if there is any truth in the statements of numerous historical writers as to Juchereau, and his fort and tannery, his buffaloes and buffalo skins, it is highly probable our little river received its name from him.

But Juchereau was not permitted to enjoy the fruits of his labors and self-imposed exile here in the wilds of North America. The Indians were here, too, as well as abundant game. They waited until Juchereau had accumulated a large stock and store of skins and furs, of every kind and description, and selecting a convenient occasion and with united forces, they made an attack upon him and his men and killed almost all of them and seized the whole of their valuable collections. Juchereau himself escaped and reached Kaskaskia, then but recently established, where it is said he died in 1705. The news of what had befallen him was carried to all parts of New France. It reached Mobile and all the southern country and much was said about expeditions to the Wabash to check, if possible, the depredations of the Indians.

In another part of the book is a list of the old maps showing a fort at this place. One rather peculiar feature of the matter is that one or two of the old maps made some years before Juchereau came here show a fort on the point between the rivers.

Father Gabriel Marest wrote from "Cascaskias, November 9," 1712, to *Father Germon* as follows:—

"About eighty leagues below, on the side of the river Illinois, that is to say, on the eastern side, (for the general course of the Mississippi is from north to south), is the mouth of again another fine river called *Ouabache*. It comes from the east-northeast and has three branches, one of which extends to the country of the Iroquois, another towards Virginia and Carolina, and the third even to the *Miamis*. It is said that silver mines have been found there. This, however, is certain, that there are in that country mines of lead and tin, and should some miners by profession come to make excavations in these lands, they might perhaps find mines of copper and other metals.

"Besides these large rivers which water the country to such an extent, there are also a great number of those which are smaller. It is on one of these rivers that our village is situated, on the eastern side, between the rivers Ouabache and Pekitanoui (Missouri). We are in the 38th degree of latitude. Large numbers of buffaloes and bears can be seen, which feed on the banks of the river *Ouabache*. The flesh of the young bears is a very delicate meat."

Father Xavier de Charlevoix's journey was from Quebec, *via* Montreal, Niagara, Erie, Detroit, Michilimackinac and Lake Michigan to St. Joseph, thence a portage to the Kankakee, thence by the Illinois and the Mississippi to Kaskaskia. Here at "Kaskasquias," October 20, 1721, he writes as follows:—

"The 10th of October, about nine in the morning, after we had gone five leagues on the Mississippi, we arrived at the mouth of the Missouri, which is north northward and south southeast. I believe this is the finest confluence in the world. The two rivers are much of the same breadth, each about a half league; but the Missouri is by far the most rapid, and seems to enter the Mississippi like a conqueror, through which it carries its white waters to the opposite shore without mixing them. Afterwards it gives its color to the Mississippi, which it never loses again, but carries it on down to the sea.

"It was about the 10th of November, at sun set, that I embarked on the little river of Kaskaskia. I had but two leagues to the Mississippi; nevertheless, I was obliged to encamp at about half way; and the next day I could make but six leagues on the river.

"The 15th, the wind changed to the north and the cold increased. We went four leagues to the south; then we found that the river turned four leagues to the north. Immediately after this reach, we passed on the left by the river Ouabache, by which one may go on up to the Iroquois when the waters are high. Its entrance into the Mississippi is a little less than a quarter of a league wide. There is no place in Louisiana more fit, in my opinion, for a settlement than this, nor where it is of more consequence to have one. All the country that is watered by the Ouabache (Ohio) and by the Ohio (Wabash) that runs into it, is very fruitful. It consists of vast meadows, well watered, where the wild buffaloes feed by thousands. Furthermore, the communication with Canada is as easy as by the river of the Illinois, and the way much shorter. A fort with a good garrison would keep the savages in awe, especially the Cherokees, who are at present the most numerous nation of this continent."

Accompanying Charlevoix's journal is a map, upon which is found a mark or X on the point between the two rivers, and the words, "A ruined old fort."

Father Vivier, in a lengthy letter of November 17, 1750, written no doubt at Kaskaskia, and to another Father of the Society of Jesus, spoke of the need of a fort at this place as follows:—

"The distance from the Akansas to the Illinois is nearly one hundred and fifty leagues; through all that extent of country there is not a single settlement. Nevertheless, to ensure us its possession, it would be well if we had a *good fort* upon the *Ouabache,* the only place where the English can enter the Mississippi."

Before getting too far along, let me note here how this immediate region of country was dealt with a century or more ago.

Illinois Land Company of 1773.—"On the 5th of July, 1773, at a public council held at the village of Kaskaskia, an association of English traders and merchants, who styled themselves, 'the Illinois Land Company,' obtained from ten chiefs of the Kaskaskia, Cahokia, and Peoria tribes, a deed for two very large tracts of land on the east side of the river Mississippi. The first tract was bounded thus: 'Beginning at the mouth of the Huron creek, called by the French the river of Mary, being about a league below the mouth of the Kaskaskia river; thence a northward of east course, in a direct line back to the Hilly Plains, eight leagues, or thereabouts, be the same more or less; thence, the same course, in a direct line to the Crabtree Plains, seventeen leagues, or thereabouts, be the same more or less; thence, the same course, in a direct line to a remarkable place, known by the name of the Big Buffalo Hoofs, seventeen leagues, or thereabouts, be the same more or less; thence, the same course, in a direct line to the Salt Lick creek, about seven leagues, be the same more or less; thence, crossing the said creek, about one league below the ancient Shawanees town, in an easterly or a little to the north of east course, in a direct line to the river Ohio, about four leagues, be the same more or less; then down the Ohio, by the several courses thereof, until it empties itself into the Mississippi, about thirty-five leagues, be the same more or less; and then up the Mississippi, by the several courses thereof to the place of beginning, thirty-three leagues, or thereabouts, be the same more or less.' The purchase of these territories was made for the Illinois Land Company, by a certain William Murray, who was then a trader in the Illinois country; and from the deed of conveyance it appears that the price which the Indians by agreement received, was two hundred and fifty blankets, two hundred and sixty strouds, three hundred and fifty shirts, one hundred and fifty pair of stroud and half thick stockings, one hundred and fifty stroud breechcloths, five hundred pounds of gunpowder, four thousand pounds of lead, one gross of knives, thirty pounds of vermillion, two thousand gunflints, two hundred pounds of brasskettles, two hundred pounds of tobacco, three dozen gilt lookingglasses, one gross gun worms, two gross awls, one gross of firesteels, sixteen dozen of gartering, ten thousand pounds of flour, five hundred bushels of Indian corn, twelve horses, twelve horned cattle, twenty bushels of salt, twenty guns, and five shillings in money. The Indian deed was attested by ten persons, and recorded, on the 2d of September, 1773, in the office of a notary public at Kaskaskia."—Dillon's History of Indiana, pages 102-104.

Soldiers' Reservation of 1787.—By an act of congress under the articles of Confederation, dated October 22, 1787, a tract of land was "reserved and set apart for the purpose of satisfying the military bounties due the late army," and the same was described as follows:

"Beginning at the mouth of the Ohio river; thence up the Mississippi to the river Au Vause (Big Muddy); thence up the same until it meets a west line from the mouth of the little Wabash; thence easterly with the said west line to the great Wabash; thence down the same to the Ohio, and thence with the Ohio to the place of beginning."

Indian Reservation of 1803.—By the Indian treaty of August 13, 1803, made by William Henry Harrison and the Kaskaskia tribe of Indians, which tribe represented the remnants of the Mitchigamias, Cahokias and Tamarois, respectively, the following described territory was set apart to the said tribes:—

"Beginning at the confluence of the Ohio and Mississippi; thence up the Ohio to the mouth of the Saline Creek, about twelve miles below the mouth of the Wabash; thence along the dividing ridge between the said creek and the Wabash until it comes to the general dividing ridge between the waters which fall into the Wabash and those which fall into the Kaskaskia river; and thence along the said ridge until it reaches the waters which fall into the Illinois river; thence in a direct course to the mouth of the Illinois river, and thence down the Mississippi to the beginning." Then follows the sixth article of the treaty, which is in the following words:— "As long as the lands which have been ceded by this treaty shall continue to be the property of the United States, the said tribe shall have the privilege of living and hunting upon them in the same manner as they have hitherto done." This treaty is an exceedingly interesting one, considered in the light of what had already taken place and what followed its conclusion, concerning the Indians.

I need scarcely say that almost all of the foregoing quotations in this chapter are from Thwaites' Jesuit Relations. I have consulted also the following named authors and have also quoted from some of them here and elsewhere:—Bancroft, Parkman, Winsor, Shea, Hinsdale, Spears, and others writing of the Valley of the Mississippi. I may here also state that I have had occasion to consult many state histories, among them Edwards, Reynolds, Ford, Breese, Davidson and Stuvé, Blancherd, Moses, Lusk, Dillon's Indiana, Collins' Kentucky, Houck's Missouri, and English's Conquest of the Northwest. Much that I have said, not of a strictly local nature, pertains to such general history of the country that citation of authors or other bibliographical reference seems almost out of place.

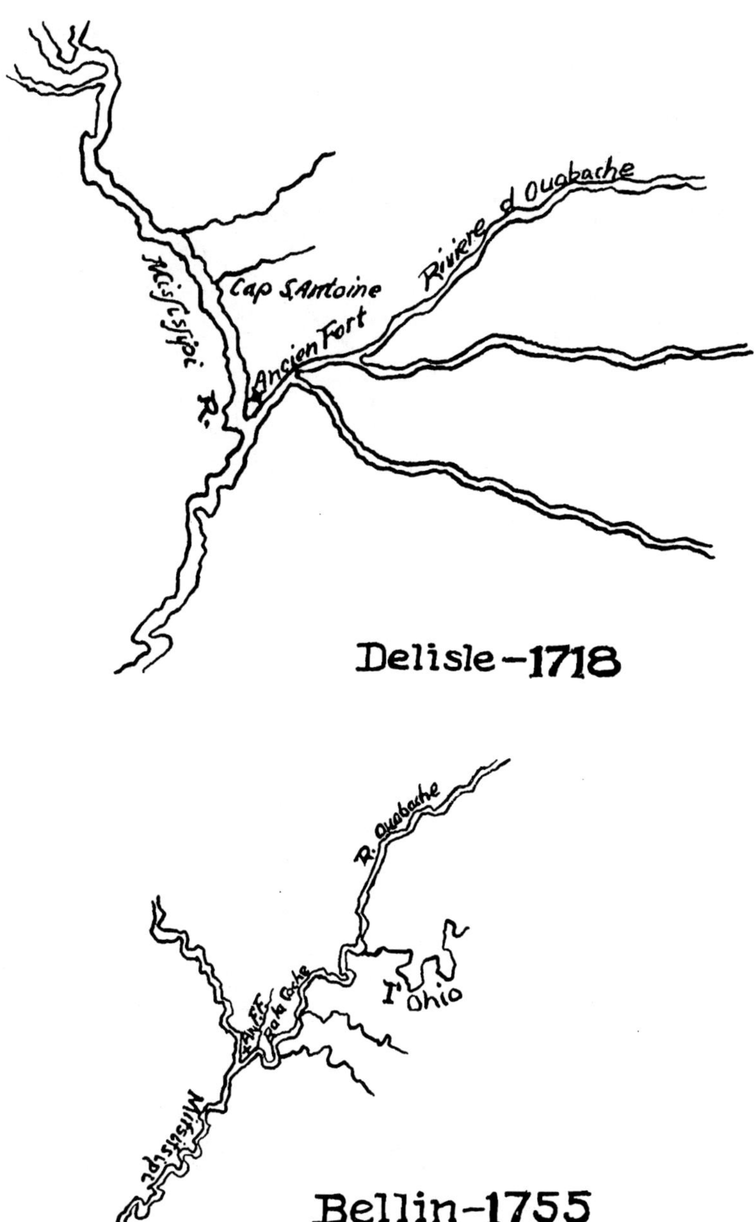

Details of Maps in Chicago Historical Library

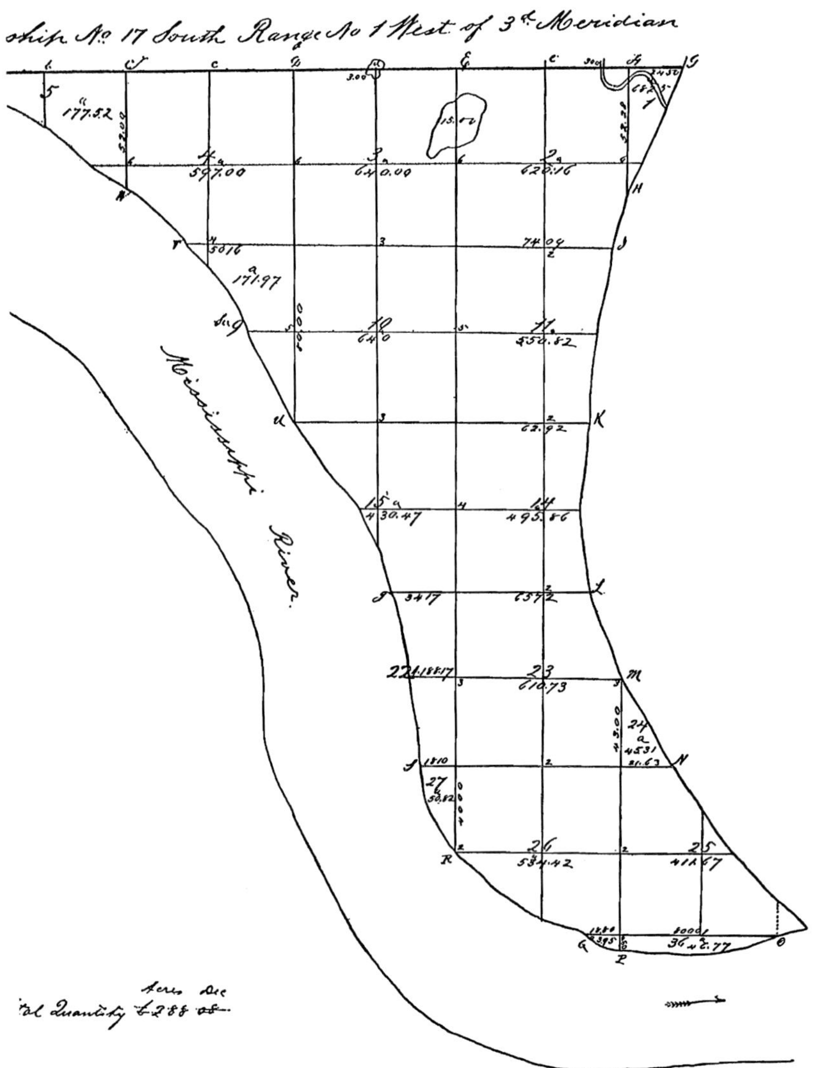

...ntract with and instruction from Jared Mansfield Esquire, Surveyor General of the United States b...
..., of 1807 I have admeasured laid out and Surveyed the above described Towns...
...it had such marks and bounds both natural and artificial as are represented on said...
...ed in the field notes made thereof and returned with this plat into the Surveyor General's Offic...

Certified this day of 1807

Anthr Henrie

First Government Survey, 1807

CHAPTER III

THE ILLINOIS TERRITORIAL GOVERNMENT

IT would be interesting to stop here and speak of the contest in and out of congress to prevent the division of the Indiana territory and the organization of the territory of Illinois, and of the public men who lost or won in the heated controversy; but space will not admit of this being done.

President Madison, March 7, 1809, appointed Nathaniel Pope, of the territory of Louisiana, the secretary of the territory; and April 24th, he appointed Ninian Edwards, of Kentucky, governor of the territory. The governor and the judges promulgated thirteen laws in 1809, twelve in 1810, and five in 1811. March 14, 1812, he ordered an election to be held the second day of April to enable the people to express their preference as to whether the government should pass from the first to the second grade; and the vote resulting in favor of the change, on the 14th of September, he ordered an election to be held October 8th, 9th and 10th, for the purpose of choosing a delegate to congress, members of the legislative council and representatives to the general assembly, of the territory. Shadrack Bond was chosen delegate to congress, Pierre Menard, Benjamin Talbot, William Biggs, Samuel Judy, and Thomas Ferguson, members of the legislative council, and George Fisher, Alexander Wilson, Philip Trammel, John Grammer, Joshua Oglesby, Jacob Short, and William Jones, members of the territorial house of representatives. Menard became president of the council and John Thomas its secretary; George Fisher became speaker of the house and William C. Greenup its clerk. The first territorial legislature or general assembly convened at Kaskaskia November 25, 1812, and continued in session thirty-two days and enacted thirty-seven laws. The salary of the Attorney General, B. M. Piatt, was $175 per annum; those of the Auditor, H. H. Maxwell, and of the Treasurer, John Thomas, were $150 each. The pay of the members of the legislature was $2.00 per day. The second session of this assembly convened November 8, 1813, and enacted thirteen laws, among them one to prevent the sale of liquor to the Indians, and another to prevent the emigration of negroes and mulattoes into the territory.

The second territorial legislature convened on the 14th of November, 1814. It made a contract with Nathaniel Pope for revising the laws of the territory. It also passed an act for the incorporation of Shawneetown, and an act authorizing the payment of $50.00 for every hostile Indian killed. On the 24th of December, it adjourned until September

4, 1815. Re-assembling, it continued in session thirty-nine days and enacted thirty-eight laws, one of which was to tax billiard tables $150 per annum; another to punish counterfeiters of bank bills by fining and whipping, and if they were unable to pay the fines, they were to be sold by the sheriff at public sale to satisfy the judgments. The third legislature sat from December 2, 1816, to January 14, 1817, and then took a recess to December 1st. It enacted twenty-eight laws at that session. One was to establish a bank at Shawneetown with a capital of $300,000. Indiana had prohibited non-resident lawyers from practicing in their courts; and in retaliation, this legislature passed an act imposing a fine of $200.00 upon any Indiana lawyer found practicing in the territory, and a fine of $500.00 against the judge who knowingly allowed the Indiana lawyer to practice in his court. At this time there was no very friendly feeling between the people of the two territories because of the contest concerning the division of the territory of Indiana. The second session convened December 1st, and enacted fifty laws, *among them the only law it ever enacted relating to Cairo,* the act to incorporate the City and Bank of Cairo. It passed both houses of the legislature and was approved by the Governor January 9, 1818. The final adjournment of the legislature took place January 12, 1818, three days after the enactment of this law concerning Cairo. The state was admitted into the Union December 3, 1818.

The map of Illinois of 1822, by H. S. Tanner, Philadelphia, found at the beginning of Chapter I, shows very well the advancement of the state at about the time of its admission into the Union.

We have thus given considerable space to our Illinois territorial government, extending from February 3, 1809, to December 3, 1818, a period of nine years and ten months. It is a meager outline, but it shows something of the general condition of what is now our part of the state, which was indeed about all there was then of it. In 1809, her population was about 11,000 and in 1818 it had increased to nearly 50,000. The territory had become the third state of the five states contemplated by the ordinance of 1787.

We cannot take leave of this subject without some suitable reference to Kaskaskia.

Cairo owes it existence chiefly to Kaskaskia men. Let me name some of them: Shadrack Bond, Elias Kent Kane, Henry S. Dodge, Michael Jones, Warren Brown, Edward Humphrys, Sidney Breese, David J. Baker, and Miles A. Gilbert. All that was done for and about Cairo, in 1817 and in 1818, was done at Kaskaskia; and the very first movement toward a second attempt to build a city here was started at Kaskaskia in 1835 and 1836, and chiefly by Breese, Baker and Gilbert. Kaskaskia was the seat of almost all of the earlier operations of the Cairo City and Canal Company, although its directors met now and then at Alton. That company's banking operations under the act of January 9, 1818, were carried on there and as late as 1839,

1840 and 1841. The Bank of Cairo, under said act, issued its notes there which recited on their face that they were issued at Kaskaskia. See two of its bank bills on another page.

But we must not say more about Kaskaskia, about which so much has been said and written. One volume could not contain it; for of and concerning it, Frenchmen, Englishmen and Americans have told their stories. Like the Indian tribe, from which it took its name, it has quite ceased to exist. The abrading waters of the great river, near to which it stood so long, cared quite as little for the Frenchmen and the Englishmen as for the Indian, and the old French post and town, standing midway between Quebec and New Orleans, is now scarcely more than a mere landmark in the center of a nation of almost one hundred millions of people. It was one of the goals of the adventurers, explorers, and missionary priests on their long and slow journeys between those distant French cities. It was indeed a resting-place, and the society and customs, the religion and amusements, they there found were to them like a return to their own beloved France. It was civilized existence again, darkly shaded, it may be, by the aboriginal life that everywhere breathed over the face of the vast country. But to those who dwelt there, and perhaps more to the sojourners for a time, the shadow of Indian life served only to brighten by contrast the short and narrow strip of country which there skirted the great river.

In the examination of our real-estate and court records here in Cairo, I have found Nathaniel Pope's name so often mentioned, that I trust it will not be regarded as entirely out of place to devote a page or two to this able man.

He was born in Louisville in 1774; resided at St. Genevieve for a while, and in the year 1808 removed to Kaskaskia; became the first secretary of the territory; was the territory's delegate in congress from 1816 to 1818; was the first United States judge in the state and held the position to the time of his death, which occurred at the home of his daughter, Mrs. Yeatman, at St. Louis, January 23, 1850. General Pope of the late Civil War was a son of the former. Judge Pope is well known as the compiler of an edition of our statutes.

We make this reference to Judge Pope chiefly to show that to him the people of the state are indebted for the extension of the state's northern boundary some sixty miles north of the southern extremity of Lake Michigan. The 5th article of the ordinance of 1787 bounded our state, or the third of the proposed states, by the Mississippi, Ohio and Wabash rivers and by a line from the Wabash to the north boundary line of the territory and made its north boundary line "an east and west line drawn through the southern bend or extremity of Lake Michigan."

When the territorial government applied for admission into the Union, Pope saw that the new state was to be shut out from the great lake, and hence he determined to do what he could to have congress extend the north boundary line of the state some distance further northward and thereby secure to the state the great commercial advantages which he was sure the lake would afford it. This desire and effort led to much controversy and engendered much bad feeling. The ordinance, like many other great instruments after it, was called a *compact* between the states and beyond the reach of congress, just as it was afterwards urged that the 6th article of the ordinance relating to slavery was a compact; but congress believed it was not bound by the lines described in the ordinance, and accordingly extended the north line of the state northward to the latitude of 42 degrees and 30 minutes, or for the distance of about 60 miles. It added about four millions and a half acres of the finest land to Illinois. Wisconsin was not a state then; but its people to this day regard that act of congress as a most flagrant breach of law and justice.

Prior to 1818, there were on the north bank of the Ohio, from the mouth of the Tennessee to the mouth of the Ohio, four or five small settlements, villages or clusters of houses, bearing the following names, Trinity, America, Caledonia, Napoleon and Wilkinsonville, and last of all Fort Massac. Trinity, America, Napoleon and Wilkinsonville have long since ceased to exist, and now few persons are living who remember anything about them. Dr. Reuben Gold Thwaites, in the year 1894, made a trip down the Ohio from Pittsburg to Cairo, described in his "On the Storied Ohio" and stopped at what was once the place or site of Wilkinsonville. It was named after General James Wilkinson, whom history connects closely with Col. Aaron Burr's scheme or supposed scheme to set up a separate government in the southwest. Dr. Thwaites took occasion to remark that he found no one in the vicinity of the old site who had ever heard of Wilkinsonville. He stopped there but a few hours, we suppose, and could have seen but a very few persons; but had he talked with many he would probably have found no one who could have told him much about the old post. Still it is somewhat remarkable; for Wilkinsonville is found in almost all of the old maps and gazetteers and in all of the Ohio River guides up to 1838 and probably later. Burr passed there in 1805, and again December 31, 1806. President Jefferson, in a message to the senate and house, January 28, 1807, informed them that Burr had passed Fort Massac December 31st with ten boats navigated by six men each. Burr and his boats and men passed this point no doubt on the first day of January, 1807. He left them somewhere down the river in the state of Mississippi and sought to escape; but he failed in this and was arrested and taken to Richmond and there tried for treason and acquitted.

General Jackson with fifteen hundred men in boats left Nashville on the 10th day of January, 1813, and reached here January 27th, where they were detained three days by ice in the Mississippi. His men were Tennesseeans and Kentuckians chiefly, and all of them riflemen by long practice as hunters. The rivers were then low. Game of all kinds abounded on the point here and in Kentucky and Missouri. Jackson always maintained excellent discipline, but he also knew very well there was such a thing as too much strictness with troops like those freedom-loving hunters of the two states mentioned; and there is no doubt but that during their three days' stay here the sharp crack of the rifle was heard everywhere over the point and across the river in Kentucky and that their camps here or over there were bountifully supplied with game.

But Indians were here also. This part of the state had been set apart to them by the Indian treaty of August 13, 1803. Most of them had gone from these parts of the country, but now and then bands of them passed through the country and often their movements were attended with the severest cruelties to the people of the settlements which lay in the line of their travels. One of their most atrocious deeds took place on the Ohio just south of Cache River, where old Trinity was soon thereafter established. It was on the 9th day of February, 1813, that ten Indians, coming along the Ohio from the Wabash country, reached the three or four families resident just south of Cache River. They represented themselves as friendly to the white settlers and were kindly received and given the food they desired. Seeing that they were stronger than the few settlers there and the latter suspecting nothing, they suddenly made an attack upon them and cruelly murdered in the most inhuman manner five or six of them. One or two of the white men escaped, and the Indians, fearing that others might soon come to the relief of the settlers, hurried away, although a very considerable number of persons assembled for their capture; but they crossed the river and escaped from their pursuers. For some little time before this and a few years afterwards such occurrences were not infrequent in the Illinois territory. One of the most notable was the Fort Dearborn massacre of August 15, 1812.

We mention these events to show something of the condition of the country just preceding the admission of the state into the Union and the commencement of the work of establishing a city here at this place.

CHAPTER IV

THE CITY OF CAIRO OF 1818

THE act of Congress of May 18, 1796, provided for the appointment of a surveyor general, and prescribed fully how surveys of the public lands should be made and for the sale thereof at not less than $2.00 an acre. This price continued until its reduction to $1.25 an acre by the act of April 24, 1820, which discontinued sales on credit. Rufus Putnam was the first surveyor general and held the office from 1797 to 1803. Jared Mansfield succeeded him and filled the position from 1803 to 1813. He was succeeded by William Rector, who held the position from 1813 to 1824. In 1807, Mansfield, in pursuance of the said act, contracted with Archie Henry, a deputy surveyor, for the survey of our township Seventeen South, Range One, West of the Third Principal Meridian, and Henry surveyed it that year and reported the acreage at 6288.08 acres or something more than one-fourth of a full township, which contains 23,040 acres. Henry also surveyed the township next north of us and the one east of that, but in the year 1810. It is interesting to look at these old surveys of one hundred years ago as they were then mapped or platted, and to see how the river boundaries now compare with the old river boundaries as then given. William Rector surveyed Township Sixteen, Range Two, West, and he also surveyed and platted those four hundred acre tracts of land on the Mississippi, known long years ago as the Flannary, McElmurry and Standlee tracts. To these tracts of land reference will be more fully made hereafter.

THE THIRD PRINCIPAL MERIDIAN.—Our system of land surveys, sometimes called the *Rectangular System,* was first authorized by an act or ordinance of congress, under the articles of the Confederation, of the date of May 20, 1785. It is not known who planned or devised the system, but the members of the committee which reported the act were Jefferson, Williamson, Howell, Gerry and Reas. The act was amended in some particulars but chiefly by the act of May 18, 1796, which prescribed fully, as above stated, how the surveys of the public lands should be made. Meridian and base lines were established in pursuance of the above acts. The first principal meridian is the dividing-line between Ohio and Indiana; the second starts at the mouth of Little Blue River in Indiana and coincides with longitude 86° 28′; the third starts at the mouth of the Ohio and coincides with longitude 89° 10′ 30″, and the fourth starts at the mouth of the Illinois River and coincides with longitude 90° 29′ 56″.

This third principal meridian may be said to start at the middle of the Mississippi River and pass northward about six or seven hundred feet east of the Halliday Hotel, leaving probably fifty to seventy-five acres of land lying east of the line and below the Halliday. It crosses the Ohio River, cutting some fifty to seventy-five acres off Kentucky near the Illinois Central railroad bridge; and again crossing the Ohio, it passess a little west of Mound City and on northward, through or near to Carbondale, Centralia, Decatur, Bloomington and Rockford, and reaches the Wisconsin line about eighty miles west of Chicago. This meridian very nearly divides equally the territorial area of the state. The base line from which the townships are numbered north and south passes across the state a few miles south of Centralia. From that line southward and adjoining the meridian on the west are seventeen townships. The seventeenth, or last one, is the one in which the City of Cairo is situated; and from that base line northward and on the same side of the meridian, are forty-six townships, the forty-sixth, or last one, having for its north line the south line of the state of Wisconsin. We thus see that there is, from Cairo to the Wisconsin line, a line of sixty-three townships, each six miles square, making the distance from the center line of the Mississippi River, Cairo's boundary on the south, to the Wisconsin line, three hundred and seventy-eight miles. This is, approximately, the actual distance.

Although this township and others were surveyed and platted so early in the last century, the Indian titles had to be extinguished before the lands could be offered for sale. Kaskaskia was made a land office by the act of March 26, 1804.

By the treaty of September 25, 1818, made by Governor Ninian Edwards and Augustus Chouteau, with the Kaskaskia tribe of Indians, and also the Peorias, which latter tribe set up claim to the territory or to an interest therein, all Indian rights and titles were relinquished in the territory above described. Among the witnesses to this treaty is the name of Reuben H. Walworth, who afterwards became the great chancellor of the State of New York. By the act of May 10, 1800, sales of public lands were to be made upon the following terms:—One-fourth within forty days, one-fourth within two years, one-fourth within three years, and one-fourth within four years, after the sale or purchase; and in default for one year after the last payment became due, the land was to be sold at public sale, and if less than what was due was bid, the lands were to *"revert to the United States."*

Before the formal and full extinguishment of the Indian titles by the treaty of September 25, 1818, namely, on the 26th and 28th days of July, 1817, John G. Comegys, of Baltimore, purchased at the land office at Kaskaskia, at which Michael Jones and Warren Brown were, respectively, the register and receiver, the *South fractional halves of Sections Fourteen and Fifteen, fractional Sections Twenty-Two, Twenty-Three and Twenty-Four, the North fractional half of Section Twenty-Five, the North half of Section Twenty-Six, and the North East frac-*

tional Quarter of Section Twenty-Seven, all in Township Seventeen South, range One West, and all amounting to Eighteen Hundred acres, "or thereabouts." Comegys made the first two payments upon his purchases, and his executors made the third payment, and for default in the making of the last payment, the lands were, no doubt, offered for sale, and for want of purchasers for the amounts due, were forfeited and reverted to the United States. These lands were afterwards, namely, in August and September, 1835, again purchased and patents issued to the purchasers thereof, who were Sidney Breese, Miles A. Gilbert and Thomas Swanwick.

Very little is now known concerning the correspondence, the conferences and other negotiations, which led up to the first attempt to establish a city here at the junction of the Ohio and Mississippi rivers. Sufficient, however, is known to authenticate fully the following account of the undertaking.

The junction of the two rivers had long been looked upon as a geographical point of very great importance. Its commercial features, great as they were, were regarded as fully equaled by the advantages it possessed for a military post or center, commanding so fully a widely extended country eastward, westward, northward and southward. This was the view taken by the early explorers, and since their time, by every traveler and writer who has spoken or written about the place. The strong and often extravagant language used may be seen by reference to some of the old circulars issued by the proprietors from time to time. It is the language of those whom we, in these modern times, call promoters; but it is the language, also, of a great many men in nowise interested, and whose language the promoters merely quoted.

But while the geographical position fully justified all that was said of it, its topographical features were largely the reverse; so much so, indeed, that the local disadvantages seemed to outweigh the advantages of the geographical position. The difficulty was obvious enough; a great central position, great rivers coming together, draining an empire in extent, but almost annually claiming dominion over the intervening land they themselves had created. It was the product or output of the rivers, and very naturally could not anywhere have an elevation above that to which the rivers themselves rose. The commingling waters could lift nothing higher than themselves; but the process had gone on for centuries, and had not the hand of man intervened, it would have gone on, no doubt, until the "made land" would have risen well nigh as high as the high-water mark of recent years, and there would have been little need of protective embankments or levees. There is no telling, of course, what the shifting Mississippi might have done with the site it had so largely created; but excepting that contingency, every overflow would have added to the elevation of the land, and in time the same would have reached the high-water line of the present annual floods. But it is quite useless to conjecture, for that great river seems now quite as hard for us to know and comprehend as it was for the

Indians, who told Joliet and Marquette of the Manitous which here and there infested its waters.

The reasons for and against occupying the site were no doubt often considered. They were so equally balanced that nothing was done. But it was not thus to go on always; for the time came when a few men reached a working belief that the advantages overbalanced the disadvantages; and hence we are now brought to the time when the work of establishing a city here was actually entered upon.

It seems to have been left to John G. Comegys, from the distant state of Maryland and of the city of Baltimore, to conclude that there was more to justify than to forbid an attempt to start a city at the confluence of the two rivers. He must have been well known in St. Louis, for we find that he was one of the witnesses to the Indian treaty made at St. Louis, in the territory of Louisiana, August 31, 1809. This treaty was signed by Peter Chouteau, and one hundred and ten chiefs and warriors of the Great and Little Osage Nation of Indians. The title of the treaty is in these words.

> Articles of treaty; made and concluded at Fort Clark, on the right bank of the Missouri, about five miles above Fire Prairie, in the territory of Louisiana, the 10th day of November, in the year of our Lord, One Thousand Eight Hundred and Eight, between Peter Choteau, Esq., agent for the Osage, and specially commissioned and instructed to enter into the same by his excellency, Meriwether Lewis, Governor, and Superintendent of Indian affairs for the territory aforesaid, in behalfl of the United States of America, of the one part, and the chiefs and warriors of the Great and Little Osage, for themselves and their nations, respectively, on the other part."

We make this quotation chiefly to show that Meriwether Lewis, of the celebrated Lewis & Clark expedition, was no doubt an acquaintance and friend of John G. Comegys. Confirmatory of this is the fact that at the sale of Comegys' personal effects by the executors of his will at Baltimore in 1819, two miniatures were sold, one that of Comegys, and the other having upon it the name "M. Lewis."

THE ACT TO INCORPORATE THE CITY AND BANK OF CAIRO.—The incorporators named in this act of the territorial legislature, of January 9, 1818, were John G. Comegys, Thomas H. Harris, Thomas F. Herbert, Charles Slade, Shadrack Bond, Michael Jones, Warren Brown, Edward Humphreys and Charles W. Hunter. Comegys was a resident of Baltimore; Bond, Jones, Brown, and Humphreys, of Kaskaskia; Hunter of St. Louis; and Harris, Herbert and Slade, of Virginia, Harris of Richmond, and Slade and Herbert of Alexandria. We give here short biographical sketches of three or four of these men, commencing with Comegys who seems to have been the leader in the first attempt to establish a city here.

John Gleaves Comegys was a native of Kent County, Maryland, across the bay from Baltimore. He was probably of German descent. The family resided near an arm of the bay into which Chester River runs, and in a region called "Quaker Neck." He was a descendant of

Cornelius Comegys, who, with his whole family and one Hans Hanson, was naturalized by a special act of the general assembly of Maryland in the year 1672, one year before Joliet and Marquette made their journey down the Mississippi and passed this point the last of June, 1673. He was probably a Quaker in early life. There is nothing in his will to show that he had ever been married. He seems to have come West very early in 1800; for he is shown to have been carrying on business in Baltimore and St. Louis some years before he applied for his Cairo charter in 1818. In a city directory of Baltimore for 1807, we find C. & J. Comegys, Merchants, No. 190 Baltimore Street; and in the directories for 1812, 1814 and 1816, we find Comegys & Falconer, Merchants, at the same number; and in the directories for 1818 and 1819 we find the same firm, Comegys & Falconer, Merchants, No. 8th St. Charles Street. In Billon's Annals of St. Louis, 1804–1821, page 112, under the heading of "Business Notices," the firm name of Falconer & Comegys is given, and it is stated that they had just received, April 19, 1809, a general assortment of merchandise. On page 116, February 22, 1810, it is stated that the firm was closing out; and on page 118, it is further noted that the firm had been dissolved and that the style of the new firm would be J. G. Comegys & Company. Mr. Falconer, of Sixth Street, in our city, now deceased, was, no doubt, of the same family of Falconers of Maryland.

The day of his death is not given, but the will bears date January 23, 1819, and was probated February 9th, following. The probate of the will was just one year and a month after the granting of the Cairo charter to him and the other incorporators, January 9, 1818.

The incorporators named in the said act of January 9, 1818, lost no time in proceeding with their undertaking; and accordingly, upon the 14th day of that month they made a trust deed conveying to Henry S. Dodge and Elias K. Kane, of Kaskaskia, the same lands precisely as those described in the said act of the 9th of January. The grantors in the deed were Michael Jones, Shadrack Bond and Achsah Bond, his wife, Warren Brown and Edward Humphreys, all of Kaskaskia, in the territory of Illinois, John G. Comegys, of Baltimore, Thomas H. Harris, of Richmond, Virginia, Thomas F. Herbert and Charles Slade, of Alexandria, Virginia, Charles W. Hunter and Martha W. Hunter, his wife, of St. Louis, in the territory of Missouri. (See book A & B, pp. 121 to 126.)

The men above named were in and by the said trust deed associated together for the purpose of laying out the City of Cairo, and by the charter were given banking privileges. The deed itself is a very lengthy one. It would require fifteen or twenty pages of this book to give it in full. It seems to have been drawn with great care and with many of the details and repetitions found in the old instruments of a hundred years ago. It conveys the lands above described which are spoken of therein as eighteen hundred acres "or thereabouts," and it recites that the Trustees accepted the trust, which required them to convey to the

President and Directors of the Bank of Cairo, provided for in the act of incorporation, so much of the said land as might be required to be divided into lots; and the said President and Directors were required to hold the land so conveyed to them in trust for the purchasers of lots. The incorporators reserved the right to survey and plat so much of the land as they deemed necessary, and the Trustees were to reconvey to them all lands not required to be conveyed to the said President and Board of Directors. An examination of the act of incorporation will show how important the banking features of the enterprise were regarded. It was, no doubt, supposed that the bank, by means of the provisions of the trust deed and other securities it might obtain, would be able to raise the necessary funds with which to construct protective embankments and otherwise improve the site of the proposed city.

Comegys and the persons associated with him, or some of them, no doubt, visited this point and became more or less familiar with its location and condition. He may have made a trip or two by steamboat from Pittsburg on his way from Baltimore to St. Louis. Steamboats had come into use on the two rivers a few years before that time. He had made many overland trips, no doubt, between Baltimore and St. Louis during the years 1805 to 1818. But whatever knowledge these men may have had of the site here, Comegys seems to have gone to Kaskaskia, or to have been there, on the 26th and 28th days of July, 1817; for on those days he made the purchase hereinbefore spoken of.

He and his associates had made these purchases as the first necessary step in their undertaking to establish a city here. Having obtained the land for a site, they seem to have lost no time in arranging to obtain legislative authority for doing what they could not well do without it. Their headquarters were Kaskaskia, the capital of the territory, and where the territorial legislature was to convene in the December of the year in which these purchases were made, the year 1817. As we have elsewhere already stated, this legislature, on the 9th day of January, 1818, enacted the first law that ever had any special reference to this place or point at the junction of the two rivers.

A reference to the prospectus of the proprietors will show that their survey and plat of the city were made as the next and very necessary step in their undertaking. It seems that a Major Duncan did this work for them. The plat or map was lithographed in Baltimore early in 1818, by Cone & Freeman. According to this plat, city lots were offered for sale, if indeed any at all were offered, as recited in the very first lines of the prospectus. The map is an interesting one, indeed. The surveyor and maker of the map no doubt saw the plat and survey made by Arthur Henry in 1807. There may have been, however, another survey by the Government authorities prior to 1818. This is spoken of in one or two places. A copy of the map introduces this chapter. It will be seen that all the streets, except Ohio and Mississippi, run at right angles and are eighty feet wide. The blocks are divided by alleys running North and South; and between Delaware and Carolina Streets is a public square lying one-half north and one-half south of

Main Street. There are four markets, each occupying a full block; No. 1, bounded by Boon, Harris, Edward and Hunter; No. 2, by Connecticut, Harris, New York and Hunter; No. 3, by Louisiana, Madison, Indiana and Jefferson, and No. 4, by Connecticut, Madison, Choteau and Jefferson. There are 290 blocks. The blocks fronting on Ohio and Mississippi Streets are not rectangular like the others, but vary in shape and size as those streets follow the river lines. Each block contains sixteen lots, except the blocks between Humphreys and North Streets, which contain twenty lots each. The lots are 66 by 120 feet. There are 4032 lots, and the numbering is from the northwest corner on the Mississippi to the southeast corner on the Ohio. The names and lengths of the streets are as follows:

East and West streets:—South, Franklin, Monroe, Madison, Jefferson, Herbert, Brown, Adams, Main, Washington, Jones, Bond, Harris, Hunter, Slade, Humphreys and North. These seventeen East and West streets, running from river to river, vary somewhat in length, the shortest being 6100 feet and the longest, the most southern, 8400 feet. It will be observed that Comegys must have supervised the making of this plat or map; for eight of the streets bear the names of his eight co-incorporators under their act of January 9, 1818, but no street is given his own name. This circumstance exhibits a trait of Comegys' character that speaks for itself.

The North and South streets are: Orleans, on the extreme southeast; next, Clay, Clark, Piatt, Howard, Wirt, Choteau, Kentucky, Virginia, Tennessee, Pennsylvania, Maryland, New York, Connecticut, Vermont, Delaware, Carolina, Georgia, Illinois, Missouri, Indiana, Louisiana, Alabama, Michigan, Edwards, Boon, Breckinridge, Pope, Ames, and Short. These thirty North and South streets vary in length from 400 to 10,150 feet. Nine of them in the central part of the town are each 10,150 feet or almost two miles. Then along the Mississippi River is Mississippi Street, along the Ohio River is Ohio Street, and they with South and North streets make one continuous street around the city of the length of seven miles.

Shadrack Bond is, of course, well known as the first Governor of the State, and little need be said of him here. He died at Kaskaskia April 12, 1832, and was there buried; but in 1881, the remains of himself and of his wife were removed to Chester, and the State there erected a monument inscribed as follows:

"In memory of Shadrack Bond,
The first Governor of the State of Illinois;
Born at Fredericktown, Maryland, November 24, A. D. 1778.
Died at his residence near Kaskaskia, April 12, A. D. 1832.
In recognition of his valuable public services,
this monument was erected by the State A. D. 1883.
Governor Bond filled many offices of trust and importance,
all with integrity and honor."

Governor Ford in his history says:—"Bond was the delegate to Congress, and while there his portrait was painted by Gilbert Stuart. It is now in the Historical Library at Chicago." The picture of Governor Bond found elsewhere is from that painting.

Shadrach Bond

E K Kane

Charles Slade was an Englishman, and came with his parents to Alexandria, Virginia. In 1816, he and his brothers, Richard and Thomas, came to Illinois and resided at or near what is now Carlyle, in Clinton County. He became a very prominent man in the politics of the State, and at the election for congressman in August, 1832, was the successful candidate. The opposing candidates were Governor Edwards, Sidney Breese, Charles Dunn, and Henry L. Webb. He took his seat in Congress in December, 1833, and upon its adjournment in March, 1834, after spending some months in the East, started home, but was taken ill of cholera, and died near Vincennes July 11, 1834. These few facts are taken from an excellent biographical sketch by Dr. John F. Snyder, of the Illinois State Historical Society. See pages 207 to 210, Publication No. 8, 1903, of the said Society.

Michael Jones and *Shadrack Bond* were, respectively, the Register and Receiver at the Land Office at Kaskaskia, which was established by the act of Congress of March 26, 1804. Jones and E. Backus, the latter of whom was the Receiver there at an early date, passed upon the claims to lands and reported them for confirmation under the act of March 3, 1791. They investigated and reported favorably the claims of the Flannarys, the McElmurrays, and of Standlee to those tracts of land lying on the Mississippi River just below Sante Fe. The surveys are numbered 525, 526, 527, 528, 529, and 684 and the claims 529, 530, 531, 680, 681, and 2564. William Rector made the surveys and this is noted on the government plat of Township Sixteen, South, Three West of the Third Principal Meridian, made in 1810. Jones was adjutant of the Randolph County regiment in the war of 1812, and a member from Gallatin County of the Constitutional Convention that framed our constitution of 1818. He was a member also of the first State Legislature and, it seems, received a vote or two for United States senator.

Warren Brown was also a Federal officer of Kaskaskia and a portion of the time the Receiver of Public Moneys there. The will of John G. Comegys recites the payment by Comegys to Brown, as Receiver of Public Moneys, upon his purchases of July 26 and 28, 1817. Edward Humphreys is spoken of by Governor Reynolds as a man of fine education and an excellent teacher. Charles W. Hunter was a resident of St. Louis. He seems to have dealt extensively in lands in southern Illinois, and our records at the court-house, both before and after 1820, show many conveyances to and from him. Of the other two incorporators, Thomas H. Harris and Thomas F. Herbert, we know very little. They and Slade had resided in Virginia.

Elias Kent Kane, one of the two trustees in the trust deed of January 14, 1818, was a native of New York and a graduate of Yale College. From New York he went first to Carthage, Smith County, Tennessee, in 1813, and in the following year he removed to Kaskaskia. He was a member of the convention which framed our constitution of 1818. He is spoken of as the controlling spirit of that body, and it is said that many of its most important provisions and in general, the whole type and character of the instrument were due to him. He was our first Secretary of State, and was appointed by Governor Bond. He was for a time editor and publisher of the Republican Advocate at Kaskaskia. He was twice chosen United States senator and was a member of the senate at the time of the death of our other senator, John McLean, of Shawneetown; and in the congressional debates for the year 1829 will be found his short but very appropriate address upon the death of his colleague, which occurred October 14, 1829. Kane died while senator and at Washington, December 11, 1835. Quite a full biographical sketch of him by Col. George W. Smith, of Chicago, is found in the Report of the Illinois State Bar Association for 1895. Many notices of him are also to be found in the publications of the Illinois State Historical Society.

Henry S. Dodge, the other trustee or commissioner in the said deed of trust of January 14, 1818, was also a lawyer, and a resident of Kaskaskia and a prominent public man. He was the father of Mrs. Helen K. Dodge Edwards, who was born at Kaskaskia in the year 1819, and who died on the 18th day of March, 1909, in her ninetieth year, at Springfield. She was the widow of Judge Benjamin S. Edwards, a son of Governor Ninian Edwards, who was long one of the most prominent men of Springfield and of the central part of Illinois.

CHAPTER V

CAIRO'S SITE AND PLACE FROM 1818 TO 1836

NOW taking leave of the City of Cairo of 1818, let us note some of the important events which took place in the state during this period, from 1818 to 1836.

During that time the administrations of Governors Bond, Coles, Edwards, and Reynolds, and two years of Governor Duncan's term, had passed. The population of the state had increased from 55,211, in 1820, to about 325,000, in 1836. Alexander County was the first new county created by the legislature. It was established by the act of March 4, 1819. Fifty other counties were established during the period above mentioned. The county seat was, by the act of January 18, 1833, removed from America, on the Ohio River, to Unity. The population of the county in 1820 was 626 and in 1830 it was 1390. The attempt to make Illinois a slave state was made in the year 1826, under the administration of Governor Coles. A number of the men who had been interested in the first Cairo enterprise were very prominent in that celebrated contest. Some of them were on the one side and some of them on the other. During this period the Black Hawk War took place. The congressional grant to aid in the construction of the Illinois and Michigan Canal was made March 2, 1827, and on March 2, 1833, the state was authorized to substitute a railroad for the canal. At the end of this period, the state was worrying along with this canal enterprise. No railroads were built or undertaken. The first railroad company, the Chicago and Vincennes, was incorporated January 17, 1835; the second, the Jacksonville and Meredosia, February 5, 1835; and the third, the Belleville and Mississippi, December 28, 1835. Fifteen were incorporated in January, 1836. They were the Alton and Shawneetown, the Alton, Wabash and Erie, the Central Branch Wabash, the Galena and Chicago Union, the Illinois Central, the Mississippi, Springfield and Carrollton, the Mt. Carmel and Alton, the Pekin and Tremont, the Pekin, Bloomington and Wabash, the Rushville, the Shawneetown and Alton, the Wabash and Mississippi, the Wabash and Mississippi Union, the Warsaw, Peoria and Wabash, and the Waverly and Grand Prairie.

Contrary to what has often been claimed, Comegys and his associates never thought of an Illinois Central Railroad nor of any railroad at all. When they procured their charter January 9, 1818, there was not a railroad anywhere in the United States nor a charter for one. If there was one in England at that time, it would not there nor here be called a railroad now. They had tram roads there then, but it was not until 1825 that a locomotive engine was used to draw cars on a railway track; and it was four or five years later that the first railroad, a short one, was put in operation in this country.

This period of eighteen years, so far as it relates to Cairo, is not a blank entirely, but it is so nearly one that little need be said of it. So little had been done under the Comegys charter of January 9, 1818, and the enterprise seemed so wholly abandoned, that public attention was withdrawn from the place as seemingly unworthy of further notice or attention. The great rivers came more and more into use, and the keelboats and flatboats were in a large degree superseded by steam vessels almost everywhere on the rivers; but as to Cairo, or what had been planned to be Cairo, it was a mere wood-yard, at which the steamboats would land to take on wood for their furnace fires, and then proceed on their journeys up or down the rivers. Besides these, there were trading boats, which, while trading very little at the point, found it a convenient place to stop for a time; for while there was no town here, or anything resembling one, the point was a central one, a kind of half-way house, at which one would tarry a while before starting out on a long river journey northward, eastward, or southward. As Major Long and his party, on their way to the Rocky Mountains in 1819, observed, the grandeur of the place fell short of what one would suppose or expect from the conjunction of two such mighty rivers, draining so much of the world's surface; but while, as they said, there was no high elevation from which one could view the approaching and uniting rivers, there was yet that strange but well-known feeling arising at the sight of the giant-like streams coming together and uniting their forces to march onward to the sea. It was the mouth of the Ohio River, an expression in daily use since the time of Joliet and Marquette. It was a great landmark, measuring off almost all river distances in one of the world's greatest valleys.

The failure of Cairo encouraged the people of Trinity and America to think they might profit by the supposed proof that no city could be built at the point. Especially was this the conclusion at America, which at once set up the claim that it was the head of navigation for the two great rivers. We speak of this somewhat fully in the chapter on Alexander County, and therefore merely mention it here. Settlements multiplied everywhere and grew larger and stronger. All fear of the Indians had passed away; but the remembrance of them long remained with the old settlers, who took real pleasure in recounting the trying and perilous times of the earlier days they remembered so well. In many cases, it had been burned into their memories, and it was a kind of relief to have occasion to tell about it. There was little to read. The mails were like angels' visits, and neighbors were few and widely separated. The Indian was therefore made the subject of conversation to pass away the long winter evenings; and in this way many traditions had their origins. They are almost all gone now. The children's children of the first narrators have all gone their way, and those of the later generations have had so much to learn and know that there remain to us now only the pages of history.

CHAPTER VI

THE CITY OF CAIRO FROM 1836 TO 1846—THE ILLINOIS CENTRAL RAILROAD COMPANY OF 1836—THE ILLINOIS EXPORTING COMPANY—THE CAIRO CITY AND CANAL COMPANY

MANY years ago I was in the office of Judge Thomas Hileman, of Jonesboro, Illinois, for whom I had charge of important litigation, to which he was a party. I was looking over the books in his office and saw a small volume which had the signature of H. W. Billings on the first blank page and the signature of D. B. Holbrook on the next page. Judge Hileman had found the book in the court-house yard, where it had been dumped with a barrel of old papers and documents. The book had probably last belonged to Mr. Cyrus G. Simons, a prominent lawyer of Jonesboro many years ago, who had also practiced law in Alexander County in the years 1840 to 1850, and represented Union county in the legislature. The book contained twenty-five separate documents or papers, all relating to Cairo. They were twenty-five small pamphlets, of various sizes, bound together. Some of them were printed by James Narine, No. 11 Wall Street, New York City, in the year 1837. Its table of contents is as follows:

DOCUMENTS PRINTED RELATING TO THE CITY OF CAIRO

19. Internal Improvement Law of the State of Illinois.
20. Map exhibiting the Rail Roads and Canals in Illinois.
21. Charter of the City and Bank of Cairo, incorporated 1818.
22. Prospectus of the City of Cairo, published by the proprietors, A. D. 1818.
23. Charter of the Illinois Central Rail Road Company.
24. Release by the Central Road Company to the State of Illinois.
25. Plat of the "City of Cairo," as laid off by the Prospectus, A. D. 1818.

As remarked about the City of Cairo of 1818, we know very little about the conferences, correspondence and other negotiations which lead up to the second attempt to establish a city here. The first attempt seems to have ended with the death of Comegys. The lands he and his associates had undertaken to purchase from the government and for which they failed to pay in full, had been forfeited, as provided by the act under which the purchases were made, and these being now gone or lost, the enterprise was wholly abandoned.

It was not until the year 1835, that the same lands again, and many others in the township, were entered and paid for as the law then required. These entries were for the same purpose as that which lead to the entries in 1817.

Following these entries, came, first of all, the incorporation of the first Illinois Central Railroad Company, January 16, 1836. Two days afterward, the legislature incorporated the Illinois Exporting Company, whose general place of business was at Alton *or elsewhere in the State as might be agreed upon.* The incorporators were James S. Lane, Thomas G. Hawley, Anthony Olney, John M. Krum, and D. B. Holbrook.

By reference to the first of these two acts, it will be seen that the railroad provided for was to "commence at or near the mouth of the Ohio river and run thence North to a point on the Illinois river at or near the terminus of the Illinois and Michigan Canal." Following the incorporation of the railroad company and the Exporting Company, came the incorporation of the Cairo City and Canal Company, March 4, 1837, the incorporators of which were Darius B. Holbrook, Miles A. Gilbert, John S. Hacker, Alexander M. Jenkins, Anthony Olney, and William M. Walker.—This company had a short but a very active career. The purchasers of those lands and the incorporators of this Company saw clearly how the establishment of their proposed city depended upon a railroad connection with the great upper country of the state; and, had it not been for outside interference, their undertaking might have fared very much better. But the spirit of enterprise that was in them was also in many other persons in the state whose actions they could not control and who thought the times required the state to enter upon a system of railroad construction worthy of its extent and the richness of its soil. One railroad from the mouth of the Ohio River to the end of the proposed canal on the Illinois River was a very small part of what it was thought the state needed; and accordingly on the 27th day of February, 1837, the legislature passed the celebrated act entitled, "An Act to Establish a General System of Internal Improvements."

To show how small an enterprise was that of the Central Railroad and the Cairo City and Canal Company, compared with that undertaken by the state, one has but to read the eighteenth section of the last-named act. It provided for the construction of eight different railroads and for the improvement of five of the rivers of the state, and for the establishment of a public mail route from Vincennes to St. Louis; and for these purposes, appropriations amounting to ten millions two hundred thousand dollars were made, a very large sum for those early days. The two hundred thousand dollar appropriation was for the benefit of counties through which none of the railroads were to pass, the same to be expended in the improvement of public roads therein. The seventh clause of the section is in these words: "The Board of Commissioners of Public Work, provided for by this act, is required to adopt measures to commence, construct and complete, within a reasonable time, a railroad from the City of Cairo, at or near the confluence of the Ohio and Mississippi rivers, to some point at or near the southern terminus of the Illinois and Michigan canal, *via* Vandalia, Shelbyville, Decatur and Bloomington, and from thence *via* Savannah to Galena; and for the construction and completion of the said railroad and appendages, the sum of three millions and five hundred thousand dollars is hereby appropriated."

The situation the passage of this act produced was very embarrassing to the Cairo enterprise and its Central Railroad. The news of its introduction into the legislature must have produced in the minds of those Cairo people a state of feeling little short of consternation. They had their acts of incorporation and could well say that the act for their railroad was a contract which the state could not annul; and, no doubt, they made this claim and argument with great earnestness. But the whole state was not to be thwarted by the comparatively small part of it down here, and the Cairo people were soon brought to terms; but it was with promises that they should have a railroad from Cairo and about on the same line as that called for by their own charter of January 16, 1836; but it was not to be their railroad, but the state's alone. On the 27th day of June, 1837, Alexander M. Jenkins, David J. Baker, D. B. Holbrook and Pierre Menard, as directors of the railroad company and in its behalf, *released* to the state their rights and privileges under said last-named act, but on the condition of the *restoration* of their rights, should the state repeal the act of February 27, 1837.

The operations of the Cairo City and Canal Company, at Cairo, and the work of the state in and about the construction of its internal improvements and especially of its central railroad, are so connected together that it is not easy to give them separate treatment, and they will hereafter be spoken of as occasion seems to require.

This period of ten years witnessed not only another attempt at establishing a city, but it was characterized by such energy and management as gave promise of great and most favorable results. The long slumber of eighteen years was followed by activities which clearly indicated that sleep and dreaming were to disappear, and give place to hard but hopeful work, conducted by men of ability and enterprise and supplied with means adequate to the great undertaking. The men and means were thought to be all that the situation required, and hence the hopes of all who were in anywise interested rose as correspondingly high as they had sunken low before.

Darius Blake Holbrook, of New York, whom we may call the successor of John G. Comegys, of Baltimore, was the man in charge and what was done and probably what was not done may be traced with a fair degree of safety and justice to him. He has been criticised much and severely, but quite unjustly, at least in some important respects. He seems to have had what may be called a local or home policy and a foreign policy as well, the former of which does not seem to have always been such as the real interests of the enterprise required. But, inasmuch as I have elsewhere given a short biographical sketch of this Cairo man of affairs, I will now proceed to relate what he did and caused to be done here at Cairo during this period.

The building of the city and of the Central Railroad was intended to be largely one and the same enterprise; but the act of February 27, 1837, in relation to internal improvements, severed the two completely, and thereafter the city and the road had to proceed as separate and wholly independent undertakings. The road, or its construction, was transferred to the state, whose interest in the city was more or less remote, whereas, before, it was in the hands of men and a company whose chief interest was perhaps in the establishment and growth of the city. In proof of this difference in interest, we may here state that in January, 1839, while work on the road was going forward between Cairo and Jonesboro and on many other parts of the line, a strong effort was made in the legislature to change the line of the road from Vandalia southward through Salem, Mt. Vernon, Frankfort, Benton and Vienna, to a point on the Ohio River near Grand Chain. The citizens of these towns had petitioned the legislature concerning the matter, and committees were appointed to investigate and report, and January 28, 1839, there were two reports in the senate, a majority report in favor of the change, and a minority report against the change; and on January 31, 1839, a strong report was presented in the House by Mr. Smith, of Wabash, insisting on the retention of the line on which the work was going forward. The reading of these reports will show what an important matter this became. Those persons favoring the new line urged strongly that the site here was most undesirable, and especially did they dwell upon the encroachments of the Mississippi River on the western side of the town. They cited what the chief engineer of the railroad, Mr. Jonathan Freeman, had written about the matter in his letter to Kinney and Willard of December 24, 1838. Had the change been made, and it seemed very probable for a time, the subsequent acts of the legislature incorporating the second and third railroad companies would have likely required the same line to be followed. It was this well-grounded fear on the part of Holbrook and those acting with him

Part of Township 17
which includes the
City Plat of
CAIRO
as Surveyed by James Thompson
1837
See the "Prospectus" of the
Cairo City & Canal Compy.
1838
True Meridian.
Variation 7° East.
MISSISSIPPI RIVER
OHIO RIVER
Sec.15
Sec.14
Sec.22
Sec.23
Sec.24
Sec.27
Sec.26
Sec.25
Sec.36
Sand Bar
The open figures shew the high water mark at the place they stand.
The black figures shew the height of the land above high water &c.

I the Subscriber have read & considered
the Deed of Trust of the Date of the fifteenth Day of
December one thousand eight hundred & thirty seven
between the Cairo City & Canal Company & the
New York Life Insurance & Trust Company, & to
which the Illinois Exporting Company has also
become a Party; & I have also read & considered the Charters of those Companies respectively
& I am of Opinion that the said Companies were
duly authorized under their Charters & the Laws
of the States of New York & Illinois to enter into
& agree to the said Deed of Trust & that the same
is valid & binding for the Objects & purposes therein declared; & I am further of Opinion that the
Holders of Bonds issued or to be issued in pursuance
of the said Deed of Trust, are & will be duly secured
in the Payment of their Bonds by the real Estate intended
by the said Deed of Trust to be conveyed, subject to
the Conditions & reservations contained therein.

New York January 12 1838 — James Kent

Chancellor Kent's Letter

that led them to insist as a condition to their surrenders to the state, one in 1837, and one in 1849, that the road should *start at and be built from Cairo*. Had they not thus insisted, the road might never have come here at all, so great were the doubts of the public at large as to the security of the Cairo site. But it was held here stubbornly and tenaciously, and to the great and lasting credit of Holbrook, which should well nigh annul all the criticisms that were ever made against him. He is indeed a wise man who knows well just what he can and what he cannot afford to surrender.

This act of February 27, 1837, establishing a general system of public improvements, gave no name to the state's railroad, nor to any of the others for the construction of which the act provided.

The Board of Commissioners of Public Works, provided for in the act, entered upon their work, and the road was commenced at and built from Cairo and most of the grading was done for the distance of twenty-three or more miles. A bridge across Cache River was partly constructed; and so on, at many places along the line, all the way up to Galena. The line of the road in Cairo began at or near what are now the freight yards of the present company between Fourteenth and Eighteenth Streets, where the state purchased ten acres of ground for station or depot purposes. From this point above Fourteenth Street, the road extended westward, curving northward, and passing not far from the present court house and on through what is now the east side of St. Mary's Park, and thence on northward and very near the present main line of the road and crossing Cache River not over one hundred feet west of the present railroad bridge. Parts of the old earth embankment are yet visible one hundred feet or less west of the present road and south of Cache River and of the levee of the Drainage District. In many places the ridges are four feet high and all of them overgrown with trees.

The seven commissioners of the Board of Public Works, one for each judicial district of the state, reported from time to time as the work progressed in their several jurisdictions. Elijah J. Willard, of Jonesboro, was the commissioner for this third judicial district. His report of December 10, 1838, sets forth many matters and things concerning the work, which we would like to give here did space permit. It gives the number of contracts made for work between Cairo and Jonesboro, through the latter of which the road was to run instead of over the site of the present city of Anna. The change of this line of the old Illinois Central Railroad of 1837 to the present line of 1851, running through Anna, occasioned a very unfriendly feeling between the two places, which did not disappear for many years if entirely gone now. The report gives the names of the contractors and of the men on the work and to whom moneys were paid. Among them were Bryan Shannessy, who took contracts Nos. 1, 2 and 3, covering the distance from Cairo to a point beyond Cache River. Mr. Shannessy is spoken of in the report as of the city of Alton. Of the two hundred or more names on Willard's pay-roll, many of them would be remembered by a few of our oldest residents. He further reports that early in 1838, a right of way was procured, by proceedings in our Alexander County Circuit Court, through or over sections 25, 26, 23, 14, 11, 3 and 2, in our Township 17, 1 West, "without any award of damages to the proprietors of the land." The foregoing information was obtained from a large volume of reports of committees of our legislature, entitled "*Reports of Session,* 1838-1839." One of the exhibits attached to Willard's report is the long letter dated at the Central Railroad office, Vandalia, December 24, 1838, and directed to the Hon. William Kinney and Elijah Willard, Committee of the Board of Public Works. This letter as above stated was written by Jonathan Freeman, the "Principal Engineer Central Railroad," and he therein sets forth at length the difficulties encountered at Cairo, selected as it had been as the southern terminus of the road. It is a most interesting letter and would be given in full did space permit. From it, those of our public men who had desired to have the road come to the Ohio at a point toward Grand Chain, obtained many of their arguments.

This work was begun in 1838 and continued until its suspension throughout the state and the final abandonment of the whole scheme of public improvements as provided for in the said act of February 27, 1837, and its amendments. The act was finally repealed February 1, 1840, at least so far as it related to every enterprise provided for therein except the Central Railroad. This short period of time, from February 27, 1837, to February 1, 1840, constitutes an era in the history of the state. We have had nothing like it since. It quite absorbed the attention of the people and the heated discussions it engendered continued for years after the scheme had broken down. A general state of semi-bankruptcy prevailed, especially on the part of the state, and repudiation was talked of and written about and actually favored by some persons of prominence in the state. See chapter 6 of Ford's History of Illinois, and chapters 37 and 38 of Davidson & Stuvé's history.

To show the importance of the Central Railroad, from Cairo to Galena, above all the other seven the state undertook to build, we may again refer to the effort made to save it from the wreck while everything else was abandoned. Col. John S. Hacker, the grandfather of our Capt. John S. Hacker, and a member of the legislature at that time, urged that the state should not give up the Central Railroad whatever of its other enterprises it chose to abandon. In the volume of reports of committees of our legislature, of 1840-1841, page 167, will be found the report of Col. Hacker as chairman of the committee on internal improvements made to the legislature January 11, 1841. It is as follows:

"In selecting the Central road, it will be seen that the committee have fixed upon the most important one in the whole system of improvements. By its completion, a continuous line of railroad communication will be made to pass through the very heart of this rich state, from the southern to the northern limits thereof. The southern portion of the state will supply the whole interior with the greatest abundance of timber for all time to come, which can be easily and cheaply transported on the railroad. And in addition to other advantages which will be conferred upon the citizens of Illinois, the building of a large commercial city at Cairo would, of itself, amply repay the expenditures of money which must necessarily attend the making of the road.

"Located at the point where the vast waters of the Ohio and Mississippi mingle in their onward course to the ocean, the city of Cairo possesses the advantages of commercial position which few cities of the earth can rival. *Neglected and abused as it has been heretofore, it nevertheless now possesses more than two thousand inhabitants, and pays into the State Treasury more than one thousand dollars in taxes.* If any man is disposed to doubt the invaluable profits to a whole state, derived from a single city within its borders, let him look at the cities of New York, New Orleans, Philadelphia, Boston, Baltimore, St. Louis, &c. Does not the city of New York pay into the State Treasury an amount of revenue almost equal to that received from the whole state besides? And is not the entire character and importance of Louisiana dependent upon the city of New Orleans? And so with other great cities. And then the incalculable and innumerable advantages, other than those of mere revenue, will be readily suggested, upon proper reflections; one of which is, that all the larger class of steamboats, which are plying between New Orleans and the ports on the upper Mississippi and Ohio Rivers, on account of the lowness of the water, and the obstructions by ice, are now discharging their cargoes at Cairo, to be forwarded to the respective places of destination by a smaller class of boats.

"We have no great commercial emporium in Illinois; and without intending to draw any invidious comparisons, or to speak disparagingly of other rising towns and cities, the committee must express their sincere belief that Cairo presents as many flattering prospects of future greatness as any other place in the state. History illustrates the high estimate which rulers have placed upon cities, in all countries; and have we, in modern times, fallen among statesmen and philosophers who can see nothing in the example of past ages worthy of their imitation?"

It was not until after this surrender of their railroad enterprise to the state, that the Cairo City and Canal Company people issued their *prospectus.* They had found it necessary to lay aside every other matter until they had ascertained what was to be done concerning a central railroad. They had to give up their own railroad scheme; but they succeeded in having their city site at the junction of the two rivers made the southern terminus of the state's railroad.

From the Prospectus and Engineers' Report relating to the City of Cairo, printed at St. Louis by T. Watson & Son, 1839, and signed by D. B. Holbrook, president of the Cairo City & Canal Company, February 18, 1839, we quote three or four pages as follows:—

The President of the Cairo City and Canal Company, having made arrangements in England for the funds requisite to carry out their contemplated improvements in the *City of Cairo,* on the most extensive and liberal scale, it is now deemed proper to give publicity to the objects, plans, and other matters connected with this great work, in order that every one who feels an interest, or has pride in the success of this magnificent public enterprise, may properly understand and appreciate the motives and designs of the projectors. The company from the commencement determined to withhold from sale, *at any price,* the corporate property of the city, until it should be made manifest to the most doubting and skeptical, the perfect practicability of making the site of the City of Cairo *habitable.* This being now fully established by the report of the distinguished engineers, Messrs. Strickland and Taylor of Pennsylvania, and also by that of the principal engineers of the state works of Illinois; the company are proceeding in the execution of their plans as set forth in their prospectus, viz.: to make the levees, streets and embankments of the city; to erect warehouses, stores and shops convenient for every branch of commercial business; dry docks; also, buildings adapted for every useful, mechanical and manufacturing purpose, and dwelling houses of such cost and description as will suit the taste and means of every citizen, which course has been adopted as the *most certain* to secure the *destined* population of Cairo within the least possible time. The company, however, wish it fully understood, that it is far from their desire or intention to monopolize or engage in any of the various objects of enterprise, trade, or business, which must of necessity spring up and be carried on with great and singular success at this city:—it being their governing motive to offer every reasonable and proper encouragement to the enterprising and skillful artisan, manufacturer, merchant and professional man to identify his interest with the growth and prosperity of the city. When the company make sales or leases of property it will be on such liberal terms as no other town or city can offer, possessing like advantages for the acquisition of that essential means of human happiness—wealth. The President of the company is fully empowered, whenever he shall deem it expedient, to sell or lease the property, and otherwise to represent the general interests and affairs of the Company. Information respecting the Company or the City, will be communicated at all times by the directors at Cairo; and also by:

Hon. Sidney Breese,
Hon. Zadoc Casey,
Hon. Joseph Duncan,
Hon. David J. Baker,
Hon. John Reynolds,
Hon. Adam W. Snyder,
Hon. William Kinney,
Mr. John Tilson,
Illinois.

Messrs. Thos. Biddle & Co.,
Mr. Wm. Strickland,
Mr. Joseph Coperthwait,
Mr. John Hemphill,
Mr. Rich'd C. Taylor,
Wm. A. Meredith, Esq.,
Philadelphia.

Mr. E. R. Biddle,
Messrs. Nevins, Townsend & Co.,
Messrs. Travis & Alexander,
New York Trust Co.,
Mr. Simeon Draper, Jr.,
Mr. Daniel Low,
New York.

Messrs. John Brown & Co.,
Samuel D. Ward, Esq.,
Amos Binney, Esq.,
Hon. Peleg Sprague,
Boston.

Col. Anthony Olney, *Acting Commissioner.*

CONSULTING ENGINEERS

William Strickland, Architect and Engineer, Philadelphia.
Major Wm. Gibbs McNeil, Chief Engineer of the Charleston and Cincinnati Railroad.

E. R. Biddle, *Treasurer, New York.*

D. B. Holbrook, *President.*

When the company are prepared to dispose of their real estate, *they will offer it on lease for a certain term of years at such rent or rents, as the business of the place will justify and warrant, conditioned,* that if the consideration agreed upon is punctually paid for and during the time stipulated in the lease, the estate in question shall become *bona fide* the property of the lessee. This will give to every one, desirous to make Cairo his permanent place of business, the opportunity of becoming the possessor of a dwelling and place of business, by the annual payment of a sum for rent, that the profits of his business will justify if properly conducted — and the company may venture to say, that the rent which may be required will not in all probability exceed the rates now paid for buildings, whether for dwellings or places of business, in the city of St. Louis. The object of this liberal policy being to offer a sufficient inducement to men of enterprise, skill and industry, to identify *at once* their interest with the growth of the city, and at the same time secure to the place a desirable population as soon as the required and necessary buildings are erected.

This last quotation from the company's prospectus contains an announcement of that policy of the company "which became the source of serious and long continued complaints, namely, the *leasing* of lots and lands instead of the *sales* thereof."

Although seemingly very much out of place, we introduce here the matter of the high water of June, 1858, when a break occurred in the Mississippi levee and caused an inundation of the city. We do this chiefly because it enables us to present a concise account of the work and operations of the Cairo City & Canal Company after its attention had been fully withdrawn from its own central railroad enterprise. The latter part of what we will now quote is our first introduction to the Trustees of the Cairo City Property.

On Saturday afternoon, June 12, 1858, in the time of what has already been called the June rise, the Mississippi levee, at or near the point where it turns and connects with the cross levee, or just west of the present Illinois Central Railroad bridge, gave way under the pressure of the great flood of water and inundated the entire city. So great was the surprise and loss of the people, and especially of the Trustees and shareholders, that the latter sent a committee of their number here to investigate and report concerning the calamity which had come to their property, and to the people here. The members of the committee were Harvey Baldwin, of Syracuse; Charles McAlister and Josiah Randall, of Philadelphia; Luther C. Clark, of New York City; Lyman Nichols, of Boston; and John Neal, of Portland. These gentlemen had been selected for this purpose under two certain resolutions of the shareholders at a meeting held at the office of the Cairo City Property July 1, 1858, in Philadelphia. On the 22d of July, the committee conferred fully with William H. Osborn, the president of the Illinois Central Railroad Company, which by its contracts with the said Trustees of June 11, 1851, and of May 31, 1855, had become almost as deeply interested in Cairo as were the shareholders and Trustees themselves.

We cannot go further into the matter here, but will say that the committee made a most thorough investigation of the situation and made their report September 29, 1858, and gave therein at considerable length very many important historical facts in regard to Cairo. If there are any errors in it we have not been able to discover the same. It was not intended to be perfectly exact as to dates and many other matters and things, but it is quite sufficiently reliable to justify including a few pages thereof in this history. Did we omit these pages we would nevertheless feel required to state the substance of them ourselves. The fact, however, that this investigation and report were made fifty-one years ago should give to it a value above anything that might be now stated as the result of present investigations. The members of the committee were shareholders and deeply interested in the situation. They were appointed June 1st and made their report September 29th and therefore had an abundance of time to make a thorough investigation. They made it and seem to have felt that the scope of their appointment or duties embraced making of a full and correct statement to the shareholders not only of the then present situation but of the history of prior undertakings to do the work in which they were then engaged. Their report, with its accompanying documents, makes a pamphlet of 105 pages, and it is entitled "The Past, Present and Future of the City of Cairo, in North America," published in Portland in 1858.

We quote from pages 14 to 19:—

As early as 1817, the great business advantages of this remarkable spot began to attract the attention of leading statesmen, capitalists, and men of business.

In 1818, a liberal charter was granted to an association, by the Territorial government of Illinois; and the territory was laid off in conformity with the charter, for the *"City of Cairo,"* with banking privileges.

Owing to deaths, commercial paroxysms, and other hindrances, nothing more was done toward carrying out the sagacious and magnificent enterprise, till 1837, when arrangements were entered into between the Proprietors holding under a charter for the "City and Bank of Cairo," and the State of Illinois; and a new charter was granted to the "Illinois Central Rail Road Company" for the construction of a Railroad, "to commence at, or near the confluence of the Ohio and Mississippi rivers, and terminating at Galena."

After this company had organized, and secured a large portion of the land they wanted, the State of Illinois undertook a large and comprehensive system of internal improvements, making the Central Railroad the basis of the whole; and the railroad company abandoned their privileges to the State upon the expressed condition, to be found in the law itself, that the Central Railroad *should begin at the City of Cairo, at or near the confluence of the Ohio and Mississippi.*

Then followed the *"Cairo City and Canal Company"* incorporated March 4, 1837, with power to purchase any part of township No. seventeen, and especially that portion thereof which was incorporated in 1818, as the *"City of Cairo,"* and "to make all improvements for the protection, health and prosperity of the City."

The stock of this new Company being all taken, and the Company itself organized, arrangements were entered into for obtaining a loan of five hundred thousand dollars "to be applied to the payment and extinguishment of such mortgages and incumbrances as might exist on the lands purchased by the Company, within Township numbered seventeen" and for further investments in land and other property, by conveying the whole proprietorship in Trust, on the 16th of Dec. 1837, to the New York Life Insurance and Trust Co., and by a supplemental deed, of June 13, 1839, to the same Company, for securing the bondholders on further loans, to be employed in large improvements at Cairo; in protecting the city from overflow, on both sides; in building a Turnpike to the State road from Vincennes to St. Louis; and in opening a canal through the city, to Cache river, a distance of six miles, which, by the help of a dam, would secure a slack water navigation of twenty miles further, into a rich agricultural and timber region.

Under this charter, the Company completed their purchases of land, amounting altogether to 9,732.4 acres, of which 3,884 acres were appropriated to the City of Cairo. The titles were investigated by eminent lawyers, and after a careful enquiry, and a comparison of prices at Alton, Chicago and other places with fewer natural advantages, the valuation of lots under the Deed of Trust, instead of being $400, per front foot, for business lots, and from $50 to $100 per foot for house lots, the prices paid in 1837 at Alton, with a population of 2,500 only, was fixed at $25 per front foot for lots of 25 by 120, on streets and squares, and $60 per front foot, for all such lots, on levees or landings.

Of the former there were surveyed 22,774 lots at $625, and of the latter 1,180 at $1,500—being 23,954 lots, which, at the valuation agreed upon, yielded an aggregate of *sixteen millions, thirty-seven hundred and fifty dollars.*

Other loans were obtained in the progress of improvement; and after bonds had been registered under the deed of Trust to the amount of £287,600 sterling, or nearly fourteen hundred thousand dollars, of which £155,800, or about seven hundred and fifty thousand dollars, had been sold, and while the company were negotiating for a further loan of £200,000, there came on that commercial crisis, which overthrew so many of the largest and wealthiest associations of both hemispheres, and completely paralyzed the business world. Thousands of merchant princes, bankers and capitalists were shipwrecked, both abroad and at home; and it being found that many of the largest, wealthiest, best-informed and most willing of the share-holders, had gone into bankruptcy; that nothing could be done with their assignees; and that the large outlays upon the city of Cairo, the buildings, levees and embankments, amounting, with interest, to about three and a half millions of dollars, might become unproductive, and all the unfinished works be rendered worthless, if immediate measures were not taken to secure the zealous and hearty co-operation of all parties interested, whether as bond-holders, mortgagees or share-holders, a proposition was made in the month of January, 1845, by the late Darius B. Holbrook, President of the Illinois Exporting Company, through whom a large proportion of these funds had been furnished, for all parties interested to unite in a sale of the whole Cairo property, *unencumbered,* to a new Company, for *seven hundred thousand dollars,* or about one fifth of the actual cost, including interest; to divide the whole stock into thirty-five thousand shares; to subscribe for one-half, or seventeen thousand five hundred shares himself, as President of the Illinois Exporting Company, and to throw a like number of shares into the market, for sale at twenty dollars a share.

This proposition being accepted, and the preliminary arrangements completed, on the twenty-ninth of September, A. D. one thousand eight hundred and forty-six, the whole Cairo City property was put into the hands of Messrs. Thomas S. Taylor, of Philadelphia, and Charles Davis, of New York, for the purposes mentioned in their Declaration of Trust, hereunto annexed, and marked D.

Under this arrangement, the beneficial interest in the Cairo City lands and property, of every description, was divided into thirty-five thousand shares, of the par value of one hundred dollars each. Certificates, representing twenty thousand shares were to be delivered by the Trustees, Taylor and Davis, to the order of the Illinois Exporting Company; certificates representing seven thousand shares, to Charles Davis, attorney in fact for certain holders of bonds issued by the Cairo City and Canal Company; certificates representing three thousand shares to Messrs. Robertson, Newbold, Cope and Taylor, Assignees in Trust, for the Bank of the United States, and holders of the Cairo City and Canal Company's bonds, which were to be surrendered and cancelled; the remaining five thousand shares to be sold by the said Taylor and Davis, and the proceeds applied to the expenses of the Trust, to the payment of five thousand dollars, advanced by Samuel Allinson, Esq., and to improvements of the Cairo City Property.

It was further stipulated that whenever thereto authorized in writing, by two-thirds of the share-holders in interest, the Trustees might enlarge the number of shares, and sell them, either at public or private sale, and apply the proceeds to further improvements of the unsold Cairo property.

On the 21st of Nov., 1850, ten thousand additional shares were authorized, making forty-five thousand in all, thirty thousand of which were received at par, to extinguish the liabilities of the Cairo City and Canal Company, and to clear off all incumbrances; while the remaining fifteen thousand shares were to be used for the benefit of the Trust, and for the improvement and protection of the property.

Of the whole 10,000 shares authorized to be issued, for these purposes, and of the other 5,000 shares appropriated under the Declaration of Trust, only 8,311 are now outstanding, and the whole number of shares now entitled to representation is but 36,491.

Under this last mentioned organization it is, that all the present shareholders in the C. C. P., now act, and while to the bond-holders and original cash creditors of the Cairo City and Canal Company the actual cost of a share, with simple interest up to this time, is about *one hundred and eighty dollars,* the cost, with simple interest to the share-holders, who bought in at one-fifth of the original cost, is only about *thirty-six dollars.*

Yet, a single share actually represents about one lot and one-twentieth of a lot, within the City, as originally laid out, with a correspondent proportion of the outside territory, equal to one and one-half lots more, of 25 feet by 120.

The sales within the city had averaged up to January last, reckoning from December 23, 1853, when the first lot was sold, about $400 per lot; and the assessed value of the lots within the city limits in 1857, based upon *sales for cash,* was $1,434,679.

This is a remarkably full and clear statement. It gives in the shortest possible space a comprehensive account of the origin of the Cairo City and Canal Company and its somewhat checkered existence, and of its merger into the Cairo City Property Trust. As in these present times, the one company had gone on as far as it could, and those in charge of its failing fortunes set about the organization of another company to take up the work the old company found too heavy to carry. New men were to be put in charge under supposedly more favorable circumstances.

But we may inquire, what did the Cairo City and Canal Company actually do and perform in the way of starting a city here? To answer this question we have not much reliable information. It exists somewhere or in many different places, no doubt, but to gather it up and put it in shape would take weeks of hard work. But much of it is not needed; an outline is about all that could be asked for. We have seen a number of original records, but they contain so little that should be stated with any kind of detail that we shall refer to them only now and then. All their books, papers and records, covering a period of ten years, if now in existence, may be in Philadelphia, or New York, or possibly they may now be among the books and papers left by Col. Taylor here in Cairo. Were they before one and gone over with some care, they would present a remarkable record of corporate activity for that decade from 1836 to 1846. They would show, much more clearly than we now see it, how one man had been invested with absolute authority; how every one yielded to him, how hard he worked, how he traveled far and near and did everything to advance the enterprise. I have said so much about this in other places that I need not say more here, except to embrace it all in one comprehensive sentence, by saying that the Cairo City and Canal Company was D. B. Holbrook, or D. B. Holbrook was the Cairo City and Canal Company.

The name of the company implied that it expected to build or start a city and to construct a canal. The canal was to extend from Cache River down to the point, a distance of about six miles, and about midway between the two rivers, and at its southern end, it was to send out arms or branches to each river. The map elsewhere found will show what was proposed. The canal part of the enterprise was abandoned. The design seems to have been to have a canal along and through the center of the city, which would very much better, as they supposed, accommodate the shipping interests than the river on either side of the city. Vessels of all kinds it was supposed could enter the wide canal either at the north on Cache or from the Mississippi or Ohio at its southern termini. The scheme must have soon appeared wholly impracticable. How the same could have ever been carried out with the rise and fall of the rivers through a perpendicular distance of forty to fifty feet can scarcely be imagined. How the water could have been maintained in the canal much higher than the level of the waters in the rivers or how the canal could have been made deep enough and yet suited to loading or unloading from vessels in the canal does not appear to us if it ever appeared plain enough to them.

To enable the men in charge of the Cairo enterprise to manage their affairs to better advantage, the legislature had incorporated the Illinois Exporting Company. There were, therefore, three companies here at Cairo on and after March 4, 1837, the day of the incorporation of the Cairo City and Canal Company. These companies were thought not only needful but sufficient to contract with and for each other in and about building a railroad and a city, and carrying on such other work or enterprises as might come within the scope of the powers of the Exporting Company, if not within the powers of either one of the other two; and accordingly, we find these companies entering into two contracts on the 26th day of June, 1837, relative to the construction of the railroad, and, in particular, relative to its being started here at Cairo and not elsewhere.

The Cairo City and Canal Company, having been relieved of all its contemplated railroad work, had nothing to do but to devote its whole attention to work here at the site of the proposed city, which was little less than a dense forest between the rivers. Levee building was, of course, the first thing to receive attention. It was useless to project anything requiring the expenditure of money without first arranging for the protection of the site from overflow by the rivers.

As elsewhere stated, they do not seem to have considered the matter of filling even a small portion of the ground to a height sufficient to dispense with levees. Their plan was to inclose a large district of country by earth embankments along the rivers and across the point, and leave the natural level of the ground just about as it was. At the outstart, they do not seem to have known much about what we now call seepage. Had they or their successors, the Cairo City Property people, adopted a different plan, that is, the plan of filling a comparatively small district of territory to a reasonably high grade, which, if requiring levees at all would have required comparatively low ones, they nor we would ever have heard of seepage water. The money expended in building levees and in a dozen different ways, made necessary by the low grounds, would have gone far toward raising the general level of a large district to the present grade of our downtown streets and avenues, and in such case we would have been spared the large expenditures we are now making to free the city from the accumulated water within its levees. But all the plans and operations of this company seem to have presupposed a great demand for city lots and for such great prosperity that any comparatively slow method of preparing a site for a city could not be entertained; and it is altogether probable that no other plan was ever seriously thought of except that of inclosing hundreds, perhaps thousands, of acres within levees along the rivers. We are impressed by nothing in all the history of those early years so much as by what seems to have been the views of the promoters of the enterprise here as to the slight depth of the water over the point when the rivers were at their highest. Much allowance must be made for men in promoting their plans and schemes, for all experience teaches us that the advantages are highly colored and the disadvantages made little of; and hence we could hardly expect that they would represent the site of the city as low as it really was or that the rivers rose as high as they really do; but making all allowances possible, it still seems remarkably strange how, as far back as in 1836 and from thence up to 1850 and even later, it was represented in every way and manner that the site was not so low and that the rivers did not rise and overflow it to any considerable depth. It is true we have a far better knowledge of the actual situation than they could have had. None of them had ever seen any very high rivers. The flood of 1844 was out of the Mississippi and could not have been very high here. The small levees then existing and inclosing 778.70 acres kept out what has always been represented as a very great flood. The flood of 1849 broke through the Mississippi levee for the distance of 1625 feet, but the record of that flood does not show it to have been a very great one. The flood of June 12, 1858, was not so high; but the levee on the west was weak and badly constructed and for that reason gave way.

Returning to the Holbrook people as they were starting out with their work, we remark that they needed large means; first, for levee construction; for it was quite useless to make any considerable expenditures here on the point until they should be protected from overflows from the rivers. The first question was then, as it is now, how much money is needed and how can it be obtained. The men in charge knew that the money could not be obtained in this country on any reasonable terms as to interest or otherwise. There was not much money in this country then, and in all matters of importance, requiring large expenditures, it was always expected that resort would be had to London, the money center of Europe and of the world then, if not quite

RAILROAD CELEBRATION.

The citizens of Galena and vicinity are respectfully invited to meet the Court-house, on Monday morning next, at 9 o'clock, for the purp of celebrating the breaking ground on the northern termination of great Central railroad. The citizens of Dubuque, Mineral Point, a the adjoining counties, are also respectfully invited to join in the celeb tion under the following order of the committee of arrangement.

ORDER OF PROCESSION

Music.

Marshal of the day.

President and Trustees of the town.

Clergy and Orator of the day.

Commissioners, Engineers and Contractors.

Second Marshal, { Laborers, with their implements. } Third Marshal.

Members of Mechanics' Institute.

Fire Companies.

Hook and Ladder Company.

Members of the Bar.

Citizens and Strangers.

President, Vice-President, and officers of the Chamber of Commerce.

Fourth Marshal. Fifth Marshal.

The committee appointed the following gentlemen to act as Marsh on the occasion:

Capt. H. H. Gear, Messrs. Philip Barry, Wm. B. Green, George I Mitchell, Legrand Morehouse.

The procession will form at the Court-house, and proceed down Ma street to the steamboat landing, where it will embark on board of bo prepared for the occasion to take them to the vicinity of the place whe the work is to commence.

A general invitation is respectfully tendered to the ladies of Galen and the surrounding country, to repair on board the boats previous the time of the procession reaching it.

☞ The business men of Galena are requested to close their stor and shops on that day.

PHILIP BARRY,
GEORGE M. MITCHELL,
JOHN L. SLAYMAKER,
JOHN H. WEBBER,
H. H. GEAR,
WM. SMITH,
Committee of Arrangement.

GALENA, *May* 23, 1838.

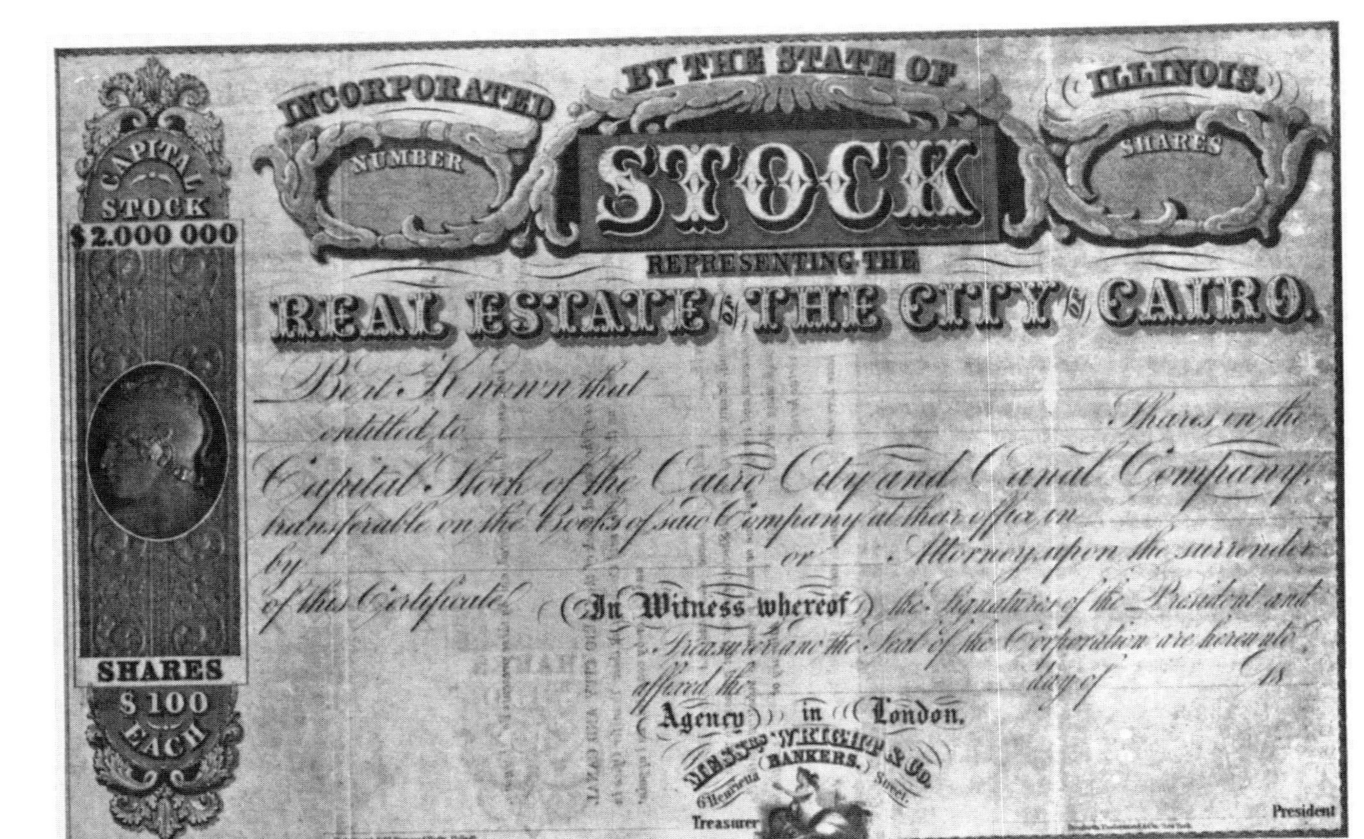

INCORPORATED BY THE STATE OF ILLINOIS.

NUMBER

STOCK

SHARES

CAPITAL STOCK $2.000 000

SHARES $100 EACH

REPRESENTING THE

REAL ESTATE of THE CITY of CAIRO.

Be it Known that
entitled to Shares on the
Capital Stock of the Cairo City and Canal Company,
transferable on the Books of said Company at their office on
by or Attorney, upon the surrender
of this Certificate. In Witness whereof the Signatures of the President and
Treasurer and the Seal of the Corporation are hereunto
affixed the day of 18

Agency in London.

Messrs. Wright & Co.
Bankers.
6 Henrietta Street.

Treasurer

President

so much so now. But to get the money anywhere, there must be good security for the interest thereon and its ultimate payment at the time stipulated. The company had only its real estate to offer as security. But as the enterprise was generally regarded with great favor, it had no great difficulty in arranging to have its monetary affairs taken in hand by competent men in this country; and therefore it arranged with the New York Life Insurance and Trust Company, in the year 1838, to secure the bonds which the company desired to put upon the market by a trust deed upon its real estate to the said trust company. That deed of trust, executed by the Cairo City and Canal Company on the 26th day of June, 1837, is found recorded in book "D" on pages 42 to 47, of our county records. It was easy enough to make a deed of trust and to prepare bonds, but to sell the bonds readily and to advantage was often very difficult. At that time, American securities were not sought after as now, and those who dealt in them abroad frequently incurred unfriendly treatment from their rivals in the money markets.

As elsewhere stated, D. B. Holbrook, the president of the Cairo City and Canal Company and the Illinois Exporting Company, proceeded to London and negotiated with John Wright & Company, Bankers, of Henrietta Street, Covent Garden, and arranged for them to take charge of the sale of his Cairo bonds, secured by the trust deed to the New York company. To arrange with these London bankers, Holbrook had to present the situation here very fully, both as to the title and value of the company's real estate as well as to the permanency of the site of the proposed city. They needed little assurance as to the geographical situation; but if the site was so low or otherwise largely unsuitable for the establishment of a city, the enterprise would be regarded with little favor. It was not to be treated as a real-estate investment alone. It was known that aside from the starting and building up of a city of some considerable size, the lands were of comparatively little value. Hence it was that Wright & Company must have been very well satisfied as to the outlook and prospects of a city here on the mortgaged property.

There were then in London Daniel Webster, our ex-governor, John Reynolds, and our United States Senator, John M. Young. Holbrook laid before Webster his papers and documents, and obtained from him a favorable opinion as to the title to the lands here, the deed of trust, etc. Holbrook was successful in raising the means he thought requisite to their enterprise for some considerable time to come. I need not speak of them here again, since the matter is set forth at length in the above report to the shareholders of the Cairo City Property in September, 1858. It is quite impossible now to tell just how the large sums of money obtained from the sale of bonds in London were expended. They must have reached New York and Cairo in various amounts from time to time. The lands embraced in the trust deed to secure the bonds were only three to four thousand acres, whereas, when the Cairo City and Canal Company sold to the Trustees of the Cairo City Property June 13, 1846, there were 9734 acres, including the more recent purchases by the Cairo City and Canal Company. If the large sum of $1,250,000.00

was expended here by that company, from 1838 to 1844, a period of six years, one can scarcely imagine for what the various expenditures were made. The levees built were the two extending up the Ohio and Mississippi rivers, the one 12,320 feet in length and the other 4780 feet, the two making an embankment of about three and one half miles. They were narrow and not very high, compared with our present levees, and could not have cost more than two or three hundred thousand dollars at the most and perhaps not so much. Labor was cheap, although in this out-of-the-way place it may have been rather high. The expenditures for lands were, as I have already stated, large. Every one thought the place had a most promising future before it, and owners of lands asked high prices; and Holbrook seemed willing to pay almost any price in order to secure well nigh exclusive ownership of everything here between the two rivers south of Cache River. Next to the purchase of lands and the construction of levees was the clearing off of a strip of ground adjoining the Ohio River, of the width of a quarter of a mile, and for the distance from the point to Twentieth Street. This expense could not have been very great. Besides these we know of little else than the large expenditures made for improvements along the line of the Ohio and on this cleared strip of land. Cottages for temporary and more permanent residence purposes were constructed. Manufacturing establishments, such as machine shops, saw mills, foundries, brick yard work, dry docks, marine ways and other appurtenances for steamboat building, and the furnishing of machinery of all kinds to equip the different manufacturing plants, these and others of a like nature required large expenditures. It is said that the most modern and expensive machinery was provided for the various establishments and that much of it came from London and other very distant points. These matters of the character of the machinery and its importation from abroad are mentioned here not as established facts, but as matters of report, not to say of tradition. And yet one can easily believe all such representations, for they comport so fully with what we know of Holbrook. Everything he planned was on a large and expensive scale. His theory was that in this way only could the country and the world be convinced that what he and his company had in hand was a great thing and was certain of a remarkable success. It is one of those strange things of human experience and observation that large and lavish expenditures of money in almost any kind of an enterprise has the effect of impressing so many people with the belief that the matter in hand is one of great merit and promise. This is somewhat natural. People conclude that others know more about the matter than they do and that the expenditures would not be made were not the enterprise a very sure one.

The manufacturing establishments were started, and work carried on for two or three years. But it could never have been to much advantage or profit. The outgo was always more than the income. The business on the river and in the vicinity was not sufficient to sustain extensive operations. For a while there was great activity, such as is always found at the first in doubtful enterprises. All of the establishments, or what are now called plants, were put in operation. The sawmills turned out great quantities of lumber for all purposes, including the building of steamboats and other kinds of watercraft. One steamboat, at least, the "Tennessee Valley," was built in 1841. Its owners resided at Florence, Alabama, and it was registered at New Orleans April 23, 1842. It was equipped with machinery furnished by the foundry and machine and boiler shops near by, just as the lumber and timbers for it came from the sawmills there at hand. The two large brick-making plants in the upper part of the little city got under way with their improved machinery and would no doubt have done good work had there been good materials for brick and a good demand for the manufactured article. It has never been supposed, however, at least in these latter days, that the point here afforded a good quality of clay for brick making.

One can tell something of what was done and carried on here in those few short years, by examining the records at the court house, found chiefly in Book D, where are recorded the mortgages and other liens given by the company to its creditors upon its property here in Cairo, its buildings, its machinery of all kinds and descriptions, its lumber and building materials generally, forms, molds, and other foundry equipment, boilers, iron of all descriptions, brick in many thousands, horses, oxen, wagons, chains, in fact, everything one would expect to find in and about such manufacturing plants.

The day of adversity had come, and those who had given credit spared no effort to secure something that would somewhat prevent a total loss. The situation was peculiar indeed, one seldom seen in the world anywhere. Cairo had been started once before and failed in the shortest possible time. It existed just long enough to spread its failure everywhere abroad. This second attempt had promised much, but when it became evident that it too must fail, a kind of frenzied feeling took possession of the people or of the creditors, of whom there were many, and the thought became general that not only the Cairo City and Canal Company was to go down, but that the whole large enterprise of building a city here was also to come to an end. It meant loss of debts and loss of home and removal to other parts of the country to commence life anew. No wonder the people or many of them exhibited a kind of rapacity of conduct as the full view of the calamity of the situation came before them.

Holbrook saw the fast approaching end probably long before anyone else, and knowing well that were he in Cairo when it arrived, he could do nothing for anyone, left the place before the storm broke upon it. He knew whom the people or most of them would look upon as responsible for their misfortunes, and that his presence here would but add violence to the probable outbreak.

CHAPTER VII

THE CAIRO CITY AND CANAL COMPANY—SUCCEEDED BY THE CAIRO CITY PROPERTY TRUST—CAIRO FROM JUNE 13, 1846, TO DECEMBER 23, 1853

HOLBROOK had taken the lead in everything relating to the organization and operations of the Cairo City and Canal Company, and now that it could go on no longer, he took the lead also in its transformation into another company or concern to take up the work the other had to lay down. He no doubt regretted the alternative of going on and into utter bankruptcy, or turning over the enterprise to others; but seeing that it was unavoidable, he accepted the situation, and, like any other brave-hearted man, sought to make the most favorable arrangement he could for the old company and its stockholders. Their enterprise had been a going one for five or six years at most, and the work of settlement and the change from the old to the new management seem to have required half of that length of time. There were many interests and persons to be consulted, both at home and abroad, and for that and many other reasons the negotiations proceeded slowly. There were creditors of every kind and description, both secured and unsecured; but as a matter of fact, those actually and well secured were very few. The first news that the enterprise was in a failing condition sent down everywhere the values of all kinds of its property. Its lands, its site for a city, could scarcely have depreciated faster or fallen lower in value; and had there been no creditors, there is no telling what could have been done. The geographical position of the place was all that saved the undertaking from complete destruction. The people interested could not come to the conclusion that they were wrong and that there was no reasonable chance to build a city here. At all events, their interests led them to another attempt under new and what seemed to be more favorable circumstances.

The nature and terms of the final arrangement are so fully set forth in the report of the committee of the stockholders of the new enterprise, made September 29, 1858, parts of which are quoted elsewhere, that we need not refer to them again.

The first thing done, in pursuance of the new arrangement, was the conveyance, June 13, 1846, by the Cairo City and Canal Company of all of its property and estate to Thomas S. Taylor, of Philadelphia, and Charles Davis, of New York City, preparatory to the formation of a trust to take charge of the property and the enterprise as described in the report of September 29, 1858, above referred to. This deed of June 13, 1846, is recorded in Register Book A, on pages 123, etc. This deed was followed by the Declaration of Trust of September 29, 1846, executed by Taylor and Davis, as Trustees, and thirteen other persons, whose names are as follows: Illinois Exporting Company, J. Robertson, Richard H. Bayard, James S. Newbold, Herman Cope, T. S. Taylor, Vincent Eyre, Thomas Barnwall, assignee of Wright and Company, John Hibbert, Henry Webb, Martha Allinson, James McKillop, and Thomas Lloyd. This Declaration of Trust is recorded in Book N, on pages 465, etc.

From the time of the Declaration of Trust, September 29, 1846, to December 23, 1853, the date of the first sales of lots in Cairo by the Trustees, we have the long period of seven and a quarter years. This delay in offering lots and lands for sale caused many complaints. The people knew something of the Holbrook plan in this regard, and it seemed to them the management was going to follow Holbrook's policy, which was to retain the title to all the real estate and give only long leases thereof. Concerning this long delay and its effect upon the people, Addison H. Sanders, in his newspaper, "The Cairo Delta," of September 20, 1849, wrote as follows, under the heading "Cairo—Good Bye To It":

> As we have before remarked, Cairo does not grow any, because no one can buy or build, the property being in the hands of a company who are not yet prepared to sell. The stockholders of this company are principally eastern gentlemen, and the company decidedly American and represented by Charles Davis, of New York, and Thomas Taylor, of Philadelphia, who hold the property in trust. We came to Cairo under the belief that the property would have been offered for sale last fall or spring. We believe that operations or improvements will be commenced next spring but can no longer await an uncertainty. If we were *sure* the property would then be offered for sale, no inducement could be offered enticing enough to urge our removal from Cairo, because we believe, we *know* in fact, that when this property is offered for sale, the lots will be snatched up at high prices and many of them by men who will guarantee to erect substantial houses on the property within a given time. From that period may be dated the rapid rise of Cairo from the village to the great and popular city. In one season the levees could be put in complete repair, and Cairo thus perfectly protected against flood, and during the same period, the ground on the inside could be raised for blocks of houses fronting on the Ohio levee.

This number of the "Delta" was the last one issued under Sanders' supervision, and contains his valedictory. He was dissatisfied and greatly discouraged, so much so that he decided to remove from the town. When he left, the Trustees had been in charge for three years and yet the people could not make purchases of real estate. He said, in the extract above given, that he supposed they would be ready to make sales in the following spring; but it was not until December 23, 1853, four years later, that they put their lots upon the market. I have already stated that this long delay may have been due to the desire of the Trustees to see what was to be done about a railroad. Col. Taylor had come west and to Chicago in the year 1846. We find his name entered on the roll of attorneys of the Supreme Court at its April term of that year, at Ottawa. At the same time the names of General Isham N. Haynie and General Lewis B. Parsons were entered upon the same roll. From that time on, Col. Taylor was hard at work in the west and perhaps in the east also for the Trustees and no doubt chiefly for and on behalf of their railroad enterprise. He had an office with Mr. Justin Butterfield in Chicago and with him and a number of others a great deal of work was done in and out of congress to further their plans for a railroad. The Trustees and shareholders in the Cairo enterprise knew very well what a railroad meant to them. They knew that from the very beginning in 1835 and 1836, the Cairo scheme was practically one and the same with, or was a part of, the Central Railroad undertaking. The two had gone along together until the upper part of the state had become able to sever them; and even then when the Cairo managers had been pushed aside, they worked on, both in the east and in the west, in season and out of season, caring only to have the southern terminus fixed at this point.

Confirmatory of what we have said above about the delay in offering lots for sale and the interest the Trustees and shareholders had in the contemplated railroad, we quote here a paragraph in a lengthy paper written by Col. Taylor many years before his death. It traces the titles to the Cairo lands and gives almost every important transaction, with the date thereof, including deeds, acts of incorporation and other laws from February 25, 1816, to June 30, 1880. The somewhat lengthy entry under date of May 10, 1876, is as follows:

> The Trustees of the Cairo City Property having expended in making material improvements about Cairo $1,307,021.42, of which the sum of $184,505.64 was expended upon the Ohio levee, the sum of $149,973.23 upon the Mississippi levee, the sum of $70,455.06 upon the protection of the Mississippi River bank, the sum of $571,534.08 upon general improvements and $330,553.41 upon taxes and assessments, found themselves unable to pay the loans negotiated in 1863 and 1867, and the mortgages were therefore foreclosed and the property of the trust sold out to the bond holders. The entire receipts of the Trustees of the Cairo City Property, from sales, rents, wharfage and all other sources have been used in improvements and other expenditures at Cairo, *except what was required to repay in New York moneys borrowed at the beginning of the trust, about 1848, to defray expenses connected principally with arrangements and legislation for procuring from congress the grant of land to the state to build the Illinois Central Railroad,* and for payment of interest on loans negotiated in 1863 and 1867.

This congressional grant of September 20, 1850, was followed by the incorporation of the Illinois Central Railroad Company February 10, 1851; and February 17, 1851, the Holbrook people surrendered all their railroad rights of every kind to the state in behalf of the new railroad enterprise; and at the end of two months more, Col. Taylor was in Cairo to take charge and push forward the matter of starting and building a city. It is thus clearly seen how all these matters and things fit together and make one and the same scheme. They could build no town—could not even start one until they knew certainly what could be told the public at large concerning a railroad. Some preliminary work had been done in the way of making surveys, plats, drawings, etc., but as for the platting or mapping for a city or for the sale of lots nothing could be safely done, except in a very provisional way. The Trustees lost no time in arranging with the railroad company for terminal facilities in consideration of obtaining good levees to protect the site from the inroads of the rivers; nor did they think it wise to offer lots or lands for sale until the levee work was well under way and assurances given purchasers of the safety of the city's site. We are thus brought down to December 23, 1853, and are shown that the plan of the Trustees was never that of the Holbrook management.

Little was done during this period, as already stated, besides preserving as best they could what was left over. It was during the latter part of this period of seven and a quarter years that an attempt was made in the legislature to incorporate the *"Cairo City Property,"* namely, in the year 1852.

The first section of the act is in these words:

> Section 1. Be it enacted by the people of the State of Illinois represented in the General Assembly that Porter William Rawle, Sidney Breese, William R. Porter, Robert J. Walker, Miles A. Gilbert, David J. Baker, Hamilton Brewer, Kenneth McKenzie, P. Strachan, Elihu H. Townsend, Darius B. Holbrook, Garret K. Barry, John A. Willink, Hiram Ketchum, F. R. Sherman, and their associates, successors and assigns, be and they are hereby made a body corporate and politic under the name of the *Cairo City Property,* and by that name and style shall be and are hereby made capable in law and equity to sue and be sued, plead and be impleaded, defend and be defended in any court or place whatsoever, to make and use a common seal, the same to alter and renew at pleasure and by that name and style be capable in law of contracting and being contracted with, purchasing, holding and conveying real and personal estate for the purposes and uses of said corporation, etc., etc.

This section restricts the right of the company to own real estate to fractional township seventeen, and, in particular, authorizes them to purchase and hold those particular tracts of land and the improvements thereon known as the Cairo City Property and then held and represented by Thomas S. Taylor, of Philadelphia, and Charles Davis, of New York, as Trustees, and to lay off said lands into lots for a town to be known as the City of Cairo, whenever a plan of said city is made. Said section further authorizes the construction of dykes, canals, levees and embankments for the security and preservation of the city and lands and all improvements thereon from all and every inundation which can possibly affect or injure the same. The second section limits the capital stock to fifty thousand shares of one hundred dollars each and vests the immediate government and direction of affairs in a board of not less than five trustees. There are twelve or thirteen sections in the act. The ninth one granted some favors with regard to taxes. The eleventh section confers the power to adopt ordinances and regulations in regard to the public health and to make and collect such charges for dockage and wharfage as the said company may deem proper, not exceeding the rates established at St. Louis. The twelfth section seems to authorize the county court of the county to erect another jail, the same to be within the City of Cairo and to be under the control of the county; but not at its expense. It seems to be implied that the company created by the act would pay for the erection of the jail.

The bill seems to have passed the House of Representatives June 11, 1851. But when it reached the Senate it was so changed and amended as to be scarcely recognizable. The whole of section ten, authorizing the company to establish and maintain ferries, was stricken out. The senator from Johnson County, Major A. J. Kuykendall, said he would vote for the bill if it could be amended in some satisfactory way. He did not want to confer upon the company "municipal powers equal to those exercised by the City of Alton." Senator Odam offered an amendment requiring the act to be submitted to a vote of the people of the county. Kuykendall's amendment striking out the provision in regard to conferring upon the company the powers possessed by the City of Alton and Odam's amendment requiring the act to be submitted to the voters of the county were adopted; and thereupon, on motion of Kuykendall, the bill as amended was laid on the table. On the motion to adopt the above amendments, eighteen senators voted for them and four against. The eighteen were Cloud, Grass, Gregg, Gridley, Kuykendall, Lansing, Mateson, Odam, Palmer, Parkes, Plato, Reddick, Stuart, Talcott, Wallace, Webster, Wood, and Wynn. Those voting the other way were Judd, Morrison, Osborne, and Richmond. It seems that the bill for an act to incorporate the City of Cairo, of which we have spoken elsewhere, was pending at this time and that the same failed of passage because of some peculiar provision relative to the selection of the first city council and their long term of office, which was to be five years.

I would like to devote more space to this period from June 11, 1846, to December 23, 1853, but I cannot do so. Judging by the attempt of the Trustees, in 1852, to have the "Cairo City Property" and also the City of Cairo incorporated and their failure as to both, and judging also by many other matters and things, it must be inferred that they were, at least in one sense of the word, *feeling* their way along. It was not until the Illinois Central Railroad was well under way of construction that the Trustees and the public began to feel strong assurance of a prosperous future for the city.

CHAPTER VIII

CAIRO'S SITE AND ITS ABRASIONS BY THE RIVERS—LEVEES AND LEVEE CONSTRUCTION—HIGHEST KNOWN FLOODS

EVER since the government survey of our township in 1807, it has been known that while the Ohio River shore remains fairly stable and unchangeable, the Mississippi, on the contrary, devours its banks and changes its current from place to place unless restrained in and by some of the various means adopted to stay its ravages. There is now no telling when it was first observed by persons in anywise interested here that the Mississippi side of this site needed to be watched and its cutting away by the river carefully guarded against. The matter received close attention at the beginning of the Holbrook administration in 1836. So carefully had the situation been examined that it was strongly urged in and out of the legislature that the southern terminus of the state's Central Railroad should be removed from Cairo to some point near Caledonia on the Ohio, twelve or fifteen miles above Cairo. See Chapter VI.

The cutting by the Mississippi had the careful attention of the Trustees, and their numerous engineers made their best efforts to devise plans to arrest it. Resort was had from time to time to spur dikes of broken stone, placed at different points on the river shore and extending down stream at a small angle to the shore line. In this way it was sought to force the current away from the bank. These dikes served a good purpose, no doubt, but they failed to prove an effective remedy. From failure to keep a close watch upon the situation or rather to make the needed repairs, the river worked in behind the ridges of broken stone, and it was not very long until the stone piles were found to be out in the stream. The situation was never very good, and it finally became so bad as to produce some considerable anxiety not to say alarm on the part of the people. They had trusted the whole matter to the Trustees, who claimed exclusive ownership of the banks and shores from Cache River on the Ohio to a point on the Mississippi opposite the present Beech Ridge. Moreover, many of the leading men in the town insisted strongly that the Trustees had obligated themselves not only to build and maintain sufficient levees but to protect them and the city from the abrasions of the rivers. It is probable that the Trustees would have done much more than they did had not their means been very limited. In the year 1874, the river seemed to have entered upon a season of unusual voracity, which it maintained steadily during the years 1875 and 1876. It pushed the rock piles out of its way or rather worked in behind them and soon undermined the levee for a long distance northward from a point where the present Thirty-Third Street, if extended westward, would intersect the present Mississippi shore. The Cairo & St. Louis Railroad, then very recently finished and extending along the Mississippi levee, had to be moved back from time to time, thus encroaching upon adjacent cornfields and other private premises. That company, like the Trustees, was too weak financially to resist the river's advances. Many of us will remember what a time it was and how the city in 1876 set about building what is now called the new levee on New Levee Street. We all then thought it was very bad; but the further we get away from it, the discouraging and dangerous situation seems to grow upon us and to impress more and more upon us the vital importance of not allowing, under any circumstances, that treacherous river to get the start of us again. It was at this time that government aid was sought, and it is due to our congressmen and a few of our leading citizens here, who worked hard and incessantly and obtained that government aid which was so greatly needed and which has had the effect of allaying, perhaps too much, all of our fears. We must not depend too much upon others. Congressional aid comes very slowly and sometimes in small quantities, and sometimes not at all. This western side of the city is its vital point. It has been that, so far as the site is concerned, for seventy years. It is time for that feature of our situation to pass away or so to change that we shall cease to have any apprehension. The government policy is not well established —not up to this time. It has to do only with the interest of navigation, it is often said, and the land-owners and others must take care of themselves.

One of Col. Taylor's reasons for his contract with the Illinois Central Railroad Company of July 18, 1872, by which that company was released from the obligations of its contracts of February 11, 1851, and of May 31, 1855, was that he expected to obtain from the Cairo & St. Louis Railroad Company a contract binding it to keep up and maintain not only the Mississippi levee, upon which its track was laid, but to protect the levee against the abrasion of the river. He failed to obtain such a contract or a contract upon which such construction could be placed; and that company, having wholly failed and all of its property having been sold in a foreclosure proceeding and transferred to the new company, the St. Louis & Cairo Railroad Company, stripped of all objections of any kind, that source of help or protection, whatever it might have been, has long since passed away. Col. Taylor knew all about the Cairo & St. Louis Railroad Company, for he was its first president. He himself knew and said it was not able to build a standard gauge railroad, but could only build one of a narrow or three foot gauge; and why he or his Trustees found it best to let out the Illinois Central, one of the strongest companies in the United States, and take in its place one of the weakest therein, is scarcely conceivable, excepting on the theory that the Trustees were in great need of the $80,000 they got from the railroad company. Those contracts were as levees to the city. They were plain enough as to all essential and vital features. The levees the railroad company was to build and maintain in perpetuity were to encompass the city or the site thereof and were to be of the width of 80 feet on the top and sufficiently high to keep out the highest waters known.

To say that the railroad company overreached the Trustees would not be correct. The latter knew what they were doing as well as the former; and these contracts, which the two made at the very outstart of their existence and which both believed to be of the utmost importance to their city, were mutually annulled to the mutual satisfaction of both of them, but to the never-ending damage and injury to the City of Cairo and its people. About the only answer the Trustees ever made to this charge was that the affair was a matter of their own business and of nobody else. From 1851 to 1860 or later, they said the very contrary in their innumerable circulars and advertising pamphlets. Col. Taylor as much as conceded that some explanation was due the public, and hence what he said about what he hoped to get from the Cairo & St. Louis Railroad Company in lieu of his contract with the Illinois Central.

Capt. Henry C. Long was the civil engineer of the Trustees and of the Illinois Central Railroad Company for many years here at Cairo. The Trustees had instructed him to make a careful survey of the site of the present city of Cairo and to report fully in regard to the same, especially in regard to river abrasions and the necessary levee construction. The work seems to have been done under the supervision of his father, Col. Stephen Harriman Long, United States Topographical Engineer and Superintendent of Western River Improvements, with headquarters at Louisville, Kentucky. His report bears date September 2, 1850, and is directed to Col. Long, and the same was laid before the Trustees, Taylor and Davis, by a letter dated at Louisville, Kentucky, September 4, 1850. It is probably the most full and carefully prepared report that was ever made relative to Cairo, its site, its dangers from abrasions, the remedies against the same, and the extent, height and width of needed levees. It would make twenty-five pages of this book and is accompanied by a number of diagrams or descriptive drawings. We give only those pages of the report describing the drawings, as follows:

Drawing No. 1.—"Chart of Cairo and its Environs." This drawing is intended to give a general view of the position and configuration of the shores, islands, etc., at the confluence of the Ohio and Mississippi rivers; it also represents the true geographical position of the city of Cairo; a general plan of its interior arrangement with reference to streets, public squares, levees, railroads, etc.; the relative distance and localities of "Ohio City," the town of "Trinity," mouth of "Cash" river etc. The scale is 1,000 feet to one inch. The lines of survey, triangulation, etc., are traced in faint dotted lines, and are sufficiently apparent on the drawing, without a more minute description.

Drawing No. 1, Fig. 2, represents on a scale of ten feet to one inch, a cross section of proposed levee, with its stone escarpment, etc., a full description of which will be given in an after part of this report.

Drawing No. 2.—"Topographical sketch of Cairo." This drawing is constructed on double the scale of No. 1, being 500 feet to one inch; it is consequently more minute in its details, representing accurately the appearance of Cairo at the time of the survey. The foundries, work shops, hotels, houses, etc., are assigned their true positions; the proportion of cultivated, cleared, and timber land is accurately given; the length, position, and general appearance of the levees are clearly defined, and in connection therewith, the true position and extent of the three natural ridges, extending across the city site. All of the topography is the result of actual survey—no attempt being made at mere embellishment, and no lines or marks introduced which a careful attention to the natural features of the ground would not authorize.

The line marked Crevasse is the one to which I would call your particular attention, as requiring immediate consideration. At this locality the abrasion is taking place. The levee at this place should be repaired, or rather reconstructed with all possible dispatch;—the distance marked is 1,675 feet, but as it is recommended to locate the new levee further from the river bank, (in the position given in Drawing No. 1,) this distance will be somewhat increased—but the entire cost of the work is trifling, as shown in the subjoined estimates, and its necessity urgent.

It may be pertinent to state in this connection, that this crevasse is said to have commenced in the spring of 1847, and has been suffered to increase since that time without any attempt at repairs. From 1843, the time of first completion of the chain of levees, to 1847, the enclosed portion of Cairo was secure from overfloods, the levees with all their imperfections having up to that time served as a complete protection.

Drawing No. 2, Fig. 2.—"Section on Crevasse;" scale vertical, 20 feet to one inch. Horizontal, 200 feet to one inch; constructed from levels taken over natural surfaces, showing the amount of embankment necessary to bring the repairs of crevasse to level of Mississippi Levee; also showing the height of Mississippi and cross levees above water surface at time of surveys.

Drawing No. 3.—"Plot of the City of Cairo." Scale 500 feet to 1 inch. This drawing gives a plan of the city on a larger scale and more in detail than represented on Chart No. 1. The blocks generally are 420 feet square, inclusive of two 20-feet alleys intersecting each block at right angles. The streets are 60 feet in width, with the exception of the avenues, which are 120 feet wide. From a careful study of the nature of the city site, and a comparison of most approved plans, this is considered the best arrangement that can be offered in point of economy of room, convenience for business purposes, perfect ventilation and drainage. From the direction given to the principal streets and avenues, they will generally command a fine breeze, which, during a great proportion of the year prevails from the south and west. The blocks designated by circles, are recommended as suitable positions for public squares. A commodious park may be obtained at the point, marked on the Plot "Crescent Park," by extending the line as shown on the drawing, and reclaiming a valuable portion of land, now entirely useless.

It is contemplated to introduce along the line of Commercial Avenue, a railroad track, which will pass northerly from the lower extremity of Cairo to a connection with the Great Western Railroad of Illinois—the depot being located at the intersection of this avenue with "Adams Avenue" on the triangular block marked on the Plot "Main Railroad Depot." Other connections can be made with the Western Railroad, as distinctly shown in Chart No. 1, giving to this city incalculable facilities of communication with the interior of the State of Illinois.

The works required in order to prevent the recurrence of the evils occasioned by the crevasse, and to afford a more perfect protection against overflows than they have heretofore imparted, are as follows, viz.:

(Here follows a detailed statement or estimate of the expense of raising the Ohio levee eighteen inches and of culverts or sewers of masonry through the Ohio levee and of the elevation of the Mississippi levee the same as the Ohio and of the construction of a new levee to connect the Mississippi levee with the cross levee about one hundred and fifty yards from the margin of the Mississippi River and parallel thereto, and of the enlargement and increased elevation of the cross levee and of the restoration of the levee where the crevasse existed on the west as shown in drawing No. 2.)

A copy of "Drawing No. 2, Topographical Sketch of Cairo," is found on another page; and I may here remark that the copies of the maps and plats contained in the book contain a great deal of information which I have not deemed necessary to state or repeat. An examination of them will answer many questions which would otherwise seem very pertinent.

Col. Long must have been, in some way or other, in the service of the Trustees, or he must have been specially directed by government authority to give careful attention to the two rivers here and the site of the city. His son, Capt. Long, as above stated, was in the service of the Trustees and just why his report, which was for them, should be directed to Col. Long, I do not know.

Col. Long was at the head of the expedition sent out to the Rocky Mountains, in 1819, by the secretary of state, John C. Calhoun, under President Monroe. The members of the party embarked on the Ohio at Pittsburg on the steamboat "Western Engineer." They reached Cairo on the 30th day of May, 1819. They seem to have stopped some time at America, which was then starting out with strong hopes of becoming quite a city, claiming as it did to be the head of navigation. While there Col. Long purchased a number of lots and two or three years afterwards purchased others. They passed Cairo and went on to St. Louis and up the Missouri River and thence to the Rocky Mountains, the highest peak of which was given the name of Long, and has ever since been called "Long's Peak." It was supposed then to be the highest peak of that range of mountains, and while it is put down upon the present maps as higher than Pike's Peak, it does not seem to be the highest. The occount of this expedition was written by Mr. Edwin James and is contained in volumes ten to fourteen of Dr. Thwaites' "Early Western Travels," now in our public library. We will refer to Capt. Henry C. Long in another chapter.

Long entertained no fear of the Ohio side of the site causing any considerable trouble. I may, however, remark here that the Ohio side was neglected so long that very considerable inroads were made a number of years ago upon the bank at a number of places, in particular, that part of the bank or shore extending from Eighth to Fourteenth Streets. Then, too, at points above the city, there have been from time to time very considerable abrasions, but none of such character as to attract much attention. The difference between the two rivers consists chiefly in the clearer water and the slow movement of the one and the more rapid and whirling current of the other, loaded down with sand and silt. On the Ohio side, between Eighth and Fourteenth Streets, nothing at all was done until it became evident Ohio Street would be cut in two and destroyed. The same thing that had taken place on the Mississippi side, in 1874, 1875 and 1876, was taking place on the Ohio shore but to a comparatively limited extent. The similarity consisted in neglect to adopt and carry out remedial measures to arrest the abrasions. On the Ohio side the danger was perhaps a little more immediate. The cutting had reached the street line and just inside of the street, of the width of eighty feet, stood the line of business houses, which would no doubt have been reached in the course of a very few years had the supineness of the Trustees, the railroad company and the city continued much longer. The situation led to an investigation to ascertain whose duty it was to protect the levee embankment and the street thereon. It seems to have been concluded that the duty rested on the railroad company and the Trustees under their contracts of June 11, 1851 and May 31, 1855. All three of the parties, however, denied liability. In this matter, as in many others, the city and the people found the Trustees and the railroad company much disposed to act together; but the situation was so plainly to be seen, so much like the midday sun in a cloudless sky, that the three parties *got together,* in political phrase, and compromised the controversy by each agreeing to pay one-third of the expense. Thomas W. Halliday was the mayor then, and friendly to Col. Taylor, the resident Trustee, his father-in-law, and also to the railroad company. Tom firmly believed that more could be done by conciliatory means, by friendly negotiations, and by compromises, than by stout words and lawsuits. This was Tom's uniform method of procedure. He did not own the city council, but had he owned it, the unanimity could not have been more unanimous. One of our newspapers called attention, now and then, to the harmonious agreement that generally prevailed under Tom's administrations, of which there were five or six. While such a state of things does not always argue well, it is, as a general rule, far better than factious opposition and frequent bickerings, conditions we often see in municipal legislative bodies.

These three parties took hold of the embarrassing situation, and no doubt did the best they could. They did nothing to the river or to the shore line or its slope. They simply constructed a stone wall at the east line or margin of Ohio Street and extended it to the height of four or five feet above the street level. It was to serve the double purpose of stopping the cutting at or near the upper line of the bank when the river was high, and to keep the water from coming over the levee should it rise above the same. It has no doubt prevented the cutting caused by high water, but it could serve no good purpose where there was under-cutting in times of low water. Fortunately there has been little of that for many years. How long the high stone wall will stand on the sloping shoulders of the river bank, no one can tell. The ever-existing danger is that its great weight, coupled with a softening bank in high water times, may carry it down. In those contracts above mentioned will be found provisions which, had they been enforced, would have saved the city its share of the expense of the stone wall and have stopped the cutting, which made the wall necessary or something else in its stead. We would quote a few paragraphs from those contracts, but it would require much space, and besides the matter is wholly one of history and need not be presented at length. It was the same old controversy that was fought over in the United States court at Springfield in the suit of the Trustees against the railroad company to recover for moneys expended which they said should have been expended by the company. That suit was compromised July 18, 1872, and the contracts annulled. The Trustees claimed that the railroad company should construct the levees and put a stop to the abrasions. The railroad company denied everything it could, especially the claim that it should protect the natural banks from the abrasions of the rivers. The two litigants seem to have cared for no one and nothing but themselves, and in effect said to the people of the city, that if they wanted levees and river-bank protections they would have to get both in the easiest and best way they could. Judge Bross, in 1863, began a suit in equity in our circuit court against the Trustees to procure, if possible, an enforcement of some of the provisions of those contracts; but he was taken off to the United States court at Springfield and found himself too weak to cope with his defendants, supported as they no doubt were by the Illinois Central Railroad Company. He had cited the multitude of circulars and other representations of the Trustees concerning the levees and levee protection and the perfect security the purchasers of lots would have against the rivers, either high or low. He insisted that the purchasers of lots had a right to rely upon the representations which had led them to make their several investments, and that to deny them that legal right would be a great injustice. The Trustees, on the other hand, replied that whatever their representations were, they were not of a *contractual* nature, and that whatever became of the levees themselves or of the natural ground upon which they rested, the lot owners could have no recourse on them, and that they must bear their losses as best they could. I must not dwell longer on this feature of Cairo's history, save only to say that if such a condition ever existed before or anywhere else, an account of the same can nowhere be found. The situation was bare of any qualifying or ameliorating features.

Returning to the Ohio River abrasion between Eighth and Fourteenth Streets, we remark that the stone wall would never have become necessary had the Trustees done what they often promised and what they started once or twice to do, and that was *to extend the wharf from 8th Street to 14th Street.* Many years ago they did a large amount of work along there to stop the cutting during low water, but they never undertook to do any systematic work in the way of filling the slope and protecting it by some system of revetment. They owned the premises and denied the right of the city to have anything to do with the river banks or the levees. They were private property to be kept up or let go, regardless of who suffered by the inroads of the rivers. In the place of an extension of the wharf and the improved state of things that its extension would have brought about, we now have that unsightly gap in the river bank and the perpendicular stone wall as a perpetual reminder of the needy condition in which the city was placed and of the parsimony of the Trustees and the Illinois Central Railroad Company. The one owned the river bank to low-water mark, and the other for all practical purposes owned Ohio Street, and the river was destroying both subjects of ownership; but the two parties knew very well who was in most danger, they or the people of the city, and hence it was easy to get the latter to compromise. The situation was not unlike that which existed in 1874, 1875 and 1876, when a long stretch of the Mississippi levee went into the river and what is now called new levee had to be built. The Trustees owned the levees which the railroad company had built for them; but their interest in their construction and maintenance seemed to change as their sales of lots and lands became less and less and their conviction increased that their Cairo enterprise would never come up to their expectations. And, therefore, some years ago they signified to the city that it could have the levees or most of them if it would assume the burden of their maintenance. The city saw that it was in a strait betwixt two, and therefore accepted the donation, which was no doubt quite as beneficial to the donor as to the donee.

As bearing on the condition of the levee or river front, from Eighth Street to Fourteenth Street, and the matter of the stone wall, I quote here from Col. Taylor's deposition taken in 1866 in a suit between the Trustees and the city, in the United States Circuit Court at Springfield, to show that it was part of the original plan, agreed upon by the Trustees and the railroad company, that the river front should be graded and paved from Eighth Street to Fourteenth Street, the same as from Fourth Street to Eighth Street:

"Since the commencement of this suit about $20,000 has been expended by the Trustees of the Cairo City Property in constructing a sustaining wall at the base of another portion of the same slope, which seemed to be necessary to preserve the river bank from abrasion. To complete the sustaining wall at the base of the remaining part below 14th Street of the levee and complete the pavement and improvement of the slope of the levee to 14th Street, so as to finish it as a wharf, will still require the expenditure of $150,000, and this amount the Trustees of the Cairo City Property had procured and had commenced to expend for the purpose indicated when their operations were arrested by the action of the City Council of the City of Cairo in providing for the collection of wharfage by the City authorities. The Trustees will proceed to expend this or any other amount necessary to complete the wharf to 14th Street as soon as their right to the levee is confirmed to them and will extend the wharf still further up the Ohio as the public wants may demand."

To much that I have said in this chapter objection will no doubt be made; but it must be remembered that I am writing a history of Cairo, and that large parts of it relate to the Trustees and the Illinois Central Railroad Company. It was their city by birth and should have been theirs for nurture and not for exploitation. I might have written a history of Cairo and filled it full of nice things about everybody, corporations, land-trusts and all; but it would not have been history. Cairo's history is a history of facts, hard facts, most of them and most of the time.

I need not say much about levee construction in addition to what is here and there found in other parts of the book.

The terminus of the Illinois Central Railroad was to be here. The company was greatly interested in the work of building a city, but to do that and to protect its own terminal property and interests it was equally interested with the Trustees in having the best of levees constructed; and hence those never-to-be-forgotten contracts of June 11, 1851, and of May 31, 1855. *By these contracts the railroad company, by the deed of October 15, 1853, had obtained extensive and very valuable grounds, five hundred acres, I suppose, and for these lands and many important privileges, it bound itself to furnish the town of the Trustees with levees encompassing the site thereof and of the width of eighty (80) feet on the top and sufficiently high to keep out the highest known floods.*

Many years ago, I procured from the Harvard College library a copy of the plat or survey of Cairo's site, made by James Thompson in 1837. I handed it to Mr. Charles Thrupp, who had resided here in Cairo since the year 1850, and requested him to indicate thereon the present lines or shores of the rivers. He did so and returned it to me, with a line drawn thereon showing how much the shore line had moved inward on both sides of the city, since 1837. According to the line drawn by him it appeared that the rivers had made inroads almost at every point except those immediately below the city, on the south and southwest. The invasion was so great that I could scarcely believe that the line was correctly drawn. And yet it would not be so difficult to ascertain the loss at almost every point. The first survey of the township was made in 1807, and the acreage given in each congressional subdivision or fractional part thereof. Other surveys were made prior to 1840 and the acreage duly ascertained; and it is very probable that Mr. Thrupp was quite well enough acquainted with the quantity of lands in the different divisions to enable him to make a fairly correct estimate thereof.

It will be observed that here and elsewhere I have said much about the abrasions of the rivers. I have done this in the hope of impressing upon the minds of the people of the city the importance of giving the closest attention to the action of the rivers upon the shores or banks adjacent to the city. It may be said that the matter is quite obvious enough. I think so; but it is nevertheless true that time and time again the beginnings of abrasions have had no attention given them until the expense of the needed work had increased many fold.

In the report of the Trustees of October 1, 1884, to the shareholders, it was stated that after the washing away of the Mississippi River bank in the fall of 1875, the government had expended in the protection of the bank up to June 30, 1880, $113,351.43, and that the expenditure was made upon about three miles of the river bank, commencing a short distance below our old cross levee and extending up stream; and further, that the abrasion where the work had been done had been entirely arrested and that whatever abrasion had taken place since was below the government work. The report further stated that since 1851, the total erosion prior to the government work had amounted to 963.69 acres, and that since the work was done most of the land had been restored to them, that is, the Trustees. The report went on to say that the government work extended but a short distance below the old cross levee and not down to the place where the levees came to the river bank.

THE HIGHEST KNOWN FLOODS. Elsewhere will be found an interesting table showing the greatest and smallest rainfalls, the highest and lowest temperatures, and the highest and lowest water in the Ohio River, at Cairo, since the year 1871. This table was prepared for me by Mr. William E. Barron, Chief of the Weather Bureau at this place, and extends over the period of thirty-nine years. We place it in the book for purposes of easy reference.

The two rivers are so close together that the measure of the elevation or level of the water in the one will do also for the other. The Ohio River water gauge, when the Ohio is high and the Mississippi low, measures for the Ohio only, and when the Mississippi is high and the Ohio low it may be said to measure for the Mississippi only. In other words, the backwater from the one or the other should not be considered as giving here the true level or height of the water in the river into which the backwater flows. It may also be remarked that while the rivers may be very high at St. Louis or at Cincinnati, Louisville or Evansville or even at Paducah, it does not follow that they will be high here at all. High water at those places seldom attracts attention here; and especially is this the case with the Mississippi River. It is the Ohio only which has ever given the city of Cairo any trouble of consequence. Even when both rivers are high at one and the same time, little or no notice is taken of the matter unless the Ohio reaches one of its very highest stages. It is the Ohio that claims for itself the right to rise and fall through a perpendicular distance of fifty feet. The Mississippi and its chief tributaries come from the cold regions of the north and their high waters do not reach Cairo until the sun is well up in the heavens to melt the northern snows and raise the rivers from the low and frozen levels of the winter. These flood waters do not reach Cairo as a general thing until about the first of June and sometimes considerably later. The Ohio, on the contrary, sends down its flood waters three or four months earlier. The highest floods ever known or recorded were those of 1882, 1883 and 1884, and the highest point reached each time did not vary twenty-four hours from February 25th of each of those years. As elsewhere stated, the Tennessee is the largest of the Ohio's tributaries. It is a large river, coming out of Virginia, West Virginia and Kentucky, crossing the state of Tennessee at Knoxville and entering the state of Alabama near Chattanooga and then running for some distance in the last named state turns northward and again crossing the state of Tennessee, passes for the distance of fifty miles through the state of Kentucky and discharges its waters into the Ohio just fifty miles by river measurement from the city of Cairo. Just above the mouth of the Tennessee, and at the distance of twelve miles, the Cumberland River also enters the Ohio. These rivers and the Ohio's other tributaries are filled full by the early spring rains, which are much heavier than further northward, and the consequence is that the Ohio at Cairo is seen to mount up at a rapid rate and rush forward into the Mississippi at a speed hardly to be expected considering its usually gentle flow.

We read accounts of great floods in the Mississippi more than a hundred years ago; but as before stated, great floods at considerable distances above Cairo, in either river, are not reliable indications of what they were here. At St. Louis and Kaskaskia or Ste. Genevieve, there were great overflows in 1785, 1815 and 1844, and at many other times since. As to the flood of 1815 at this place, it is said that the water was so high that persons rode in skiffs or other boats out as far as Charleston. Many times since 1815, the water across the river in Missouri has extended far out over the adjoining country, but none so far as Charleston, we suppose. In 1785, Augustus Chouteau went by skiff or other small boat over the American bottom from what is now East St. Louis to Kaskaskia; but it is also stated that the flood of 1844 was higher by two feet than that of 1785, in that region on the Mississippi. The overflow of 1844 could not have been, for this region, very high; for it seems to be a well established fact that the Cairo levees withstood that flood and securely protected the city, which by that time had been reduced to very small proportions, but for other causes than high rivers or inundations. It is exceedingly difficult, if not quite impossible, to reconcile the accounts found here and there concerning the great floods in the Ohio and Mississippi from Cincinnati and St. Louis to the mouth of the Ohio River. When we consider the fact that we have no very reliable information as to the exact height of the water here at Cairo prior to 1867, we must concede the difficulty of obtaining exact information at other points. Such information would be found to exist only where immovable monuments of some kind could be found upon which the different heights of the water had been carefully inscribed.

THE FLOODS OF 1832 AND 1840.—The English bond-holders, in 1840, sent to Cairo Mr. Septimus Worsley, of London, to examine and report the condition of things he found here; and in a letter dated Cairo, Illinois, July 14, 1840, he says, speaking of the levees:

"The measures, as stated by Mr. Strickland, are perfectly correct, and I have practical proof that if the proposed bank had been completed, the site of the City of Cairo would have been perfectly protected from this year's flood, the greatest that has been known for eight years—the waters at their highest stage not having reached within two feet of the top of the levee, which has not yet in any place been carried up to its proposed height; it was also ascertained, that whilst the waters higher up the river were rapidly increasing, the waters around Cairo, after they had attained a certain height, did not rise more than an inch during the day."

THE FLOOD OF 1844.—As elsewhere stated, Mr. Miles A. Gilbert came to Cairo in June, 1843, and during the remainder of that year he constructed the cross levee extending from a point near Eighteenth Street and Ohio levee out westward and then bearing northward and connecting with the Mississippi levee. The length of this line was 8670 feet. That work was no doubt well done, for it and the other levees seem to have withstood the high water of 1844. If the reader will turn to the topographical map of Cairo made by Mr. Henry C. Long September 2, 1850, he will see the lines of the Cairo levees and what is said thereon regarding the height to which the water arose. It must have been thought very extraordinary that Cairo should escape that flood when at so many other places it had caused great loss and damage.

THE FLOOD OF 1849.—We hear nothing more of overflows or high rivers until the year 1849. Regarding the effect of the flood of that year upon Cairo, we give here an extract from the "Cairo Delta," of March 20, 1849, entitled "High Water":

> The rivers have been higher during the past week at this point than they have been since the construction of our levee. Had several hundred dollars been expended last winter in repairing a break in the Mississippi levee, repairing the sewers and elevating slightly portions of the Ohio levee, the spectacle would have been presented of this being the only point in this region of country on the rivers, not more or less inundated. The public would have beheld a place, which for years back has been ridiculed above all others, through unfair prejudices, as a point subject to frequent inundations—standing alone and singular, almost the only dry and perfectly protected town on the Ohio or Lower Mississippi rivers. But through the negligence or inattention of the company owning this valuable property—or probably from their ignorance of the real want of such expenditure—these trifling repairs and improvements were not made, and Cairo, like almost every other place above and below on the rivers, has suffered from the floods. The flood first poured through the old break in the Mississippi levee till the waters inside the levees became higher than the Ohio river, and finally reached such a height as to overflow the Ohio levee in different places. Our stores and the Delta office have not been much discommoded by the flood.
>
> We trust and hope that the repairs so much needed will no longer be postponed. We are satisfied that if the company were fully aware of the injury

inflicted upon their interests here, by this deferred expenditure, it would no longer be withheld. The expense of making repairs is now much increased. The immense value of this property, and the high prices lots would undoubtedly bring if offered for sale, might warrant any expenditure for its protection.

We hear of immense destruction of property on almost every western river. The coast below is suffering severely, and the prospects of many extensive sugar planters are blasted for two seasons to come. Never before have we heard of so great a rise in all our rivers taking place at one time. The noted floods of 1844 cannot compare with the memorable floods of 1849.

We have seldom heard anything much about the flood of 1849; but Editor Ad. H. Sanders seems to have had an excellent newspaper and to have treated everything he took in hand with sound judgment. But at this distance of time, we cannot be very certain about any such matter or thing occurring that far back. The Trustees of the Cairo City Property were in charge. They were endeavoring to perfect their land titles, and were doing many other matters and things of a preliminary nature. Even at that time, they had strong hopes of an Illinois Central Railroad, whose terminus would be here at Cairo, and which would aid them in putting up high and strong levees; and it may be that they did not care to spend considerable sums on the levees as they then existed. Still, we can see no good answer to what the editor has said regarding what might have easily been done to prevent the disaster.

The high water of 1858, which broke through the Mississippi levee on the afternoon of Saturday, June 12, 1858, was not of extraordinary height. It is said the levee had been badly constructed, at least in places; that those persons having that part of the levee in their immediate charge left stumps and logs in the line of the levee and had used the same so far as they would go instead of well selected earth. Col. Taylor was here on the ground and this was his statement both to the public generally and to the committee of shareholders sent here to investigate the calamity. Col. Taylor and Mr. H. C. Long were here all the time during the construction of the levees by the Illinois Central Railroad Company. The contracts of June 11, 1851, and May 31, 1855, provided that the engineers of each party should co-operate with each other in carrying forward that great and most important work of levee construction. Who used the logs and stumps as a part of the levee construction and whose duty it was to know what was being done and prevent the wrong, need not at this distant day be considered. But if there was more than a grain of truth in what Col. Taylor said was the cause of the inundation of the city, it should have aroused the indignation of the twenty-five hundred people then in Cairo. It no doubt led to a better supervision of the work; for since that day we have never heard of anything like it occurring again.

THE FLOOD OF 1862.—On the 20th and 21st days of July, 1863, two large public meetings of the citizens of Cairo were held at the court house to consider the condition of the levees. Col. John S. Hacker was the chairman and David J. Baker the secretary of the meetings. Among the men present and taking a part were Daniel Hurd, Robert H.

Cunningham, Dr. E. K. Hall, John W. Trover, Peter Neff, John Howley, Martin Egan, David T. Linegar, and Joseph McKenzie. The proceedings of the meetings were published in the Cairo Daily News of July 27, 1863. The resolutions adopted were long and wide in scope and ladened with severe complaints against the Trustees. Portions of the speeches are given. I quote two or three of the preambles and a sentence or two from one of the speeches to show their references to the floods of 1858 and 1862.

> And whereas, this said temporary levee did, in the year 1858, give way, and the city was thereby submerged to an average depth of twelve feet, causing a loss of life and the destruction of property to the amount of hundreds of thousands of dollars, besides a vast deterioration in the value of real estate, and a loss of confidence in the practicability of building a city at this unrivalled commercial point;
>
> And whereas, the rivers did, in the year 1862, rise to a height of fourteen inches above the present levees, and the city property was greatly endangered, and was only saved by the industry of the citizens by turning out and erecting and guarding temporary levees on the top of the present Ohio river levee;
>
> And whereas, the levee on the Ohio river, between the graded part thereof and the Illinois Central freight depot, has caved and is still caving to an alarming extent, and to the great detriment of property holders; * * * In 1862, the levee was again found to be insufficient. You all remember the consternation that spread among the inhabitants, and how all packed up and fled to the levee for safety. You also remember how the people took the matter of defense into their own hands, and worked almost day and night at the false levees that finally saved us. Had it not been for these efforts we would have been overflowed, and worse disasters and a greater destruction of property would have taken place than in 1858.

It will be here seen that as far back as that early day the bad condition of the river front from Eighth Street to Fourteenth Street was being complained of as the source of much trouble to the city. Those contracts of June 11, 1851, and May 31, 1855, between the Trustees and the Illinois Central Railroad Company provided for the extension of the work all the way to Fourteenth Street; but it was never done, and after many years the situation became so bad as to necessitate some remedy or other, *and hence the present stone wall* on the river front.

The Flood of 1867.—Mr. Barron, in speaking of the River Gauge, in Chapter XI, says that the flood of March, 1867, reached a stage of 51 feet, measured by the present gauge. This information may have come from Col. Taylor or from some one else who had preserved a mark of the same on some building or structure that was still standing in 1871, when the gauge was first put in or established.—It was indeed a trying time to the people, not unlike what it was in 1862, to judge by the proceedings of those public meetings just referred to.

The writer had not been here long and this was the first high water he had seen at Cairo. But for another reason he remembers its occurrence. He had charge of a stock of drugs for sale, and had advertised the same somewhat extensively, with the result that James S. and Philander W. Barclay, the former of Chicago, and the latter from

Bowling Green, Kentucky, came here with a view of purchasing the same and locating in Cairo. They purchased the stock and thus began their wholesale and retail drug business which they conducted here for so many years. Besides recording the fact that this sale was consummated only a few days after the water had reached its highest mark, I desire to record here also my high esteem and regard for those two men. The population of Cairo was long made up of people who were born elsewhere; but of all who came hither and made their homes here, it would be hard to mention citizens of higher character and standing than these two Kentuckians. Whether it was due to their state, or their town, or their parents, or the general environment in which they grew up or were trained, they bore the true stamp of character, to bear which ought to be the proudest possession of any man. James removed from Cairo to Oak Park in the year 1892, and there, ten years afterward, he and his wife died within a few weeks of each other. The other brother remained in Cairo until the time of his death July 6, 1907. He had long been a prominent Mason, and had, some years before his death, reached the thirty-third degree, a very high honor indeed in that ancient order. A biographical sketch of him, but all too meager, is found in Volume I, Templar History, Illinois, 1857-1881. There were six of the Barclay brothers, a picture of whom, taken in Louisville in 1901, is now in the possession of Mr. Phil C. Barclay. Of those six brothers, but one, Jo C. Barclay, is now living. Elsewhere I have spoken of the five Halliday brothers, of whom Major Edwin only is now living.

With reference to those floods in the early eighties, it may be said that the first of the three was the only one that caused the people of Cairo any serious apprehension, and that arose almost chiefly from the fact that a part of the levee on the westerly side of the city was of recent construction, and was made to take the place of a portion of a much older levee that had been undermined by the abrading waters of the Mississippi. This new levee had not become sufficiently firm and solid as to wholly prevent the sliding down of the inside slopes here and there. Even this would not have occurred had not the builders of the levee excavated too close to it, and the consequence was that water accumulated in these excavations and so softened the foot of the levee inside that at one or two places very considerable portions of the inside of the levee slid down into the excavations below. The people were very much alarmed by this. The water in the Mississippi was very high and of the width of at least a mile or more; and the heavy winds blowing northeastward pressed the waters with great force against the levee. The situation looked very bad indeed; but when the flood subsided and the waters were withdrawn into their natural boundaries every one saw that the city was in much less danger than the people had supposed. That new levee had been constructed with a long fine slope and it was seen how the great flood of waters that seemed to be pressing against the levee was simply resting upon the long slope. But after all is said it was a remarkable time, such as every one hoped would not be seen again. Had the levee been as weak as it looked it might have given away entirely; but the faithful and untiring efforts of the citizens of the town so strengthened and fortified the weak place that all fear was largely removed. The strong men who had charge of that work were Capt. Halliday and Mayor Thistlewood, or Mayor Thistlewood and Capt. Halliday. I know not which of them I should name first.

Junction of Rivers, 1858

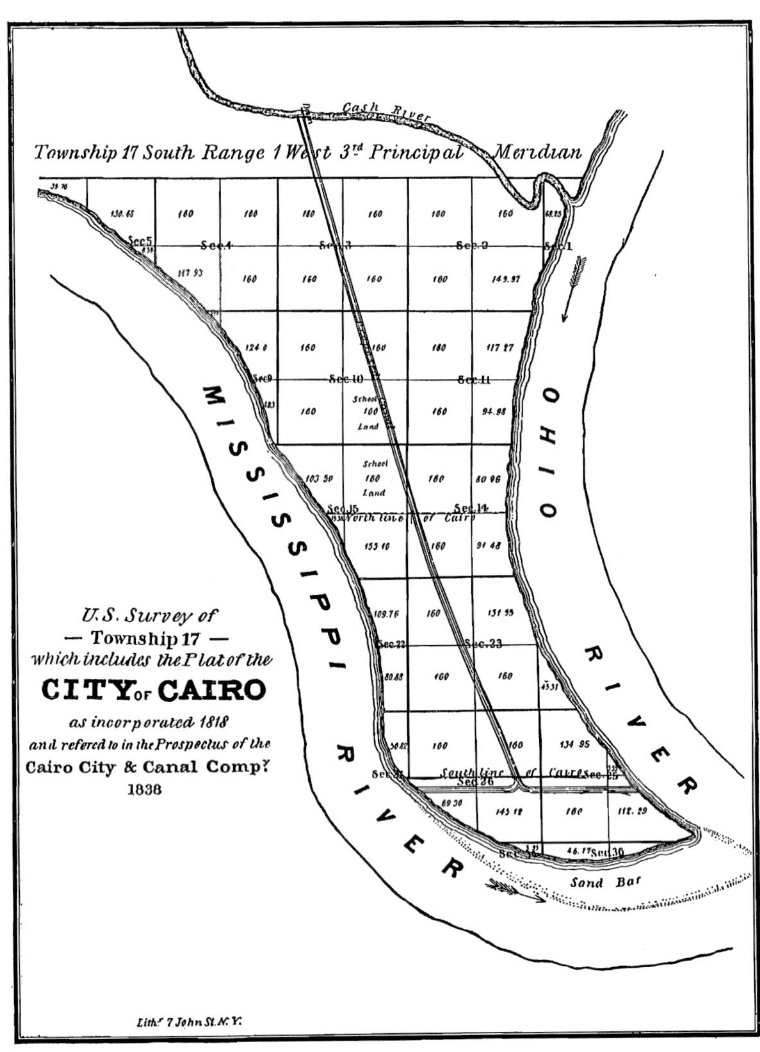

Proposed Canal Between Rivers, 1838

CHAPTER IX

LOW LOTS AND GROUNDS—SEEPAGE—THE LINEGAR BILL—STREET FILLING—CITY INDEBTEDNESS

WHILE our levees have effectively protected the city from overflow for fifty years, we have not been able to adopt any plan to prevent seepage. The underlying strata of sand at and below a certain depth are full of river water, whose level rises and falls with the rise and fall of the waters in the rivers. The rivers unite in these subterranean waters. The natural earth surface of the city presents a number of ridges, generally extending across the city in a southeast and northwest direction. One crosses 3d, 4th, 5th, and 6th Streets diagonally; one, two or three blocks further north; one, still further north and extending on northwestward to and beyond block numbered four, in the third addition to the city; and one from the vicinity of the stone depot on the Ohio at Fourteenth Street and out by the office building of the Trustees and Mr. J. B. Reed's residence. From thence up to the vicinity of Twenty-Eighth Street, the natural ground is generally very low. In these ridges it is claimed that much more underlying sand is found near the surface than in the much lower and level ground, and that these ridges are the chief sources of the seep water. The seepage is due to the pressure of the high waters in the rivers upon the water in the underlying sand, and the latter is forced up to the surface through the porous earth or sand or through openings caused by the decayed roots of trees or otherwise. If the underlying water is much nearer the surface in the ridges than in the low grounds, then indeed more water may seep from the ridges than elsewhere; but this is counteracted by the increased height to which the water must be forced or lifted. It is well remembered that in the days of driven wells, iron pipes of two inches diameter were driven into the earth to the depth of sixty to eighty feet, and when the rivers were high these pipes would send out constant streams of water. Hence those ordinances of the city forbidding excavations in the earth for any purpose to any considerable depth.

In times of very high water in the rivers, the city is much like an empty basin sunken almost to its brim. The minutest opening in the bottom of the vessel will permit a stream of water to shoot up almost to the level of the brim. To prevent this, there is but one effective or practical remedy, and that is earth filling. It is the process of stopping the openings in the surface of the ground within the city. The only other method ever suggested was to stop or keep the river water from getting under the city. That is undoubtedly the best of the two or the best of all methods or remedies; but as a working method or theory, it is so wholly impracticable as to be worth very little. It assumes that the sources of the underground supply of water from the rivers are few and easily reached and stopped or shut off by what is called *sheet piling.* With a river shore line of seven to ten miles and the whole site of the city nothing but an alluvial plain resting on sand, very much like the Illinois Central bridge piers which rest on nothing but sand, how one could expect to keep the river water from finding its way everywhere under the city is hard to understand. The driven wells in all parts of the city north and south exhibited the same water connection with the rivers and no doubt had hundreds of places of supply. They simply tapped the river water right under them and conducted it to the surface. It was forced to the surface in the city by the pressure of the higher water in the rivers. The water was simply seeking its level. The city protected itself against those sources of water from the river by requiring the driven well pipes to be plugged.

In the selfsame way, the method to stop the seepage was to stop the innumerable openings throughout the city, reaching down to the waters beneath, by filling the low grounds with earth to such depth as would prevent the penetration thereof by the upper pressure of the water. Were it practicable to fill with earth all the low grounds within the city to a depth of four to six feet or to the grade of the filled streets in the lower part of town, we would be free forever from the great evil to which the seepage has so long subjected the people of the city. No one has ever seen any seepage, not the smallest quantity, making its appearance on any of the filled streets in the city or where the natural surface has been covered with earth to the depth of four or five feet. The expense of this process has been the only thing in the way of putting the city beyond the reach of this great annoyance. The low site of the city has always been its chief drawback. Earth filling has been the great need, almost the only need. Such work is the work every one should want done. It is simply making the site of the city just what every one would have it to be,—higher and higher than the rivers left it when they were shut out by the levees.

Earth filling is the need, not sand. In all those parts of the city now filled or being filled with sand, the seepage will rise just as high as before the filling. The water will come up through it just as it comes up to the natural surface through the sandy strata extending down to the river waters. Were our levees sand only the waters would not be kept out of the city. Earth embankments are used for dams the world over, because the water will not penetrate them. So, also, a few feet in depth of earth filling will keep down the upward pressing seepage water. But the earth here is a poor quality even for levees. It has too much sand.

The Linegar Bill.—Under Mayor Charles O. Patier's administration, an attempt was made to test the legality of the act of our legislature passed May 19, 1883. It was called the "Linegar Bill" because David T. Linegar, the county's representative in the lower house of the legislature, had drawn it. Its provisions show that it was carefully drawn. It provided for the filling of the low lots and grounds of the city and charging the expense thereof upon the lots and grounds filled. Doing this, however, was dependent upon its being shown *that the rain and seepage accumulated on such lots and grounds and became stagnant and injurious to the public health and that such lots and grounds with the stagnant waters thereon were nuisances.* The people, with few exceptions, were heartily in favor of the bill and of proceedings under it to abate the evil, which was one to be gotten rid of, if it were possible, upon any reasonable terms or conditions. It had existed ever since the town and its levees had existed; and strangers and visitors were amazed that we could not devise some means to rid ourselves of these annual invasions.

Mayor Patier started out to ascertain whether the Linegar Bill was worth anything or nothing. An ordinance was adopted October 17, 1892, describing certain very low lots and providing for their filling and for steps to be taken to collect therefrom the costs of the work, which were made a lien on the lots. Lots fourteen and fifteen, in Block fifty-one, First Addition, were selected for the making of a test case. Among the few persons in the city who opposed the bill or the doing of anything under it, were Col. Samuel Staats Taylor and Capt. William P. Halliday, in most respects the two most prominent men in the city. Col. Taylor's reasons for opposing it no doubt arose from the fact that his Trustees owned more low lots and grounds than almost all the other people in the city, and that the assessments thereon would become a heavy burden, very difficult to be borne by them. Capt. Halliday could have had no such reasons for his opposition; for he owned few such lots. He wrote or had written a lengthy article which he published in the Cairo Daily Telegram of June 20, 1891, in which was set forth at large his reasons for claiming that earth filling was not our remedy for seepage. He insisted that to prevent the water from the rivers entering the sand ridges in the city we should resort to sheet piling, cuts of which were given in the Telegram. He took the strange ground that filling the low grounds with earth would actually increase the quantity of seepage and would not keep it from coming in but would add to its depths in other parts of the city and send it to quarters where it had not formerly gone. In a word or two, his reasons were, first filling the low places with earth would make matters worse, and second, the Linegar Bill was unconstitutional.

Patier, however, was pushing the slow proceedings along to test the validity of the bill, when he was succeeded in office by one of our citizens who cared less for the undertaking than he did; and so the proceedings were not carried further; and to put a final quietus to the matter, that is, to the *danger* incident to filling the low grounds with earth, Capt. Halliday applied to the source from which the law emanated and had it repealed, April 24, 1899. We do not know what the *considerations* were which moved the legislature to this repeal; but whatever they were, their act was in the nature of a calamity to the city. The members who were solicited to procure the repeal should have said that the act seemed to them a good one and that if it was unconstitutional it could be shown before the city could proceed more than a few steps in their undertaking.

Thus came to an end one of the most important proceedings ever undertaken for the good of the city and its people. The principles of the bill had been sustained time and time again in a number of cases in different states, where large lots and tracts of land in and adjoining cities had been filled in precisely the same way and to remove the same evils. *Wilson v. Board of Trustees,* 133 Ill. 443; *Dingley v. City of Boston,* 100 Mass. 544; *Grace v. Board of Health,* 135 Mass. 490; *City Council of Charleston v. Werner,* 38 S. C. 448; *same case* 17 S. E. R. 33; 24 S. E. R. 207; *Sweet vs. Rechel,* 159 U. S. 380. Other cases might be cited, but those given will enable anyone to trace the authorities. It is a little remarkable that when this matter was before the people men were to be found in the city who claimed that the seep water was a good thing to have in the city and that it was not a nuisance to be abated. Few persons, however, went so far as to object to its being pumped out of the city and into the river. We have never had anything in the city which developed so many queer, not to say absurd, theories as did this seepage question and the remedies for the same. The low grounds were objectionable in every view of the case, and to get them higher and above seepage and accumulated rain water was a need too plain for argument. The low site of the city has been the only thing which has prevented it from being four or five times as large as it is.

It may be said, it serves no good purpose now to dwell at such length upon such a past matter as this; but the city still stands in the greatest need of earth filling; and it is to be earnestly hoped that it is not too late to obtain, in some large measure, the object the bill was intended to secure. As elsewhere remarked, next to protecting the site of the city from the abrasion of the rivers, comes the matter of raising the site by earth filling.

But if earth cannot be gotten or gotten only at too high a price, sand should, of course, be used. We have seen that it can be *pumped* into the city at rates much less than those required for earth, and hence the inducement to use it. It will not keep the seepage out or down, but it will keep it out of view, and it will so raise or lift the earth surface that for many purposes it will be as useful as the higher grounds of the city.

Street Filling.—Whatever may have been thought by the people generally as to the need of filling with earth and raising the site of the town, all were agreed as to the importance of filling the streets and bringing them to a proper grade or level. In their natural condition they were and some of them are almost impassable some portions of the year. Very little of this kind of public work had been done prior to the year 1863, when the city authorities took the matter in hand, and

July 15, 1863, contracted with Capt. William P. Halliday to fill with earth Commercial Avenue to 20th Street, Washington Avenue and Poplar Street to 18th Street and all the cross streets from 1st to 18th Streets, both inclusive. The contract provided that the filling should be made to the present grade of those avenues and streets and at the cost of thirty-five cents per cubic yard. The contractor gave a bond in the sum of $25,000.00 for the faithful performance of the work.

It seems, however, that the contractor, after filling part of Commercial Avenue, found that he had taken the work at too low a price, and differences arising between him and the city, the contract, on the 23d day of June, 1864, was rescinded and the bondsmen released by the city council of the city. The Trustees in their report to the shareholders, September 29, 1864, speak of this matter as follows:

"So, also, from inability of the contractor to do the work at the contract price, the contract for filling the streets at 35 cents the cubic yard has been annulled, and a new contract made by the city council for doing the same work at 60 cents the cubic yard. This contract for filling the streets only embraces streets up as far as Twentieth Street."

A short time after this, namely, on the 10th day of November, 1864, the council let the same work to George Odiorne at 60 cents per cubic yard, but Odiorne does not seem to have given the required bond of $25,000.00, and the arrangement failed. Afterwards, and on the 25th day of February, 1865, the council let the work to Fox, Howard & Company, of Chicago, but at the price of 74 cents a yard. That was forty-five years ago and we do not know what the actual facts and circumstances of the situation were which made it necessary or important to let go the one contract and bond and take up the others. Something over eighteen months elapsed from the first to the last letting. These somewhat peculiar proceedings seem to have been entirely fair and proper, judging by the well known names of the persons in charge of the matter. David J. Baker, whom every one esteemed very highly, was the chairman of the board of public works.

Fox, Howard & Company proceeded with the work and in its prosecution used a steam shovel for excavating the earth and filling their long line of tram cars to haul the same into the city and along the different streets to be filled. The work was pushed forward rapidly, and completed late in the year 1866, or early in the year 1867. The assessments for paying for the work were levied upon the abutting lots according to the frontage principle and as provided for in the laws then in force regarding such matters, but this method of assessment having been held unconstitutional under our then existing constitution of 1848, in the case of *Chicago vs. Larned,* 34 Ill. 203, the collections of the assessments had to be abandoned, with perhaps almost one half of the assessments unpaid.

Upon it becoming known in the city that these assessments were not legally made or levied, all payments of the same immediately ceased; and the question at once arose as to the liability of the city to refund to the owners of property the assessments they had paid. Two cases were begun against the city to test the question, the one by Capt. Walter Falls and the other by Patrick Mockler. The Falls suit only was tried. Judge David J. Baker, our circuit judge at that time, heard the case without a jury, and decided that the city was not liable to refund the payments, chiefly on the grounds that the payments were voluntary and there had been no failure of consideration, for the filling had been done and the benefits thereof conferred upon the property upon which the assessments had been made and had been paid. Capt. Falls took his case on to the supreme court, where the judgment of the circuit court was affirmed. See *Falls vs. City of Cairo,* 58 Ill. 403.

The payment of assessments having ceased, the city was without means to pay the contractors, and they therefore brought suit against the city for the balance due them, and on the 29th day of April, 1868, obtained judgment for the sum of $110,390.09.

The city taking no steps to pay the judgment, they applied directly to the supreme court for a writ of mandamus to compel the city council to make a special levy of taxes to pay the same. The court awarded the writ, but the matter was adjusted, under Mayor John H. Oberly's administration, without further proceedings, by the issuance to Fox, Howard & Company of eight per cent twenty year city bonds to the amount of $123,000,00. The interest on these bonds was paid for a few years only. The city in 1876 stopped payment of the interest on these bonds and on all of its other bonds, the larger portions of which were railroad bonds. Extensive litigation then ensued and continued for many years, resulting finally in compromises and settlements, generally by exchanging new city bonds for the old ones on terms agreed upon from time to time by the holders and the city authorities. The city had undertaken to carry too heavy a load. It and the county had issued to the Cairo & Vincennes Railroad Company and the Cairo & St. Louis Railroad Company (narrow gauge) bonds to the amount of $385,000.00. The six and eight per cent interest had accumulated rapidly; and when the city and county ceased payment in 1878, their bonded indebtedness amounted to the large sum of $765,373.30.

This bonded indebtedness trouble of the city hung upon and clouded it for many years beginning with 1876. The county united with the city in attempts to obtain relief from burdens concededly too heavy to be borne; and the writer takes occasion here to remark that the services of the Hon. William B. Gilbert in his representation of the city and county in the litigation with bond-holders and in the various methods of compromises and settlements were of the greatest value. With the greatest tenacity of purpose and the most unremitting and persistent efforts on his part, he brought the city and county out of one of the most embarrassing financial situations in which such municipalities could possibly be placed.

CHAPTER X

THE WHARF AND WHARFAGE—RIPARIAN RIGHTS

THE paved wharf as it now exists extends from the south line of 4th Street to the north line of 8th Street, a distance of ten hundred and eighty (1080) feet. The paved face of it extends nearly to low-water mark on an angle of about eleven degrees to the plane or level of Ohio Street adjoining; and the distance from the street line to the paving at or near low-water mark is about two hundred and ten (210) feet. There are, therefore, about 24,000 square yards in its surface or about five acres or as much as two of our largest city blocks.

Looking at the wharf now and at the river bank above and below it, we can easily see what the river landing was prior to the construction of the wharf, which was begun in the year 1857. Prior to that time and for thirty years, the flatboats, keelboats, and other like water-craft, and the steamboats, wharfboats, barges, &c., had to land at and be tied up to the bank, and there were, therefore, the most primitive and temporary means for loading and unloading and caring for passengers and freights.

Hence, arose at a very early day in Cairo's history, the question of the ownership of the river banks or shores, and of the right of the owners to collect wharfage or dues for the privilege of landing and tying up to the shore for a greater or shorter time. The collection of wharfage seems to have begun as far back as 1843, possibly earlier. By the act of February 17, 1841, the Cairo City and Canal Company had been vested with all the powers of the City of Quincy; and on the 23d day of May, 1843, the Company passed an ordinance providing for the collection of such dues, a photograph copy of which, signed by D. B. Holbrook, is given on another page. At this time the town had fully entered upon its decline. No more funds were to come from England, nor were they expected to come from American sources; and it may be that this ordinance had its origin in the hope that some small amounts might be obtained from water-craft, which would enable the landed proprietors to hold out a while longer, or until substantial aid came from other quarters, or until they could sell out the whole enterprise. So far as we know, the ordinance probably had little other effect than to prejudice still further the growing river interests against the town.

Very soon after Col. Taylor's arrival here in 1851, the matter of collecting wharfage dues was again taken up; and the Trustees, whom he represented, were proceeding to make these dues an important source of their needed revenues. Many of the leading people of the town believed the Ohio River shore or wharf, such as it was, belonged to the public and that the Trustees had no legal right to claim the same or to charge or to collect wharfage dues thereat. They seem to have claimed, first, that the title of the Trustees did not extend further than high-water mark, and, second, that the Trustees and their predecessors had dedicated the wharf and landing to the public by doing this and that, and especially by the making of maps and plats showing the river front and other places in the city to be public grounds and property.

The city, or that which we have called a city all the time, became incorporated as a town in March, 1855; and on the 27th day of March and the 2d day of April, 1855, the trustees of the town passed two ordinances, the one imposing a fine of $50.00 a day for maintaining at the landing any wharfboat, flatboat, storeboat, floating dock, flat, barge, keelboat, or other water-craft, without license or permission from the city, and the other, a fine of $75.00 for making sales on such boats or keeping hotels thereon. On the 16th day of April, 1855, Solomon Littlefield and Samuel Wilson, the latter of whom is well remembered by scores of our citizens, filed their bill in chancery in the circuit court of the county at Thebes against the said town trustees, who were Samuel Staats Taylor, Bryan Shannessy, Peter Stapleton, Louis W. Young, Moses B. Harrell, and Robert Baird, constable, to enjoin them from enforcing the said ordinances. The injunction was issued, and the case came up for a hearing on demurrer by the trustees, before Judge William H. Parrish, the circuit judge of our county at that time, and said to have been a very able man and judge. William A. Denning, before that time one of the judges of our supreme court, was the attorney for Littlefield and Wilson, and John Dougherty and Cyrus G. Simons, the attorneys for the town and its trustees. Among the papers in this chancery suit are printed copies of those two ordinances and of two others dated March 31st and April 4, 1855. The four ordinances are signed or attested by Edward Willett as clerk. Judge Parrish seems to have disposed of the suit in rather short order, and held that Littlefield and Wilson had not stated a case entitling them to any relief, and dismissed their bill.

The town trustees elected March 10, 1856, seem to have differed widely from those of the preceding year. They were Thomas Wilson, Cullen D. Finch, McGuire Phillips, Samuel S. Taylor and Charles Thrupp. The judges of the election were Bryan Shannessy, Robert H. Cunningham, and Edward Willett, and the clerks Henry H. Candee and John Q. Harmon. The election was by ballot and not by *viva voce* votes, and hence there was probably more freedom in voting than at the election the year before. The issue seems to have been the same as that made in the Littlefield and Wilson suit, and the election must have gone in favor of what they represented, although they had lost in the circuit court. This new board of trustees had a strange habit, as Col. Taylor says, of frequently holding meetings without notifying him. On the 24th day of May, 1856, they passed an ordinance aimed at Col. Taylor's Trustees, just as the former board had passed the two ordinances of March and April, 1855, which seemed aimed at certain citizens who had wharfboats at the landing. Under this ordinance, just mentioned, George D. Gordon, whom a few of our citizens well remember, was appointed wharfmaster and was to collect the wharfage dues. Under the ordinance and the efforts made to enforce it, a confused state of things arose. Gordon was able to collect only about $400.00 of wharfage during his term of service, during which time as much as $8000.00 in dues had accrued, almost all of which was lost both to the city and the Trustees. The Trustees, to defeat the attempt of the town trustees to enforce this ordinance of May 24, 1856, obtained an injunction against them in the United States Circuit Court at Springfield.

This suit was no doubt still pending when the first election came on March 7, 1857, under the city charter of February 11, 1857, and which resulted in the election of Col. Taylor as mayor and the following named aldermen: Peter Stapleton, Peter Neff, Patrick Burke, Rodger Finn, John Howley, Henry Whitcamp, Christopher M. Osterloh, Martin Egan, Timothy N. Gaffney, C. A. Whaley, William Standing and Cornelius Manley. Quite a majority of these aldermen seem to have been favorable to Col. Taylor and the policy of the Trustees, and they lost no time in wholly undoing what the last Board of Town Trustees had done regarding wharfage, for on March 11th, four days after their election, they repealed all ordinances relating to wharfage, and thus ousted the wharfmaster, George D. Gordon. At this election Mr. Henry H. Candee was chosen city treasurer and John Q. Harmon clerk. March 9th, they were directed to demand of the town trustees all books and records of every kind and all moneys and funds, belonging to the town government. Whatever became of the books and records of the former town government I do not know. I have seen no record indicating anything concerning them.

Whatever, also, became of the suit in the Federal court to enjoin the town trustees of 1856, we do not know, but we find that within a few weeks after the voters of the city had substituted David J. Baker as mayor in place of Col. Taylor, another ordinance was passed by the council to take charge of the wharf or of the collection of wharfage. Following the passage of this ordinance, Fredolin Bross brought a suit against the Trustees to obtain an enforcement of the contracts of June 11, 1851, and of May 31, 1855, between the Trustees and the Illinois Central Railroad Company. (We have referred elsewhere to this suit of Judge Bross.) In the report of the Trustees to the shareholders, September 29, 1864, we find these references to this Bross suit and to the ordinance last mentioned:

In May last, a bill was filed in Chancery, by F. Bross, who purchased a lot, in 1856, from the Trustees, praying the court to compel the performance, by the Trustees, of the contract entered into by them with the lot purchasers, as he claims, to build the levees provided for by the first agreement between the late Trustees and the Illinois Central Railroad Company. Our counsel are of the opinion, that there is no good ground for any such claim or suit. The case will be removed, at the proper time, from the local court in which it was instituted, into the United States Court, at Springfield.

In April last, the City Council of the City of Cairo passed an ordinance providing for the appointment of a Wharf Master, and the collection of wharfage at our levee wharf. The Trustees immediately restrained the operation of this ordinance by an injunction, issued out of the United States Court. The injunction was granted about three weeks before a regular term of the court, at which it would have been proper for the City to ask for a dissolution of the injunction. But at the time of granting it, the counsel for the City asked for time beyond the term of the court to answer the bill upon which the injunction was founded, and then, July 1st, asked for further time, until October 1st, to make this answer. The only foundation that the Trustees are aware of for the claim advanced by the City for the wharf, is set forth in a resolution adopted at a citizens' meeting, in July, 1863, of which the following is a copy, viz.: That as the Ohio and Mississippi rivers are public commercial highways, and the landing at this city a public landing, that can only be controlled and regulated by the public, or those authorized by the Legislature of the State; therefore, the authority claimed and exercised by the Trustees of the Cairo City Property, in the collection of wharfage, etc., is a gross violation of the rights of the City, a fraud upon the city treasury and an usurpation of power.

Our counsel have not a doubt of the ability of the Trustees to maintain their right to the wharf, and to defeat the City in its pretended claim.

In this Springfield suit, brought by the Trustees in April, 1864, there was filed as an exhibit to Col. Taylor's deposition, a large map or plat of the City of Cairo, made by William Strickland, architect and engineer, and Richard C. Taylor, engineer and geologist, probably in 1838, to which exhibit was attached the following affidavit, subscribed and sworn to before John W. Ash, Notary Public at Alton, February 22, 1866.

"My name is Miles A. Gilbert. My age is 56 and my present residence is in Saint Mary, state of Missouri. I moved to Cairo, Illinois, in the year 1843, and took possession and charge of all the property there belonging to the Cairo City and Canal Company, acting as their agent up to June, 1846, the time the property was transferred to the Trustees, Thomas S. Taylor and Charles Davis. From that period, I acted as agent for said Trustees up to April 18, 1851, the time S. Staats Taylor, Esqr., came and took charge of the trust. I resided at Cairo from 1843 to the latter part of 1846; from 1846 till 1851 was at Cairo a considerable portion of the time. During the aforesaid periods, as agent, I exercised control and authority over the high river bank and strips of land lying between Levee Street in the City of Cairo and the Ohio River, and during the whole time made and asserted continuous public and notorious claim to said ground. As agent had notices stuck up in several of the most public places in Cairo, requiring trading, boarding, family and flat boats and other similar water craft landing at or moored to the shore to pay wharfage. In some cases I collected wharfage and in others remitted it when business was dull and they could not afford to pay. As agent I pointed out places for trading boats, flat boats and other water craft to land at and use for the time being. Also pointed out a certain location to be used especially for steamboats to land at, and often, when trading boats and flat boats would land at the place, assigned for steamboats I required such trading and flat boats to remove to some other place, which I pointed out, they usually doing so without trouble. I frequently employed men to clear off logs, drift wood and other obstructions lodged on the levee, and generally during the entire period spoken of exercised exclusive control and ownership over the entire river bank and levee at Cairo, from the confluence of the Ohio and Mississippi rivers for about three miles up the Ohio.

"I was one of the incorporators and also a director of the Cairo City and Canal Company from its inception, during the entire period of its existence and was familiar with its operations. I was and am familiar with the map made by Mr. William Strickland, the engineer of that company. He never made but one plan and no plat. The plan accompanied a report made by him to the company in 1838 and was made to illustrate his recommendations as to the best method of building a city and improving and developing the property at Cairo. This report was printed and the map was engraved on different scales and some attached to the printed reports. I hereto annex one of the plans and reports marked Exhibit Y; also one of the plans on a large scale marked Exhibit X. This plan was never adopted by the company as *a plat of the city;* the city was never laid out according to it; no survey was made by authority of the company under it, and no lots sold under it. It was a sketch of a proposed plan for a city, to be adopted or not as the company might thereafter determine.

MILES A. GILBERT."

This suit also seems to have determined nothing, for Col. Taylor, with the aid of certain influential friends here, prevailed upon the city council to withdraw its defense to the suit. This action of the council only put off the day of the decision of the question; for it came up again in the *quo warranto* suit brought in the name of The People on the relation of John W. Trover against Marmaduke S. Ensminger, wharfmaster, in 1868. This suit finally settled the question of the right of the Trustees, *as riparian owners,* to the wharf and to collect wharfage, after the matter had been pending in one form or another since 1855. This ruling of our supreme court in the Ensminger case was, by the Supreme Court of the United States in *Barney vs. Keokuk,* 94 U. S. 384, held applicable only in those States where it had become a rule of property or where the restrictions of the riparian owner to high-water mark would be an interference with vested rights.

With the exception of certain river frontage or lands fronting on the one or the other of the two rivers which have been sold, the Trustees must be now regarded as the owners of all the river frontage on the rivers. Their titles extend on the west, to the *middle thread* of the Mississippi, and on the east, to *low-water mark* on the Ohio. In the old city charter of February 11, 1857, the legislature extended the city's boundaries to the middle of the main channels of both rivers, but this it could not lawfully do as to the Ohio. See "The Ohio River as a Boundary" in a subsequent part of the book.

CHAPTER XI

GEOLOGICAL FORMATIONS—THE SIGNAL STATION—THE RIVER GAUGE—TEMPERATURES AND RAIN-FALLS

THE geological formations of that part of the valley of the Mississippi extending from a point or line a few miles north of Cairo to the Gulf, and of the width of a few miles at Cairo and of many miles at the Gulf, is well known. This long strip of land or country is a kind of widening trough, into which the flowing waters have carried an ocean of sand and silt for ages. It is said that an arm or bay of the Gulf, in very early times, extended to the chain of hills a few miles north of us and constituting a part of the present Ozark range of mountains. It is further said that the Ohio River once ran some miles north of its present course from the hills in Pope County, and following somewhat the course of the little French River, the Cache, united with the Mississippi some distance above its present place of union with that river; and also, that the Tennessee and Cumberland rivers united at Paducah, and followed the present course of the Ohio from there to Cairo.

May it not be reasonably well supposed that the tendency of uniting rivers is to extend the point of junction further and further in the direction of their resultant course? Be that as it may, it is well established that this part of the great valley for hundreds of feet in depth consists for the most part of alternating strata of sand and gravel of varying degrees of fineness, that is, of very fine to very coarse sand and gravel. Many of us remember the first driven wells we had in Cairo and of the one or two very deep wells sunken by Mr. Jacob Klein, one of which was of the depth of 300 feet or more. Mr. Gerould, of the gas company, had charge of this work for Mr. Klein. It was indeed interesting to see the character of the pure and almost white sand brought from the depths below, varying in little else besides its degree of fineness. For a few feet more or less it was very fine and then very coarse.

We cannot devote much space to this matter, but beg the privilege of quoting a few pages from the report of Mr. L. C. Glenn, of the United States Geological Survey, entitled "Under-ground Waters of Tennessee and Kentucky West of Tennessee River, and of an Adjacent Area in Illinois." It is Water-Supply and Irrigation paper No. 164, Government Printing Office, Washington, 1906. The theory of the course of the Ohio River ages ago is regarded as probably but not certainly true, as therein given.

Embayment Area in Illinois.—"In Illinois, the Gulf Embayment Area includes the south-eastern part of Alexander County, all of Pulaski

County south of the chain of swamps in its northern portion, and a very narrow strip in Pope County along its southern boundary.

"This area in Illinois may be divided into two portions that differ from each other in their surface topography and elevation. One portion comprises the low, flat alluvial plains of the Mississippi and Ohio rivers. The other portion is a rolling to hilly upland.

"*Flood plain.*—The alluvial plains extend as a broad belt from Santa Fe down the Mississippi to Cairo and thence as a narrow belt up the Ohio to a point a few miles above Mound City, where the upland bluffs on the Illinois side close in on the river and continue with but slight interruption to a point a short distance north of Metropolis. There the flood plain again begins and widens as it extends up the river until it attains a width of several miles in the bend at Paducah. This flood plain extends up the Ohio beyond the limits of the gulf embayment region.

"The elevation of this low plain is about 320 feet at Cairo and about 340 or 350 feet along the edge bordering the upland. In places the alluvial plain and the upland meet along a sharply defined line, the upland surface rising abruptly as a steep-sided bluff. In other places, the two types of surface meet and merge with gentler slopes.

"*Cache River Valley.*—The flood plain of Cache River below Ullin is a part of this alluvial plain and is covered by backwater during floods. Above Ullin, the valley of the Cache is a continuation of the same plain, though it is bordered on the south by a rolling upland that rises a hundred feet or more above it.

"The Cache River valley is an abandoned valley of Ohio River, and to this fact it owes its width, flat surface, and low grade. The Ohio formerly turned westward three or four miles below Golconda and followed the valley of Big Bay Creek for some distance, then continued westward to the present Cache River through the depression now occupied by the chain of swamps in northern Massac County. The Cumberland and Tennessee rivers then united at Paducah and followed the present course of the Ohio from there to Cairo.

"*Uplands.*—The upland region includes all of Pulaski County lying southeast of the Cache River valley and north of the Mississippi and Ohio flood plain, which extends, as has been stated, a short distance north of Mound City. It also includes all of Massac County south of the chain of swamps which crosses its northern part, except the strip of Ohio flood plain in its southwestern part, and a small area of Pope County adjacent to the Massac County line. The upland has a rolling to hilly surface whose average elevation is 375 to 450 feet above sea level."

As to other geological features of this locality, the reader is referred to the tables or logs taken from the above described government publication. They relate chiefly to the artesian wells in the city and in the Cairo Drainage District. I am indebted to Major Edwin W. Halliday for the pamphlet containing the above information and table.

For information about almost everything of a practical nature, most of us have been accustomed to go to Major Halliday.

The Signal Station.—The two following papers were very kindly furnished me by Mr. William E. Barron, the local forecaster of the Weather Bureau of Cairo.

"The Weather Bureau is a branch of the U. S. Department of Agriculture, established July 1, 1891, to take charge of the meteorological work of the Government which had grown up since 1870, under the Signal Service of the War Department.

"The first reports of this service were gathered Nov. 1, 1870, from twenty-four stations. The station at Cairo, Illinois, was established June 1, 1871. At that time there were only forty-nine stations; now (1910) there are over two hundred regular observing stations, besides a large number of special and co-operating stations of various kinds. Sergeant Henry Fenton was the first officer in charge at Cairo and the office was located in the old City National Bank building on the Ohio levee. It has been in the present location in the Custom House since July 1, 1877.

"Cairo is situated in latitude 37° 00.8′ N., longitude 89° 11.6′ W. Local mean time is three minues faster than Central Standard or 90th meridian time.

"The instruments in use at the Cairo station are as follows: Maximum and minimum thermometers, dry-bulb and wet-bulb thermometers, psychrometer, Richards thermograph, mercurial barometers, Richards barograph, anemometers, anemoscope or wind vane, self-recording rain gauge, snow gauge, electric sunshine recorder, and meteorograph or triple register."

Accompanying this paper was a very interesting table giving the highest and lowest temperatures and the dates thereof, the highest and lowest water in the rivers and the dates thereof, and the rainfalls, since the establishment of the Station in 1871, up to the present year, a period of thirty-nine years. It will be found in the last chapter of the book. I am sure it will be found very useful to almost every person of this section of the country.

The River Gauge. We have to thank Mr. Barron, also, for the following paper concerning the River Gauge:

"The river gauge is located on the Ohio levee at the foot of Fourth Street. It was established in 1871 by Col. William E. Merrill, Corps of Engineers, U. S. A. The high water of March 20, 21, and 22, 1867, was equivalent to 51.0 feet on this gauge. The portion of the gauge above the 9-foot mark was reconstructed by the Weather Bureau in 1903, and from 9 to 50 feet consists of steel I beams laid in a bed of concrete nearly flush with surface of the levee, making an angle of about 11° 15′ with the horizontal. The zero of the gauge is 270.9 feet above mean tide level at Biloxi, Mississippi. The gauge is graduated in feet and tenths of elevation from —2 to 55 feet."

ARTESIAN WELLS

In and near Cairo several deep wells have been sunk. The location and logs of several of them are as follows:

The first deep boring is at the power station of the Cairo Electric Light and Power Company, on lot 29, city block 26, and was drilled in 1896-97 to a depth of 1,040 feet. The diameter is 10 inches at the top and decreases to 6½ inches at the bottom. The log is as follows:

LOG OF WELL OF CAIRO ELECTRIC LIGHT AND POWER CO., CAIRO, ILL.

	Thickness	Depth
	Feet	Feet
Soil	4.5	4.5
Sandy blue clay	50.5	55
Sand and gravel, similar to river deposit	60	115
Sand with kaolin partings	15	130
Kaolin	4	134
Sand with a few thin layers of kaolin and traces of shale and lignite	240	374
Shale or marl, slate colored	124	498
Very soft sand	20	518
Partings of shale and lignite	5	523
Chert of "Elco" gravel	177	700
Chert pebbles	5	705
Hard, reddish calcareous sandstone; no water in it	335	1,040

From the sand at 498-518 feet water rose to the surface and flowed about a gallon a minute. The following sanitary analysis of this water was made at the University of Illinois by Prof. A. W. Palmer:

ANALYSIS OF WATER OBTAINED BETWEEN 498 AND 518 FROM WELL OF CAIRO ELECTRIC LIGHT AND POWER COMPANY, CAIRO, ILL.

	Parts per million
Nitrogen as free ammonia	0.35
Nitrogen as albuminoid ammonia	.022
Nitrogen as nitrites	.009
Nitrogen as nitrates	.204
Chlorine as chlorides	83
Oxygen consumed	3.4
Total solids by evaporation	365
Fixed residue	348
Volatile matter (loss on ignition)	17.1

Comments of analyst: "Too much time—ten days—had elapsed between collection of analysis to be sure of sanitary condition, though it is probably satisfactory. The mineral matter consists mainly of carbonate of lime, with some sodium chloride and very little sulphate. Not excessively hard. Not likely to form a hard scale in boilers."

Professor Palmer also analyzed the water from the 705-foot level, with the following results:

ANALYSIS OF WATER FROM DEPTH OF 705 FEET IN WELL OF CAIRO ELECTRIC LIGHT AND POWER COMPANY, CAIRO, ILL.

(Parts per million)

	1	2
Nitrogen as free ammonia	0.36	0.36
Nitrogen as albuminoid ammonia	.016	.02
Nitrogen as nitrites	None	None
Nitrogen as nitrates	.06	.06
Chlorine as chlorides	110	110
Oxygen consumed	1.4	1.2
Total solids by evaporation	356	353
Fixed residue	346	339
Volatile matter (loss on ignition)	10	14
Hardness	115	

Comments of analyst: "Of exceptional purity and perfectly safe and wholesome for drinking. Hardness is quite moderate." The two samples were taken at the same time.

The Halliday Hotel well, on lot 24, hotel addition to city of Cairo, has practically the same log as the one given above. The boring went to 824 feet, but there was no increase of water below the 700-foot level. It was drilled in 1897; diameter at the top 8 inches, at the bottom 4½ inches; temperature 62° F.; head 12 feet above the surface.

A well on the W. P. Halliday estate, near the mouth of Cache River, in about the center of the NE. ¼ sec. 2, T. 17 S., R. 1 W., in Alexander County, had the following log:

LOG OF HALLIDAY WELL IN THE NE. ¼ SEC. 2. T. 17 S., R. 1 W., ILLINOIS

	Thickness	Depth
	Feet	Feet
Soil and blue clay (buckshot)	40	40
Sand and gravel; drift with kaolin partings	104	144
Brown shale or marl	112	256
Gray sand	54	310
Chert, fractured—"flint rock"	72	382
Dark brown sand	10	392
Chert fractured—"flint rock"	34	426
White sand	42	468
Flint rock with slight fractures	62	730
Flint pebbles	7	737
Flint Rock	69	806

From the last 7 feet water with a head of 12 feet flows at an estimated rate of half a million gallons a day. There was no increase in water below 735 feet. Drilled in 1898; temperature 62° F.

Another well at E. W. Halliday's residence on lot 16, block 70, between Ninth and Tenth and Walnut and Cedar Streets, in Cairo, had the following log:

LOG OF WELL AT RESIDENCE OF E. W. HALLIDAY, LOT 16, BLOCK 70, CAIRO, ILL.

	Thickness	Depth
	Feet	Feet
Soil and friable blue clay (loess or terrace)	50	50
White sand with thin partings of kaolin (Lagrange)	325	375
Gray shale or marl (Porters Creek)	130	505
Fine, closely compacted white sand (Ripley)	24	529
Flint rock, but slight fractures (Paleozoic)	220	749
Flint pebbles	4	753
Hard calcareous sandstone	58	811

From the 753-foot level there is a flow of 60 gallons per minute, with a head of 12 feet above the surface. The temperature is 62° F. Four hundred gallons per minute may be pumped.

There are other similar wells at several manufacturing establishments in Cairo and the records run much the same. The temperature seems to be 62° F. in each case, and the static head is the same. The material described as flint is a very light colored chert of Mississippi age that is exposed in a 150 or 200 foot face at a quarry between Tamms and Elco, from which it is extensively shipped for railroad ballast and road material. In this locality it is highly fractured, so that it is virtually of macadam size without crushing. As struck in wells it is in some places massive and solid, while in others it is seamed and broken, and is then called gravel by the drillers, though in neither wells nor in the Elco gravel quarry is the material waterworn or rounded, being simply mechanically disintegrated chert still in place.

We know very little concerning the site of the city, save that it is of very recent origin. The point between the rivers may have had a very slow southward movement or been now and then cut off and moved back northward. Certain it is, that what was the point sixty years ago was the point one hundred and three years ago when the first government survey was made. From the most southern east and west line of that survey, within a few hundred feet of the point, to the foot of the yellow clay and gravel hills at Mounds, we have the distance of seven or eight miles. These hills, which extend north of Villa Ridge and over to the Ohio River, are old compared to the alluvial plain south of Mounds. They have, no doubt, the same origin as that of the Wickliffe and Columbus hills in the so-called Gulf embayment area. At no distant time in the past the two rivers may have united just south of Mounds. Their present general direction at Mound City and at or near Beech Ridge, where the distance between them is about six miles, would indicate that they may have once united just below Mounds or some six or seven miles north of us. The site of the city may have existed a number of centuries, save that it has been narrowed and widened from time to time and elevated somewhat by the rivers. The grounds south and west of the Mississippi levee afford us a good illustration of *made land,* as it is sometimes called. None of it is one hundred years old. It would require a hundred years yet to make it what the site of the city was in 1818, so far as the timber growth is concerned.

CHAPTER XII

THE ILLINOIS CENTRAL RAILROAD

IT may be said we need nothing more concerning the early history of the Illinois Central Railroad, so much having been already written. We think, however, that what we shall say herein about the road and especially about its origin, will be found neither superfluous nor inappropriate.

A full and complete history of the road might be written which would contain little about the city of Cairo; but a history of Cairo with little therein about the road would be unworthy of its title. As I have before remarked and shown, the present Cairo owes its origin to the Trustees of the Cairo City Property and the Illinois Central Railroad Company. To make the statement a little more complete and accurate, it may be said it owes its origin to Darius B. Holbrook and his Cairo City and Canal Company of March 4, 1837. But this leads us still a little further back and requires the statement to be made that Cairo and the Illinois Central Railroad, in their respective origins, were largely Kaskaskia enterprises. Nor must I fail to notice in this chapter the part taken by the Trustees of the Cairo City Property in the work of procuring government aid to build the railroad.

This close connection of the starting of the city of Cairo with the origin or starting of the Illinois Central Railroad, I will now proceed to set forth as briefly as a clear understanding of the matter will allow. I cannot do this, however, without frequent references to Judge Breese and Senator Douglas, whose correspondence, in December, 1850, and January, 1851, furnishes quite an outline history of legislation concerning this railroad. So much has been said about the congressional land grant of September 20, 1850, and so little about the many years of hard and persistent work which led up to the grant, that one would suppose the road had its origin in that enactment; and hence a very imperfect view of the matter has been quite too generally taken and credit given and credit withheld contrary to and against the actual facts of the history of the enterprise.

It now and then occurs that in the hour of exultant success they are forgotten who had borne the burden and heat of the day and made possible the success credited to others. Lapse of time may separate the first movers in the enterprise from those last in it and present at the finish; but when the clouds and dust of noisy triumph have lifted and cleared away, the final award will go without dissent to those in whose minds the great undertaking first took shape and by whose hands it was first started towards an actual existence.

That a magnificient *donation* of lands was obtained instead of pre-emption rights merely, that it was to the state and not to a private corporation, were matters of importance; and that the work and management bestowed upon their procurement deserve high marks of recognition no one would deny; but in looking around to find to whom credit and honor should be given for the completed enterprise, it was very unjust that the award should extend no further than the finishing workmen. The man who plans and builds up to the laying of the corner-stone, if no further, should not be forgotten when the capstone is hoisted into its place and the celebration begins. Even if some changes were made in his plans as the work progressed, and even though he may have died and been years in his grave, yet the injunction still obtains that tribute and honor must go to whom tribute and honor are due. But I must not delay showing Judge Breese's connection with the starting of Cairo and with the beginning and growth of the Illinois Central Railroad enterprise.

Judge Sidney Breese was the originator of the Illinois Central Railroad. Others completed the great undertaking; but he had carried it on so long and faithfully that the work remaining to be done was neither very long nor very difficult. He had gone from New York to Kaskaskia a year or two prior to the admission of the state into the Union, and there began the reading of law in the office of Elias Kent Kane. He must have been familiar with all of the proceedings of the legislature then taking place, and especially with the preparation of the act of January 9, 1818, incorporating the city and bank of Cairo, and also with the proceedings of the convention which there drafted our state constitution of 1818 and in the making of which Kane took so prominent a part. We read how he and his ox team conveyed the state records from Kaskaskia to Vandalia in 1821, and of the numerous offices he filled in early life and of his steady advancement in the esteem and favor of the people. He was no doubt well acquainted with John G. Comegys and his Kaskaskia associates and with what they did and were unable to do with their Cairo enterprise of 1818, at which early day there was no railroad anywhere in the United States nor in England, if anywhere else.

Passing over a few years and many events, and premising that Breese kept well and fully abreast of the times with their then very promising outlook, we come to the year 1835, in the months of August and September of which he and Miles A. Gilbert and Thomas Swanwick, of Kaskaskia, entered the south halves of sections fourteen and fifteen, the east half of section twenty-two, all of sections twenty-three and twenty-four, the northeast quarter of section twenty-six and the west half of the northwest quarter of section twenty-five, of township seventeen south, range one west of the third principal meridian. A month or two later Anthony Olney and Alexander M. Jenkins entered other lands in the same and other sections, and David J. Baker still others in the same and other sections. The whole of the entries amounted to about twenty-three hundred acres. Quite a large part of these lands are now embraced in the present city of Cairo.

I must not proceed further before joining the name of Darius B. Holbrook with the names of the men already mentioned,—Breese, Baker, Jenkins, Gilbert, Olney and Swanwick. I will let Judge Breese tell us how Holbrook came to be one of the Cairo men of whom I am now speaking. In his letter of January 25, 1851, to Senator Douglas, we find the following:

"At the called session of the legislature which followed it in '35-'36, I found Mr. Holbrook at Vandalia, then a stranger to me, endeavoring to procure charters for manufacturing purposes, as I understood. Believing him to be the man of great intelligence and expanded views, I unfolded my plans to him and seizing upon the project, which had been started in 1818 to build a city at the mouth of the Ohio, which the projectors, Gov. Bond, and others, had then denominated 'Cairo,' he fell into my views, and being a man of great energy, *he proposed the formation of a company to construct the road and build the city.*"

These entries of lands may be said to be the beginning of the second attempt to start a city here; and we shall now see how closely the starting of the Illinois Central Railroad followed the entry of the lands; for in the state senate, at Vandalia, on the 29th day of December, 1835, Col. John S. Hacker, representing Alexander and Union Counties, introduced a bill to incorporate the Illinois Central Railroad Company. The persons named therein as incorporators were Alexander M. Jenkins, David J. Baker, John S. Hacker, Henry Eddy, Wilson Able, Richard G. Murphy, Pierre Menard, Miles A. Gilbert, Francis Swanwick, John Reynolds, Harry Wilton, Sidney Breese, John M. Krum, D. B. Holbrook, Simon M. Hubbard, James Hughes, Albert G. Snyder, and forty other persons, all of whom with a few exceptions lived in the southern part of the state as it was then known. Some amendments were made to the bill, but it soon passed both houses and was approved January 16, 1836, a day on which eight other railroad companies were incorporated by the legislature.

No time seems to have been lost by the men who made these land entries and procured this incorporation of the railroad company; for on the 13th day of the February following, the board of directors held a meeting at Alton, and no doubt having in mind that canal donation act of March 2, 1827, and its allowance by the act of March 2, 1833, for a railroad in lieu of a canal, proceeded at once to draw up a memorial to congress for aid in their railroad undertaking, and deputed the president of the company, Alexander M. Jenkins, and the treasurer of the board, D. B. Holbrook, to proceed at once to Washington to present their application for government aid. At that meeting of the directors, Breese was no doubt present; nor can there be any doubt as to the part he took in the preparation of the memorial. Miles A. Gilbert was the secretary of the company and of that meeting and his name is affixed to the papers accompanying the memorial, one of which is his certificate of the appointment of Jenkins and Holbrook to present the memorial to congress. It is an able paper and would probably fill eight or ten pages of this book. It is Document No. 121 of House Reports of the second session of the 24th congress, pages 305, 519, etc.

This memorial was very probably the first request ever made of the general government for aid in the construction of a railroad. The act of March 2, 1833, granting to the state the right to use the grant of March 2, 1827, for the construction of a railroad in lieu of the canal, is not a like case. There the donation had already been made. Jenkins and Holbrook proceeded to Washington almost immediately, and placed the memorial and accompanying papers in the hands of the Illinois members, who at once laid the same before congress and had the proper reference made; and on March 31st, only two and a half months after the act of incorporation had been passed, a favorable report was made and a bill presented to congress making a pre-emption grant. Considering the means of travel at that early day, it will be seen that these Southern Illinois and Illinois Central railroad men pushed forward their scheme for government aid with a zeal seldom equaled. The prayer of the memorial is in these words: "In conclusion, your memorialists for the foregoing reasons, and many more which the subject itself will suggest to the wisdom and foresight of congress, pray that such a *donation of lands* as the importance of the subject may indicate as reasonable and proper may be made to said company; and that a pre-emption right to the whole or a portion of the public lands lying immediately on the route of said road, within a distance to be specified on each side thereof may be secured to them for a reasonable time within which it may be practicable to complete the same." (Signed) "A. M. Jenkins, President of the Illinois Central Rail Road Co." (and) "D. B. Holbrook, Treasurer of the Illinois Central Rail Road Co."

The bill was printed, but congressional action was soon arrested by the state's embarking upon a system of railroad construction for itself and this led our members of both houses of congress to withhold their support from this particular enterprise. Douglas and Breese knew all about the internal improvement scheme. Douglas always led, seldom followed; and it is altogether probable that to him more than any one else that ruinous policy of state railroad building was undertaken. He voted for the bill of February 27, 1837.

I have neither time nor space to take up and consider the various bills introduced by Breese and by Douglas, and possibly one or two other persons at the instance of the one or the other senator. It is sufficient to say that Douglas reached the senate in December, 1847, and that he worked diligently for government aid for an Illinois railroad. That there were jealousies between them and others interested in the work, is somewhat fully set forth in Wentworth's Congressional Reminiscences in Fergus's Historical Series No. 24. This is an exceedingly interesting paper, giving his account of this railroad enterprise in congress during his service of eight years in the lower house.

But Senator Douglas neither wanted nor sought an Illinois central railroad. The road he wanted was a Chicago road, a road running direct from the mouth of the Ohio to Chicago, and which would have had four-fifths of the state west and north of it; a road which would have left Vandalia, Decatur, Bloomington, and LaSalle far to the westward. The road he insisted upon all the time was one from Cairo direct to Chicago *and thence to the upper Mississippi.* That was the way he desired to connect the upper and lower Mississippi with the Lakes. He and his Chicago associates, strongly supported by their eastern friends, wanted to draw all the business to Chicago, whence, after reaching there, it would go eastward, and little if any of it towards the Gulf. They would have succeeded with this plan had not our other members in congress plainly said that they would not stand for such a road, which could not in any view be called a central railroad. The old line of road from Cairo to Galena had been before the people too long, and had been insisted upon so strongly that to give up the line wholly for another which had in view only the interests of one city in the state was quite out of the question. Douglas' constant insistance on the Chicago road weakened the enterprise of a central railroad all the time. He and Breese had found their plans in whatever shape presented meeting with successful opposition all the while. One wanted more, and the other less because of the great doubt as to their being able to get anything at all. Breese believed in asking less and getting something, rather than asking more and getting nothing.

This leads to the inquiry, how did Douglas at last get his donation of September 20, 1850? The history of it is told by his brother-in-law, Col. J. Madison Cutts, of the Army, in that large government volume entieled "Public Domain, 1884, by Thomas Donaldson, 262-264." Douglas seems to have come finally to Breese's belief and to have found that government aid would have to be given up unless the scheme could be so presented as to look like something entirely new. He knew quite as well as any one else how solid the Democratic-South was against his railroad land grant and that unless he could fall upon a plan that would appeal to their self interest, there was little use of keeping the matter longer before congress. He, therefore, went south, to Mobile and two or three other cities, and laid before the proper parties his Illinois railroad scheme, so modified as to take in the entire country from the Ohio River to Mobile, although there were no government lands either in Kentucky or Tennessee. This was something that had never been offered before. The southern senators, especially those in Alabama, Mississippi and Kentucky, were kept in ignorance of the object of Senator Douglas' visit to the south; and it was only after they were importuned by many of their constituents that they consented to abandon their long continued opposition to a government grant. It was something new to these southern men in and out of congress and it led to a new view of the matter of government aid. All Douglas had to do and all he did do was to take some one of his or Breese's old and beaten bills, change its title and add section seven to bring in Mississippi and Alabama as donees, and the work was done. In this way the old *status in quo* of fifteen years was so immediately changed that one must have wondered why it had not been thought of long before. The short and simple title of the old bill, making a grant of lands in Illinois in aid of a central railroad was changed to "An act granting a right of way and making a grant of land to the states of Illinois, Mississippi, and Alabama in aid of the construction of railroad *from Chicago to Mobile.*" This title of Senator Douglas' donation act of September 20, 1850, is a fair and just representation of his attitude towards an Illinois central railroad. All he wanted was a road to Chicago. This bill would have been, throughout, just what its title indicates, had not our other members of congress insisted that the grant should be for a railroad substantially as provided for in the acts of 1836, 1843 and 1849.

But we must submit proof of Douglas' opposition to a central railroad. In his letter of January 5, 1851, to Breese, he says: "You can learn, if you will take the trouble to inquire of the Hon. Thomas Dyer, who is now a member of the Legislature with you, that in the month of September, 1847, I urged him and many other citizens of Chicago to hold public meetings and send on memorials in favor of a donation of lands to the state to aid in the construction of a central railroad, with one terminus in Chicago. It was necessary that the road connect with the Lakes, in order to impart nationality to the project and secure northern and eastern voters. The old line from Cairo to Galena parallel with the Mississippi, with both termini on that stream, was regarded as purely a sectional scheme, calculated to throw the whole trade upon the Gulf of Mexico at the expense of the Lakes and the Atlantic Sea Board."

Did this statement of Senator Douglas as to the line he desired the road to follow need confirmation, it is found in the proceedings of a public meeting at Chicago January 18, 1848, presided over by the Hon. Thomas Dyer, just mentioned in his letter. The proceedings were published in a small pamphlet, a copy of which is now in the possession of the Hon. William B. Gilbert, who received it from Col. Taylor. The following is a copy of one or two of its pages:

"Proceedings and resolutions of a public meeting held at Chicago on the subject of *a railroad to connect the upper and lower Mississippi with the great lakes,* printed at Chicago by R. L. Wilson, Printer, Daily Journal Office, 1848.

"A public meeting was held at the court house January 18, 1848. Thomas Dyer, Chairman; Dr. D. Brainard, Secretary; Col. R. J. Hamilton, J. Butterfield, M. Skinner, A. Huntington and E. B. Williams were appointed by the chairman a committee to report resolutions; which were reported and unanimously adopted. John S. Wright, M. Laflin, J. Frink, J. Rogers and William Jones were appointed a committee to confer with citizens. [The last resolution of the five offered is in these words:]

"Resolved that our senators and representatives in the congress of the United States, be requested to use their best exertions to secure the passage of a law granting to the State of Illinois the right of way and public lands for the construction of a railroad to connect the upper and lower Mississippi with the lakes at Chicago, equal to every alternate section for five miles on each side of said road."

The remainder of the pamphlet of 16 pages is taken up with Mr. Butterfield's address. In that address is found the following:

"It is proposed to construct a railroad, to connect the upper and lower Mississippi with the great lakes. This railroad to *commence at the confluence of the Ohio and Mississippi rivers at Cairo; thence to proceed to Chicago, the head of lake navigation, and from thence to Galena on the upper Mississippi."*

Let us now show what connection the Trustees of the Cairo City Property Trust had with the above Chicago meeting and the general work then going on to secure government aid for an Illinois central railroad. This land trust company was an association of New York, Philadelphia, Boston, Portland, Syracuse and other men, owning about ten thousand acres of land between the Ohio and Mississippi Rivers and at their junction, and who were lavishly spending their money east and west to obtain national aid for a central railroad, which they well knew was necessary to their Cairo enterprise.

The western representative of these men was Samuel Staats Taylor, of New Brunswick, New Jersey, long connected with the United States Bank. His headquarters were at Chicago, where he remained from 1846 to April, 1851, and until the hard and long protracted work at Washington and Springfield had been brought to a close. The Cairo men, or men interested in Cairo, beginning with Breese, Holbrook, Jenkins, Gilbert and others, and ending with the Cairo City Property people, had been working, many of them continuously, for fifteen years, to obtain a central railroad, in furtherance of their city enterprise here at the junction of the two rivers. To show what Taylor was doing at Chicago as the representative of the Cairo City Property, I give here two separate statements made in his own handwriting fifty years ago. They were entered by him on the large sheets of an abstract of the title to the lands of the trust here, and are as follows:

"Public meeting of citizens of Chicago held January 18, 1848, at the Court House, pursuant to public notice, to consider the feasibility of constructing a railroad to connect the upper and lower Mississippi with the Great Lakes, recommending that a grant of public lands be made to the State of Illinois for the purpose. This meeting was gotten up at the instance of Justin Butterfield, who prepared and delivered at it an elaborate speech (a copy of which see on file), copies of which and of the proceedings were sent to the different County Seats along the proposed line of the road, and public meetings held at them advocating the project and instructing their representatives in Congress to support it. Mr. Butterfield in this acted upon the suggestion of S. S. Taylor, agent of the Trustees of the Cairo City Property, who occupied an office in Chicago with Mr. Butterfield; and those Trustees paid all the expenses attendant upon the movement."

"The entire receipts of the Trustees of the Cairo City Property, from sales, rents, wharfage, and all other sources have been used in improvements and other expenditures at Cairo, *except what was required to* repay in New York moneys borrowed at the beginning of the trust, about 1848, to defray expenses connected principally with arrangements and legislation for procuring from Congress the grant of land to the State to build the Illinois Central Railroad."

The receipts of money from the sources above enumerated were probably a million and a half to two million dollars, and all of it was expended here at Cairo, *"except what was required to repay in New York, etc."* This excepted amount is not given, but it would not have been mentioned at all, had it not been up in the tens of thousands. Holbrook was one of the very largest shareholders, and never expected to do or effect much without the use of money. He and his Trustees of the Cairo City Property, from the time of their appointment, September 29, 1846, worked on and constantly for the road, being very willing to get a Chicago road, if not an Illinois central road. They did very little at Cairo during the intervening four or five years and not until they were assured of a great road to the north. Just how much money they spent, or how it was spent, or to whom or where it was paid, there is no one now living who can tell much about it; but Breese's letter to Douglas above referred to, contains this significant passage:

"In the passage of the present law, I had no share, nor have I claimed any; but *you know and I know how it was passed.* * * * As great as may be the credit to which you are entitled, and I will not detract from it, you know that it received its most efficient support in the house, from a quarter where neither you nor any of your colleagues, save one perhaps, had much if any influence. It was the votes of Massachusetts and New York that passed the bills, and you and I know how they were had. I venture to say, the much abused Mr. Holbrook and Col. Wentworth contributed most essentially to its success."

This language of Judge Breese's is most suggestive. Observe some of its clauses: *You know and I know how it was passed* * * * from a quarter where neither you nor any of your colleagues, *save one, perhaps,* had much if any influence * * * It was the votes of Massachusetts and New York that passed the bills, and *you and I know how they were had.* I venture to say the much abused *Mr. Holbrook and Col. Wentworth contributed most essentially to its success.*

We will now let in a little more light on these suggestive statements of Breese to Douglas. For their illumination, we will refer to Wentworth, Holbrook, Webster, Congressman Ashmun and possibly one or two others.

Wentworth was in congress from December, 1843, to September, 1850; and in his Reminiscences, we are giving much concerning the last days of the congressional struggle for aid for an Illinois central railroad. It seems to come from one who knew much about what was going on for and against the scheme. He enlarges on the part the great Massachusetts senator took in the matter; how the eastern men going to Washington inquired for him, then Secretary of State under President Fillmore; how Webster gave them assurances and turned them over to Ashmun, whom he regarded as equal to almost any emergency; and then how things moved on rapidly under Ashmun's lead to the triumphant end. Back of it all were Webster and Ashmun, and a few other Massachusetts and New York men, with none of whom, Breese says, Douglas had much, if any, influence. But there was another man there, a member of the third house, Darius B. Holbrook, as smart and as wise as almost any of them and far shrewder than most of them. He had known Douglas long and well; he knew Ashmun, a Massachusetts man like himself; he knew everybody worth knowing in such an enterprise as they had in hand; but above all, he knew Webster, had known him as a client knows his lawyer for fifteen years, perhaps many more. He had paid Webster a good round fee in London, August 23, 1838, for his opinion as to the validity of the Cairo bonds Holbrook was putting on the London market. See the opinion at the end of this chapter. Holbrook was far better acquainted with the whole history of the railroad enterprise than Douglas. He had been with it all the time, fifteen years, instead of three or four, and a directly interested party. He could reach the Whigs in congress easier than Douglas, a bitter partisan all his life. Holbrook went to the fountain-head of whiggery, and enlisted a simon-pure section of it in his behalf, which Douglas never could have done. He had no doubt spent all of his London money of 1838, but its place was well supplied by money from Cairo men, that is, men of Boston, New York, Philadelphia, Portland and Syracuse, shareholders in Cairo City Property Trust, whose western representative in Chicago was Col. Samuel Staats Taylor, of New Brunswick, who arranged the Butterfield public meeting there January 18, 1848, and who knew all about the expenditures of the Trustees from September 29, 1846, to February 10, 1851, and from that time to 1896. From the one date to the other, these Cairo trust gentlemen did nothing at all at Cairo besides preserving their Cairo property and working for the railroad land grant, on which they knew their Cairo city so largely depended.

No one can be found who would desire to detract from the credit or honor due Senator Douglas for his work and management which brought the long drawn out matter to a successful end. But almost every award or suggestion of honor to him has somehow seemed a denial of honor to all others. He seemed quite willing to accept the tender of exclusive honor and credit, although in his correspondence with Judge Breese in 1851 he seemed willing to accord the latter a fair share of what was being lavishly bestowed upon him. He knew all about Breese's commencement of the work, his efforts in and out of congress and that only the vicissitudes of politics removed him from his cherished work in that body. He well knew that he had only taken up and carried through successfully the undertaking Breese had planned and carried forward a decade before he took hold of it. He knew that the chief difference between them was that Breese did not believe a donation of lands to the state could be gotten and both knew that one of the bed-rock principles of their party was opposition to such government aid or aid of any kind for such enterprises. In Judge Breese's letter of January 25, 1851, in reply to Douglas' of the 5th of that month, he presents at some length this difference between himself and Douglas as to the line to be adopted for the road. Douglas failed to draw the whole road over to Chicago and had to content himself with a branch, which differed very little from the branch road provided for in Breese's and Holbrook's act of February 10, 1849, which was for a road from Cairo to Chicago, *via* the southern terminus of the canal. Breese and Holbrook were compelled to yield to Chicago's demand that the road should not go on northward to Galena or Dubuque; but in the final outcome, the other members of congress were able to draw the line back to the old route.

Col. Wentworth either knew nothing about the senator's trip to the south or credited it with no great results. At all events, his account so fully corroborates what Breese said to Douglas, in his letter of January 25, 1851, as to whence the needed aid came, that we must be pardoned for quoting somewhat at length from the same.

I have alluded to the superior confidence which all capitalists had in the opinions of Mr. Webster. This was of inestimable service to the Illinois delegation in the House of Representatives in securing our early railroad grant. I accent the word *early* because, since the census of 1850, the numerical strength of the Western States has been so greatly increased that liberal grants have been secured without difficulty. During the period in which we were struggling for our grant, we had, at different times, for senators, four able and influential men who had been upon our Supreme Bench together, James Semple, Sidney Breese, Stephen A. Douglas, and James Shields. But, as the new States had the same number of senators as the old ones, they did not meet with the same obstacles that we did in the House. Yet they were very sensitive as to any one's having superior credit over the others for extra efforts. Gen. Shields, at his last visit to Chicago, complained to his friends, that, as a member of the committee upon public lands having charge of the bill, he had not had sufficient credit for his efforts in the matter. "But," said he, "so thought each of the others, and no one was upon speaking terms with all the others at the time of his death." There was never any serious controversy in the Senate about the passage of the Illinois Central Railroad Grant, as the Senate journals and the congressional Globe will show. The jealousy of our senators in respect to each other's credit for the passage of the bill in the Senate, arose from the indiscretion of friends in claiming too much for their favorite, and yet with no disposition to injure the others. But in the House we could secure nothing of this kind to quarrel about. We labored, and labored, and labored; but it did no good. There was a great sectional and political barrier which we could not overcome. Members from the old States opposed offering governmental inducements for western emigration, and the Whig party wished the lands sold and the proceeds distributed. Thus matters had continued from my entrance into Congress, in 1843, up to

September, 1850. Fortunately, our canal had been intrusted to a company upon terms which caused our canal indebtedness to appreciate and secured its ultimate payment. As some of the holders of our canal-bonds were also holders of our other bonds, and as they mostly were residents of the older states and members of the Whig party, whence came the opposition to our grant, the thought occurred to me that we could utilize such bond-holders in securing our land grant. A correspondence ensued, which resulted in a committee being sent to Washington. I met them at the depot, and their first inquiry was for Mr. Webster. I could receive no encouragement from them until a consultation with Mr. Webster was had. I afterwards found out that their original designs were to have the grant made directly to a company; but Mr. Webster satisfied them that a provision in a charter, like that which was inserted eventually, making the money payable to the State solely applicable to "the payment of our interest—paying State indebtedness until the extinction thereof," could not be repealed. I went with them to the Secretary of State's department, and Mr. W. received us very cordially. He knew all about our contract with the canal company, and he had been consulted as to its irrepealability. He said there were a great many measures that ought to be adopted by Congress, and which could be if a spirit of compromise could be brought about. He said the new States wanted land grants and the old States wanted some modification of the tariff laws; but there were members who cared for neither, and who could defeat both unless the friends of both would adopt that spirit of concession and compromise that had been so happily brought to bear in the adjustment of the slavery question. "Now," said he to me, "my friend George Ashmun is a man of remarkably practical good sense and discretion and, if men of conflicting interests would rally around him in a spirit of compromise, he is capable of doing a great deal of good. I will advise him to call upon you," and then he made an appointment for the gentlemen at his residence. I knew Mr. Ashmun's relation to Mr. Webster from seeing him take Mr. Webster's seat in the Senate when he arose to make his celebrated 7th-of-March speech, in that year; and Mr. Ashmun handed him his books of authority, opened at the appropriate page, as he progressed. He will be remembered as the president of the national convention which first nominated Mr. Lincoln. One Saturday, Mr. Ashmun says: "Mr. Webster thinks that you and I, by acting in concert, can do our respective people and the country at large a great deal of good. What do you say?" I said: "You know what we Illinois men all want. Lead off." "Now," he says, "help us upon the tariff where you can, and where you can not, dodge. And have all your men ready for Tuesday." Promptly upon that day, 17th September, 1850, Mr. Ashmun made the motion to proceed to business upon the speaker's table, and when our bill was reached, so well did I know our original force, I could estimate the value of recruits. And when I saw our old opponents voting for the bill in such numbers, I was so confident of the result that I ventured to telegraph the bill's passage to Chicago, and it was known there quite as soon as the speaker declared the result—101 to 75. But for Mr. Webster and Mr. Ashmun, I am confident we should have had to wait for a new apportionment, and then our company would have had to compete with the owners of other land-grant roads in the loan market. And Webster would have been dead.

But I must bring this chapter to a close, already too lengthy for a local history like this. I cannot do so, however, without stating some of the conclusions which the foregoing pages clearly establish.

1835. First:—The present city of Cairo and the Illinois Central Railroad were started at the same time and by the same men, Breese, Baker, Jenkins, Gilbert, Olney and Swanwick, who entered the Cairo lands in August and September, 1835. In the December and January following, they joined Holbrook with them and procured the Illinois Central Railroad charter of January 16, 1836. The second day afterwards, namely, January 18, 1836, Holbrook procured his charter for the Illinois Exporting Company, the incorporators of which were

James S. Lane, Thomas G. Hawley, Anthony Olney, John M. Krum, and himself, Holbrook. Breese says that in those months, he found Holbrook at Vandalia, and that he there unfolded his plans to him, and that the result was the proposal to *"form a company to construct the road and build the city."*

1836. Second:—Within the first three months of the year 1836, the board of directors of the railroad company met at Alton, prepared their memorial to congress for government aid, sent Jenkins the president, and Holbrook the treasurer, of the company, to Washington, who presented the same and had a favorable report thereon, and had a bill introduced for aid, as prayed for; and all this within less than three months after the passage of the railroad charter of January 16, 1836.

1837 and 1838. Third:—Following this railroad work came the purchase of other Cairo lands and the incorporation March 4, 1837, of the Cairo City & Canal Company, which was to Cairo what the act of January 16, 1836, was to an Illinois Central railroad. The intervention of the state, February 27, 1837, with its scheme of internal improvements, arrested and well nigh upset all these plans for railroad and city building by those Cairo men. It halted everything in congress for government aid; but while the Cairo men were pushed aside as to their own railroad plans, they accepted the situation and did all they could for the state central railroad from Cairo to Galena, and went on with their city work here at home and in London.

1839 and 1840. Fourth:—The State's railroad and river improvement work was tottering to its fall when John Wright & Company, of London, financing the Cairo enterprise, failed November 23, 1840; and then ensued a general state of business illness almost everywhere and especially in Cairo, followed by a protracted convalescence of three or four years.

1843 to 1846. Fifth:—Breese entered the senate and Douglas the house in December, 1843, and the former at once set to work again for government railroad aid, the latter doing little else than opposing the former's plans. Holbrook was at work to get his Cairo city work again under way and arranged for the transfer, September 29, 1846, from the Cairo City & Canal Company of everything it represented, to the Cairo City Property Trust, composed of New York, Philadelphia, Boston, Portland, and Syracuse men, thus making the enterprise largely American instead of English.

1846 to 1851. Sixth:—During part of this time Breese and Douglas were together in the senate, still differing about the kind of government aid they should ask. Shields succeeded Breese in December, 1849, and the Illinois senatorial differences ceased. The Trustees of the Cairo City Property, one in New York and one in Philadelphia, by direction of those eastern share-holders, sent Samuel Staats Taylor, of New Brunswick, to Chicago, and he there occupied one of Butterfield's offices, and managed the western branch of the business of getting a railroad land grant. Holbrook devoted his time to the same work in New York, his home, in Philadelphia, Boston and Washington, supervising almost everything that was done and seeing that there was no lack of money where money was really needed. He and Wentworth enlisted Webster and Ashmun in their railroad and city scheme and thereby reached Massachusetts and New York men, sufficient in number and ability to assure the passage of the bill. If we are to accept what these two men have said about the matter, the great railroad land grant of September 20, 1850, became a law because of aid which was brought to it from Massachusetts and New York, rather than from the south.

I have thus established the fact that the work of securing an Illinois central railroad and that of building a city here, were but the two parts of one enterprise, carried on almost continuously from August, 1835, to February, 1851, and chiefly by men east and west interested in the city here. It is also further shown and clearly proven that Judge Sidney Breese was the originator of what is now the great Illinois Central Railroad.

Daniel Webster, as before remarked, knew all about Holbrook's scheme of city and railroad building, knew it as far back as 1839; and when the matter was again brought to his attention in 1850, when he was Secretary of State, he pointed out the way to success. Holbrook knew Webster's great influence with eastern public men and of their advocacy of internal improvements as well as of a protective tariff. Following the advice of Webster, Holbrook and Wentworth sought and obtained the aid of Ashmun, and the long pending and almost hopeless bill for government aid became a law. Breese said to Douglas: "I venture to say, the much abused Mr. Holbrook and Col. Wentworth contributed most essentially to its success."

Webster and Holbrook's acquaintance and relations are shown by the following letter:

London Augt 3rd 1839

I have perused and considered two Indentures of deeds of trust, as printed in a book laid before me, which book is marked on one side "City of Cairo," and on the other "Messrs. Wright & Co," (and on which book I have written my own name, at the end of one of the deeds of trust, page 10) viz

One Indenture made and executed on the Sixteenth day of December One thousand eight hundred and thirty seven, between the Cairo City and Canal Company, and the New York Life Insurance and Trust Company, and to which Indenture the Illinois Exporting Company also became party:

And on the other Indenture called a "Deed Supplemental," made and executed on the thirteenth day of June One thousand eight hundred and thirty nine, between the said Illinois Exporting Company, the said Cairo City and Canal Company and the said New York Life Insurance and Trust Company

And I am of opinion:

1st. That the conveyance made to the said New York Life Insurance and Trust Company by the said Cairo City and Canal Company by virtue of said Indentures and deeds, is a good and valid conveyance, and effectually vests the property intended to be conveyed in the said New York Life Insurance and Trust Company for the purposes and the trusts in said Indentures mentioned and set forth.

2nd. That by these Indentures and deeds, the said New York Life Insurance and Trust Company has become bound, and is legally obligated to all holders of bonds, issued in pursuance of said Indentures, for the faithful administration and fulfillment of said trust, by the payment of the interest and principal of such bonds, according to their terms, to the full extent of all the proceeds of the property conveyed as aforesaid

Danl Webster

Legation of the U States
London Augt 3rd 1839

This certifies that the foregoing signature is known to me to be the proper handwriting of the Hon. Daniel Webster, Counseller at Law, and a member of the Senate of the United States now in London

In the absence of the Minister.
Benjamin Rush
Secretary of Legation

(Seal)

We attest the foregoing as being a true copy of the original

10 September 1839

P. O. Donohoe
Chas Marshall
Clerks to Messrs Few & Co
Solctrs
Covent Garden London

Aliens by the Statute laws of the State of Illinois can purchase and hold real Estate (Land) and may afterwards dispose of it by Will, Deed of Conveyance, or otherwise, without any limitation or restriction whatever and if the purchaser should chance to die intestate, it would descend to his heirs or next of kin of equal degree in equal proportions (the law of primogeniture not being in force in that Country) saving to the Widow, if any, in such cases the one third part of the land as dower during her natural life, and in respect to heirship, it makes no difference whether the children or next of kin of such Purchaser are at the time of his decease citizens of the United States, or subjects of Great Britain. It may not be unimportant also to know that land purchased originally from the United States at any of the Government Land offices in Illinois (there yet being a large portion of the public domain in that State unsold) is not subject to taxation for any purpose whatsoever until the expiration of five years from the day of the purchase. This exemption is in consequence of a special compact between the United States and the State of Illinois, in consideration of certain immunities granted by the former to the latter.

Richard M. Young
of Quincy—Illinois
and at present a Senator from that State
to the Congress of the United States

London Oct 25th 1839
267 Regent Street

Honor to Whom Honor is Due.—This scriptural injunction was forgotten when some of Senator Douglas' Chicago friends proposed a celebration in his honor for the great work *he had accomplished.* It was to be for him and him only. Douglas himself saw this and protested somewhat in favor of others. He did not, however, even mention Breese, who, in any view of the history of the great work, should have been mentioned along with himself if not first of the two. Breese seeing the slight put upon him, like any other man of spirit, addressed to Douglas the letter of January 25, 1851, a few lines of the introductory part of which are as follows:

"I thought I had discovered a studious endeavor on your part, and on the part of those with whom you have acted, to conceal from the public my agency in bringing the measure into favor, and in opening the way for successful legislation in regard to it. In none of the speeches and letters you and others who have your confidence, have made and written, has there been the least allusion to the part I have acted in the matter, nor in any of the papers in the state, supposed to be under your influence. Seeing this, and believing there was a concerted effort to appropriate to yourselves, exclusively, honors, to which I knew you were not entitled, I deemed it my duty, for the truth of history, to assert my claim, and in doing so, have been compelled, much against my will, to speak of myself, and of my acts in regard to it."

In the language of lawyers, I respectfully sumbit that all that Judge Breese ever claimed for himself in regard to the Illinois Central Railroad has been fully established in the foregoing pages.

Sidney Breese

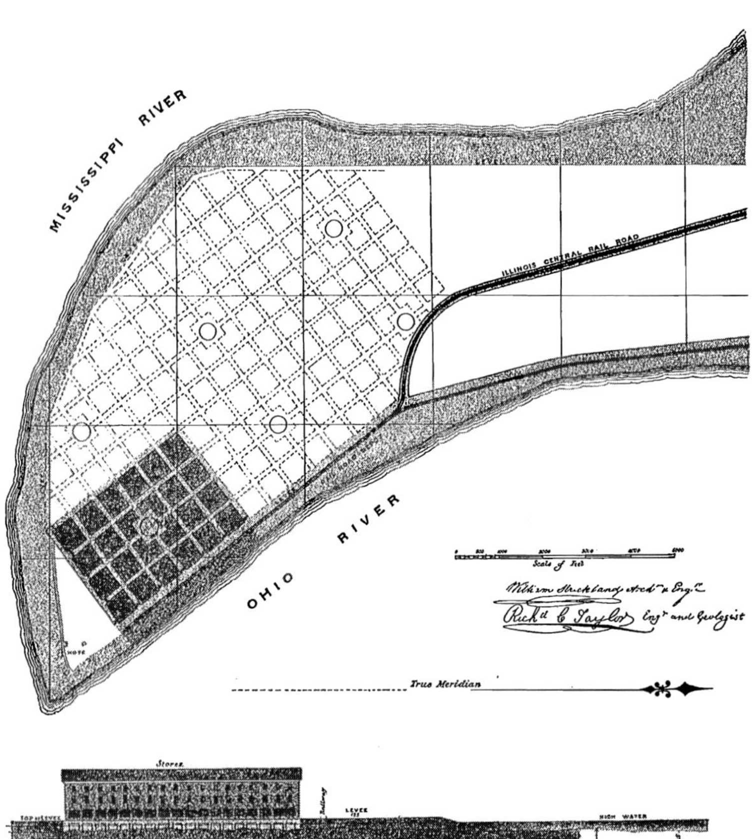

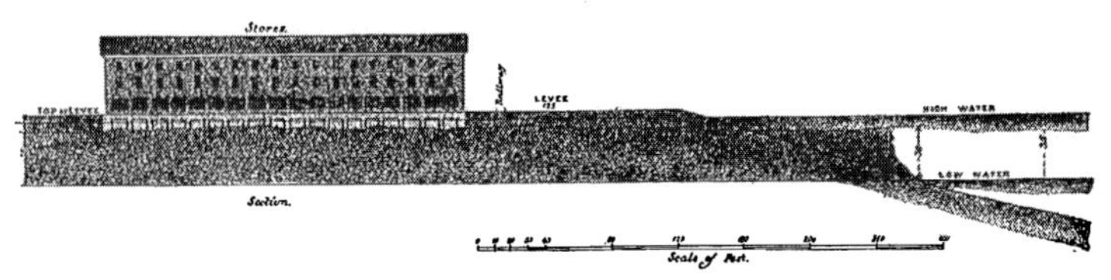

Plan of Cairo, 1838

CHAPTER XIII

MAPS AND PLATS

BEFORE referring to the maps and plats of Cairo as made by the land companies which desired to start and establish a city here, I desire to call attention to a list of old French and English maps which show the early existence here of a *French fort,* probably the very first structure ever erected at this point or place. These old maps might have been very properly given in that part of the book where I have spoken of *Sieur Charles Juchereau de Saint Denis* and his fort and tannery, but I have thought it best to include them herein.

I have made a very careful investigation of the matter of the existence of an old French fort here or within a few miles of the place, not further off, certainly, than the hills which approach close to Cache River about six miles north of us. I have done this in order to ascertain if the old fort could probably have been the later Fort Massac, forty miles up the Ohio River from us. In volume No. 8, pp. 38 to 64, of the Publications of the Illinois Historical Society, is found an able paper by Mrs. Mathew T. Scott, of Bloomington, entitled "Old Fort Massac." In this paper Juchereau is frequently spoken of and his fort mentioned as the early or first Fort Massac. Mrs. Scott's quotations from the Margry papers, especially her quotations *in the original French,* pp. 57 and 58, tend strongly to show that Juchereau's fort was not on the Ohio River forty miles from its mouth, but was at or very near to the mouth of the river; otherwise, it is very hard to account for such language as this: *"A la rivière de Ouabache dans le lieu ou elle se descharge dans le Mississippi"* and *"à la embouchère de la rivière d'Ouabache sur la Mississippi."*

Fort Massac was, of course, at first and for a long time, a French fort or post; and the generally accepted authority about the matter is that it was established at that place or point on the Ohio to protect the French northwestern country from the strong and warlike tribe of Cherokee Indians. These Indians dwelt along the line of the Tennessee River, which, for a long time in the earliest history of the country, was called and put down on the maps as the Cherokee River. The fort was on the first high ground below the mouth of that river and was well located to defend against incursions of these Indians into the northwest country. I have made inquiries at many places and have been uniformly told there can be little doubt as to this old fort being at or near the mouth of the Ohio River and not at the site of Fort Massac.

The site of the old French fort is indicated on the old maps by a cross or star on the point where the two rivers unite. The list of thirty-five to forty old maps, procured by me from the Library of Congress and the Historical Library of Chicago, show an old fort here, with such descriptive words as these: Old Fort; Vieu Fort; French Fort Ruined; French Ft.; Ancient Fort; Fr. Ft.; Altes Fort; The Fort; Ancient Fort; Fort; The Fort; French Fort; French Fort Destroyed; Ruined Fort; Ancient Fort Francois; 1755, An. Ft., R., a la Cache; 1765, Lieut. Ross, Ancient Fort Destroyed; Delisle, 1718; Homann, 1730; Popple, 1733; Le Roque, 1742; Seale, 1744, D'Anville, 1746; Jeffreys, Bellin, London Magazine, 1755; Rocque, Overton and Sayer, 1755 to 1766; Rhode, 1758; Homann, 1759; Bowen and Gibson and Bowles, 1763; Kilian, 1764; Delarochette, 1765; D'Anville and Seale, 1771; Pingeling, 1776; 1777, 1778, 1783, 1784, 1785, 1796 and 1798, D'Anville Lodge, Beaurain, Walker, Boudet, Gussefeld, Wilkes, Sayer and Bennett, and Phelipean.

The first map or plat of Cairo was made in the city of Baltimore in 1818 by Cone & Freeman. John G. Comegys no doubt had charge of the work. A Major Duncan had made, it is supposed, the necessary surveys; but it is not certain that surveys were made. They may have made the plat to represent what they thought would represent the plan of the city when the surveys were made for streets, blocks, lots and public grounds. We present elsewhere an exact copy of this plat, which is also somewhat fully described in Chapter IV.

The Cairo City and Canal Company made a few maps of the site as they proposed to lay it out for a city; but it is said no actual surveys were made and that all that was done was the making of outline plans, showing streets, blocks and public grounds, but no lots. Their first civil engineers were William Strickland and Richard C. Taylor. The former styled himself architect and engineer, and the latter engineer and geologist. A copy of one of these maps is found elsewhere, and a copy of the survey by James Thompson, made in 1837, for that company, and also a copy of a map showing the line of their proposed canal. This company never in fact reached a stage of platting for the sale of lots or other property. This seems always to have been a matter of the future; and their long delay in offering property for sale was the cause of many complaints and kept the people who were here in a very unsettled condition. The situation or site did not admit of an easy platting into satisfactory subdivisions for a city; and hence the divers kinds and descriptions of plats made by the different proprietors.

It is not until we reach the Cairo City Property people that we find almost a penchant for city map-making. Col. Taylor in his deposition, already referred to, states that their first plat was filed and became a public record December 10, 1853, and that all maps or plats made before that time were merely provisional affairs and bound no one. In the suit in which that deposition was taken, the city's attorneys produced a map which they claimed showed that the wharf or river frontage and certain other grounds were public property or had been dedicated to the public. The proof on this point does not seem to have been very strong, and Col. Taylor's testimony seems to have been quite sufficient to overcome it. The earlier maps of Col. Taylor's Trustees exhibited many features which did not appear on the one filed for record in 1853, or on any others subsequently filed. On the earlier ones, a number of public parks were indicated, among them Crescent Park, at what was then the southern point of the city; Townsend Park, of considerable size, north of 17th Street and adjoining Cedar Street on the west; Delta Park, in the curve of the Mississippi levee as it turns northward out near the river; and St. Mary's Park extended from the present Park Avenue all the way over to Washington Avenue. As thus laid out or marked on the plat, this park was more than twice its present size; but the Trustees seem to have felt that their lands were too valuable to admit of so much thereof being devoted to the uses of the public.

Holbrook Avenue once bore the name of Schuyler Avenue, after Robert Schuyler, the first president of the Illinois Central Railroad Company; but Schuyler having fallen into disrepute, the name of the avenue was changed to Holbrook. On one of these early plats the lines of the old Holbrook levees up the Ohio and Mississippi rivers are indicated, and the cross levee built under the supervision of Mr. Miles A. Gilbert from a point near the intersection of 18th Street and Ohio Street on the Ohio River to a point where Thirty-fourth Street, if extended, would intersect the Mississippi shore. The land inclosed by these three levees seems to be spoken of as the original city or the first division thereof.

West of Holbrook, Park Street extended to the Park and from thence it was called Park Avenue. Further on West were Mulberry Street, Cypress Street, Oak Street, Papaw Street, and last of all was Metropolitan Avenue. On this plat there was no street east of Commercial Avenue. The cross streets extended to what is now the railroad bridge embankment and the last of them was platted *47th Street.*

Maps with these parks indicated thereon as above described and attached to the lengthy notices advertising the city were circulated all over the country as late as 1855 and 1856; and is it to be thought strange that the people, when they saw that these public places, supposedly dedicated to the public, were one by one being withdrawn or erased from the city plats, were more and more confirmed in their opposition to the policy and management of the Trustees? This feature of the situation furnished one of the chief grounds for the suit instituted by Judge Fredolin Bross against the company in the year 1864, and which is more fully referred to elsewhere.

One map, a very large one and which Mr. Miles A. Gilbert, in his affidavit given in the chapter on the "Wharf and Wharfage," says is a copy of the small one made by Strickland & Taylor, was on file in the circuit court of the United States at Springfield in the suit begun by the Trustees against the City of Cairo in 1864. I have obtained leave from the Hon. J. Otis Humphrey, judge of the said circuit court, to withdraw the same for presentation to the A. B. Safford Memorial Library.

Explanations of Maps.—Henrie's survey of our township was made in 1807, and when it was a part of the Randolph County of Indiana Territory, and when the Indians were to be seen almost everywhere. The frightful massacre in the township just this side of the mouth of the Cache River took place February 9, 1813. Some of the Birds were probably here then and very near the point. Col. Taylor, in his deposition taken in 1866 in his suit against the city in the United States court at Springfield, said that when he came here in April, 1851, only about fifty acres of the land on the Ohio and near the point had been cleared and that the remainder of the country in this vicinity was covered with very dense woods.

Comegys' or Major Duncan's map of 1818 was made in Baltimore that year by Cone and Freeman, and is fully explained in Chapter IV.

James Thompson's survey of the township in 1837 was accompanied with the fullest possible field notes and explanations, contained in the small book described in Chapter VI.

Strickland and Taylor's map of the city and the map showing the plan of the canal of the Cairo City and Canal Company, both of the year 1838, need no explanation further than to say that they were provisional representations of what the city was to be as planned by the Holbrook administration, from 1836 to 1846. They are interesting for a number of reasons, chiefly, perhaps, for showing the line of the state's Illinois Central Railroad under the act of February 27, 1837.

Long's topographical map of July, 1850, is but one of the four which were on file in the War Department at Washington. The other three could not be found. I regret very much I was not able to get trace of the one which showed the full and complete plan of the city as laid out by Long in 1850. It no doubt differed very materially from the official map of the Trustees filed at the court house December 10, 1853. The topographical map shows what the city of Cairo was when it came into possession of the Trustees of the Cairo City Property. Long was here at work two or three years before Col. Taylor came. One of his letters to Taylor & Davis at Philadelphia is numbered 149 and is dated October 10, 1854. The map shows the old hotel nearest the point, the post-office and stores, the foundation of the great warehouse, sometimes called the London warehouse, the machine shop, the saw-mills, the foundry, the brickyards, the taverns and the groceries, and the cottages of the company standing back somewhat from the Ohio levee. I need not go further. The map speaks for itself. You see the small space of cleared land and the wide extended and dense woods; the three levees of 12,320 feet, 4,789 feet and 8,670 feet, respectively, the latter built by Judge Gilbert in 1843, all inclosing 778.75 acres of land; also the crevasse in the Mississippi levee of the length of 1,675 feet, made by the great flood of March, 1849, of which Editor Sanders speaks in his Cairo newspaper, "The Cairo Delta," of March 20, 1849.

The Picture of Cairo in 1841—This picture is the earliest representation of what is set forth in Long's map of July, 1850. It is taken from "The Valley of the Mississippi Illustrated," December number 1841, published at St. Louis, Missouri, by J. C. Wild, at the Republican Printing Office. This publication was in magazine form and contained from time to time series of views of the principal cities, towns, public buildings and picturesque scenery on the Ohio and Mississippi rivers. The literary department was under the charge of Mr. Lewis F. Thomas and the drawing and lithographing under that of Mr. J. C. Wild. Mr. S. R. A. Holbrook, of Boston, sent this particular number to Mr. M. Easterday some years ago, and to the latter I am indebted for its use here. This number contains three other fine cuts, a splendid river view at Grand Tower, a view of Selma, Missouri, and one of Prairie Du Rocher and Darbeau's Creek where it enters the Mississippi in Illinois. The picture shows most of the buildings as they appear on Long's map. It also shows that few changes had taken place from December, 1841, to the time Long made his map. In both the picture and map are seen the old and noted hotel at the point spoken of by Mr. D. S. Crumb as being there May 29, 1836; then above, the postoffice building and stores; the large long house fronting the Ohio, no doubt Holbrook's, or erected by him; then the low cottages; next the three-story machine shop, which Judge Gilbert defended so strongly against Cairo's first mob; then the saw-mills with their slanting log-ways to the river; then the large foundry; then in the picture, the steamboat "Tennessee Valley," built the latter part of 1841 and early in 1842, and enrolled at the New Orleans custom house April 23, 1842. This vessel was built and equipped at Cairo, the timbers furnished directly from the saw-mills and the machinery from the foundry, there and nearby. The owner and Captain, Samuel G. Patton and M. W. Irwin, lived at Florence, Alabama. (See the certificate from the Bureau of Navigation at Washington, dated the 3d day of February, 1910.) This steamboat was on the ways, as seen in the picture, or had but left them a short time before Charles Dickens arrived at Cairo on the steamboat "The Fulton," Saturday, April 9, 1842. He undoubtedly saw what is seen in the picture, except possibly the steamboat. Almost everything seen in the picture was there when Long made his map. There was indeed not much of a city here in April, 1842; but Dickens' representation as to what he saw is so far from the truth that it cannot be accounted for on any other theory than that he did not want to state the situation as he actually saw it for the hour or two he was here.

The other cuts, pictures and representations in the book so fully explain themselves that I need not say anything in reference thereto.

I take the liberty of suggesting to the purchasers of this book the careful preservation of the maps. Some of them can be easily torn in the folding and the unfolding. They are very important and valuable parts of the history because they show the actual situation and condition of things at the various times they were made. They set forth clearly and fully a great deal in the city's history that could not be so well presented by merely written descriptions. To remove them from the book would leave it in many respects very incomplete.

CHAPTER XIV

THE OHIO AND MISSISSIPPI RIVERS—THE TERRITORY DRAINED—THE OHIO RIVER AS A BOUNDARY

IN July, 1847, the Trustees of the Cairo City Property issued their first pamphlet circular, entitled "CIRCULAR AND OTHER DOCUMENTS RELATING TO THE CAIRO CITY PROPERTY AT THE CONFLUENCE OF THE OHIO AND MISSISSIPPI RIVERS, ILLINOIS;" New York: H. Cogswell, Printer and Stationer, 19 & 21 Merchants Exchange, 1847. The pamphlet contains 41 pages, and its table of contents is as follows: 1st, Skeleton Map of the United States; 2nd, Circular by the Trustees, 14 pages; 3rd, Map of the Site of Cairo, 2 pages; 4th, Report of William Strickland and R. C. Taylor, engineers, 5 pages; 5th, Extract from a Report by J. Freeman, engineer, to Legislature of Illinois, 2 pages; 6th, Extract from Report of Committee of Congress, 1 page; 7th, Extract from Report of Committee of Legislature upon Central Railroad and Cairo as the terminus, 2½ pages; 8th, S. Worsley, engineer, Report to English Proprietors, 4 pages; 9th, Letter of H. Baldwin, Esq., to Trustees, 1½ pages; 10th, Another Letter by him to same, 1 page; 11th, Extract from Western Review, 6 pages; 12th, Extract from S. A. Mitchell's work on Illinois, 1 page; 13th, Names and lengths of western rivers, 1 page.

The following is the last page, page 41, of the pamphlet with the names and spelling just as given therein.

MEMORANDUM

TAKEN FROM PECK'S GAZETTEER OF THE LENGTH OF THE OHIO AND MISSISSIPPI RIVERS AND THEIR TRIBUTARIES, ABOVE THE CITY OF CAIRO. (A. D. 1847.)

RIVERS AND RECIPIENT.	MILES.	RIVERS AND RECIPIENT.	MILES.
Alleghany, Ohio	300	Missouri, Mississippi	3,217
Cumberland, Ohio	450	Ohio, Mississippi	945
Grand Kanawha, Ohio	327	Ouisconsin, Mississippi	380
Grand Miama, Ohio	174	Rock, Mississippi	285
Green Run, Ohio	308	Rum, Mississippi	127
Guyandot, Ohio	134	St. Peters, Mississippi	400
Hocking, Ohio	100	Salt, Mississippi	200
Kentucky, Ohio	312	Turkey, Mississippi	135
Licking, Ohio	204	Upper Iowa, Mississippi	180
Little Kanawha, Ohio	127	Big Sandy, Tennessee	160
Monongahela, Ohio	216	Clinch, Tennessee	230
Muskingum, Ohio	203	Duck, Tennessee	185
Salt, Ohio	110	Elk, Tennessee	125
Sciota, Ohio	200	Halston, Tennessee	230
Tennessee, Ohio	850	Caney Fork, Cumberland	100
Wabash, Ohio	477	S. Fork Cumberland, Cumberland	105

Rivers and Recipient.	Miles.	Rivers and Recipient.	Miles.
Au Canoe, Missouri	100	Des Plaines, Illinois	100
Chariton, Missouri	143	Fox, Illinois	104
Crow Wing, Missouri	115	Kankakee, Illinois	143
East Fork, Missouri	145	Mackinaw, Illinois	113
Gasconade, Missouri	204	Sangamon, Illinois	175
Grand, Missouri	272	Spoon, Illinois	125
Grand Nemanha, Missouri	220	Embarras, Wabash	135
Konzas, Missouri	1,200	Little Wabash, Wabash	200
Nodaway, Missouri	115	Missineway, Wabash	100
Osage, Missouri	293	White, Wabash	260
Wood, Missouri	120	East Fork, White (In.)	228
Chippewa, Missouri	200	West Fork, White (In.)	225
Des Moines, Mississippi	400	French Road, Holston (Tenn.)	176
Forked Deer, Mississippi	114	Grand, Osage	134
Great Maquanguetois, Mississippi	120	North Fork, Osage	130
Illinois, Mississippi	400	Greenbrier, Kanawha	130
Kaskaskia, Mississippi	250	Kaskiminetos, Alleghany	103
Lower Iowa, Mississippi	237	Long Beach, Grand	130
Maramic, Mississippi	184	Miss. Gulf of Mexico	3,000
Nolicuchy, French Broad	125	New, Great Kanawha	115
Pickamink, Kankakee	100	Pine, Ouisconsin	125
Powells, Clinch	105	Rufus, Chippewa	100
	9,754		13,045
			9,754
		Total miles	22,799

The rivers less than 100 miles long are omitted.

It may be remarked that there are other rivers, longer than 100 miles, whose names are not given; for instance, the Youghiogheny River, which rises in Maryland and flows 150 miles to its junction with the Monongahela, some little distance southeast of Pittsburg. The Allegheny rises in Potter County, Pennsylvania, flows northward into New York, then southward into Pennsylvania again and reaches Pittsburg, 350 miles from its source. This river is regarded as the extension of the Ohio from Pittsburg northward.

Waters from fourteen states reach the Mississippi and pass Cairo, namely, Missouri, Kansas, Colorado, Nebraska, Iowa, Wyoming, Montana, South Dakota, North Dakota, Minnesota, Michigan, Wisconsin, Illinois and Indiana. Waters from thirteen states reach the Ohio and pass Cairo, namely, Illinois, Indiana, Ohio, New York, Pennsylvania, Maryland, West Virginia, Virginia, North Carolina, Georgia, Alabama, Tennessee, and Kentucky. These make twenty-five states, counting Illinois and Indiana but once. Waters from some of these states flow in other directions; but making all due allowances, it will be seen what a drainage area is here presented! And is it any wonder that almost always in the springtime and at other times, now and then occurring, we may expect these two vast water-sheds to pour down upon us, or at our very feet, their accumulated floods? If we were upon a rock-ribbed promontory instead of a tongue of alluvium and sand, we might defy their threatenings. We are not so situated, however, and hence it is a vital condition to our existence that these monster rivers, fed from the mountains and the skies, should be kept always and safely at bay.

THE OHIO RIVER AS A BOUNDARY.—The word *northwest,* as applied to this territorial district of our country, has come down to us from the old Virginia charter of 1609. The grant was of "all that space and circuit of land, lying from the sea coast from the *precinct* aforesaid, up to the land throughout from sea to sea, *west and northwest.*" The territory was west and northwest, and embraced what is now Kentucky and what has always been known as the northwest territory. The Kentucky country was afterwards known as the southwest territory, to distinguish it from the territory north of the Ohio River. Virginia retained the southwest or Kentucky territory or country, and granted to the Federal Government the territory *northwest* of the Ohio. This left the Ohio River wholly within her own territorial boundaries. In all the acts of congress and of the states, in reference to the matter, the south or southeastern boundary lines of Ohio, Indiana and Illinois have been spoken of as the Ohio River or the "northwestern shore" thereof.

The question as to what jurisdiction the states north of the Ohio River had upon or over the same arose at a very early day, and the decisions of the Virginia and Kentucky courts tended strongly to establish an exclusive jurisdiction on the part of those two states respectively. The very first reference was, of course, to the 11th section of the Virginia act of December 18, 1789; *13 Hening's Va. St. At Large, 19.* This act is entitled an act concerning the erection of the district of Kentucky into an independent state, and the 11th section thereof is in these words:

"SEC. 11. The use and navigation of the river Ohio, so far as the territory of the proposed state, or the territory which shall remain within the limits of this commonwealth lies therein, shall be free and common to the citizens of the United States. And the respective jurisdictions of this commonwealth and of the proposed state, on the river as aforesaid, shall be concurrent only with the states which may possess the opposite shores of the said river."

The Virginia and Kentucky courts held that this section of the Virginia act gave jurisdiction to the three states north of the river, but they made so much of the Virginia and Kentucky jurisdictions that what was left to the states north of the river could serve few practical purposes of any kind. In some of their decisions, it was said that the concurrent jurisdiction was *legislative* only and that the courts of the states on the north side had no jurisdiction at all. The arguments were elaborate and the reasons various. The later cases cited the constitutions of Illinois of 1818, 1848 and 1870, and called attention to the difference in the language of the first from that in the other two. The result, however, was the same in almost all cases; and it was not until 1896 that a case arose which reached the supreme court of the United States in 1903, and which resulted in a decision of that court February 23, 1904, which practically annulled one or two score of state cases on the subject. It is the case of *Wedding vs. Meyler, 192* U. S. 573. Wedding, of Indiana, sued Meyler, of Kentucky, in the Vanderburg County superior court, May 27, 1896, and the summons was served on Meyler on a steamboat on the Ohio and beyond low-water mark on the Indiana side and within the county of Henderson in the state of Kentucky. The Indiana court sustained the service and rendered judgment against Meyler; and Wedding having sued Meyler on this judgment in the circuit court of Warren County, Kentucky, said court sustained the Indiana judgment and rendered judgment against Meyler, and the latter appealed to the court of appeals of Kentucky, which reversed the circuit court. Wedding, thereupon, appealed from this judgment of the court of appeals to the supreme court of the United States, which reversed the judgment of the court of appeals and sustained the rulings of the said superior and circuit courts. The decision of the Federal supreme court was without dissent. Judges Hobson and Burnham of the court of appeals dissented from the other five members of that court. The supreme court, near the conclusion of the opinion, quotes and adopts Chief Justice Robertson's definition of jurisdiction as given in *Arnold vs. Shields,* 5 Dana (Ky.) page 18.

It is not easy, always, to state the extent and operation of a judicial decision; but it seems that if civil process may be properly served on the Ohio River and beyond low-water mark fifty or one hundred feet and within the territorial jurisdiction of a Kentucky or West Virginia county, there is little reason why it may not be served anywhere on the river within fifty or one hundred feet or less of low-water mark on the Kentucky or West Virginia side. And if civil mesne and final process may be so served and executed, why may not criminal process, also? It must be observed, however, that the jurisdiction is *on the river* and does not extend to the bed of the river or to permanent structures attached thereto. In the briefs of counsel in this Federal case are cited almost all of the decisions of the state and Federal courts on this subject.

Mr. Justice Holmes, speaking for the Federal supreme court, concludes his opinion as follows:

" But so far as applicable, we adopt the statement of Chief Justice Robertson in *Arnold vs. Shields,* 5 Dana, 18, 22; 30 *Am. Dec.* 669, 673: 'Jurisdiction, unqualified, being, as it is, the sovereign authority to make, decide on, and execute laws, a concurrence of jurisdiction, therefore, must entitle Indiana to as much power—legislative, judicial, and executive—as that possessed by Kentucky over so much of the Ohio river as flows between them.'

"The conveniences and inconveniences of concurrent jurisdiction both are obvious, and do not need to be stated. We have nothing to do with them when the law making power has spoken. To avoid misunderstandings, it may be well to add that the concurrent jurisdiction given is jurisdiction 'on' the river, and does not extend to permanent structures attached to the river bed and within the boundary of one or the other state. Therefore, such cases as *Mississippi & M. R. Co. vs. Ward,* 2 Black, 485, 17 L. Ed. 311, do not apply. *State v. Mullin,* 35 Iowa, 199, 206, 207.

CHAPTER XV

THE HEALTH OF THE CITY

LIKE many other things which were once true of the city but which have largely passed away, the health of the place, in early times, was by no means good; but it was never as bad as was represented. The ground was low and the point for six or eight miles up the Ohio River and twelve to fifteen up the Mississippi was covered with a very dense growth of trees of all sizes and kinds known to this section of the country. The undergrowth was almost impenetrable, so much so that one wonders how Arthur Henrie and his assistants worked their way over the point in 1807 when they made the first government survey and plat of the township. Such was the growth upon this tongue of land that the hot sun of the summer was needed to dry up effectually the fallen rain water and that which might be left by the receding rivers. But this was not so extreme as has been generally supposed. The nature of the ground was such that when the rivers reached their lower stages, the surface water sank rapidly through the sandy soil and soon reached the level of the water in the rivers. Just as the high rivers force the subterranean waters through the porous soil and up to the surface, so the falling rivers no longer sustain the surface water in place but allow it to pass back freely the way it came. The rain water follows in the same way. To this is due in large part the healthfulness of the city now. The sandy and gravelly nature of the whole site of the city, for hundreds of feet in depth, permits the easy passage of the water through the ground and to the level of the river waters, and in this way the unhealthful accumulations on the surface are dissolved and to a great extent carried away. In very wet seasons or years, the water may have stood here and there possibly for the whole season or year; but Cairo was never a marsh or anything like one. The pervious nature of the ground would not admit of it. But there were and are low grounds and some marshy lakes in Missouri and Kentucky, across the two rivers, and these with the dense growth upon the point could not fail to cause ill health to a greater or less degree; but when the Cairo proprietors began cutting out lanes and roads through the woods for streets through which a free circulation of air was obtained across and along the neck of land between the rivers, the health of the place became very much improved. Col. Taylor, who came here in April, 1851, and remained here until his death in 1896, frequently spoke of this matter as the reason for the improved health of the town.

When the troops came here in 1861, there was still considerable standing timber and under-growth; but contrary to the expectations of the whole army force here, the soldiers were found to have no cause to complain further than as to the ordinary risks incident to soldier life. The troops in Cairo had better health than those on the higher grounds near the rivers, north and south of Cairo.

Then, too, it must be remembered that the two rivers are great bodies and streams of water of very different temperatures. The Mississippi up to the very point of junction often freezes over hard and solid, but the Ohio never. The water in the one comes from the distant north while that in the other comes largely from the south. The Tennessee is the largest of the Ohio's tributaries and comes out of north Alabama, crosses Tennessee and, flowing for a short distance through Kentucky, empties into the Ohio at Paducah, forty miles on an east and west line from Cairo. The winds are uniformly from the southwest to the northeast, and crossing the Mississippi and then the Ohio must in the nature of things carry away from the city exhalations which would otherwise, at least to some extent, produce ill health.

But however we may reason about the matter, the writer can say that he has now resided in the city forty years, and that having before resided many years in one of the best counties of central Illinois, he is strongly of the belief that there is not anywhere in the state a more healthful place or city than the city of Cairo. He would not, however, have any one believe that the climate here is all that could be desired. For a northern town, Cairo is far south, as far as Richmond and Norfolk. The summers begin early and end late, making the long or hot season a long one comparatively. There is, also, malaria here, quite sufficient for home consumption. One feels less active here and must take things somewhat more moderately than further north. In a word or two, the geography and topography of the place make it more of a southern than a northern town. It must be added, however, that so far as the diseases of typhoid fever, pneumonia, and consumption are concerned, there is not one case here to four or five in central Illinois, supposedly a healthful part of the state.

In March, 1856, the Trustees published and circulated extensively an interesting pamphlet of twenty pages of large letter sheet size, printed on blue paper, a copy of which was sent to me from Cleveland. Besides its two pages of introduction, it contains eleven different headings as follows:

(1) Railroad facilities possessed by Cairo.

(2) The advantages possessed by Cairo by her river communication with the Gulf of Mexico.

(3) Cairo as a commercial city.

(4) Identification of the interests of the Illinois Central Railroad with those of Cairo.

(5) Immunity of Cairo from inundation.

(6) Drainage of Cairo.

(7) *Health of Cairo.*

(8) Supply and quality of water at Cairo.

(9) Abundance of building materials at Cairo.
(10) Cairo as she is.
(11) The future of Cairo.

That part of the pamphlet relating to the health of Cairo is as follows:

Health of Cairo.—So much has been written on the unhealthiness of the Western cities; so many terrible pictures have been painted of the fever-stricken and ague-suffering inhabitants; so many fancy sketches have been drawn of the fearful mortality which has attended the pioneers of civilization on the banks of the Mississippi,—that truth has a hard battle with misrepresentation and prejudice in her efforts to establish the facts. Yet we can scarcely wonder at this, when we see a writer like Charles Dickens, who, in his descriptions of the springs which actuate the lower strata of English society, is unequaled and unapproachable,—deliberately, to gain the applause of the bigoted portion of his countrymen, misapply his talents by seeking to vilify and abuse our rising cities of the West. From the personal testimony of all who have resided there, and who, by their connection with the city, are the best qualified to judge, we unhesitatingly assert that not only is this point one of the healthiest in the valley of the Mississippi, but that Cairo is as healthy as New York. The salubrity of the climate will compare favorably with the healthiest cities of the West. This is proved by the testimony of residents, whose families present a picture of robust health, not exceeded by the inhabitants of any other district, West or East; and a short acquaintance with the locality will not fail to satisfy every one of the fact.

Dr. James C. Cummings, now of Portland, Maine, who resided in Cairo for some years, practicing there as a physician, says,— "Yellow fever and consumption are unknown. There is not a swamp within miles of the city, and the rivers being a mile or more in width, Cairo has nothing to fear from the miasma of the Kentucky or Missouri shores. There is, generally, a refreshing breeze from one river to the other. The climate is delightful. The summers are long and by no means extremely hot. The atmosphere is generally clear, and there are usually refreshing breezes. The winters are short and mild; snow is seldom seen and lies but a short time. The water is excellent. Shippers say it is the best in the world. After a heavy rain of days even, twenty-four hours of clear weather will generally make the walking good in any direction."

Since the departure of Dr. Cummings, the Trustees have cut down the timber on the flats, from river to river, for a considerable space, and this permits of the free circulation of air, and has driven away the miasma, which might have produced chills and fever. Last summer, when there was so much cholera in the other towns on the Ohio and Mississippi, there was not one case of it among the inhabitants of Cairo. In fact, Cairo is far enough north to avoid the discomforts and fevers of a southern climate; and far enough south to avoid the frost, which, during a portion of each winter, binds in fetters the giant streams of the great West. The salubrity and healthiness of Cairo is officially recognized by the United States Government, and steps are now taking for the establishment of a U. S. Marine Hospital at this point, to humanely meet and protect diseased emigrants, and sailors navigating the Mississippi from below, during the summer season.

The Yellow Fever: The ten days beginning with July 9, 1878, were probably the hottest ten successive days in the history of the city. During that time the writer was kept at home by an attack of illness and was treated by Dr. W. R. Smith, whom most of us remember as one of our most prominent citizens and physicians. On entering the room one of those days and while wiping the perspiration from his face, he said, " John, we are likely to have yellow fever in the south within a month or two." The doctor's prophecy came true. The first case occurred in the south about the first of August. It moved on northward and soon appeared at Natchez, Vicksburg, Memphis, and Hickman, and reached Cairo September 12th. It is said by many persons that Mr. Oberly, the father of the Hon. John H. Oberly, died of the fever a few days before the 12th. On the 12th there were two deaths; one of them Mr. Thomas Nally, editor of the Bulletin, and the other Mr. Isaac Mulkey, a son of Judge John H. Mulkey, and also of the Bulletin office. Those deaths caused a panic in the city, and the afternoon and evening of that day witnessed the departure of hundreds of people from the city. For some three or four weeks prior to that time there had existed in the city an unseemly controversy as to whether the fever would probably reach Cairo or not. Were one to turn to the files of the Bulletin and the Cairo Evening Sun for the last half of August and the first twelve days of September of that year, he would see what a state of feeling existed in the city; the one party insisting that there was little or no danger and the other that there was very great danger and that every possible effort should be put forth to keep the dreaded disease out of the city. The Bulletin led off as was its custom and criticised with unnecessary severity every one who chose to differ with it. It was strongly supported by a few of our prominent citizens who felt that it was their duty to maintain our supposed immunity. I can best describe that peculiar state of things preceding September 12th by saying that it was not quite as bad as the yellow fever itself. I had been attending court at Jonesboro and was told by the conductor, on offering to go aboard the train at Jonesboro to come home, that he could not take me on account of the quarantine at Cairo. I prevailed upon him and came, and on reaching the northern part of the city I saw the levees patrolled by armed guards. One or two of them went through the train to ascertain who might and who might not be permitted to go on into the city. When I reached the city, I was surprised beyond measure to see the state of things prevailing. On every hand were seen all kinds of vehicles carrying trunks and every other description of baggage to the railroad stations. They were driven, some of them, almost at furious rates of speed. In a word, there was a panic, which I need not attempt further to describe. I left on the same Illinois Central train about eight o'clock that evening, on which were Mr. Oberly and hundreds of other citizens of the town. I remained away until the 2d day of October, when I returned home, having seen in the Cairo Evening Sun, of September 24th, the following notice:

"The Cairo public schools will open on Monday, September 30th, under the superintendency of Prof. G. G. Alvord. Mr. F. Korsmeyer, clerk of the Board of Education, furnishes us with the following list of persons who are to teach this coming year. Misses A. Rogers, K. A. Thompson, N. J. McKee, L. M. Walbridge, E. F. Armstrong, Henrietta Foss, E. Kratzinger, Mary Hogan, S. N. French, H. W. French, Mary Burnham, and Mrs. P. A. Taylor; Mr. Jesse Newsome, Miss Newsome, Miss Sarah Rose, Miss Ida Christy and James Nott. The last five are the names of the colored teachers." The schools opened at the time announced, but were discontinued October 4th. On Sunday and Monday, October 6th and 7th, there were six deaths, among them Miss Maroe Powers, one of the public school teachers. These deaths occasioned another exodus, not quite so panicky nor quite so large; and it was not until the latter part of October that the people began returning home, and it was not until far into November that all had gotten back.

The Bulletin had suspended publication with its issue of September 12th, and did not resume publication until the first day of November. Mr. D. L. Davis, the editor of the Cairo Evening Sun, and his family had also gone from the city, and had left Mr. Walter F. McKee in charge of the paper. Walter, for most of us were accustomed to address him by that name, remained at his post and gave the city a very faithful account of what was daily taking place. As bad as the news often was which it contained, the residents were eager for its appearance in the evening, and most of them forwarded copies to their friends who had gone from town and who were anxious to know the state of things at home. Mr. Davis removed from Cairo to Chicago a few years afterwards, and kindly handed to me all the numbers of the "Sun" which covered that yellow fever period. Of the one hundred or more cases there were about fifty deaths. The names of those who died are as follows:

Thomas Nally, Isaac Mulkey, John Crofton, John Bloom (Blohim), Mr. Reice, Richard Nason, Mrs. R. Nason, Miss Nason, Mr. Clark, Michael Dugan, Miss Dugan, Mrs. P. Corcoran, John Petry, Mrs. John Petry, Miss Louise Petry, Patrick O'Laughlin, child of Mr. and Mrs. Stapleton, child of John Oakley, child of J. J. Balfry, Mrs. J. J. Balfry, Robert Hart, Thomas Cook, Mr. and Mrs. Jerry Murphy, and child, Thomas Healy, Miss Kate Healy, Miss Maroe Powers, Mrs. Fitzpatrick, Huston Dickey, W. H. Wilcox, D. William Hamlin, Phillip K. Howard, Mrs. Shurburn, John McEwen, Dr. Roswell Waldo, Timothy Conners, Anthony McTigue, John Warren (colored), Annie Davis, Clara Keno, Mrs. W. H. Stoner, Mary A. Sampson, John Keho, Mrs. Stephens, Samuel Nealy, John Stanton, Miss Sullivan, Miss Anthony, John Sullivan, and Miss Mary Sweney. The seven last names were not found in the Daily Evening Sun from September 1st to November 12th, but it is said the whole list as above given was made up by Drs. William R. Smith, J. J. Gordon and Mr. Alonzo Daniels.

I give here the number of cases and the number of deaths in a few of the southern cities during the months of August, September, October and November; for the disease prevailed in the south far into November. At Baton Rouge, number of cases 2,716, deaths 201; Greenville, Miss., cases, 1,137, deaths 387; Grenada, Miss., cases 1,468, deaths 367; Holly Springs, Miss., cases 1,240, deaths 346; Memphis, cases 17,600, deaths 5,150, ratio of mortality to cases, 1 in 3.3; Hickman, Kentucky, cases 454, deaths 180; Gallopolis, Ohio, above Cincinnati, population 3,700, cases 51, deaths 31.

The above statistics are taken from the history of the "Yellow Fever Epidemic of 1878 in Memphis," by Mr. J. M. Keating. It is a volume of 454 pages and contains a full history of yellow fever, beginning as far back as the year 1600. It says that on the 14th of August in that city, the panic among its citizens first began, and that the last week of that month the panic was over and that all had left who could, and that all were in camp who would go; and further, that on the 14th day of September, the second day after the fever reached Cairo, the heaviest mortality occurred. It gives the names of the persons who died in Memphis and other cities and places in Tennessee. Necessarily many errors would occur in the collection of such information. For instance, the population of Cairo is given as 6,300, the number of cases 43, the number of deaths 32. This is a higher rate of mortality than any occurring at any of the other seventy-five to a hundred places mentioned. The fact is just as above given. There were about one hundred cases and about fifty deaths. This book gives a full account of the tow-boat John D. Porter, which it calls a floating charnel house, all the way from New Orleans to Gallopolis or Pittsburg. A number of our citizens will remember when it passed Cairo.

I have devoted these few pages to the epidemic of the fever because it was an era in the city's history. One third of the people left the city. Many remained who could and should have gone. Their reasons for remaining were various; and sometimes they could give none at all. It was a simple disinclination to leave home. There was a continuing hope that the danger would soon pass, but it persisted instead. To some it was a question of means; for to go and remain away even for a short time required money for the trip and board. Many had no friends or relatives to whom they could go. Few persons in the surrounding country desired to see any one from Cairo. Many whole families would not go because they could not decide who should remain, and they feared leaving their homes unprotected. Business was suspended; only just enough done as seemed actually necessary for the people at home. The days were unusually bright, in sharp contrast with the doubly dark and silent nights. Part of the time persons could not be abroad at night without passes of some kind from the authorities. In a word, everything spoke plainly of the reign of pestilential disease. The city government of course went on. It had to. Mayor Winter was equal to the occasion, and to be equal to such an occasion seems capability for almost anything, but he seemed made for it as for some special occasion. Jack, like so many public men of the country, liked to do things in a kind of showy way, not exactly spectacularly, but that word expresses something of the idea. Jack had been so harrowed by the Bulletin and others about the fever, that he seemed somehow to be glad that they and not he had been proven false prophets; and when the fever came he met it with an undaunted face. He could not rescue its victims; but he and the few trusty men he had buried them in the shortest possible time and yet with all the care and ceremony of which the deadly situation would admit. But I must not go on further or attempt to describe the pestilence that walked in darkness or the destruction that wasted at noonday.

Jack Winter was no better than many of the rest of us; but if at the end of all things there is a balancing of accounts for every man, Jack's account will have opposite September and October, 1878, a very large credit. Of the rather few persons on whom he relied for attention to families in need and for other aid to the city authorities, I may mention Mr. William H. Schutter. I do so because of my personal knowledge of much of his work. Of the many persons who remained out of a sense of duty to those who could not go or did not choose to go, I may mention the Rev. Benjamin Y. George, of the Presbyterian Church, and Father Zabel, of St. Joseph's Catholic Church, of whose constant care and devotion to the stricken families of the town it would be impossible to say too much. Doctor Roswell Waldo, of the Marine Hospital, gave up his life in the work he did, which extended alike to all persons needing his services. He died at St. Mary's Infirmary October 18th, after a long illness which kept the community alternating between hope and fear for his life. The Sisters of St. Mary's Infirmary did everything in their power, as they always do. It may not be so, but it sometimes seems that they take pleasure in such times as those were. They look upon every opportunity for doing good as a blessing to themselves. Did not this happiness come to them, how could they devote their lives to such work?

The Sun of Monday, November 25, 1878, gives an account of the presentation to Dr. J. J. Gordon of a gold medal in recognition of his very faithful services during the prevalence of the fever. The presentation took place at the Arlington House, afterward The Illinois, and now The Marion. It gives the names of the thirty-five donors, and speaks of Mayor Winter, the Rev. Mr. George, and other persons present.

Many of the older residents of the city remember that during the yellow fever epidemic that prevailed in many cities of the south in September and October, 1873, we had six or seven deaths here in Cairo, which were probably the result of that disease. Keating says there were seventeen deaths here from yellow fever. This is another error in what seems to be a valuable publication. Among those who died were Christian Pitcher, James C. Arrick, James Hughes, Francis M. Hundley, Mr. Powers, and Mr. Fielding. Almost all of the persons who died were employed upon some one of the wharf boats, or were in some way engaged in work on or near the river. At that time, as well as in 1878, there was quite a controversy as to whether the disease was yellow fever. The funeral of Hundley was held at the Methodist Church and quite a large number of persons attended the same. The funeral of young Arrick, who died September 16, 1873, was held at the residence of his father, Mr. A. A. Arrick, on 20th Street, and a large number of persons attended the same and went to the burial, which was at Beech Grove. It seems, however, that by the last of September the Bulletin came finally to the conclusion that the disease was yellow fever.

It is supposed that the yellow fever has been banished from the United States, if not also from Cuba. If this claim is well founded, or reasonably well supported, why may we not also hope for the banishment of other diseases? If one so deadly as this one which has penetrated even into the heart of the country may be permanently expelled, how is it that the expulsion or prevention may not sooner or later extend to other diseases—others prevailing almost all the time and almost everywhere?

CHAPTER XVI

CAIRO DURING THE WAR
1861-1865

IT is quite impossible to say much concerning Cairo during this period of four years without also saying much about the war. Those years, however, were so full of events relating directly to the city as to require a separate if not a somewhat full account.

The census of the year 1860, one of the most remarkable years in the country's history, shows the population of Cairo to have been 2,188, of whom 55 were negroes. It had no doubt increased a few hundred and probably had reached 2,500 in the month of April, 1861. Its population in 1870 was but 6,267. At the very opening of the war, it was seen that Cairo was to become one of the most important points on the long line of division between the revolting and the adhering states. The two great arteries of commerce united here and took their course southward through almost the heart of the then hostile country. Charlevoix, Governor Hamilton, of Canada, General George Rogers Clark and many others had spoken of the importance of the position as a means of defense against foreign foes; but few, if any, had ever spoken or thought of its strategic advantages in case of civil or domestic war. It is true, the Mississippi River had now and then been cited as a kind of bond of union between the states, but such references were little more than mere figures of speech, and when it became apparent that we were likely to have a civil war, the country turned at once to a careful study of the geographical features of the border states. Illinois extends far down into the Southern country and Cairo was and is about on a line with the south line of Kansas, the old well-known Missouri compromise line of 36-30, which was less than forty miles north of the south line of Virginia and Kentucky. The two slave states of Virginia and Missouri extended north of Cairo 200 and 300 miles, respectively, and three-fourths of the state of Kentucky lay north of it. But its chief importance lay in its position at the junction of the two great rivers, from which it was supposed large control might be obtained and exercised over the united streams flowing into the Gulf and almost equally dividing the country in revolt.

At the general election November 6, 1860, Lincoln received 76 votes in Cairo, and 106 in the whole county; Douglas 347 in the city and 684 in the county; Bell 91 in the city and 178 in the county, and Breckinridge 73 in the city and 79 in the county. In Union County, Lincoln's vote was 157, Douglas' 996, Bell's 58, and Breckinridge's 819. In Pulaski, Lincoln 220, Douglas 550, Bell 45, and Breckinridge 9. In Johnson, Lincoln 40, Douglas 1,563, Bell 0, and Breckinridge 9. In Pope, Lincoln 127, Douglas 1,202, Bell 83, and Breckinridge 1. In Jackson,

Generals Grant and McClernand, 1861

River Gunboats, Cairo, 1861

Lincoln 315, Douglas 1,556, Bell 147, and Breckinridge 29. In Williamson, Lincoln 173, Douglas 1,835, Bell 166, and Breckinridge 40. In Massac, Lincoln 121, Douglas 873, Bell 84, and Breckinridge 0. In Hardin, Lincoln 107, Douglas 499, Bell 62, and Breckinridge 0. In Saline, Lincoln 100, Douglas 1,338, Bell 113, and Breckinridge 15; and in Perry, Lincoln 649, Douglas 1,101, Bell 138, and Breckinridge 1.

In the twenty-seven counties lying along the line and south of the railroad from East St. Louis to Vincennes, the whole vote for the four candidates was about 60,000, of which Lincoln received a little less than one-third. The only counties in which he received more votes than any other candidate were Edwards, Madison, and St. Clair. Breckinridge's vote in Union County of 819 was about three times as great as his vote in all the other twenty-six counties. In Edwards, Hamilton, Hardin, Lawrence, Monroe, Massac and Washington, he did not receive even one vote.

It is well known that the people generally, or a large majority of them, in the southern and southeastern part of the state, sympathized with the south but not largely to the extent of disunion. They had voted for Douglas, who had in some vital matters broken with the southern leaders, and when he, seeing that war was inevitable, declared that there was but one thing for loyal men to do and that was to support the government, these southern Illinois people laid aside their radical democratic views and with remarkable unanimity rallied to the support of the Union. The Illinois and other troops who first came to Cairo in April and May, 1861, came there with the belief that its residents were, with a very few exceptions, southern sympathizers if not *rebels* at heart. They had known of the town only as a very hard and a very unhealthy place, and seeing the low site, the unfilled and muddy streets, the poor houses and still poorer sidewalks, their impressions, which they wrote back home, were in substance much like those of Dickens, if not always expressed in the same fine language. For a time the officers and men treated the people as if they were across the Ohio and in Kentucky. The little city government, with Samuel Staats Taylor at its head as mayor, became smaller and smaller and shrank almost into invisibility. It seems all the while, however, to have maintained itself *de jure,* but as for a *de facto* existence it had little if any at all in the midst of so many captains, colonels, generals, and armies of soldiers, equipped with muskets and cannon of every description. In the midst of arms the laws were silent. But this unavoidable state of things soon settled down into a condition or type of administration that seemed entirely natural, and to which the people of the little city adjusted themselves with becoming grace and contentment. It was soon seen, because practically demonstrated, that to carry on war much money was needed, and Cairo having become a great military station and depot, money soon began to make its appearance in a way never dreamed of by any one in the town, nor, for that matter, by any of the somewhat visionary founders of the place. Rents went up higher and higher, new but rather temporary buildings rose in great numbers and in every quarter. Prices of all kinds of goods advanced beyond precedent, and it was supposed that the future of Cairo was now well assured. This change in values and advance in prices were seen and felt everywhere in the country, with the fall in the face value of all currency and the constant and unlimited demands by the war for all products and manufactures. Many persons became comparatively wealthy who had never expected to attain unto more than a comfortable competency. It was a time of great prosperity, and very naturally sympathy with the south and opposition to the war became things of the past. The two newspapers here then received from time to time friendly suggestions from the generals commanding the post, who for the most part were treated as editors in chief. The city jail or calaboose now and then contained a soldier, but the coming morning generally witnessed his transfer to the proper military authorities, which in most cases was regarded as best for all parties, especially the city and its people.

Fort Sumter was fired upon April 12, 1861, and was surrendered the next day. On the 15th President Lincoln called for the 75,000 three months' soldiers and on the 23rd, the first soldiers of Illinois arrived in Cairo. This is what is said about their arrival by Mr. A. H. Burley, of Chicago, in his account of"The Cairo Expedition."

April 21 (1861), the expedition started from the Illinois Central Railroad station (Chicago) . . . . The military train passed unheralded the length of the State, and rolled into Cairo to the astonishment of all and rage of many of its citizens. . . . . Knowing the sentiment of the people, the fear was that they would destroy the long, wooden trestle-work across the Big Muddy River, which they could have rendered impassable, in an hour, by burning it. There was also fear that the rebels would seize Cairo, as being a point of great strategic importance. It was afterwards learned that Cairo would have been seized in forty-eight hours, had its occupation been delayed. . . . . The first armed force sent out in the West was that sent to Cairo, and it was sent from Chicago.

The following three or four pages are from the report of Allen C. Fuller, adjutant general, for 1861-1862, dated January 1st, 1863, and addressed to Governor Richard Yates:

On the evening of April 15, 1861, the following dispatch was received: "Washington, April 15, 1861. His Excellency, Richard Yates: Call made on you by to-night's mail for six regiments of militia for immediate service. Simon Cameron, Secretary of War." . . . . Washington, April 19, 1861. Governor Yates: As soon as enough of your troops is mustered into service, send a Brigadier General with four regiments at or near Grand Cairo. Simon Cameron, Secretary of War.

The importance of taking possession of this point was felt by all, and that, too, without waiting the arrival and organization of a brigade. Accordingly, the following dispatch was sent to Brigadier General Swift, at Chicago:

"Springfield, April 19, 1861.

General Swift:

As quick as possible have as strong a force as you can raise, armed and equipped with ammunition and accoutrements, and a company of artillery, ready to march at a moment's warning. A messenger will start to Chicago to-night.

RICHARD YATES,
Commander-in-chief."

At eleven (11) o'clock on the twenty-first, only forty-eight hours after this dispatch was delivered, General Swift left Chicago with a force of 595 men and four six pounder pieces of artillery. Capt. Houghtaling's battery, of

Ottawa; Capt. Hawley's, of Lockport; Capt. McAllister's, of Plainfield, and Capt. Carr's, of Sandwich, did not arrive in Chicago in time to join the expedition, but followed it the next day. The expedition consisted of the following forces:

Brig. Gen. Swift and Staff	14
Chicago Light Artillery, Capt. Smith	150
Ottawa Light Artillery, Capt. Houghtaling	86
Lockport Light Artillery, Capt. Hawley	52
Plainfield Light Artillery, Capt. McAllister	72
Co. A, Chicago Zouaves, Capt. Hayden	89
Co. B, Chicago Zouaves, Capt. Clyborne	83
Capt. Harding's Company	80
Turner Union Cadets, Capt. Kowald	97
Lincoln Rifles, Capt. Mihalotzy	66
Sandwich Company, Capt. Carr	102
Drum Corps	17
Total	908

Captain Campbell's Ottawa Independent Artillery, with about twenty men and two six-pounder cannon, joined the force about the 28th of April."

This expedition, indifferently armed with rifles, shot-guns, muskets and carbines, hastily gathered from stores and shops in Chicago, arrived at Big Muddy bridge, on the Illinois Central Railroad, at five o'clock, A. M., April 22d, and detaching Capt. Harding's company at that point, arrived at Cairo at eight o'clock the following morning. The batteries were unprovided with shell or canister, but slugs hurriedly prepared—and some of which were subsequently used at a critical time, and with terrible effect, by one of these batteries at Fort Donelson—answered the purpose of all.

This command was reinforced, on the twenty-fourth, by seven companies from Springfield, under the command of Col. Prentiss, who relieved Gen. Swift, except as to that portion—who did not desire to muster into the United States service—commanded by Captains Harding, Hayden and Clyborne, who returned to Springfield on the second of May, to join a regiment organizing here. These last companies, however, arrived too late, and were mustered out of the State service, with allowance of one month's pay, under an act of the Legislature then in session.

The importance of an early occupation, by our forces, of Cairo, was not overestimated. Situated at the confluence of the Ohio and Mississippi rivers, and commanding the navigation of these waters, its possession in a strategical point of view, was absolutely necessary to our safety. The state governments of Missouri, Tennessee, and Kentucky were controlled by disloyal men. Governor Magoffin had, on the 16th of April, said to the President, in reply to his call on that state for troops: "Your dispatch is received. In answer, I say emphatically, Kentucky will furnish no troops for the wicked purpose of subduing her sister Southern states." Governor Harris, of Tennessee, on the 18th, in reply to the call upon his state said: "Tennessee will not furnish a single man for coercion;" and on the same day Governor Jackson, of Missouri, said: "Requisition is illegal, unconstitutional, revolutionary, inhuman, diabolical, and cannot be complied with."

By taking possession of this point, at so early a date, our forces were enabled to prevent a traffic with the rebellious states in contraband property. This traffic was being actively carried on between Galena and St. Louis, with towns on the Mississippi below Cairo. The execution of the following telegraphic order was the first arrest made to this traffic:

"Springfield, April 24, 1861.

Col. B. M. Prentiss, Cairo:

The steamers C. E. Hillman and John D. Perry are about to leave St. Louis, with arms and munitions. Stop said boats, and seize all the arms and munitions.

Richard Yates.
Commander-in-chief."

On the evening of the 24th and morning of the 25th, as these boats, bound for southern ports, neared Cairo, Col. Prentiss directed Captain Smith, of the Chicago Light Artillery, and Captain Scott, of the Chicago Zouaves, to board them and bring them to the wharf. His orders were executed, and large quantities of arms and munitions of war were seized and confiscated. Though this seizure was not expressly authorized by the War Department, the act of seizure and subsequent confiscation was approved. Further shipments were all forbidden soon after, as appears from the following dispatch:

"Washington, May 7, 1861.

Governor Yates:

Circular has been sent to collectors forbidding shipments intended for ports under insurrectionary control. Stop such shipments from Cairo.

S. P. CHASE."

The Legislature having met on the 23d of April, proceeded at once to provide for the organization of these six regiments, and, on the 25th, an "act to organize six regiments of volunteers from the State of Illinois and provide for the election of regimental officers and a Brigadier General," was approved and became a law. Under the old militia laws of the state a company of infantry consisted of one captain, one first, one second and one third lieutenant, four sergeants, four corporals, one drummer, one fifer, and not less than forty-six nor more than one hundred and sixteen rank and file. A regiment consisted of one Colonel, one, two or three Majors (as the case might be), the senior to be Lieutenant Colonel, with a regimental staff, to be appointed by the Colonel, to consist of one Adjutant, who should act as regimental judge advocate, one Quartermaster, one Paymaster, to rank as Captains, respectively; one Surgeon and Surgeon's Mate, one Sergeant Major, one Quartermaster Sergeant, one Drum Major and one Fife Major.

The regulations of the Secretary of War for organizing these regiments required each regiment to consist of one Colonel, one Lieutenant Colonel, one Major, one Adjutant (a Lieutenant), one regimental Quartermaster (a Lieutenant), one Surgeon, one Surgeon's Mate, one Sergeant Major, one Drum Major, one Fife Major, ten Captains, ten Lieutenants, ten Ensigns, forty Sergeants, forty Corporals, ten drummers, ten fifers and six hundred and forty privates.

The law provided that "in token of respect to the Illinois regiments in Mexico," these regiments should be numbered seven, eight, nine, ten, eleven, and twelve; and that when organized they should be known as the "First Brigade Illinois Volunteers." Under the provisions of this law they were organized and mustered into service and ordered to duty as follows:

The Seventh, Colonel Cook, was mustered at Springfield, April 25th, and ordered to Alton the 27th.

The Eighth, Colonel Oglesby, was mustered the same date, and ordered to Cairo the 27th.

The Ninth, Colonel Paine, was mustered at the same place, April 26th, and ordered to Cairo May 1st.

The Tenth, Colonel Prentiss, was, with a part of his command, ordered to Cairo, April 22d, and was, on the 29th, mustered at Cairo.

The Eleventh, Colonel Wallace, was mustered at Springfield, April 30th, and ordered to Villa Ridge, May 5th.

The Twelfth, Colonel McArthur, was mustered at Springfield, May 2d and ordered to Cairo, May 10th.

As has already been remarked, Cairo was soon seen to be one of the most important points on the dividing-line between the northern and southern states. It was the most important point in the whole Mississippi valley and in many respects a key to the wide extended country, and both sides, seeing the advantages of its possession, sought to occupy it. The Confederates pushed up into central Kentucky and at the same time occupied Columbus, only twenty miles below us, and they would have been in Cairo and have held it, at least for a time, had not Governor Yates rushed his very first soldiers to its defense against the Confederate approach.

As illustrating the view taken of this important position at Cairo, I quote a few lines from General Clark E. Carr's book, "The Illini," on page 357, where he says:

"Governor Yates received a telegram from the Secretary of War requesting him, as soon as enough Illinois troops were mustered in, to send a force to occupy Cairo. He did not wait for troops to be mustered in. In less than forty-eight hours, he had General Swift, of Chicago, flying down, upon a special train of the Illinois Central Railway, with four batteries of artillery and six companies of infantry, and the most important strategic point west of the Alleghanies was safe in our possession. Cairo was from that time forward the central point of all the movements of our armies on the western rivers. The movement for its occupation was not made a day too soon."

Major General George B. McClellan was, in April, 1861, assigned to the department of the Ohio, consisting of the states of Ohio, Indiana, and Illinois, and in his book entitled "McClellan's Own Story," he says, on page 45:

"In the course of May and June, I made several tours of inspection through my command. Cairo was visited at an early day and after a thorough inspection, I gave the necessary orders for its defense, as well as that of Bird's Point which I also visited. Cairo was then under the immediate command of Brigadier General Prentiss, and, considering all the circumstances, the troops were in a remarkably satisfactory condition. The artillery, especially, had made very good progress under the instruction of Colonel Wagner, a Hungarian officer, whom I had sent there for that object."

In Col. Taylor's lengthy letter of September 6, 1858, to the Trustees of the Cairo City Property, concerning the inundation of June 12, 1858, wherein he states that the break in the levee occurred near where it curves into the cross levee towards the Ohio River, there occurs this passage: "When the levee broke, no one was in sight of it that I can ascertain. Captain McClellan, the Vice-President and General Engineer of the Illinois Central Railroad, and myself, had passed over it on foot within two hours before it occurred, and the watchman whose duty it was to look after it was over it about twenty minutes before, but to none of us was there any appearance of weakness. After leaving the location about twenty minutes and being distant less than one-fourth of a mile, the watchman heard the roaring of the waters running through the crevasse, and when I reached it, three-fourths of an hour afterward, the water was running through to the full width of three hundred feet and in an unbroken stream, as if it was to the full depth of the embankment. The probability is, I think, that, aided by the stumps and roots in the embankment and it is possible some other extraneous substances, the water had found its way through the base of the embankment, and had so far saturated it as to destroy its cohesion with the natural ground below, and then the weight of the water on the outside pushed it away."

Less than three years from this time, the great Civil War, the greatest of modern times, had begun, and Captain McClellan was at the head of the Union army as Major General.

In saying much about Cairo during the war one would likely say much more about the war than about Cairo. The Cairo of that time could be disposed of in a few pages more than Dickens used in 1842, although its population in April, 1861, was just about ten times what it was in April, 1842. Anthony Trollope was here two or three days in February, 1862, and he wrote much more and much more painfully about the town than did his facile penned countryman. (Trollope's "North America," vol. 2, chapter 6.) This much, however, can be said in palliation of Trollope's description of Cairo, and that is, it must have looked even worse in 1862 than in 1842. Cairo during the war was hardly Cairo at all. It was a great military camp, set down in a low flat plain and surrounded by high levees from which you descended to the town's level by long flights of wooden steps at the intersection of the unimproved and often very muddy streets. Trollope never tired of talking of the mud. The town was, as now, in a basin, whose rim was a high earth embankment, seven or eight miles in circuit, and over which one could not see either river unless upon a building or other elevation. Inside of these levees and along the same were the camps or barracks of the soldiers. At the junction of the rivers they constructed Fort Defiance. It was not of great extent. It was simply a large flat-topped mound, on which the cannons were placed, so as to command effectually the junction of the two great streams. Two or three miles lower down and on the Kentucky side of the Ohio and at a point very near where the waters of the Mississippi first push over to the Kentucky shore, Fort Holt was erected. It was named for the judge advocate general of the United States army, General Joseph Holt, of Kentucky. This point or place was subsequently called Fillmore. Fort Holt commanded not only the mouth of the Mississippi but commanded also the approach from the south on that river. Fort Defiance was also well situated to defend against vessels coming up the Mississippi and entering the Ohio. There was also a fort, for a time, at Bird's Point or rather at the site of Ohio City, somewhat east or further down the river. These three forts were intended to protect Cairo by commanding the adjacent parts of Kentucky and Missouri.

During the early part of the war the expression "Border States" meant very much indeed. These border states were slave states. The free states just north of them were scarcely ever spoken of as border states. These border states were a sort of neutral zone or a zone in which the people were pretty equally divided between union and secession. This equality of division led to a desire for neutrality, that is, freedom from invasion by either side. Had this been carried out or been assented to, we would have had no war; but the neutral zone could not be maintained. The Confederates pushed up into Kentucky as a kind of matter of course or of right, she being a slave state; and before the year 1861 closed, they had secured and fortified Columbus twenty miles below us, the Tennessee and Cumberland Rivers, and Bowling Green, all in that state. They had two forts on the Tennessee, Fort Hieman on the west side and Fort Henry on the east side, just a little below; and just across the narrow space of ten or twelve miles, they had their Fort Donelson on the Cumberland, inclosing one hundred acres of ground, and occupying a high position on that river. At Columbus they had the advantage of the very high bluffs just above the town.

With this well-selected line of advance toward the north, it was quite impossible, so long as it was maintained, for the northern forces to proceed a foot southward in this region of country. On their way northward, the Confederates would not have stopped at Columbus but would have occupied and held Cairo with all the advantages the place afforded, had they moved a month sooner or had moved with a stronger force either by land or by river. This early advance into Kentucky had for its main object the drawing of that important state into the Confederacy. Had not General Grant come this way, there is no telling how far the enemy's line would have gone northward, perhaps to the Ohio River. Grant not only stayed its advance but pushed it far southward as we will now proceed to show.

Ulysses Grant was born in Ohio April 27, 1822; graduated at West Point in 1843; was for many years in the regular army and was in the Mexican War; was a farmer near St. Louis in the years 1855-57; in the real estate business in St. Louis in 1858; moved to Galena in 1859, and there was a clerk in his father's tannery that year and 1860; appointed colonel of the twenty-first regiment of Illinois volunteers in May, 1861; brigadier-general of volunteers at Mexico, Missouri, in July, 1861, and major general of volunteers at Fort Donelson February, 1862; had his headquarters at Cairo from September, 1861, to April, 1862; was appointed major general in the regular army on the capture of Vicksburg July 4, 1863, and lieutenant general in 1864, and general of the army in 1867; and was elected President in November, 1868. Few men at home or abroad, at any time in history, have risen through so many grades and so high as this; from a clerkship in a tannery to the presidency of the United States within less than eight years.

Captain Grant was appointed colonel of the twenty-first regiment of Illinois Infantry in May, 1861, and leaving Springfield with his regiment, he entered the state of Missouri in the vicinity of Quincy or Hannibal, and was first stationed at Jefferson City. In a very short time, he was transferred, and given the command of southeastern Missouri and southern Illinois. He made his headquarters at Cape Girardeau. At this time, July and August, 1861, Jeff. Thompson and other Confederate officers were operating all over the southern part of

Missouri and to them the Federal commanders were giving more or less attention. On the 4th day of September, 1861, Grant came to Cairo, and this place remained his headquarters until the northern line of the Confederate forces had been pushed far southward. Col. Oglesby was in command at Cairo when Grant arrived. On the second or third day after his arrival, he assembled a few vessels and hurried up to Paducah and took possession of the place. Had he delayed as much as eight or ten hours, the Confederates would have had possession of that city. Three to four thousand of their soldiers were on their way from Columbus and were within a few miles of Paducah when Grant entered and took possession. He had sent Oglesby with three thousand men into the state of Missouri, along the line of the present Iron Mountain Railroad, and on the 6th of November he proceeded down the Mississippi, as far as or near Columbus and Belmont, with two or three gun-boats and about three thousand men. This movement, which led to the battle of Belmont November 7, 1861, was intended to detain at Columbus the Confederate forces and thereby protect Oglesby and his troops. Grant says that had not this movement been made Oglesby's forces would no doubt have been captured.

The entrance of the Confederates into Kentucky at different points was but an invitation to the Union forces to enter and occupy the state so far as they might be able. To break this central hold of the Confederacy on Kentucky, Grant saw that the rivers afforded him the very best available means. By the close of the year 1861 quite a large number of war vessels suitable for river service had been assembled at Cairo and Mound City, where, under the supervision of Captain William L. Hambleton, the government had built eight or ten gunboats, one of which Commodore Foote named The Cairo. These and many other vessels were ready for service late in 1861. They were first brought into service at Belmont November 7th; then at Fort Henry February 7th; then at Fort Donelson February 16, 1862. The capture of Forts Henry and Donelson led to the evacuation of Bowling Green; and as the vessels proceeded on up the Cumberland to Nashville, the latter was also evacuated by General Albert Sidney Johnson. Then came the evacuation of Columbus. Following these events came the great battle of Pittsburg Landing or Shiloh and the retreat of the Confederates to Corinth. Before the end of the month of May, Corinth was given up to the Federals, and this was followed, June 6th, by the evacuation of Memphis. Thus within the short space of four months, Grant had pushed the Confederate line from central Kentucky down to the south line of the state of Tennessee.

Following Nashville, Memphis and Corinth, came Knoxville and Chattanooga; and though the progress southward was or seemed slow, yet by the end of another year, namely, July 4, 1863, fifteen months from the battle of Pittsburg Landing, Vicksburg had fallen. This led to the junction of the Union forces from the north and from the south and the full and complete possession of the Mississippi River from its source to its mouth; and along with this came the possession also of all the states on the river south of Cairo, Kentucky, Tennessee, Mississippi, and Louisiana on the east, and on the west, Louisiana, Arkansas, and Missouri. The Confederacy was thus severed in twain, divided as along the median lines.

Although the red line of war moved southward from Cairo, she continued to be the great point of departure for everything bound southward, as she was the point of arrival for everything going northward. The southern armies were pushed backward, but the people within the reclaimed territory were as a general thing no friends of the Union cause, and hence everything south of the Ohio had to be held by arms. Cairo thus continued to be throughout the war the most southern point in the great valley adhering heartily to the Union. Through the city there was almost a constant stream of soldiers bound northward or southward. A few days after the battle of Fort Donelson fifteen thousand Confederates were brought to Cairo and sent northward to the different prison camps. Over thirty thousand came also from Vicksburg. Some of our older citizens remember how the steamboats or other transports seemed covered and alive with them, dressed as they all were in their brown or butternut suits. And so it continued throughout the war.

Before closing this chapter I must speak of the gun-boat The Cairo, so named October 29, 1861, by Commodore Foote, who was so long here and held in such high esteem by our citizens. This vessel was one of six or eight built at Mound City, as above stated. Her commander was Lieutenant Nathaniel C. Bryant. He was assigned to the command of this vessel by Commodore Foote. It was badly disabled at Fort Holt by an accident. It was at Fort Henry and also at Fort Donelson and went on up the river to Nashville. It was also at the siege of Vicksburg, and was destroyed while in the mouth of the Yazoo River about the 12th of July, 1863, by a torpedo, which it encountered in moving about in that river.

I cannot say much of the town itself during this period of four or five years, for the soldiers were here and passing and repassing far up into the year 1865, and perhaps later. Had we the registers of the old St. Charles Hotel from April 15, 1861, when the war began, to April 15, 1865, when the President was assassinated, how many scores of distinguished names we would see therein written. In number and prominence they would be exceeded only by those at the capital of the Nation for the same period.

I cannot devote more space to this subject; nor is it necessary. Cairo's importance during the war was due to her situation at the junction of the Ohio and Mississippi Rivers, and perhaps more relating to the city will be found in the records of the navy than of the army. See especially vol. 22, series I, of the records of the Union and Confederate Navies, in our Public Library.

CHAPTER XVII

CHURCHES

ST. PATRICK'S ROMAN CATHOLIC CHURCH.—Under the supervision of Rev. C. M. Collins, C. M., of Cape Girardeau, who occasionally visited Cairo to minister to the Catholic people here, a frame church building, about thirty-six feet square, was erected upon posts at the intersection of 18th and Ohio Streets, in 1838. The bell was hung in the forks of a tree in front of the church. This was no doubt the first church building of any kind erected in Cairo. The records of St. Patrick's parish show that Father Collins baptized nineteen persons in 1840, eighteen in 1841, four in 1842, and three in 1843. This falling off was due to the failure of the Cairo company and the consequent abandonment of the town, practically, in 1843. On Christmas day 1844, the Rev. J. P. McGerry, C. M., baptized Mary Ann Lefcovitch, John Shannessy and John Corcoran. There seems to be no record of Catholic church matters in Cairo from February, 1845, to November, 1853; and from this last date the same records show that Rev. P. McCabe had charge here until December, 1858. From the "Cairo Times" of 1854, it appears that St. Patrick's church building, thirty-five by seventy feet, with a large roomy basement, was completed under the supervision of Father McCabe and services held therein on Sunday, June 25th, of that year. The contractor was John Saxton, of St. Louis, and the cost of the building about five thousand dollars.

Father McCabe was succeeded by Rev. Thomas Walsh, who continued as pastor until his death, March 15, 1863. Rev. Louis A. Lambert was assistant to Father Walsh from April, 1859, to the September following, and upon the death of Father Walsh, he, then pastor at Shawneetown, was transferred to St. Patrick's church here. In May, 1868, he resigned his charge and went to New York, and was succeeded by the Rev. P. Brady, his assistant, who remained until October, 1869, when he was transferred to Springfield. Rev. P. J. O'Halloran was next in succession and continued until November, 1873, when he and Rev. Francis H. Zabel, D. D., of East St. Louis, exchanged places. Father Zabel remained until September, 1879. Our older citizens remember him and especially his devoted self-sacrificing labors during the yellow fever of 1878. He was a man whom every one in the city esteemed very highly. Rev. Thomas Masterson came from Mound City to take his place and remained until July, 1882. He was succeeded by Rev. J. Murphy, who remained until November, 1885. Rev. Charles Sweeney succeeded him and remained until November, 1889. Then came Rev. James Eckerle, who was pastor until December, 1890, and who was succeeded by the Rev. T. Day. The latter was transferred in November, 1891, and upon his departure the Rev. Charles J. Eschman took charge of the parish. During Father Eschman's pastorate, and in 1894, the present fine stone church was built. In March, 1902, Father Eschman and Rev. James Gillen, of Prairie du Rocher, exchanged places. Father Gillen remained in charge until May, 1904, when he was assigned to St. Joseph's parish, and Rev. James J. Downey succeeded Father Gillen as pastor of St. Patrick's, and he is now in charge. Shortly after he came he built the new rectory, and later on installed the fine pipe organ now in the church.

Until 1879, St. Patrick's had a large congregation, being attended by all but the German Catholics of the city. In that year the bishop divided the city into two parishes, making Fifteenth Street the boundary line. This division reduced the size of the congregation by more than half, as most of the Catholic people resided in the upper part of the city.

The Church of the Redeemer (Episcopal).—Origin of Parish: A letter, December 1, 1840, Rt. Rev. Philander Chase, bishop of Illinois, to J. P. T. Ingraham, appointing him "a lay reader among the Episcopalians of Cairo;" a meeting April 18, 1841, the bishop presiding, at which was formed the "Parochial Association of Christ Church Cairo;" organization of "Church of the Redeemer" November 3, 1862; incorporated April 25, 1864, under the title "Rector, Wardens, and Vestrymen of the Church of the Redeemer, Cairo, Illinois." Subscription started May 2, 1858, to erect church; foundation partly laid and destroyed by high water; enclosed fall 1862, occupied several weeks for government hospital, then finished; occasional services by Rev. S. Y. McMasters and other army chaplains; first regular services February 8, 1863. Building substantial frame 44 x 70 feet, wooden tower, cost $3,000.00, erected on 14th Street (lots 35 to 39, block 44, City, donated by Trustees of the Cairo Trust Property); sold July 2, 1886, to Rt. Rev. George F. Seymour, bishop of Springfield, in trust for "St. Michael Mission" (colored Episcopal) now occupying same. Present Church of the Redeemer, N. E. corner of Washington Avenue and Sixth Street (lots 24 to 39, Block 24, City) a beautiful brown stone edifice, slate roof, cupola, gold gilt cross, cost including furnishings and memorials, $30,899.49, commenced September 28, 1886; cornerstone laid December 7, 1886; finished April 9, 1888; first services April 10, 1888; consecrated by Bishop Seymour November 13, 1892. Rectors of the parish, with time of service: Isaac P. Labagh, November 16, 1862, to January 18, 1864; Thomas Lyle, May 2, 1864, to February 1, 1867; W. W. Rafter, April 29, 1867, to September 16, 1867; J. W. Coe, September 21, 1867, to October 30, 1869; Edward Coan, April 10, 1870, to March 9, 1873; Charles A. Gilbert, November 1, 1873, to January 1, 1877; David A. Bonnar, November 2, 1879, to December 11, 1880; Frederick P. Davenport, June 1, 1881, to November 28, 1891; Fr. A. De Rosset, October 31, 1892, to September 3, 1901; E. L. Roland, November 12, 1902, to November 12, 1906; A. H. W.

Anderson, May 1, 1907, to December 1, 1908; George M. Babcock, present rector since May 5, 1909. Wardens: Samuel S. Taylor, Henry S. Candee, 1864 to 1867; Horace Wardner, Samuel B. Halliday, 1867; Horace Wardner, W. W. Thornton, 1868; W. W. Thornton, Henry L. Halliday, 1869; Horace Wardner, Henry L. Halliday, 1870 to 1872; Henry H. Candee, William B. Gilbert, 1872 to 1897; William B. Gilbert, Miles Fredk. Gilbert, 1897 to present time. Vestrymen: (Six elected annually since 1862 in addition to the wardens) have included many substantial citizens, among whom, for want of space, can only be mentioned the old familiar names of Robert Jennings, Alfred B. Safford, Wm. P. Halliday, Charles Thrupp, Jesse B. Humphrey, Wm. H. Morris, David J. Baker, Alex. H. Irvin, John Q. Harmon, C. W. Dunning. Present incumbents are Henry S. Candee, Joseph W. Wenger, Frank Spencer, Henry E. Halliday, John T. Brown, C. Fred Galigher. Present communicants 222.

The Presbyterian Church.—On the 20th day of December, 1882. this church celebrated the twenty-fifth anniversary of its organization. On that occasion Mr. George Fisher, then the editor and publisher of the "Weekly Citizen," presented to the congregation an historical sketch of the church. At the annual meeting of the congregation in 1885, he added a supplemental account, together with a very short manual prepared by the Rev. Albert H. Trick, then the pastor of the church. All these Mr. Fisher caused to be printed in a pamphlet of 35 pages; and it is from this pamphlet that almost all of the following information is obtained.

The church building was erected in the year 1855, and dedicated the first Sabbath of January, 1856, but the lots, 31, 32, 33 and 34, block 50, in the city, were not conveyed to the trustees of the church by the Trustees of the Cairo City Property until February 12, 1856. The Rev. Robert Stewart, through whose efforts the building had been erected, preached the sermon at the dedication. Most of the money for the erection of the church came from Presbyterians of the city of St. Louis. The ladies of the Presbyterian church at Alton gave the funds for the furnishing of the church. The names of the pastors of the church and the length of their terms of service are as follows: Rev. Charles Kenmore, October, 1856, to June, 1857; Rev. A. G. Martin, December, 1858, to March 1861; Rev. Robert Stewart, June, 1862 to November, 1864; Rev. H. P. Roberts, January, 1865, to February, 1867; Rev. C. H. Foote, February, 1867, to November, 1871; Rev. H. B. Thayer, January, 1872, to March, 1875; Rev. Benjamin Y. George, October, 1875, to October, 1883. From that time to November, 1884, the church was without a pastor, but was supplied almost all the time by ministers from other places. The Rev. Albert H. Trick was pastor, December, 1884, to November, 1890; Rev. Charles T. Phillips, April, 1891, to September, 1897; Rev. J. T. M. Knox, January, 1898, to May, 1905. The Rev. A. S. Buchanan became pastor in November, 1905, and is now the pastor of the church.

The names of the elders of the church and when chosen are as follows: Edward P. Wilcox and James McFerran, 1861; William Cunningham, 1863; Daniel W. Munn and Walter Hyslop, 1865; Joseph B. Reed and John M. Lansden, 1868; George Fisher and Reuben S. Yocum, 1880; Edmund S. Dewey, William White and Slater S. Bossinger, 1890; M. Easterday, 1893; Charles P. Simons, 1896; William H. Gibson and Julius G. Holman, 1904; William S. Dewey and Rollo H. Spann, 1906; and Jesse W. Rule, 1908. The present elders are William White, M. Easterday, William H. Gibson, William S. Dewey, Rollo H. Spann and Jesse W. Rule. The present trustees of the church are Charles Cunningham, William S. Dewey, William J. Buchanan, William H. Sutherland, Arthur B. Turner, Walter H. Wood and Quinton E. Beckwith.

In 1893, the congregation decided to erect a new church building, and many of the members residing in the upper part of the city, it was thought best to build further up town, and accordingly lots 14, 15, 16, 17 and 18, in block 51, in the First Addition to the city, on the southeast corner of Eighteenth Street and Washington Avenue, were purchased June 10, 1893; and on the 23d day of December of that year, the lots on Eighth Street and the building thereon were sold and the proceeds, with the subscription moneys, used in the erection of the church on the lots named. The Eighth Street lots had been conveyed to the church for church purposes, with a clause in the deed providing for a reversion. To extinguish this right so as to enable the congregation to sell, they paid the sum of one hundred dollars per lot. The new building and the manse property were completed in the year 1894, under the pastorate of the Rev. T. C. Phillips, who took up the work of the new church enterprise with great earnestness and carried it on to a successful and speedy completion. The present membership of the church is three hundred and ten.

The Methodist Episcopal Church.—The few early Methodist families in Cairo were served by missionaries who made occasional visits in 1852 and 1853. The earliest of these were Revs. Henry C. Blackwell and T. C. Lopas, who held services and preached to the six or eight Methodist families at that period.

Rev. Ephraim Joy visited Cairo and preached a few times later. The First Methodist Episcopal Church society was organized in 1855, and proceeded to raise funds for the erection of a church. They were successful in their efforts and work on the building was begun in the summer of 1856. It was used for services in February, 1857. The church was of Gothic style, 38 feet wide by 60 feet in depth, with a 20 foot ceiling. A Mr. Van Ness was the architect, and McKenzie & Carnahan were the builders.

Rev. G. W. Hughey was pastor during the building of the church. He was succeeded by Rev. R. H. Manier in 1856. A revival was held in the new church beginning in February, 1857.

The church was dedicated on March 1, 1857, in the presence of a gathering of about two hundred persons. Rev. Dr. Akers preached the dedicatory sermon from the text, "And he was afraid and said this is none other than the house of God, and this is the gate of heaven." Rev. Mr. Shumate followed in a short sermon, in which he appealed to the sympathies of his audience regarding the church debt. He succeeded in raising a collection of $43. Subscriptions were also made amounting to $375.00.

During the Rev. Mr. Hughey's pastorate, toward the close of the Civil War, a frame parsonage was built at a cost of $2,300. In 1891, the present brick church edifice was erected at a cost of nearly $11,000. The building committee in charge at that time was composed of George Parsons, Wilton Trigg and W. H. Oakley.

The pastors of the church from the organization of the society up to the appointment of the present incumbent have been as follows, viz.: G. W. Hughey, in 1855; R. H. Manier, 1856; J. A. Scarritt, 1857; C. Babbitt, 1858; G. W. Jenks, 1859; L. Hawkins, 1860; J. W. Lowe, 1861; G. W. Hughey, 1863 to 1865; M. A. Bryson, 1866; John Vancleve, 1867; Erastus Lathrop, 1868; F. M. Van Treese, 1869-70; F. L. Thompson, 1870-73; J. L. Waller, 1873-75; J. D. Gillham, 1875-77; A. P. Morrison, 1877; W. F. Whitaker, 1878-80; J. A. Scarritt, 1881-83; E. A. Hoyt, 1884-86; J. W. Phillips, 1887-89; S. P. Groves, 1890-93; F. M. Van Treese, 1894-97; J. A. Scarritt, 1898-1905; and W. T. Morris, 1905-08; Rev. J. G. Dee, the present pastor, succeeded Rev. Mr. Morris on September 22, 1908. In 1909, the present parsonage was built at a cost of about $3,000.00.

The present church membership is 250, with a Sunday-school enrollment of 400 and an average attendance of 250. Prof. T. C. Clendenen is president of the board of trustees, and Edwin Bond, Sunday-school superintendent.

The Immanuel Lutheran Church.—The Immanuel Lutheran Congregation of Cairo was organized in October, 1866, by Andrew Lohr, Christian Schulze, Robert Bribach, Henry Harris, Gustave Beland, Henry Miesner and Fred and Henry Whitcamp. Services were at first held in the hall of the Relief Fire Engine House on Seventh Street, the first pastor having been Rev. J. Dunsing. About five years after the society was organized, it purchased a frame building on Douglas Street, west of Washington Avenue, which had previously been used as a Baptist church. The congregation occupied this building until 1896, when the present handsome brick church was erected. This edifice is 30 by 50 feet, a semi-circular altar recess in the rear, an organ recess on the left, and a library room on the right. The cost of the building, and its furnishings, was $10,000. Two years after the church was erected, a primary class Sunday-school room, 16 by 30 feet, was built in the rear of and connected with the church. This was a gift from Mr. and Mrs. A. Lohr.

The first service in the new church was conducted by Rev. J. G. M. Hursh. The dedication of the building took place on May 9, 1897. Rev. S. S. Barnitz officiated, and was assisted by Revs. H. L. McGill, E. H. Kitch and D. C. Hurst.

Rev. G. P. Heilbig, the second pastor, assumed charge in January,

1870, and remained until December, 1872. Rev. C. Duerschner was pastor from April, 1873, until January, 1879. Next came Rev. E. Knappe in May, 1879, and remained until November, 1881. Rev. Carl Schuart was in charge from July, 1882, until his death on August 4, 1885. Rev. W. Englebracht served from September, 1885, to November, 1888; and Rev. J. F. Moenkemueller, the last of the German pastors, from July, 1889, to July, 1892. At this time the congregation decided to become English speaking and it united with the Evangelical Lutheran Synod of Southern Illinois.

Rev. H. C. Grossman, the first English-speaking pastor, assumed charge in January, 1894, and resigned in November, 1895. Then came Rev. W. C. Seidel, serving until July, 1896. Rev. J. G. M. Hursh was pastor from January, 1897, until February, 1903. He was succeeded by Rev. George A. Bowers, D. D., who resigned in April, 1904. In August, 1904, Rev. C. H. Armstrong accepted a call and continued until December, 1909.

St. Joseph's Roman Catholic Church.—St. Joseph's church was built by the German Catholics of Cairo, and was completed in the spring of 1872. Lots were secured in the summer of 1871, on the southeast corner of Walnut and Cross Streets. In September the contract for building the church was let to R. M. Melcher and Son, of St. Louis, for $15,500. The corner-stone was laid on Sunday, October 22, 1871, Rev. D. S. Phelan, of St. Louis, preaching the sermon. The first mass was celebrated in the new church on Sunday, April 22, 1872, it being a solemn high mass. Rev. C. Hoffman was the first pastor, and remained about two years. William Kluge and Peter Saup were the first lay trustees. St. Joseph's continued as a German church until 1879, when Bishop Baltes divided the city into two parishes, making Fifteenth Street the boundary line. He then designated St. Joseph's as the parish church for all Catholics, regardless of nationality, residing north of the boundary line. Several years later, Seventeenth Street was made the dividing line. Since Father Hoffman's departure, the successive pastors have been: Rev. G. Hoppe for two years; Rev. Louis Lammert for three years; Rev. Thos. Hogan, one year; Rev. O. O'Hare, three years, having died in 1883; Rev. C. Sweeney, two years; Rev. L. Hinsen, one year, and Rev. J. B. Diepenbrock from November, 1886, to May, 1904. Rev. James Gillen, the present pastor, succeeded Father Diepenbrock in May, 1904. During Father Gillen's pastorate, a fine modern two-story brick school-house has been built in the rear of the church at a cost of $18,000. It was completed in the winter of 1905-6. In 1907, the congregation purchased a modern residence for the pastor adjoining the church property.

The Christian Church.—The Christian church in Cairo was organized in May, 1866, with the following charter members: Mr. and Mrs. S. R. Hay; Mr. and Mrs. A. B. Fenton, Mr. and Mrs.

Morrison, Mr. and Mrs. McCauley, Mr. and Mrs. Trumbo, Mr. J. C. Talbot, Mr. and Mrs. Robert J. Cundiff, Mrs. Mary E. Clark, Mrs. White, Mrs. Brown, Mrs. Gilkey, Mrs. Henderson, Mrs. Seely, Mrs. Wilson, Mrs. Layton, Miss Gilkey and Miss Smith. Rev. G. G. Mullins, of Chicago, was the organizer. S. R. Hay, A. B. Fenton, and Mr. Cyrus were made overseers, and J. C. Talbot and R. J. Cundiff, deacons. The Trustees of the Cairo City Property donated the society four lots on the north side of Eighteenth Street, between Washington Avenue and Walnut Street. A frame church building 36 by 55 feet was soon erected at a cost of $4,500.

In 1894, the congregation secured a new site on the northwest corner of Sixteenth and Poplar Streets, and the church was moved there. In 1909, work was begun on the new brick church. For various reasons work has been delayed, and the church is yet in an unfinished condition. It is estimated that the cost of the new church will approximate $25,000.

The former pastors of this church have been as follows: Revs. L. S. Brown, John Friend, R. B. Trimble, F. A. Sword, C. W. Marlow, C. S. Townley, E. W. Simmons, W. G. McColley, Clark Braden, L. D. Hill, W. F. Wieland, R. A. Sickles and Mr. Carpenter. Rev. Frank Thompson is the present pastor.

The Cairo Baptist Church was organized on Monday evening, Oct. 26, 1880. The council was composed of Rev. W. F. Kone, of Huntsville, Ala., and Revs. Geo. L. Talbert and A. J. Hess, of Columbus, Ky. The organizers were George W. Strode, Mrs. Mary P. Strode, C. B. S. Pennebaker, Isaac N. Smith, Mrs. Louise E. Smith, A. J. Alden, Mrs. B. E. Alden, Hasen Leighton, Mrs. Sarah E. Parks, Mrs. M. J. Dewey, Mrs. Martha Whitaker, Mrs. William Martin, W. C. Augur, Mrs. Julia C. Augur, Mrs. N. E. Caster, and Mrs. Sarah S. Stickney. Elder A. J. Hess was the first pastor and remained until January, 1883. Elder A. W. McGaha served as pastor from March, 1883, to October, 1883. He was succeeded by Elder John F. Eden, who remained one year.

The church was without a regular pastor from Elder Eden's departure until June, 1886, when Elder A. J. Brown was secured, and he continued as pastor until June, 1887. In September, 1887, Elder R. H. McNemer took pastoral charge and remained four years. Elder W. B. Morris was next in service, and served the church from August, 1891, to October, 1893. Elder Geo. P. Hoster was pastor from March, 1894, to September, 1897; Elder W. Sanford Gee, D. D., from January, 1898, to January, 1903; and Elder T. J. Porter, from April, 1903, to September, 1906. The present pastor, Elder S. C. Ohrum, assumed charge in January, 1907.

Soon after the church was organized, the trustees purchased the Turner Hall property, a frame building and three lots on the northeast corner of Tenth and Poplar Streets for $2,500.00.

The building was converted into a church edifice and so used until 1894, when it was removed to the rear of the lots and a new brick church erected.

On June 8, 1897, a fire destroyed the frame house and left only a portion of the walls of the brick building. The brick church was reconstructed during the fall and winter of 1897, and was opened for worship on January 1, 1898. In the spring of 1903, the church purchased a house and lot on Poplar Street, adjoining, and remodeled the building for a parsonage. In 1908-9, an annex was built to the church at a cost of $7,000.00. A fine pipe organ was placed in the church in January, 1910, at a cost of $2,000.00.

The present officers of the church are: Trustees, C. B. S. Pennebaker, Dr. A. A. Bondurant and George A. Hilburn; clerk, F. W. Cox; and treasurer, John C. Gholson. The present membership is about 400.

The Calvary Baptist Church.—This church was organized September 8, 1897, in the hall room of the Hibernian Engine House at the corner of Washington Avenue and Douglas Street, by Elder J. W. Hunsaker, of Anna, as moderator, and Elder E. B. Sullivan, pastor of the Lake Milligan church, as clerk, and assisted by J. B. Anderson, F. D. Atherton, and W. R. Lane, as Deacons, also of the Lake Milligan church. Eighty-one persons became members at the organization—charter members, as they are sometimes called—almost all of them being well-known citizens of Cairo. Quite a majority of these persons had been members of the Cairo Baptist church, the first Baptist church organized in the city, whose church building is at the corner of Tenth and Poplar Streets.

The following named ministers have been pastors of the Calvary church, for the times stated: The Rev. Geo. P. Hoster, D. D., until October, 1900; the Rev. W. C. Rutherford from thence until March, 1903; the Rev. R. A. Sickles until August, 1904; the Rev. S. P. Mahoney until February, 1907; the Rev. L. D. Bass, D. D., until March, 1908, at which time he was succeeded by the present pastor, the Rev. L. G. Graham.

The first board of trustees were J. L. Sarber, J. W. Burns, and F. W. Koehler; financial secretary, J. A. Cox; treasurer, W. F. Gibson, and church clerk, John C. Gholson. The congregation continued to worship in the hall of the said engine house until August, 1898, when they removed to their new church building at the corner of Poplar and Sixteenth Streets.

The present officers, besides the pastor, are: J. A. Cox, E. G. Hoppe, W. F. Gibson, W. T. Landon, T. W. Benson, Henry H. Stout, and J. D. Gill, deacons; trustees, T. O. Webster, Claude C. Stanley, and O. B. Archibald; treasurer, E. G. Hoppe; clerk, J. L. Benson; Sunday-school superintendent, J. E. Neff; assistant, T. W. Benson.

I have not been able to secure any account of the Southern Methodist Church, whose place of worship is in the upper part of the city, and hence its absence.

Besides the eleven foregoing church organizations, there are also eleven organizations of and for the colored people. These are given on page 20, of our present city directory. Almost all of them have their own church buildings, some of which are a great credit to their congregations, such as the First Missionary Baptist Church, at the corner of Walnut and Twelfth Streets; the African Methodist Episcopal Church, on Seventeenth Street between Washington Avenue and Walnut Street; the Missionary Baptist Church, at the corner of Nineteenth and Walnut Streets, and St. Michael's Episcopal Church, on Fourteenth Street between Washington Avenue and Walnut Street.

One will see in Chapter XXV how the colored population of the city and county has increased since the year 1861. They are as likely to remain here and grow in number just the same and as long as they do further south. So far as the churches are concerned, the colored people have received little aid or guidance from the white people, notwithstanding their great need. The former have not repelled the latter. It has been a matter of aloofness, rather, on the part of the white people.

Cairo is a southern city, not only geographically but racially. In the latter respect, it is not much more likely to change than in the former. The colored people are here to stay, just as they are throughout the South. The situation is not of our nor of their making. To make the best of it, both races should do all that can be reasonably expected of them. The white people claim to be the superior race. Let them prove their superiority by showing that they can do more than the other race for the situation, concededly more or less difficult and embarrassing. If the colored people of our city, with all the advantages of education provided for them by the white people, if they, their church members and preachers included, have been bought and sold at election times until the elective franchise in their hands seems to be a travesty, they can very truthfully reply that the white people, the office-seekers and the so-called politicians, have been their purchasers. Whatever may be said of their weakness or of their ignorance or of their poverty, one thing at least can be safely said, and that is, quite too many white people among us have sought by the use of money and other like inducements to take advantage of their weakness, their ignorance, and their poverty. Too much of the influence of the white race upon the colored has been debasing instead of elevating. More to the same effect and tenor might be said, but the above is broad enough to sustain very many specific charges.

On the other hand, the colored people have scarcely furnished any kind of a man or leader to rise up and utter a protest that would reach the ears of his own people or those of the other race. Few white people seek to help them and they seem to be without any real leaders to conduct them on to a better state of things. What they most need seems to be protection against office seekers. Self-protection is best and most needed. But it is scarcely to be hoped for. Is it not clear that this rising up and protesting against the widespread venality of our elections should come first from us who are most at fault?

There are a large number of worthless and debased negroes in our population. The occurrence of last November, resulting in the lynching of James, should not be unduly charged to the colored race; but the demeanor of a great many of them as exhibited just following the crime and during the presence of the soldiers here indicated quite too much a sort of indifference to the situation instead of indignation against the crime and the criminal. It will be well for both peoples, especially for the colored people, to observe that the experiences of our city during the last eight or ten months have separated them still further apart. It has come to be generally believed that the white women of the city must exercise more care. There may be a little more risk or danger than during years past, but the one dreadful occurrence has effected a great and perhaps a needed change. It is very manifest that this whole matter to which I have thus briefly alluded furnishes an important not to say a striking lesson to both races in our community, more especially to the colored race or people, who perhaps find themselves quite too often the greater sufferers.

NOTE.—A number of the sketches of the churches, contained in this chapter, were prepared, at my request, by members of the organizations. I asked for very condensed statements; hence their brevity. I may also here state that the church property of St. Patrick's Church represents an expenditure of not less than fifty thousand dollars, that of the Presbyterian Church of about thirty thousand, that of the Cairo Baptist of about twenty thousand, and that of St. Joseph's Church, including its school property, of fifty-five thousand.

CHAPTER XVIII

THE SCHOOLS OF THE CITY

DURING the existence of the Holbrook administration from 1836 to 1842, when the population of the town ranged from less than a hundred to two thousand people, there were no doubt one or two schools in Cairo. They were private schools, sustained by the individual subscriptions of the parents of the pupils. We have not been able to find any record or writing about such schools; but Mr. Moses B. Harrell, in his short history of 1864, names one or two individuals who taught school here then. As in many other cases, a very thorough search would no doubt bring to light information now deemed as non-existent; but it is quite impossible to devote more than a reasonable amount of time and labor to going over and through sources which might be supposed possibly to contain historical facts of some importance. We must gather diligently that we may have the opportunity of choice, and we must sift carefully that the best only may be preserved.

We have a fairly full record of what was done for the maintenance of schools in Cairo commencing with the year 1853. Much of it is found in a large book called the "Journal," containing pages 632, which was opened for the Trustees of Schools for that year by Mr. Moses B. Harrell their treasurer and secretary. The Trustees were Bailey S. Harrell, William Dickey and P. Corcoran. At the commencement of that year they had no school-house, and their first step was to apply to the legislature for leave to use the interest on the funds obtained by the sale of school lands above town for the erection of a school house *"for the inhabitants of the township."* On the 10th day of February, 1853, the legislature passed the act they requested; but it required the Trustees to conform to section 81 of the act of February 12, 1849, which provided that when the trustees desired to have a school-house built they should have a public meeting of the voters and ascertain their wishes in regard to the matter. This was done, and on the 21st day of May, 1853, the voters assembled and held their meeting, of which Samuel S. Taylor was the chairman and J. J. Rutter the secretary. The resolution drawn up and offered for the building of the school-house at the cost of not exceeding five hundred dollars, was unanimously adopted; and on the 31st day of May, 1853, Bryan Shannessy was given the contract to build a school-house, twenty-five by forty-five feet and twelve feet high, for five hundred and seventy-five dollars. The specifications for the building, furniture, etc., are all found set out in full in the said Journal, as are also the notices and all other proceedings. Shannessey was required by the written contract to complete the house by the 15th of October, 1853.

The trustees, Bailey S. Harrell, William Dickey and P. Corcoran, on the 27th of August, of the same year, entered into a contract with Charles T. Lind to teach the school for one year, commencing September 1st, for six hundred and twenty-five dollars, payable in quarterly instalments. He was to furnish all the fuel, and was to insure the house for one year for the use of the trustees. He taught the school and was paid, as required by the contract. The record of all these proceedings, as entered in the said Journal, shows that the school-house was to be built upon a lot to be donated by the Trustees of the Cairo City Property. The deed was made December 22, 1853, the day before the Peter Stapleton and John Howley deeds were made for lots down on Third Street near Commercial Avenue, and is for lot numbered thirty, in block numbered forty-seven, in the city of Cairo. It is on the north side of Eleventh Street about one hundred and fifty feet east of Walnut Street. The building at this time standing there and used for colored children is the same one contracted for and built in 1853; and the first school taught therein was by Charles T. Lind, commencing September 1, 1853. It has been used almost continuously for the long period of fifty-six years. Few of us know of the memories and associations connected with the little building. We must call attention, however, to the strong provision in the deed to the effect that the lot was conveyed to the Trustees of Schools of the township " for the purpose of establishing and maintaining a common school in the city of Cairo," and for no other purpose or use whatsoever and only so long as the same should be used by the inhabitants of the said district for said purpose and use aforesaid and no longer. While this restricted use is stated in strong language, there is no provision or language for its reversion to the grantors or any one else in case it should be used for other than school purposes. The whole of the property of the Trustees of the Cairo City Property was sold in 1876 and a new trust formed, called the Cairo Trust Property. We do not remember that the decrees and conveyances made at this time provided in any way that reversionary interests in property like this should go to the new trust or to any one else; and we venture to say that it is highly probable that the Trustees of Schools now have and hold an absolute and indefeasible title to the said lot, and that they may deal with it as with any real estate conveyed to them without any conditions whatsoever.

The record book above spoken of, called the "Journal," contains nothing more regarding the employment of teachers. It seems that there were no school directors at that time and that the trustees acted as directors. We have found a number of old schedules kept by teachers, beginning with the year 1855. Some of the teachers seem to have been employed for two or three or more years. We give their names up to the year 1865, although it may be there were some whose names we have not obtained.

Some time ago I had prepared a number of pages in outline, expecting to fill the blanks therein with information I supposed I could easily obtain. The pages commenced with the Douglas School building on Walnut Street between Douglas and Fourteenth Streets, which was erected in 1864 by Messrs. Rankin, Wood and Wickwire, under the supervision of directors Daniel Hurd, William J. Yost and Moses B. Harrell, and came on up to the Elmwood School building, erected in 1908-1909 by Mr. Frank Ferguson, under the supervision of Mr. Casper Kusener, architect, and the Board of Education, composed of the Hon. Walter Warder, president, Edward L. Gilbert, H. H. Halliday, P. H. Smyth, Mary B. Wenger, E. D. Carey, J. H. Galligan, Anna G. White, C. B. S. Pennebaker and W. F. Gibson; but I have found it so difficult to obtain the necessary information that I have not been able to complete the statements. Mr. Edward L. Gilbert, a member of the present board, and for many years its secretary, informed me that he had made a long and diligent search but could not find the record or minute book or books of the board prior to April, 1902, at which time the present book began. I regret this very much; for the people of Cairo have taken a very great interest in their public schools, and I desired to embrace in this history as much concerning them as their importance would seem to require. Not being able to present a reasonably full account, I have thought best not to undertake to present one in a very imperfect form.

The members of the board from its establishment, almost forty years ago, have uniformly endeavored to do the very best they possibly could for the people of the city in the support and maintenance of our schools.

There has been a steady and wholesome growth in the schools all the time. The expense of their maintenance has been comparatively large, not to say heavy, especially when the ordinary expenses have had to be increased by large sums required for new buildings. It is well known that the expenditures have been larger because of the fact that the colored people are not possessed of property subject to taxation to such an extent as to meet what would be regarded as their proportionate share of the burden under ordinary circumstances. The white people have had in large measure to maintain schools for both races. The law made it their duty, and it is only simple justice to them to have it said that they have cheerfully borne the burden of the additional expense. If there has ever been any lack upon the part of our boards of education to discharge fully the duties owed by the public to the colored people we do not know when it has occurred. All our citizens have felt that it was a matter of very great importance that all of the children in the city, without distinction of race, should be afforded ample opportunity for securing an education. They have looked upon it as absolutely necessary in any view that might be taken of the needs of the city and the public at large. Under these circumstances, with so large a proportion of colored people in the city, our boards of education have had no easy task to perform. They have endeavored to please, so far as it was in their power, both the white and the colored people, the latter of whom have at times made complaints, but it is believed that in very few cases, if any at all, was there any just ground for dissatisfaction.

It was not until the year 1865 that the directors chose a superintendent of schools. Our first superintendent of schools was Mr. E. A. Angel, who had charge of the schools from the summer of 1865 to the summer of 1866. The superintendents succeeding him with the terms of service are as follows: E. P. Burlingham, 1866-1869; Joel G. Morgan, 1869-1870; H. S. English, 1870-1871; W. H. Raymond, 1871-1872; George G. Alvord, 1872-1881; M. Bigley, 1881-1882; E. S. Clark, 1882-1883; B. F. Armitage, 1883-1886; and Taylor C. Clendenen, 1886 to the present time, a period of twenty-four years. Of these nine superintendents, whose services have extended over a period of forty-five years, only four served more than one year. They were E. P. Burlingham, three years; Prof. Alvord, nine years; Prof. Armitage, three years, and Prof. Clendenen, twenty-four years as above stated Prof. English died here while superintendent. Only a very few of our people remember Professors Angel, English and Raymond. Professors Burlingham and Alvord are remembered by a great many. Prof. Burlingham seemed to be a great favorite with all the teachers and the pupils. He seemed to have given character to the schools, which continued for some time. It was of a kind that seemed to meet with pretty general approval, but was somewhat criticized by others. It was remarked that on all public occasions his pupils appeared to great advantage. This was true, but I do not suppose that persons so speaking of the schools meant to imply that they were in any other respects inferior. Prof. Alvord, here nine years, seemed to impress upon the schools something of his own individuality. He was a remarkably affable and well-appearing man, and I have no doubt that under his supervision the schools were well conducted. Mrs. Alvord was a very talented lady and a fine teacher. Prof. Armitage left us and went to Mattoon in 1886. He was also liked very much, but for reasons of health, I believe, he desired to go elsewhere. Prof. Clendenen has been here almost three times as long as any of the former superintendents. This speaks much more for him than anything I might say. He has gone forward, year after year, in his own way of management and according to his best judgment, and that he has been successful in his long and arduous work, no one can doubt. No one knows better than the superintendent what the duties are which such a position imposes. To have been at the head of schools, such as we have had here for a quarter of a century with the children of the two races to be educated and trained, signifies hard and exacting work and faithful service.

The names of the present Board of Education are as follows: H. H. Halliday, President; Edward L. Gilbert, Secretary; Mary B. Wenger, Anna G. White, C. B. S. Pennebaker, James H. Galligan, W. F. Gibson, Walter Wood, W. M. Hurt, P. T. Langan, Herman

C. Schuh and J. J. Rendleman. The names of the present teachers in the public schools are as follows: Superintendent, Taylor C. Clendenen; Supervisor of Music, Laura A. Miller; Supervisor of Drawing, Pauline Vanderburgh. Cairo High School: J. Earl Midkiff, Commercial; Margaret Wilson, English; Elizabeth Smith, History; G. Pearl Mulberry, Domestic Science; Clara B. Way, Latin; C. O. Gittinger, Mathematics; Sheldon R. Allen, Manual Training; Maude Hastings, Latin and English; and E. H. Carlson, Science. Douglas School: Henry E. Alvis, Principal; assistants, Margaret Leuschen, Zulima M. Smith, Allie Chambers, Ethel Barry, Reta Cohn, Jennie E. Dewey, and Anna Riley Redman. Safford School: Ella Hogan, Principal; assistants, Maude Ehlman, Pearl Cohen, Julia Farrin, Maude Palmer and Carrie J. Miller. Lincoln School: I. H. Hook, Principal; assistants, Laura I. Milford, Katherine Walbaum, Alice Wenger, Emma Carey, Bessie Batterton, Helen Lippitt and Frances W. Bennett. Elmwood School: Ralph W. Jackson, Principal; assistants, Mabel Lancaster, Margaret Whitaker, Ella Armstrong Blauvelt and Ellen B. Fisher. Woodside School: Della Hurst.

Sumner High School: John C. Lewis, Principal; Ben H. Mosby, English, History, and Athletics; Mabel C. Warrick, History and Domestic Science; assistants, Cordelia O. Lewis, Eva C. Self, Mattie E. Guy Lott, F. F. Bowlar, Alma Partee, Lydia Amos, Lida Tyler, and Ida M. Bedford. Garrison School: Emma L. Minnis, Myra V. Scott, Josie Ruffin and Nancy A. Bugg. Greeley School: Ernestine Jenkins, Principal; assistants, Azalea Dumas, Georgia Bugg and Araminta Taylor. Bruce School: H. S. Sanders, Principal; assistants, Edmonia A. Watkins and Amelia Pearson. Phillips School: Hannah M. Harper.

During the last thirty or more years, there have also been one or more private schools in the city. For many years the Catholics maintained a " Female Academy of the Sisters of Loretto." The prospectus of the institution will be found in the "Cairo Morning News" of September, 1864, setting forth that the institution would open on the first Monday in October. They purchased block seventy-eight in the First Addition to the city of Cairo and erected on the westerly end thereof excellent buildings for their school purposes. It was patronized largely by Cairo people and also by many persons living in the adjacent parts of the country. It was discontinued many years ago, but for what reasons I am not able to state. It may have been because of the influence and growing strength of other similar institutions which drew from the same fields of support.

The Germans also maintained for many years a school for the teaching of German to their own children and such others as their parents desired to send to their school. The Catholics have always had one or more private schools, and they have now two flourishing schools, the one under the care of St. Patrick's church, and the other under the care of St. Joseph's church.

First School House, 1853. Oldest Building in Cairo. Sign: "For Sale by School Board," September, 1910

The A. B. Safford Memorial Library

CHAPTER XIX

THE A. B. SAFFORD MEMORIAL LIBRARY—ST. MARY'S INFIRMARY—THE UNITED STATES MARINE HOSPITAL

THE Woman's Club and Library Association was organized in 1875, and in 1877 it established a subscription library in one of the rooms of what is now the First Bank and Trust Company Building. In 1882, the club tendered the library to the city for the use of the people as a free library; and the city, highly appreciating the offer thus made, accepted the same by the passage of ordinance No. 88, July 1, 1882, entitled "An ordinance to establish and maintain a public library and reading room in the City of Cairo, for the use and benefit of the inhabitants of said city,"—and July 6, 1882, Mayor Thistlewood appointed the following named persons members of the board of directors: Mrs. Anna E. Safford, Mrs. Henry H. Candee, Mrs. William R. Smith, Mrs. Philander W. Barclay, Mrs. P. A. Taylor, and Rev. Benjamin Y. George, the Hon. William H. Green, Mr. William P. Halliday, and Mr. Wood Rittenhouse.

Mrs. Safford, seeing the great need of a suitable home for the new public library and earnestly desiring to honor the memory of her deceased husband, Mr. Alfred B. Safford, purchased the easterly end of block forty-two, fronting two hundred feet on Washington Avenue, 16th and 17th Streets, had the ground filled to the city grade, erected thereon the present handsome library building, and at once conveyed the property to the city for the purpose for which the first gift was made. The corner-stone was laid October 30, 1883, by the Alexander Lodge I. O. O. F., of which Mr. Safford had long been an earnest and honored member. The building was dedicated July 19, 1884, on which occasion Mrs. Safford delivered an interesting address, at the conclusion of which she tendered the property to the city. The same was accepted on behalf of the city by the Hon. Thomas W. Halliday, mayor, in a very appropriate address of thanks. On the tablet, set in the wall on the stairway, is the following inscription: "This A. B. Safford Memorial Library Building was erected in memory of Alfred B. Safford, born January 22, 1822, died July 26, 1877, by his wife, Anna E. Safford, A. D. 1883."

At the time of the gift of the library to the city, it contained 1583 volumes. At the present time, it contains 16,157 volumes. The library occupies the south side of the main floor, and across the hall are the reading and reference rooms. The lecture hall on the south side of the second floor is a fine room. The north side of this floor is occupied by the museum and club room of the Woman's Club.

It would be hard to find such an institution which has been more useful to the community in which it exists. The people of the city regard it as one of the greatest means of education and entertainment which could in any way have been procured for them. They look upon the building and beautiful grounds as a great credit not only to the donor and the city but in a measure to themselves. This is due no doubt to the fact that the property is the gift of one of our own citizens whom they esteem so highly. Mrs. Safford in erecting this memorial to her husband has erected in the hearts of the people of Cairo an equally enduring memorial.

The present directors of the library are: Mrs. Anna E. Safford, president; Michael J. Howley, vice-president; Mrs. Samuel White, secretary; Mrs. Walter H. Wood, Mrs. Isabella L. Candee, Mrs. Kate F. Miller, Reed Green, Herman C. Schuh and Philander C. Barclay. Mrs. P. E. Powell, the librarian, has held this position continuously since the establishment of the library as a public institution. Misses Effie A. Lansden and Marie C. Glauber are her assistants.

THE WOMAN'S CLUB AND LIBRARY ASSOCIATION, as above stated, was organized in 1875. Its charter members were Mesdames Anna E. Safford, Isabella L. Candee, Kate B. Gilbert, Charles Thrupp, Phillip H. Howard, Charles Pink, Amarala Martin, Carrie S. Hudson, John H. Oberly, Horace Wardner, William R. Smith, Catherine C. E. Goss, William Winter, Samuel P. Wheeler, Al Sloo, and C. C. Alvord. The first officers were Mrs. Oberly, president; Mrs. Candee, vice-president, and Mrs. Goss, secretary and treasurer of the club. The club was incorporated Februray 9, 1877, under the general act of the legislature for the incorporation of such bodies. Mrs. Candee, Mrs. Goss, and Mrs. Ford made the necessary certificate for its incorporation. The trustees for the first year were Mrs. Oberly, Mrs. Smith, Mrs. Wardner, Mrs. Winter, Mrs. Safford, and Mrs. Adele Korsmeyer. (See record book No. 8, page 28, at the court-house.)

I do not know how I can better express the good this club has done for the people of the city than by asking what our condition would now be had it never existed. What we could or would have had in its place I do not know. Perhaps nothing. Too many of us do not stop to consider the influence it has had upon the people of the city. The roll of its members is indeed an honored one. I know of nothing that can be pointed to, in our city, which can approach it in this respect. They have placed it upon a firm foundation, as enduring, I hope, as the city itself. It will, I am sure, interest all the members of the association to give here the names of the deceased members. They are as follows:

MRS. MARY J. ADAMS
MRS. M. A. ARTER
MRS. MARY C. BARCLAY
MISS IDA BARRETT
MRS. I. N. CARVER
MRS. N. R. CASEY
MRS. JENNIE M. DEWEY
MRS. EDITH ELLIS
MRS. SUSAN G. FISHER
MRS. EMMA B. FRANK

Mrs. Jennie M. Galligan	Mrs. F. J. Peter
Mrs. C. C. E. Goss	Mrs. P. A. Taylor
Mrs. Mamie H. Gordon	Mrs. W. W. Thornton
Mrs. Emma Goldsmith	Mrs. Christine Woodward
Mrs. Annie Holmes	Mrs. Adele Korsmeyer
Mrs. John H. Oberly	Mrs. J. A. Scarritt
Mrs. Ada V. Parsons	Mrs. Herman Meyers
Mrs. W. H. Stratton	Mrs. John M. Lansden
Miss Hattie Smith	Mrs. W. B. Gilbert
Mrs. Herman C. Schuh	Mrs. E. M. Starzinger

Mrs. J. D. Ladd

Nothing can stay this growing list; but as name by name is added thereto, the honored roll will reflect honor, more and more, upon the institution of which they were members.

St. Mary's Infirmary.—In 1861, on a call from Governor Morton, of Indiana, the superior of the Order of the Holy Cross at Notre Dame sent out sisters to act as nurses, some of whom were stationed at hospitals at Cairo and Mound City. At the close of the war, many citizens of Cairo, including Dr. Horace Wardner, who had been associated with the sisters in their hospital work, urged the Order to establish a permanent infirmary in the city; Mother Angela, then mother-general of the Order, came to Cairo in October, 1867, and with the assistance of Dr. Wardner secured a temporary location on Eleventh Street, between Commercial Avenue and Poplar Street, and placed Sister M. Augusta and Sister M. Matilda in charge. On January 1, 1868, they removed to a larger building, known as the Pilot House, on Washington Avenue, where the present Armory building now stands. In 1869, the Trustees of the Cairo City Property donated to the Order block numbered eighty-nine, in the First Addition to the city, on upper Walnut Street, for hospital purposes; and that year they erected a large frame building thereon, and furnished and equipped it as St. Mary's Infirmary. In 1870, Sister Augusta was recalled for promotion, and Sister M. Edward succeeded her, and continued in charge until the summer of 1877, when she was succeeded by Sister Anthony. In 1866, Sister Anthony was recalled, and Sister M. Adela, who had been an assistant in the infirmary for some years, was made superioress.

In 1892, a handsome three-story brick addition was erected in front of the main building, at a cost of seven thousand dollars. In 1901, the present three-story brick addition, extending almost the entire width of the block, was built at a cost of twenty thousand dollars. Rev. Charles J. Eschman, then pastor of St. Patrick's church, superintended the construction of the building, and the same was dedicated February 18, 1892, by Right Rev. John Janssen, bishop of Belleville, assisted by the local pastors, Rev. C. J. Eschman, Rev. J. D. Diepenbrock and by Rev. F. Pieper, Rev. William Van Delft, Rev. C. Goeltz and Rev. William Goeltzhauser.

The chapel in the infirmary was the gift of Rev. C. J. Eschman, as were also the altar, pews, organ, and stained glass windows. Dr. W. F. Grinstead has furnished two private rooms, a surgical ward and an ambulance, and has also added a new operating room and furnished the same, at the cost of about two thousand dollers, and borne one half the cost of the fine and substantial iron fence around the grounds. Dr. W. C. Clarke has given a fine X-ray apparatus, as a memorai to the late Dr. W. W. Stevenson, who was a strong friend of the infirmary; among the many others who have remembered the institution in a very substantial manner may be named Dr. A. A. Bondurant, Dr. John T. Walsh and Dr. James McManus, Mrs. Eliza Halliday, Mrs. M. E. Feith, Mr. John S. Aisthorpe, Mr. P. T. Langan, Mr. Frank Howe, and the Rhodes-Burford Company.

At present Sister M. Asteria is superioress, besides whom there are eighteen other sisters in the infirmary. Five hundred and thirty-nine patients were treated in the infirmary during the year 1909. All the leading physicians of Cairo comprise the medical staff.

United States Marine Hospital.—Capt. John R. Thomas, our congressman in 1882, procured, in that year, the enactment of a law appropriating sixty thousand dollars for the purchase of grounds and the erection of buildings for the hospital, and in September of that year, Surgeon-General Hamilton came here and he, together with Mr. George Fisher, the surveyor of the port, and General C. W. Pavey, the collector of internal revenue, looked over the city with a view to choosing a site for the same. The matter was not definitely decided, it seems, until some time in 1883, when the present grounds between Tenth and Twelfth Streets and Cedar Street and Jefferson Avenue were chosen and purchased of the Trustees of the Cairo Trust Property for the sum of $14,000.00. The grounds include seventy-two lots. The buildings, practically as they now stand, were finished in 1885, but the hospital was not formally opened until some time in February, 1886. Up to that time patients had been taken care of by the Sisters of the Holy Cross; and they for a time conducted the new hospital, under the supervision of Dr. Carmichael, who was the first surgeon in charge. The names of the surgeons and passed assistant surgeons in charge are as follows: Duncan A. Carmichael, Passed Assistant, January 25, 1885, to January 25, 1888; James M. Gassaway, Surgeon, January 25, 1888, to June 14, 1890; Rell M. Woodward, Assistant Surgeon, June 14, 1890, to March 18, 1894; Ezra K. Sprague, Assistant Surgeon, March 18, 1894, to November 24, 1894; James M. Gassaway, Surgeon, November 24, 1894, to July 25, 1897; Parker C. Kallock, Surgeon, July 25, 1897, to January 9, 1899; W. A. Wheeler, Surgeon, January 9, 1899, to May 4, 1899; H. C. Russell, Assistant Surgeon, May 4, 1899, to December 5, 1899; John M. Holt, Assistant Surgeon, December 5, 1899, to April 25, 1901; James H. Oakley, Passed Assistant, April 25, 1901, to June 11, 1903; Gregorio M. Guiteras, Surgeon, June 11, 1903, to April 30, 1907; Julius O. Cobb, Surgeon, May 9, 1907, to April 22, 1908, and Robert L. Wilson, Passed Assistant, April 22, 1908, to the present time.

St. Mary's Infirmary

Cairo in 1841

CHAPTER XX

THE TRUSTEES OF THE CAIRO CITY PROPERTY—THE TRUSTEES OF THE CAIRO TRUST PROPERTY—SOME OF THEIR CIVIL ENGINEERS—CAIRO NEWSPAPERS

WITH the exception of Col. Samuel Staats Taylor, none of the Trustees have ever resided in Cairo. All of the others have resided in New York City, except Thomas S. Taylor, one of the first two, who resided in Philadelphia. The trustees, or some of them, may have visited the place now and then; but we have nowhere seen any notice of the fact. Mr. Miles A. Gilbert was in charge here from June, 1843, to April, 1851, about eight years, although during the last three or four years of the time he resided at St. Mary's but visited the place from time to time to see that affairs were going on properly. After building the cross levee in 1843, Mr. Gilbert could not have done a great deal here besides taking care of the lands and other property of the Trustees. It was a period of waiting, and it seems to have taken a long time to finish the preliminary work and make the necessary surveys and plats for starting the city again. Mr. Gilbert's lengthy stay here enabled him to become perfectly familiar with everything about the place during those important years from 1843 to 1851, and had we from him a somewhat full and detailed account of that period I am sure it would be very interesting. It began with the failure of the Holbrook administration, the ruin of business and the dispersion largely of the people, and ended with the actual beginning of what is now our City of Cairo.

We have before remarked that no city in the country has been so identified with a land trust and a corporation as has been the City of Cairo with the Trustees of the Cairo City Property and Illinois Central Railroad Company. The first of the two bought all of the lands here between the rivers, and the other having had this point made the southern terminus of its railroad, the two very properly undertook the task of building the city. The land company owned nearly ten thousand acres of land, and depended chiefly upon the sales of the same in city lots for the profits of their investment. The railroad company could not deal in lands, but to have a prosperous city at its southern terminus in Illinois meant large profits in the transportation business. Not to dwell here and to express the thought in a word or two, Cairo was their town, and it is for this reason that I have had so much to say about the two in this historical narrative of the place.

Thomas S. Taylor, of Philadelphia, was Trustee from September 29, 1846, to April 6, 1859, when he was succeeded by Mr. John H.

Wright. Charles Davis was Trustee from September 29, 1846, to September 29, 1860, when he and Wright were succeeded by Samuel Staats Taylor and Edwin Parsons. The court and other records here seem to show proceedings for the removal of both Davis and Taylor and the matter as to the former seems to have been pending for some time, but I have not deemed it of sufficient importance to search out the details and give them here. We may remark, however, that his widow, who subsequently married a Mr. Mayo, sued the Trustees, Samuel Staats Taylor and Edwin Parsons, in the United States Court at Springfield, and recovered a judgment for $12,957.57. The Trustees appealed the case to the Supreme Court of the United States and that court affirmed the judgment of the circuit court February 4, 1884. The case, entitled "Taylor and Another vs. Davis' administratrix," is found in 110 U. S. 530.

It seems that on the 21st day of December, 1875, Edwin Parsons conveyed all his interest as Trustee to Samuel Staats Taylor. This was no doubt done as a preliminary step to the subsequent proceedings in the United States Court at Springfield to foreclose the Ketchum mortgages. The Trustees by authority of the shareholders issued bonds to the amount of two hundred thousand dollars in October, 1863, and secured the same by the execution of a mortgage to Hiram Ketchum, as Trustee, upon the property of the trust; and again in October, 1867, they issued other bonds to the amount of fifty thousand dollars and secured the same by another mortgage to the same Trustee, upon the same lands and lots; and in 1875, Charles Parsons, who had succeeded Ketchum as Trustee for the bond holders, began his suit in the United States Circuit Court at Springfield against Samuel Staats Taylor, Trustee, and at the January term of the court, 1876, a decree of foreclosure was entered, and on the 10th day of May of that year the mortgaged property, excepting such lots and lands as had been in the meantime released from the liens of the mortgages, were sold by Mr. John A. Jones, Master in Chancery of that court, to Charles Parsons as Trustee on behalf of the said bond holders. This deed is recorded in book 7, on pages 214, etc.

On the 20th day of June, 1876, Charles Parsons, as such Trustee, conveyed the property to Samuel Staats Taylor and Edwin Parsons as Trustees of the Cairo Trust Property, and on the same day they as individuals executed a declaration of trust showing that the lots, tracts and parcels of land had been conveyed to them for and on behalf of the uses, purposes and trusts in the said instrument set forth. This declaration of trust is recorded in said book 7, on pages 270, etc., and shows that the beneficial interest in the trust property was divided into thirty-six thousand (36,000) shares of the par value of ten dollars each, but subject to assessment to an amount not exceeding in the aggregate five dollars per share.

Let us recur for a moment to the Cairo City and Canal Company and the Trustees of the Cairo City Property and compare their respective high capitalizations with the capitalization of the Cairo City Trust Property.

The capital stock of the Cairo City and Canal Company was two million dollars, divided into twenty thousand shares, of one hundred dollars each. The lands the company owned, as the sole basis of the value of the stock, amounted to about four thousand acres. These lands were mortgaged December 16, 1837, to the New York Life Insurance and Trust Company to secure the former company's bonds, from the sales of which it expected to obtain all the funds it needed for starting and establishing a city here. The four thousand acres would have to have been worth five hundred dollars per acre to justify a capitalization of two million dollars; but from that day to this the property, exclusive of the city proper, has never been worth any such sum.

As before stated, this company was succeeded in 1846 by the Cairo City Property Trust, which purchased more land, and issued stock to the amount of three million, five hundred thousand dollars, half of which Holbrook agreed to take in behalf of the Illinois Exporting Company. On November 21, 1850, ten thousand additional shares were authorized, thus making forty-five thousand shares in all, thirty thousand shares of which were to be received at par to extinguish the liabilities of the Cairo City and Canal Company and to clear off all incumbrances; and the remaining fifteen thousand shares were to be used for the benefit of the trust and for the improvement and protection of the property. Just what the circumstances were that seemed to require or justify this increase in the stock we do not know. It seems to have been a mere matter of more water; and yet the outlook in 1850 may have been very promising. One is almost amazed at the extravagant language used by the proprietors in 1818 and again in 1836 and 1837; but that of the proprietors of 1846 seems to have been of the same tenor and effect. One would suppose that twenty or more years of experience here with the low site and the ever threatening rivers would have tended to some moderation in the description of the situation. This capitalization in 1846 and 1850 of four million, five hundred thousand dollars was at the rate of four to five hundred dollars per acre for the 9743 acres.

We do not get down to anything like actual values for safe capitalizing purposes until we reach the year of 1876, when the present trust was created and which since June 30, 1876, has been known as the Cairo Trust Property. While a large number of city lots had been sold by the Trustees of the Cairo City Property, very small quantities of its lands above town had been disposed of at the time of the foreclosure of the Ketchum mortgages. There was then on hand almost all of the lands, probably nearly seven thousand acres, and also the wharf property and almost every foot of the river frontage on both rivers; and at the time of the sale, in the foreclosure suit in May,

1876, there was due upon the first mortgage of two hundred thousand dollars the sum of $39,305.00; upon the second mortgage of fifty thousand dollars the sum of $58,375.00, and there was also due to the Trustees about $27,831.00. These sums made the whole amount of the indebtedness for which the remaining real estate was sold $125,511. At the sale May 10, 1876, Charles Parsons, as Trustee for the mortgage bond holders, bought the property for $80,000.00 free and clear of all rights of redemption. The whole proceeding from beginning to end must have been in the nature of a friendly suit by and for the immediate parties in interest, otherwise it is hard to account for the absolute sale for $80,000.00, and the immediate capitalization of the property at many times that amount.

We have before spoken of the protracted efforts of Holbrook to arrange for the taking over of the assets and estates of the Cairo City and Canal Company by the Trustees of the Cairo City Property. His work culminated in the deed of June 13, 1846, and the declaration of trust of the 29th of the September following. This trust instrument executed by Thomas S. Taylor, of Philadelphia, and Charles Davis, of New York City, will be found recorded in the book " N " on pages 465, etc., of our county records. It is a very interesting document made sixty-four years ago, and constituting, for all practical purposes, the foundation of all our real estate titles. No one now seeks to trace his title beyond this instrument or rather that of June 13, 1846. When the United States government, in 1871, purchased from the Trustees block thirty-nine (39), for the erection of the custom-house and post-office building, Colonel Taylor was required to make a showing of title beyond those instruments, and the same has been required by purchasers in one or two other instances.

The land described as held in trust amounted to 9,743.01 acres. Something more than half of this was in township sixteen, most of the latter in Pulaski County. The instrument described by metes and bounds that somewhat noted ten-acre tract of land, a part of which is now embraced in the Illinois Central Railroad freight yards on the Ohio River between Fourteenth and Eighteenth Streets.

Let me stop here and speak of that ten-acre tract of land. Jeremiah Diller, on the first day of April, 1835, entered the northeast fractional quarter (5.55 acres), and the east fractional half of the northwest fractional quarter (54.99 acres), of section 25-17-1 west. The first tract lies in a triangle on the Ohio just below the stone depot of that railroad company, and the other now embraces its freight yards and the Halliday milling property, between Fourteenth and Twentieth Streets. September 14, 1837, Diller sold ten acres of the last described tract to William Day, a captain of the United States Army at St. Louis. Day seems to have sold to Ethan A. Hitchcock, also of the United States Army at St. Louis, and on the 7th day of August, 1838, the latter sold the ten-acre tract to Elijah Willard, commissioner of the board of public works of the third judicial district of the state under the general improvement act of February 27, 1837. The railroad enterprises of the state having broken down within a year or two, the state seems to have held this ten-acre tract of land and the right-of-way of the old Illinois Central Railroad in the county *in trust* for a number of years; and finally in the incorporation, February 10, 1851, of the present Illinois Central Railroad Company, it was provided that these lands should be transferred to the latter company. The state, had, some years before, arranged for their conveyance to the Great Western Railway Company incorporated in 1843 and 1849, to build a central railroad.

It seems that on the 13th day of July, 1876, for the consideration of fifteen thousand dollars, Samuel Staats Taylor, as Trustee of the Cairo City Property, conveyed certain property to Charles Parsons, trustee for the second mortgage bond holders of the Cairo City Property and the same is recorded in book 9, page 193. On the 31st day of October, 1895, Samuel Staats Taylor conveyed his interest as Trustee under the declaration of trust to Henry Parsons and Edwin Parsons, Trustees; and on the 9th day of November, 1895, Mary Llewellyn Parsons, administratrix, and Charles Parsons, administrator, conveyed to Henry Parsons and Edwin Parsons, as Trustees of the Cairo Trust Property. The instrument recites the death of Edwin Parsons August 21, 1895, and the resignation of Samuel Staats Taylor, and that the shareholders had chosen Henry Parsons and Edwin Parsons, the latter a son of Mr. Charles Parsons, successors of the said Samuel Staats Taylor and the former Edwin Parsons; and these gentlemen, the cousins of our present Mayor, the Hon. George Parsons, are now the present Trustees of the Cairo Trust Property and have been such since the 9th day of November, 1895.

It will be remembered that on the 13th day of June, 1846, the Cairo City and Canal Company conveyed its property to Thomas S. Taylor and Charles Davis, Trustees as above stated, and that in the following September the latter made the declaration of trust above referred to. It will therefore be seen that from the formation of the trust of the Cairo City Property September 29, 1846, to the formation of the trust of the Cairo Trust Property of June 20, 1876, we have the period of about thirty years and that from the formation of the last named trust, namely, the trust of the Cairo Trust Property, to the present time we have the period of thirty-four years. To the public the change in the trust has been wholly personal. The trust has been continuous from September 29, 1846, to the present time, a period of sixty-four years. At the outset it owned the whole country here, except one or two small lots or tracts of land. It sold nothing until December, 1853, since which time it has from year to year sold more or less of its property. For the first few years after 1853 many sales were made and generally for good, not to say high, prices. Much of the property on the levee and in other parts of the town in 1856 and 1857 sold for very high prices. The most desirable lots and property having been sold within the first few years, the sales thereafter became fewer in number and the prices very much lower. Prices advanced from time to time as the outlook for the city became now and then brighter, but as a general thing, the situation was not encouraging if we except the stimulus which war times gave the town. Many years ago it became evident that the growth and prosperity of the town had ceased largely to depend upon the Trustees and that the people must look to themselves and make the most out of the growth which the city had attained. The trust still owns a large amount of property, the most valuable being, we suppose, the levee and frontage along the two rivers, carrying an exclusive right to wharfage charges. It seems somewhat remarkable, if not unfortunate, that the city nowhere owns a foot of river frontage. This is a fair representation of the city's environment, a cramped one indeed; but it has been that so long, that were enlargement or freedom to come to it now, it would feel that somehow or other something strange had happened to it, and that it was not in its natural and proper position.

THE CIVIL ENGINEERS OF THE TRUSTEES.—Going back to 1818, we have elsewhere shown that the first map or plat of the City of Cairo was probably made by a Major Duncan for Mr. John G. Comegys and his associates. I have not been able to find anything concerning him further than what is said in the Prospectus of those early proprietors.

Coming on down to 1836 and 1837, we find that Mr. James Thompson made a survey and plat of the township, an exact copy of the plat being found elsewhere in this book. The field notes accompanying this plat or map were very full and complete indeed. They are part of the small book mentioned in Chapter IV as given me by Judge Thomas Hileman. I have not been successful in ascertaining whether Mr. Thompson was a resident of southern Illinois or of the west anywhere or of the east. I have not made as careful a search for information concerning him as I would like to have made.

William Strickland and Richard R. Taylor, both probably of Philadelphia, were the first and perhaps only engineers and surveyors here during the Holbrook administration. The reader is referred to other parts of the book for information as to the work done and maps made by them. They may have done some work before the Trustees of the Cairo City Property came into possession here about the middle of the year 1846.

Mr. Henry Clay Long, a son of Stephen Harriman Long, was in charge of the engineering department of the Trustees for many years. He seems to have been an able man in his line of work and profession. Other parts of this book will show much about him and his father, Col. Long, chief of the corps of topographical engineers of the government, whose headquarters were, in 1850, at Louisville. I have referred to the report made by Henry C. Long to S. H. Long concerning the site of the city as probably the most important engineering work ever done for the city. It was in many respects the basis for all other plans, plats and work of the Trustees from 1852 or 1853 onward.

In 1884 Mr. Harvey Reid published a biographical sketch of Enoch Long, an Illinois pioneer, which seems to have been taken from Appleton's American Cyclopedia. In this account it is stated that Henry Clay Long was born near Philadelphia February 18, 1822, and that he became a civil engineer, and died while in the employ of the United States government on board the United States steamer Montana at LaCrosse, Wisconsin, April 10, 1871. In the sketch of Enoch Long referred to, the names of other members of the Long family are mentioned as living at Alton, Illinois, where Stephen Harriman Long died. While Long was here at work helping the Trustees to start their city, Mr. Charles Thrupp came here, probably in the year 1850, and was assistant to Long for some years. Mr. Thrupp, whose death occurred on the 15th day of July, 1900, was probably better acquainted with the City of Cairo in all its somewhat varied features than any other person, excepting Colonel Taylor. He was for a long time in the service of the Trustees after that early period, and was almost the first man to be inquired of concerning corners and boundary lines and other like matters in our city. He and Mrs. Thrupp were English people and up to the time of their respective deaths they were well known and highly esteemed in the city.

There were a number of other persons who occupied the position of civil engineers for the Trustees, but their terms of service were generally of limited duration and arose long after most of the important work of that nature had been fully completed.

I have elsewhere spoken of Mr. John Newell, who was for a year or two in the service of the Trustees, embracing the year 1855; and I have also in another place told of General McClellan's presence here so often when the levees were in the course of construction and when he was vice-president and chief engineer of the Illinois Central Railroad Company. I have often spoken of the offices of the Trustees as containing so many documents and records of a highly important nature. They often seem to me as in the nature of public offices; and I am quite sure that so far as historical facts or information are concerned they contain a hundred-fold more material than can be found at any or all other places in the city, excepting possibly the court-house, where the records are far more complete from the time of the organization of the county, in 1819, than can be found in almost any other of the older counties.

Cairo Newspapers.—The whole of Chapter VI of that part of the "History of Alexander, Union and Pulaski Counties" which relates to Cairo is devoted to Cairo newspapers. It begins with the first one published in 1841 for a short time under the Holbrook administration, the name of the paper not being given, and ends with the "Cairo Daily Argus." The chapter is very full and we suppose complete, and were we to go over any part of that period from 1841 to 1883, it would be but to copy from that history.

Since that time, we have had published here "The Citizen," "The

Evening Citizen," a daily, "The Cairo Telegram," "The Peoples' Paper" and "The Weekly Star." If there were other papers started and published for a time, I am not able to recall the names thereof. Mr. Henry F. Potter continued the publication of the "Cairo Daily Argus" up to about the first of October, 1907, at which time he was compelled to discontinue its publication solely on account of failing health. Few persons can realize the very exacting duties imposed by the publication of a daily paper. The daily demand, while not always severe, sooner or later becomes very trying where so much of the responsibility falls upon one person. Mr. Potter's experience as a publisher and editor at Mound City and Cairo made him one of the best of writers. An able and forceful man naturally, his newspaper training developed all his intellectual faculties and gave him a strength of character which no other training probably would have afforded him.

"The Cairo Telegram" was established by Mr. Eugene E. Ellis in the year 1887. He conducted it along with his long established jobbing office, but in the year 1906, after nineteen years of existence, he discontinued the paper. Different persons were its editors from time to time, but he always exercised a direct supervision over its columns and made the paper a strong force in the community and a great credit to the city. It was with the "Telegram" that Miss Bessie M. Turner began her newspaper work. She was also with the "Bulletin" a number of years and until she became Mrs. Jean M. Allen. It was with regret that the public gave her up.

"The Peoples' Paper" was edited, and I believe published, by Mr. Solomon Farnbaker, whose parents were among the very oldest residents of the city. It was started in June, 1886, and was published a number of years. It was a kind of free lance, cutting in almost all directions, but not always with fine discrimination. Like many of the newspapers found in almost all the cities of the country, it seemed to be most at home or in its proper line of duty when criticising some one or something. We found a large number of clippings from it among Col. Taylor's papers, which were and are as innumerable as the sands of the seashore.

"The Citizen" was established October 1, 1885, by Mr. George Fisher, who had been for a number of years and up to that time the surveyor of the port of Cairo and long a practicing lawyer of our city. He began the publication of "The Evening Citizen," a daily, October 1, 1897, and carried on the publication of the two papers up to the time of his death, which occurred on the 19th day of December, 1900. Since then, his son, Mr. John C. Fisher, has continued the publication of the two papers, and it is believed with a success that is a credit alike to him and the people of the city who have supported the papers. They have always been strongly republican, strong party papers, but their management has seldom, if ever, been subject to just criticism. As favorably as "The Citizen" is regarded as a newspaper it cannot be said that it is not fully deserved. Its value to the people of the city can in no sense of the word be measured by its cost to them.

Mr. Thomas W. Williams, long connected with "The Cairo Bulletin," purchased in 1905 "The Weekly Star," at Thebes. The "Star" was the successor of "The Thebes Record." Mr. Williams continued the publication of the paper at Thebes until 1906, when he removed it to Cairo, and since that time he has continued its publication here. Its circulation is confined largely to the county, and, we are glad to say, it seems to be well sustained. Mr. Williams has become well and favorably known throughout the city and county and is at present a member of our city council and represents the third ward.

"The Cairo Bulletin," first published in 1868, is still one of our city papers. It is now in its forty-second year. This says so much for the paper that little more is needed. Sometime before the year 1883, when Mr. Bradsby wrote, Mr. Oberly had sold out his interest in the "Bulletin" to Mr. E. A. Burnett, now of St. Louis, and removed to Bloomington, where he began the publication of the "Bloomington Bulletin." Mr. Burnett, in the year 1903, sold the "Bulletin" establishment to Harry E. Halliday, Henry S. Candee and David S. Lansden, and they continued its publication up to the year 1908, when Mr. Lansden disposed of his interest. In 1904 they published for six to nine months an evening paper called "The Evening News." Mr. Samuel J. Stockard was the editor of the "Bulletin" for a year or two. He was a good writer and esteemed very highly not only as a writer but as a man and citizen. Mr. Edward W. Thielecke has been in charge of the editorial department of the "Bulletin" longer than any one else. He was in the city of St. Louis during the editorship of Mr. Stockard and returned here in the year 1905. He has been connected with the "Bulletin" in his present capacity for the period of twenty-four years. He has shown himself an able writer, and I think an able editor. My first recollection of him extends back to the time when he had not even thought of becoming a writer or an editor. If any one supposes his position, or the position of editor of "The Citizen," or of any other such paper, is easy to fill he is very much mistaken. Few persons are qualified for such positions. We are too often ready with our criticisms when, if we would but take the places of the persons criticized, we would soon see how unequal we were to the demands of the places we had assumed to fill. Many of us might, in a kind of flabby way, edit a mere newspaper, but to make the paper anything like what it ought to be in a community we would find ourselves largely, if not totally, insufficient. Whatever may be said for or against Mr. Thielecke's general course as an editor this at least can be safely said that he has learned to write clearly, strongly and fearlessly. Without the latter qualification the so-called editor is little else than a mere excuse. His long editorial connection with the "Bulletin" is far better evidence of his standing as an editor than anything I might say.

Now leaving this subject of Cairo newspapers, may I not be permitted to say that we have perhaps a better state of things regarding them than has existed in Cairo for many years? Most of the time have we not had too many newspapers; too many for the people to take and too many among which newspaper support had to be divided? As a general rule our Cairo newspapers, whether many or few, have been quite as good as could possibly be expected, considering the support due them from the public. With our daily morning paper and daily evening paper, the people of the city get all the city news, and their support enables the publishers to do better for their readers, and in this way the people are served to the best advantage. They obtain the best newspaper service at lowest reasonable rates.

CHAPTER XXI

CAIRO IN SERVITUDE TO LAND COMPANIES

IN law we have what are called dominant and serviant estates. Cairo's existence, both corporate and otherwise, has always been that represented by the latter of these conditions. The limitations upon her corporate life and action and upon her people have been of a peculiar nature, and have to a greater or less degree interfered with her growth and prosperity. These have changed somewhat from time to time, but have not yet disappeared. She never had a civil government of her own until 1855, when she was thought entitled to become a town or village. This form of civil administration was superseded, about two years later, with a city government, whose fifty-three years of experience under its limitations ought to be of considerable municipal value.

Cairo was *started by a land company* three several times. To a limited extent, at least, this explains why it had to be started so often. It is very true, the natural difficulties of the situation were great, and it may be that the enterprise could not have gotten under way at all except by means and methods in the nature of corporate initiatives. This, however, is but accounting for a condition of the things necessary in itself though unfortunate. The lands were entered in 1817 for the purpose of building a city. They were soon forfeited to the government and the attempt abandoned. In 1835, the lands were again entered for the same purpose; and with the year 1836, began an actual and most earnest attempt to build a city, worthy somewhat, at least, of its remarkable geographical position. This decade of years, ending with 1846, was in many respects the most important of all in the history of the city. It was in many respects a stirring time, a time of great things, under the lead of a man of character and great enterprise, above any one, no doubt, who has ever had the interest of the place in his charge. But it was a land company, a company that did not want to sell any of its lands until after it had gotten its city under way; and during the whole period of its ten years of existence, it sold neither lands nor lots, until it found that it also had to retire out of being, and turn over all it had, both real and personal, to another and third land company, which likewise found it necessary to invest no one else with ownership of real estate until the lapse of eight years, ending with December, 1853. We thus have the long period of eighteen years, ending with the year 1853, during which these land companies of 1836 and 1846 held all the lands and country here as in a kind of *mortmain* or dead hands. No protest or remonstrance could avail anything at all. The land companies had mapped out their policies, which were essentially one and the same, and that was to hold on to everything they had until they had a city of tenants who might be induced to buy on terms largely dictated by the landed proprietors. I have carefully examined the real estate records of the county from 1836 to 1854, and with the fewest possible exceptions, I have been unable to find that the Cairo City and Canal Company, during its life of ten years, or the Trustees of the Cairo City Property, from 1846 to 1854, sold any town or city lot or land to any one.

As much as they may have desired to see the place grow and prosper and to induce people to become residents, they retained in their private ownership the whole river frontage on both rivers, aggregating a distance of twelve to fifteen miles, over which no one scarcely might or could pass for water or for any other purpose whatsoever, without becoming a trespasser, either in an actual or legal sense. This exclusive dominion over approaches to the rivers has always enabled them to lay under tribute all the commerce of the rivers; and this became a matter of serious complaint by the river interests, which demanded free or cheap wharfage. Their complaints often degenerated into abuse, but it was against the city itself, between which and the landed proprietors they made no distinction; for as a general rule they knew of none. These complaints, of every kind and nature, were carried up and down these great rivers and their tributaries and were thus widely disseminated; and to them is due, in no small part, the reputation in which the city was so long held. These landed proprietors, with one or two possible exceptions, were merely foreign landlords, whose interests somehow seemed to be one thing while that of the people here seemed to be quite another. Very naturally, there arose at the very outset a want of sympathy and co-operation, to remove or change which the landed interests made little or no effort.

In the last days of the Cairo City and Canal Company, when the proprietors, or their representatives, were taking their departure, what they had left here was seized upon and made way with without ceremony or any form of legal proceedings. The people were little or no part of the enterprise. This they well knew and fully realized. They had acquired no lands nor lots—could acquire none; and now that the city, or what was left of it, was to be abandoned, they found themselves unexpectedly fortunate in not being incumbered with anything but movables to prevent their departure to other parts of the country; and so it was easy enough for the number of people in the place to fall in a comparatively short time from two thousand to the two hundred which was the population of Cairo when Col. Taylor arrived here April 15, 1851.

To further establish what is said above about the policy of the land companies, we refer to the editorial in the "Cairo Delta," of September 20, 1849, quoted in Chapter VII. Judging from what Editor Sanders said, the people had hoped that the administration of the Trustees of the Cairo City Property would differ widely and favorably from that of the Holbrook administration; but they seem to have been disappointed. The change was but from one land company to another, and the end and means thereto seemed strikingly alike. The Holbrook enterprise of 1836 to 1846 was largely western; that of the Trustees was more largely eastern. The Trustees tightened their hold on the river frontage and brought the river interests into satisfactory subjection to their demands of wharfage dues. This seems to have been their legal right, and the matter could only be questioned on the ground that it was most unfavorable to the public and to the general interests of the city.

CHAPTER XXII

THE AMERICAN NOTES

CHARLES DICKENS landed at Boston the 21st of January, 1842, and returned home from New York about the same date in the following June. He was, therefore, in the United States five months. He came in a steamer and returned in a sailing vessel. His reception at Boston was altogether a hearty one. The banquet given him at New York on the eve of his departure was all that he and his closest friends could have hoped for. He came to lecture and to stimulate the sale of his books, but chiefly in the interest of international copyright. His early letters home were friendly enough; but by the time he left Baltimore for his western trip he had found it difficult and probably impossible to arouse in the public mind the interest he felt in copyright matters, and the tone of his letters changed to accord with his feeling of disappointment. His unfavorable impressions of the country deepened as he dwelt on the obstinacy of the American people; and to this is due, largely, the spirit the notes everywhere manifest. It was to be expected, of course, that he would on his return home write a book—an account of his experiences and impressions while in the United States; but it was not supposed that the volume would be filled with sneers and caricatures.

In a letter to Macready, written at Baltimore March 22nd, he named the cities he expected to visit on his western trip. He was to go from Baltimore to Harrisburg, and thence by canal and railroad to Pittsburg, thence down the Ohio to Cincinnati and Louisville, and to the Mississippi, up the same to St. Louis, over the prairies to Chicago, and thence eastward, through Canada, to New York. He left Pittsburg on the Messenger April 1st, Cincinnati on the Pike April 6th, Louisville on the Fulton April 7th and reached Cairo the forenoon of Saturday, April 9th. He arrived at St. Louis Sunday evening, April 10th, at about ten o'clock. He was not detained at Cairo by low water or by ice. He was here but an hour or two. His account of what he saw here was colored much more by his feelings than by his vision. There were then 1500 to 2000 people here. A million and a quarter dollars of English money had been spent in the purchase of lands and the making of improvements, all of which was then beginning to be lost by the failure, November 23, 1840, of his countrymen, John Wright & Company, Bankers, of Henrietta Street, Covent Garden, London. The Cairo improvements had been planned by Holbrook and his associates on the faith and belief that Wright & Company would furnish all the means necessary to make their enterprise a success. The bonds which Wright & Company handled were secured by a trust deed to the New York Life Insurance & Trust Company on all the lands of the company here between the two rivers. But other London financiers, disliking Wright & Company's handling of American securities, turned against them, broke them down entirely and forced them into bankruptcy and out of business; and with their retirement went down also the Cairo enterprise. Dickens kept along with the times too closely to be ignorant of these facts when he reached Cairo. The American publishers were, he said, growing rich on the sale of his books and he getting nothing, and the sight of Cairo only brought to mind the fact that many other Englishmen had fared badly in this country. He was in such temper of mind that nothing was needed to stimulate to unfriendly and unjust criticism.

The following letter of May 1, 1842, to Henry Austin, his brother-in-law, will show his degree of ill humor when here April 9th,—three weeks before the letter was written.

"Is it not a horrible thing that scoundrel booksellers should grow rich here from publishing books, the authors of which do not reap one farthing from their issue by scores of thousands; and that every vile blackguard and detestable newspaper, so filthy and bestial that no honest man would admit one into his house for a scullery doormat, should be able to publish those same writings side by side, cheek by jowl, with the coarsest and most obscene companions, with which they must become connected, in course of time in people's minds? Is it tolerable that besides being robbed and rifled an author should be forced to appear in any form, in any vulgar dress, in any atrocious company; that he should have no choice of his audience, no control over his own distorted text, and that he should be compelled to jostle out of the course the best men in this country, who only ask to live by writings? I vow before high Heaven that my blood so boils at these enormities that when I speak about them, I seem to grow twenty feet high, and to swell out in proportion. 'Robbers that ye are,' I think to myself when I get upon my legs, 'here goes.' "

The following are extracts from the Notes:

"Nor was the scenery, as we approached the junction of the Ohio and Mississippi Rivers, at all inspiriting in its influence. The trees were stunted in their growth; the banks were low and flat; the settlements and log cabins fewer in number; their inhabitants more wan and wretched than any we had encountered yet. No songs of birds were in the air, no pleasant scents, no moving lights and shadows from swift passing clouds. Hour after hour, the changeless glare of the hot, unwinking sky, shone upon the same monotonous objects. Hour after hour, the river rolled along, as wearily and slowly as the time itself.

"At length, upon the morning of the third day, we arrived at a spot so much more desolate than any we had yet beheld, that the forlornest places we had passed, were, in comparison with it, full of interest. At the junction of the two rivers, on ground so flat and low and marshy, that at certain seasons of the year it is inundated to the house-tops, lies a breeding-place of fever, ague, and death; vaunted in England as a mine of Golden Hope, and speculated in, on the faith of monstrous representations, to many people's ruin. A dismal swamp, on which the half-built houses rot away; cleared here and there for the space of a few yards; and teeming, then, with rank unwholesome vegetation, in whose baleful shade the wretched wanderers who are tempted hither, droop, and die, and lay their bones; the hateful Mississippi circling and eddying before it, and turning off upon its southern course a slimy monster hideous to behold; a hotbed of disease, an ugly sepulchre, a grave uncheered by any gleam of promise; a place without one single quality, in earth or air or water, to commend it; such is this dismal Cairo.

"But what words shall describe the Mississippi great father of rivers, who (praise be to Heaven) has no young children like him! An enormous ditch, sometimes two or three miles wide, running liquid mud, six miles an hour; its strong and frothy current choked and obstructed everywhere by huge logs and whole forest trees; now twining themselves together in great rafts, from the interstices of which a sedgy lazy foam works up, to float upon the water's top; now rolling past like monstrous bodies, their tangled roots showing like matted hair; now glancing singly by like giant leeches; and now writhing round and round in the vortex of some small whirlpool like wounded snakes. The banks low, the trees dwarfish, the marshes swarming with frogs, the wretched cabins few and far apart, their inmates hollow-cheeked and pale, the weather very hot, mosquitoes penetrating into every crack and crevice of the boat, mud and slime on everything; nothing pleasant in its aspect, but the harmless lightning which flickers every night upon the dark horizon.

"For two days we toiled up this foul stream, striking constantly against the floating timber, or stopping to avoid those more dangerous obstacles, the snags, or sawyers, which are the hidden trunks of trees that have their roots below the tide. When the nights are very dark, the look-out stationed in the head of the boat, knows by the ripple of the water if any great impediment be near at hand, and rings a bell beside him, which is the signal for the engine to be stopped; but always in the night this bell has work to do, and after every ring, there comes a blow which renders it no easy matter to remain in bed."

Dickens after his arrival at St. Louis decided to return the way he came, at least as far as Cincinnati, and journey thence to Sandusky and thence into Canada, but before doing so, he went over to Belleville, which he described with much the same temper and language as that shown and used about Cairo. He went as far as Lebanon, in St. Clair County, to get a better view of the prairies. From Lebanon he returned to St. Louis and there took the same steamboat, the Fulton, for Cincinnati. Passing Cairo on his return trip he gave it a parting shot in these miasmatic words:

"In good time next morning, however, we came again in sight of the detestable morass called Cairo; and stopping there took in wood, lay alongside a barge, whose starting timbers scarcely held together. It was moored to the bank, and on its side was painted 'Coffee House'; that being, I suppose, the floating paradise to which the people fly for shelter when they lose their houses for a month or two beneath the hideous waters of the Mississippi. But looking southward from this point, we had the satisfaction of seeing that intolerable river dragging its slimy length and ugly freight abruptly off towards New Orleans; and passing a yellow line which stretched across the current, were again upon the clear Ohio, never, I trust, to see the Mississippi more, saving in troubled dreams and nightmares."

What Dickens wrote about Cairo was no more true than the following he wrote about Belleville:

"Belleville was a small collection of wooden houses, huddled together in the very heart of the bush and swamp. Many of them had singularly bright doors of red and yellow; for the place had been lately visited by a traveling painter, 'who got along, as I was told, by eating his way.' The criminal court was sitting, and was at the moment trying some criminals for horse-stealing; with whom it would most likely go hard; for live stock of all kinds being necessarily very much exposed in the woods, is held by the community in rather higher value than human life; and for this reason, juries generally make a point of finding all men indicted for cattle-stealing, guilty, whether or no.

"The horses belonging to the bar, the judge, and witnesses, were tied to temporary racks set up roughly in the road; by which is to be understood, a forest path, nearly knee deep in mud and slime.

"There was an hotel in this place which, like all hotels in America, had its large dining-room for the public table. It was an odd, shambling, low-roofed out-house, half cow-shed and half kitchen, with a coarse brown canvas table-cloth, and tin sconces stuck against the walls, to hold candles at supper-time."

"The American Notes" is one of the poorest of his books. Macaulay was requested to write a notice of the book, but after reading it declined, saying:

"I cannot praise it, and I will not cut it up. I cannot praise it, though it contains a few lively dialogues and descriptions; for it seems to me to be, on the whole, a failure. It is written like the worst parts of ' Humphrey's Clock." What is meant to be easy and sprightly is vulgar and flippant. What is meant to be fine is a great deal too fine for me, as the description of the Fall of Niagara. A reader who wants an amusing account of the United States had better go to Mrs. Trollope, coarse and malignant as she is. A reader who wants information about American politics, manners, and literature had better go even to so poor a creature as Buckingham. In short, I pronounce the book, in spite of some gleams of genius, at once frivolous and dull."

In *"Martin Chuzzlewit"* we find Dickens still caricaturing the United States and its people; and Cairo especially, under the name of "Eden," comes in for a large share of attention. It would seem that the one book, the "American Notes," would have been sufficient to satisfy his resentment, for such it seems to have been. Every one must, however, admire his wonderful writing. Then, too, we must remember that when he was here and for many years afterwards, Great Britain was hated and abused everywhere and by fully one-half of the people of the country.

In the will of Lieutenant-Governor William Kinney, dated August 9, 1843, and probated in St. Clair County October 18th of that year, we find this clause: "I give R. K. Fleming, in consideration of his copying and writing for me a pamphlet against Charles Dickens, and other articles, one hundred dollars in cash." See volume IX, pp. 441-444, of the Historical Publications of the Illinois Historical Society. A certified copy of the will was filed in the recorder's office of Alexander County, October 1, 1909.

Now, taking leave of Dickens, let us say that in his letters to Forster and others, he made it clear that when he reached home he would, to use his own fine language, stretch himself "twenty feet high and swell out in proportion," in railing at the American people.

After twenty-five years, he came back to lecture, or rather to read. He landed at Boston, as before, but with feelings of anxiety about the reception that would be accorded him. What he had written in 1842 was much in his way in 1867. The incongruity of his second visit with his account of the first one was apparent; but his desire for money was too strong to forbid him asking the favor of the people whom he had so deliberately and maliciously traduced and insulted.

If in man there are two natures, the one good and the other evil, it may be safely affirmed that out of the latter in Dickens "The American Notes" issued.

But Cairo had a hard name before Dickens saw it. It had a hard name because it was a hard place. On the rivers were and always have been many hard characters. The central location of the place drew many of them here. River craft of every existing kind and pattern and doing all kinds of trading and business landed here. The site was low and often overflowed, and hence the long absence of improvements and settled inhabitants. The failures of land companies to overcome the natural obstacles in the way of establishing a town or city added to the unfavorable reputation the place bore. It was a low and a decidedly uninviting point, and the travelers upon the rivers never spoke well of it. They could not. They all seemed to think that at the junction of two such great rivers as the Ohio and Mississippi there ought to be a fine, not to say a grand city.

The hard name arose in part from a hard state of things, but quite as much from the temper and disposition of some of the early Cairo inhabitants, who were jolly good fellows in their off-hand and don't-care sort of a way, and who, instead of trying to improve the reputation of the town, seemed to have sought to keep alive the unfavorable opinions of it by all sorts of remarkable stories and accounts of crimes and offenses which never had any existence save in their fertile brains.

I might close this chapter without saying anything more concerning the reputation which our city has so long borne; but to do so would not be correct historical treatment. Historical silence is not allowable save in cases of want of information. It is seldom attributed to ignorance or oversight. Most of us who live here know better than other people what has so generally been said of our city and is still often if not quite so generally said. The person spoken of is much more likely to remember what was spoken than the speaker where what was said or spoken is of an uncomplimentary nature. Cities, large and small, are not unlike individuals; but an individual may live down, so to speak, the bad reputation he has borne; but for this much time is often required. May not cities do the same? The public is often very incredulous and often demands a long period of probation. It is not admitting too much to say that our city should have made more progress in getting a good or a better name. The change has been slow but most of the time hopeful. It may be that the ground gained has all been lost by reason of the recent mobs and lynchings and their attendant circumstances; but if so, it is only another evidence that a re-established name is much easier lost than one which had never needed re-establishment. The hindrance to our acquiring a better reputation has generally been ourselves. We have persistently denied that anything was needed here that was not equally needed in almost all other cities—river cities, especially. This is but saying that if Cairo is not worse than other places, there is no ground for complaint or need of improvement, nor is there any reason for being told we ought to be better. This fatal view of the matter hinders every effort for advancement.

If one's reputation is what one's neighbors say of him, why may we not say a city's reputation is what its neighbors and the people generally, elsewhere, say of it? Whether they speak the truth or not is not very material in law or in the courts. There is absolutely no remedy other than the adoption and the faithful following of such course of conduct as will convince the public generally that we are better than we once were and deserve a better name. Some of our citizens lose all their patience when this matter is spoken of. Some say it is a falsehood and that Cairo is all right. Others say it has always been rather a wide open town, and it is useless to try to make it anything else. Others say Cairo is a city, and we must expect to have the usual city characteristics, and that vices of all kinds exist everywhere, and one hurts the town and business by talking about it; and that if it is such a place as is represented, one should not publish it abroad and keep people from coming here and investing in business enterprises and making the city the home of their families. And finally, others say, we don't care, Cairo is good enough for us; if one does not like the town as it is, let him go elsewhere; the world is wide.

But not to pursue the matter further, Cairo is not the hard place it is so often represented to be. Many towns and cities in the state deserve no better name or reputation than our city. Let us cease, however, enjoining silence about evils whose existence or extent we should be able to deny. Let us, along with our great material improvement, seek also to improve, in corresponding degree, those other features of city administration which every one knows are of far greater importance than are matters of a wholly material nature.

CHAPTER XXIII

THE TOWN GOVERNMENT OF TWO YEARS AND THE CITY GOVERNMENT OF FIFTY-THREE YEARS—THE SEVENTEEN MAYORS

ALTHOUGH generally spoken of as a city, Cairo never became a city until the passage of the act of February 11, 1857. An attempt was made in 1852 to incorporate the town or village as a city, but the Trustees, having the bill in charge, desired to include in it a clause requiring the first board of aldermen to be chosen by the legislature and to hold their positions for five years. The member of the legislature who presented and urged the bill, C. G. Simons, of Jonesboro, admitted that this requirement was a very unusual one, but he said it was regarded as a necessary protection to foreign real estate owners. This reference could only have been to the Trustees or to those whom they represented. The bill failed of passage. Andrew J. Kuykendall, then in the senate from Vienna, seems to have been the chief opponent of the bill. He subsequently became our member of Congress. He seems to have been interested in Cairo; for on the first sale of city lots by the Trustees, namely, the 23rd day of December, 1853, he bought lots one and two, in block fifty-one, in the city. He paid $500.00 for the lots. The Alexander Club now owns these lots.

On that somewhat celebrated day, seven years and a half after the Trustees acquired their title, June 13, 1846, from the Cairo City and Canal Company, they began their first sale of real estate to the people. Is it any wonder that the people lost patience and that the editor, Add. H. Sanders, took himself and his newspaper, "The Cairo Delta," to another part of the country? But the circumstances must always be considered. The Trustees had indeed undertaken a seven-year task.

Cairo under the Town Government.—Under the Holbrook administration, from 1836 to 1846, the people had no kind of civil local government except such as came from the county and state. There may have been some kind of township, school or road district government, but we have not come upon anything of the kind. The county records may, however, show something of that description. How the people managed to get along from 1846 to 1855, it is not very material now to inquire. They did not seem to have needed or wanted anything besides what the county and state could afford them until 1855; for in that year, at an election held in the railroad station house, it was decided that they would establish a town government, and on the 8th day of March they held an election for town trustees. The law then applicable to such matters provided for a vote *viva voce* at the polls; and at the election, 135 voters went to the polls and openly announced their respective preferences or votes. There were five Trustees to be elected, and each voter was required to give the names of the five persons he desired to become Trustees. The persons chosen were S. S. Taylor, Bryan Shannessy, Peter Stapleton, Louis W. Young and M. B. Harrell. Only two of the voters declined to vote for Col. Taylor. They were I. Lynch and E. Babbs.

It is altogether probable Col. Taylor was strongly in favor of this movement for a local government for the town. At all events, a majority of the Trustees were favorable to his policies or that of the Trustees.

The next year, however, the election held March 10, 1856, resulted in a choice of men, a majority of whom were not kindly disposed toward the management of the Trustees. The men chosen Trustees at this election were Thomas Wilson, Samuel Staats Taylor, Cullen D. Finch, Moses B. Harrell and Charles Thrupp.

We have been unable to find the records or papers of the town Trustees for either of the years of 1855 or 1856, except the poll book of the election just mentioned, and possibly one or two other papers which were of little or no interest. These records should have passed to the city government, which began in March, 1857; but the present city clerk, Mr. Robert A. Hatcher, has told me that he had made a careful search for the same but found none.

The most important matter with which the town Trustees, of both years, seem to have had to deal was the wharf and wharfage question. We have presented this matter somewhat fully under that heading and need not refer further to it here.

It seems highly probable that the town government scheme was taken up by the Trustees upon their failure to procure the incorporation of the city of Cairo and the Cairo City Property or the Cairo City Property trust; and the experience of the Trustees under the second year of the town government, when Thomas Wilson was president of the board, was so unsatisfactory that they were led to seek an incorporation of the city in the usual way, and hence the act of February 11, 1857, was passed, the city's first charter.

The city made its start under this act by holding an election March 10, 1857, the poll book of which is found elsewhere. With this poll book, the reader, if acquainted in Cairo, can see who of the voters of 1857 are still with us.

This act remained in force ten years, or until it was superseded by the act of February 18, 1867, drawn by David J. Baker. An important amendment was made to it February 10, 1869, by which the city was provided with two legislative bodies instead of the one only. The new or upper body was called the *select council,* and the lower the *board of aldermen.* This amendment of twenty-eight sections was prepared by Judge H. K. S. O'Melveny, Judge William J. Allen, and Mr. Louis Houck, under the general supervision of Col. Taylor, who always took the greatest interest in all legislative matters relating in anywise to the city. Mr. Houck was then Judge O'Melveny's partner. The need of this amendment arose out of the setting aside by the supreme court of the city's method of making assessments for street filling and other local improvements. (The City of Chicago *vs.* Larned, 34 Ill., 203.) Very little, however, if anything at all, was done under this amendment; for within a year or two, the legislature adopted an entirely new method for making assessments for local improvements. It was article nine, of the act of April 10, 1872, for the incorporation of cities and villages. The city adopted the article before it became incorporated under the act, which was January 7, 1873. It may be here remarked that neither of the charters of 1857 or 1867 or the amendment of 1869, required the mayor or aldermen to be citizens or electors of the state. A property qualification only was required. This general act of April 10, 1872, has been adopted by almost all of the cities of the state, and the same, amended from time to time, has been found very satisfactory indeed. The city is still incorporated under that act.

Under the first and second city charters, the mayor was elected annually, and Col. Taylor, the first mayor, succeeded himself five several times, beginning with the election in March, 1857, and ending with the election in March, 1862. H. Watson Webb was chosen mayor in March, 1863, without opposition. At the election in March, 1864, Col. Taylor again became a candidate for the office, but was defeated by David J. Baker. This contest is said to have been a very unusual one and the result very unexpected to Col. Taylor's friends. Baker, however, was a very popular man with the Democrats as well as with Republicans. Moreover, from the earliest time in the city's history to the present time, politics have never played any very important part. It may also be stated that the people probably thought that Col. Taylor had been quite sufficiently honored by his prior six elections.

At the risk of taking too much space, I give here the number of votes Col. Taylor and his competitors received at each of the elections of 1857 to 1864, and the names and lengths of terms of all subsequent mayors.

1857—Samuel S. Taylor, 211; W. J. Stephens, 159.
1858—Samuel S. Taylor, 382; Barney Mooney, 10.
1859—Samuel S. Taylor, 290; John Howley, 200.
1860—Samuel S. Taylor, 299; Jno. W. Trover, 230.
1861—Samuel S. Taylor, 361; W. R. Burke, 319.
1862—H. Watson Webb, 345; no opposition.
1863—Samuel S. Taylor, 389; Thomas Wilson, 298.
1864—Samuel S. Taylor, 354; David J. Baker, 380.

Thomas Wilson, mayor from February, 1865, to February, 1867.
John W. Trover, mayor from February, 1867, to February, 1868.
Alexander G. Holden, mayor from February, 1868, to February, 1869.
Jno. H. Oberly, mayor from February, 1869, to February, 1870.
Thomas Wilson, mayor from February, 1870, to February, 1871.
John M. Lansden, mayor from February, 1871, to April, 1873.

John Wood, mayor from April, 1873, to April, 1875.
Henry Winter, mayor from April, 1875, to April, 1879.
N. B. Thistlewood, mayor from April, 1879, to April, 1883.
Thomas W. Halliday, mayor from April, 1883, to September, 1892.
Chas. O. Patier, mayor from September, 1892, to April, 1895.
Corodon R. Woodward, mayor from April, 1895, to April, 1897.
N. B. Thistlewood, mayor from April, 1897, to April, 1901.
Marion C. Wright, mayor from April, 1901, to April, 1903.
Claude Winter, mayor from April, 1903, to April, 1905.
George Parsons, mayor from April, 1905, to present time.

The city has, therefore, had seventeen several mayors during a period of fifty-three years, beginning with Col. Taylor's election in March, 1857, and ending with the election of George Parsons in April, 1909. Thistlewood, Woodward, Parsons, and the writer are now living. Of Col. Taylor I have elsewhere given a somewhat lengthy biographical sketch.

H. Watson Webb was city attorney two or three times after serving one term as mayor. He lived many years in the city. He was a son of Col. Henry L. Webb, a very prominent man in his day, and was born at Trinity, the now almost forgotten town on the Ohio just south of the mouth of Cache River. The Webbs were of the celebrated family of Webbs in New York, one of whom was James Webb, for years prominent in New York politics. Mr. Webb left Cairo many years ago and went to San Francisco and there remained some considerable time. Subsequently he removed to Portland, Oregon, and there died a few years ago. In both cities, as here, he practiced his profession of the law.

David J. Baker succeeded Mr. Webb and was mayor from 1864 to 1865. He was liked by every one, just as he seemed to like every one else, such was his good nature. He was a good lawyer and an able judge. He served on the circuit and appellate court benches many years, and one full term of nine years on the bench of the supreme court of the state. If any trait of his character seemed in anywise to be above or superior to his intellectual abilities as a lawyer and a judge, it was shown in his great desire to get at the truth and the right of matters and to decide fairly and justly. He was not a brilliant man as the phrase goes. He was something more and better than that. While he enjoyed eloquent speech and fine writing, he liked best those simpler methods of speech by which truth is brought to light and error disclosed. Somewhat like Judge John H. Mulkey, whom he succeeded on the supreme court bench, he was distrustful of first impressions, and always waited until his mind had obtained a full view of the whole matter in hand before he proceeded to pronounce judgment. His opinions while supreme judge extend through forty-two volumes of reports.

Thomas Wilson succeeded Judge Baker and was mayor from 1865 to 1867 and from 1870 to 1871. He was a large, fine looking man. In natural abilities and force of character, he was not behind any one of those seventeen. He was as strong mentally as he was large and strong physically. Had he been favored with the advantages of a thorough educational training, and had sought wider fields of activity, he would have stood in the very front rank in the political world, if not also in the business world. I am not speaking of him when I say some men like a little education, a little better than much. Much is dangerous and should be avoided. We hear this quite too often. A little learning with them is not a dangerous thing. The danger is in much. They reverse Pope, and say that the danger is in drinking deep of the Pierian spring. This view that one may know too much, may be too well informed, may have his mind broadened and strengthened too much, may be too much of a man mentally, sets a premium on ignorance and would level to the ground well nigh every high institution of learning in the country. I would say, "Do not be afraid of getting too much education. It is like the fresh air; one cannot get too much of it." Wilson was fairly well educated; but had he gotten anywhere, or by any means, a good college education or its equivalent, he could have stood before kings. It would have developed all of his splendid natural faculties. It would have given him confidence, without which men never can do their best. It would have lifted him higher in his own good and sound judgment, and have equipped him well for successful work with great men almost anywhere. He never came to a full knowledge of the extent and character of his natural endowments. It may have been best. It is sometimes. Feeling strongly what one might be, yet never being it, can never be a happy thought.

John W. Trover succeeded Wilson and was mayor from 1867 to 1868. He formerly lived in the central part of the state, perhaps in Cass County, the county from which Robert W. Miller came. He was president of the First National Bank of Cairo. He was a Republican in politics and was successful in his race for mayor against Judge H. K. S. O'Melveny, who ran as a Democrat. Judge O'Melveny judged the Cairo democracy by the Marion County democracy. Up there they always voted the ticket, and he supposed the same was the rule down in Alexander. But he had been here but a short time and did not know the habits of the people in their local elections. Trover was one of the boys, and the boys and Trover won. Judge O'Melveny's defeat wounded him severely. He had not sought the office and did not want it at all; but a number of his Democratic friends said he must make the race and he did, with the result stated. He removed to Los Angeles in November, 1869; and after I had been elected city attorney in February, 1870, he wrote me and said he could not see how I could get the consent of my mind to trust my chances for an office to such unreliable voters as we had here in Cairo. At that election in 1870, Fountain E. Albright was the candidate against me. It was known that very soon the colored people of the city were to have the right to vote, and on the day of the election Fountain went about telling his friends that they must come out and vote, for this election, he said, was to be the last white man's election we would have. Since that time, about thirty-eight years ago, we have not indeed had a white man's election—an election at which only white men could vote. I must not omit to say that Judge O'Melveny was a splendid man, an able lawyer, and an able circuit judge, and one would have to go very far and inquire very diligently to find a man of superior character or more exemplary personal conduct.

Alexander G. Holden succeeded Trover, and was mayor from 1868 to 1869. Like Judge O'Melveny, Doctor Holden did not want the office; but his friends insisted that there was nothing that could possibly be said against him and that he must make the race. He yielded. His friends judged rightly, and he was elected. He gave all the time he could to the discharge of his official duties. He was careful and painstaking and ventured little without first getting the best advice obtainable.

John H. Oberly succeeded Dr. Holden, and was mayor from 1869 to 1871. He came to Cairo from Memphis soon after the war began. It seems that his views concerning secession and the war were not favorable to his longer remaining there. He became identified with the "Cairo Democrat" soon after leaving Memphis. In 1868 he started the "Cairo Bulletin"; and after editing and publishing that paper a number of years, he removed to Bloomington and there engaged in editing the "Bloomington Bulletin." He was also a member of the legislature from this county in the years 1872-1874; and in the years 1877-1881 he was a member of the Board of Railroad and Warehouse Commissioners. Still later, he became commissioner under President Cleveland, of the Indian schools. He was a man of versatile talents. He had been an editor almost all his life. He wrote well, few editors better. He was much given to severity of criticism, so much so that his friends did not always escape. It seemed sometimes to be a mere matter of exercising his pen. Even Secretary Vilas came in for a share, and he was so affected by it that President Cleveland said there was no use appointing Oberly to another office while Vilas was in the senate. He had gone there soon after he left the cabinet. This trait of Oberly's character was much in his way to the success he should have won; for he was indeed a man of brilliant endowments. Nature had not stopped short of making him a genius. He was of a happy and genial temperament and exceedingly interesting in conversation. He made a good mayor, but complaints were made that he was too strongly inclined toward Col. Taylor and the Trustees of the Cairo City Property. Let me add that Mrs. Oberly was equally talented. The whole family, indeed, was one of unusual intelligence.

John M. Lansden succeeded Oberly, and was mayor two terms, that is, from February, 1871, to April, 1873. By the city's changing its incorporation, under the act of 1867, to incorporation under the general act of 1872, his second term of office was extended two months, that is, from February to April, 1873.

Col. John Wood succeeded Lansden, and was mayor from 1873 to 1875, one term. He had been in the war, and came to Cairo a short time

Mayors of Cairo

Mayors of Cairo

before its close. He was a contractor for some years before he went into the milling and wholesale grocery business. He was a member of the city council two or three or more terms before he became mayor. He was regarded as one of the most independent and outspoken councilmen and mayors the city ever had. The most serious objection any one ever heard made to him as a man, councilman or mayor, was that he was so hard to move from any position he had taken. He was a Scotchman. His term of office was so satisfactory to the people that had there been a higher position for bestowment on any one, he would have received it.

Henry Winter succeeded Wood, and was mayor from 1877 to 1881, two terms. He was an Englishman, and came to Cairo in 1856. He carried on many branches of business; was highly public spirited; was the father and promoter of the whole business of fire protection; was kind and charitable in every way and manner, and took great interest in all public matters. He had not much use for strict laws in infringement of personal liberty in this democratic country of ours. He was an anti-Taylor man, and yet thought a great deal of Col. Taylor and Taylor of him. He was tenacious enough, and had run for mayor two or three times before his election in 1877. He had a strong personal following, more than any of the others ever had. He was mayor in the epidemic of the yellow fever in 1878, and had the mayor been any one else, there is no telling how the city or the people thereof would have fared.

N. B. Thistlewood, our present congressman, succeeded Winter and was mayor from 1881 to 1885, and again, from 1897 to 1901, four terms. He had not been here a great many years when he was first elected, but he took such great interest in the public matters of the city and of the people that they felt they could not do better than to intrust him with the chief charge of its affairs. What he undertook he always did well. He was never satisfied with half-way or half-done work. He soon became a Cairo man and has always been that. He looked upon the town as so situated that the rules applicable to most places not larger could not be closely applied to it. As to city government, he has always thought that strict laws of a sumptuary nature often defeated themselves. Had he chosen the Latin with which to express his idea about the matter, he would have said *medio tutissimus ibis,* that is to say, the middle course is the safest. Of all who have come here in these many years, few, if any of us, could name a more desirable or public-spirited citizen. I have before referred to Mayor Thistlewood when speaking of the flood of 1882.

Thomas W. Halliday succeeded Thistlewood at the expiration of his second term, and was mayor from April, 1883, to August, 1892, almost nine and one-half years. He was chosen mayor five successive times, one less than his father-in-law, Col. Samuel Staats Taylor, whose terms, however, were only one year each. On two or three occasions, Halliday had no opposition. He died in August, 1892. Had he lived there is no telling how long he would have been continued in the office. Frequent elections to office generally indicate the high regard of the people. His must be attributed largely to the easy and friendly terms he always succeeded in maintaining with almost every member of his various city councils. He knew and fully realized that without the hearty co-operation of the members of the legislative body of the city, he himself could not do much. Hence, his constant endeavor was to obtain and keep the friendly feeling of the city's ward representatives. And it therefore followed, very naturally, that these ward representatives were generally for him when the mayor's election came on. He was very successful in making it appear that almost everything that came up and went through, was really the measure of some one of the councilmen. He kept himself somewhat in the background, but not so much so as to be quite out of sight of a clear-visioned man.

Halliday took great pleasure in being mayor, although it added largely to his other rather hard work. He laudibly liked to have the good will and approval of the people of the city. I cannot enumerate the measures he started and carried through for the material improvement of the city. I can only say that he was a strong friend of public improvements, and that too, when our laws were in a poor shape to facilitate public work. Tom was a Halliday man and a Taylor man, of course. To outsiders, this may not mean much, but to Cairo people it is a little volume. Tom steered his official craft around among the breakers and reefs with a success that surprised both sides, and thereby largely obtained their favor. It was administrative ability of the highly useful variety, which is the only kind really ever needed. He was a member of the lower house of our legislature in 1879; and the writer has often heard members from the upper part of the state speak in the highest terms of his services in that body.

Charles O. Patier was selected by the city council to fill out the unexpired portion of the term of Halliday, that is, from August, 1892, to April, 1893, when he became a candidate for election to that office. He was successful, and gave the city his very best services. Although disagreeing with his immediate predecessor in many things, he nevertheless admired him, and more especially his successful management of city council work. Halliday had become so familiar with city matters that many of the aldermen looked to him for guidance, if I may be permitted to use such a word. Patier liked Halliday and yet he did not, very much as Captain Halliday liked David T. Linegar and Linegar him, and yet they did not. Patier diligently sought information; that is but saying he wanted to be right. He thought the town was too low and that if it needed anything at all that thing was earth filling; and he accordingly decided to try his mayor's hand on the important matter of filling the low lots with earth under the Linegar bill, of which we have before spoken. He knew that Linegar had worked hard to draw up a good and sound bill, and thought it should at least be given a fair trial. This he started out to do, as we have already set forth in Chapter IX; but he was succeeded in office by one of our citizens, who was lukewarm about the matter, although quite active about many other things; and so the work Patier started was dropped; and shortly afterwards Capt. Halliday gave the act itself its death-blow up at Springfield, that is to say, he procured its repeal by the legislature. I need not repeat it here, but concerning Patier it may be well and truly said that he undertook to do one of the very best things that was ever undertaken in Cairo, and that he failed was not his fault; it was the city's misfortune. Charlie justly prided himself on his military record, which extended through the war. I might say the same as to his being one of the 306 delegates who voted in the Chicago convention for a third nomination of General Grant for President.

Corodon R. Woodward succeeded Patier, and was mayor from 1895 to 1897. He had resided in Cairo a long time, but had never cared much for office. His business had grown under his careful and wise management and to such proportions that he felt he could safely undertake the duties of the mayor's office. He ran and was elected, to the surprise of some and to the joy of others; for many persons thought that a new man in a place new to him might bring about a change, productive of good to the city. He took hold of city affairs in his own way, that is, very much as though no one had ever been mayor before. He did not care to be bound by what is called precedents or old methods. In a word or two, every one expected that he would turn over a new leaf of some kind. I cannot stop to enter into details, but will speak of one change he made, a change back to a former state of things in the city.

In 1865 and 1866, the city expended very many thousand dollars at the intersection of Ohio and Tenth Streets for pumps to lift the seepage water over the levee and back into the river; but after a few years of use and owing to the great expense of operation and maintenance, they were abandoned and the valuable machinery and implements sold. The writer well remembers hearing Capt. Halliday say at the time that the city would some time regret the destruction or abandonment of its pumping plant. Woodward returned to the work of pumping our seepage water into the river, but with new and far better pumping machinery, and the success of the work was such that one had but to go up to the intersection of those streets to see a great stream of water five or more feet wide and one or more deep, plunging over the levee and back into the river, whence it had stealthily come. It was a kind of revelation; and although Woodward himself has gone away, yet the system will no doubt be maintained until we have banished the seepage water by filling up the places which it annually invades. Before passing on to another mayor, let me say that the pump has now been running ten years, when needed, and no one now doubts its efficiency. It is no doubt a patented machine, but with us it ought to be called Woodward's pump.

Capt. Thistlewood succeeded Woodward, and was again mayor, and from 1897 to 1901, as above stated. He thus held and filled out four full terms of two years each. I need not repeat here what I have before said of him. By his frequent elections one would suppose, and no doubt very properly, that the only condition to his election to the chief office of the city was his allowance of his name to be used as a candidate.

Marion C. Wright succeeded Capt. Thistlewood, and was mayor from 1901 to 1903. He had long been a resident of Cairo and a very busy man. For much of his life, he had charge of important branches of Capt. Halliday's extensive business enterprises, and no one supposed that he had any kind of a taste or turn for public office. He, however, took the office and held it but one term, declining to be persuaded into standing for the place again. He had found the duties of the office so out of keeping with everything with which he ever had anything to do in a business way, that he wanted no more of office-holding. Before the close of the term of his office, he undertook a reform movement in the city, and cleared out, at least for the time being, a certain central location in the city. His motives were challenged and said to be bad, just as would have been the case of any one else who had undertaken to do and had done what he did. I am not able to speak of Wright's motive, but whatever it was, the thing done was little, if any, short of the very best thing ever done in the city, in a moral sense. When a good thing is done, it is generally a poor and silly thing to say the motive was bad. A blind man, whose sight had been given back to him, once said in substance, that he did not know who he was who healed him nor what his motive was, but one thing he knew and that was, whereas, he was once blind, he now could see. I need not speak of the undoing of what Wright did, with his good or bad motive, whichever it was, nor of the majority by which the undoing was ordered. The straight-forward and honest thing for his critics to say was that what Wright did was wrong and should be undone, and the former condition re-established, just as it was. It was not a question of motives at all.

Claude Winter succeeded Wright, and was mayor from 1903 to 1905. He was Cairo born and has been an industrious and hard working boy and young man, always cheerful, friendly and accommodating. He made friends easily and retained them quite as well and probably better than most persons. His father had been mayor, and a more or less prominent man in Cairo for very many years; and Claude was justly ambitious to reach the mayor's office. He was full of energy, and pushed everything he took hold of, and became very successful in business, and very naturally with this success came the desire to obtain some formal recognition of himself and his faithful attention to his duties as a citizen and as a business man of the city. It was to be supposed that his views of city government would not differ widely from those of his father, whose views concerning the same, as we have before stated, were of a very liberal character. Claude's administration of the office accorded fully with the views of his supporters and tended strongly to show the kind of a city government he thought the people of Cairo wanted. I must not omit to say that Claude Winter did everything he possibly could to start and carry on public improvements. Just as soon as the legislature provided for the making of public improvements without petitions of property holders, he took hold of the matter and was getting very much of the preliminary work done for a large number of the streets in the upper part of the city, when the supreme court held the law unconstitutional, and thus put an end to the improvement work going on under him.

George Parsons succeeded Claude Winter as mayor in April, 1905. He was re-elected in April, 1907, and again in April, 1909, and is now entering upon the sixth year of his terms of service. It is said by many persons that his *pledges of reform* secured him his first election. Some persons do not like the word *reform.* The expressions, *reform movement,* reform party, platform of reform, sound badly in their ears. They say the word repels people. The reason for this, if there is any, is that so many reform movements turn out to be no reforms at all. The word is a good one and does not deserve to be thus thrown into the scrap heap of desuetude. People who are scared off from any good movement because of the words by which it is described might as well be openly against it. And yet, I suppose, there is something in a name. It ought to be a reasonable something, however.

The writer does not recall the fact that Mayor Parsons was elected as a reform mayor. If he was, the reform never came. Matters concerning which the word reform is generally used went on in the city the same as before; nor has there been up to this time any change worth mentioning. The fact is, there has never been much of a change in the general character of the city's police administration. At times it has been better and at times worse, but its general tenor has never been of a high grade. The people, or a great many of them, have wanted a rather free and easy administration of police matters, a kind of administration that is likely to become entirely too free and easy, even for the advocates of the free and easy policy. A sound head and a strong hand are needed to administer city affairs where the police policy is of the free and easy order. To see just where *liberty* ends and *license* begins requires discrimination. Some see the boundary line and some do not; but whether seen or not, the line is quite too often disregarded and passed over with impunity. Mayor Parsons and his chiefs of police have said they were giving the people of the city the kind of police government they wanted, and that they were serving the people, or a large majority of them, very acceptably. It has not been a question of what was really best for the people generally or what was lawful under the city laws or whether the laws of the city should be enforced, but what did the people or a majority of them want. This, however, has left them pretty much the sole judges of what the people wanted. They have failed to remember that what the people wanted, or are supposed to want, is found in the laws of the city and state. Outside of these, it is difficult, if not impossible, to ascertain what the people want. They, the mayor and the police, have not wanted a wide open town but one that was somewhat open. The door somewhat open, or the lid somewhat lifted is the proper figurative expression. But as above remarked, to open the door just enough and keep it from being pushed wide open requires sound judgment, great strength and inflexible purpose. These are qualifications not often found in combination.

I have said this much about our present city administration now in its sixth year, because so much has been said about it during the past year or two, and because, too, I have desired to express my own views of such matters without any regard to particular persons. It would be quite unjust for me to close this short notice of Mayor Parsons without presenting some other features of his administration besides the important one above given. In every city, in every community, the moral and the material must go along side by side. The importance of each requires both to be kept ever in mind. In every city there should be good schools and other institutions of learning, good churches, good societies and other means and sources of culture and entertainment, the least of drinking or drunkenness, of gambling and of other evils, and on the other hand, plenty of good water, good lighting, good streets, good street cars, and other like improvements. These all seem to be the needs of satisfactory city life. In Cairo, our greatest and longest existing material want has been good streets, the very first distinguishing features of the city after the houses are built. The streets, more than almost anything else, speak for or against the city. Mayor Parsons fully realized this and at once entered upon a policy of street improvement. To judge somewhat of the work done we have but to look at Ohio Street, Twenty-Eighth Street, Sycamore Street, Washington Avenue, Poplar Street, Thirty-Fourth Street, Elm Street, Second Street, Walnut Street and Twenty-First Street, all now paved, and it is believed in the most substantial and permanent manner. Then, too, we have had the very large sewer on Commercial Avenue from Second to Thirty-Eighth Street and the outlet sewer on Tenth Street to the river and the various lateral sewers connecting with the main sewer on said avenue. Other works and improvements of an important nature I need not enumerate here; but it is well worthy of mention that what he has done has resulted in establishing a most satisfactory spirit of public improvement in the people of the city, and now with the important works already projected and under way, we may be well assured that this important matter of city improvements will go on to completion, when, for the great change made in the appearance of the city, it will scarcely be recognized as the place it was five or six years ago. It will, perhaps, add something to what I have already endeavored to express by saying that the expenditures for lasting and permanent improvements made during the last five years exceeds very considerably all of the expenditures that were made in the city for like improvements during the preceding forty-five or fifty years, or since the city's organization in 1857.

While the chief credit for all this very desirable work must be set down to Mayor Parsons, yet it must not be forgotten that he has been highly seconded by the Board of Local Improvements, the city council and their legal adviser, Mr. Angus Leek, to whose skillful and painstaking attention large credit is due. Nor does it detract from the work of any of these gentlemen to say that much also is due to the spirit and wishes of the people of the city, who so far and during the entire time have in every way encouraged the carrying on of the good work.

Then, too, Mayor Parsons has added about thirty-five thousand dollars to the city's annual revenues by obtaining an increase of the saloon license fee from five hundred to one thousand dollars. I cannot admit that this was a bad thing to do, considering the strongly expressed desire of the people to have saloons and not prohibition in the city. If we are to have them at all, the higher the license the better, even if raising it to the maximum should reduce the number of saloons to the minimum. Many persons think that every community should have its proper complement of saloons and that without them men cannot secure happiness or even contentment. I cannot agree with this view; but I am but one of many thousand, and cannot complain if other persons differ with me and are in the majority.

Although I have extended this notice of Mayor Parsons' administration further than I had intended, I may be permitted to say that while he has done so much, as I have above set forth, the inquiry very naturally arises, could he not have done it all and at the same time not have incurred the somewhat severe criticism which has been made upon his more recent management of city affairs?

Of the 135 voters at the election for town trustees March 8, 1855, mentioned on page 177, I know of none now living. Of the 391 voters who voted at the first city election March 7, 1857, I know certainly of but six who are now living, or living here: Thomas Meehan, James Quinn, Captain William M. Williams, John Sullivan, Jacob Lehning, and Charles W. Henderson. These 391 names are found on pages 273 and 274.

CHAPTER XXIV

DARIUS B. HOLBROOK, MILES A. GILBERT, SAMUEL STAATS TAYLOR, WILLIAM P. HALLIDAY, HALLIDAY BROTHERS

DARIUS BLAKE HOLBROOK.—The second attempt to establish a city here seems to have been begun by Darius Blake Holbrook, of whom we have already frequently spoken. He was not an adventurer, a dreamer, or a man of schemes merely. Force of character, strong will, ceaseless activity and enterprise, initiative, ability to bring others to see things as he saw them, were only some of his remarkable endowments. These characteristics were noticeable at all times. Nothing within the bounds of reason seemed too hard for him. Where others drew back he pushed forward. He had no patience with men who floated with the current. He would take advantage of it if it carried him toward the goal of his plans but if in the other direction, he turned against it and buffeted its waves with a faith and belief that seemed unconquerable.

He must have known all about this place or geographical point before he came here. He knew of the attempt and failure of 1818. He knew or soon ascertained who were the owners of the lands between the rivers; for nothing could be safely done without first acquiring good titles to the lands. He knew the low site, the river floods, the abrasions and inroads upon the shores, the need of strong levees and of the clearing off of the dense woods. He knew that while the geographical point was all that could be desired, the proposed city must have a secure foundation, a safe and enduring site. It was more than starting and building a city. A site had to be first provided. But he seems to have firmly believed that he and those associated with him could bring moneyed men to such a belief in the feasibility of the enterprise as would lead them to make all necessary advances of means. It was then as it was in 1818 and is now, a question of money. As the first promoters in 1818 left everything to the control and management of Comegys, so in 1836 to 1846, Holbrook seems to have been invested with unlimited authority. He was said to be not merely the chief representative of the companies but the companies themselves. If such was the case, it must have been due to the very general belief that what he wanted was needed and what he did not want was to be laid aside. He made two or three trips to London, and the great banking house of John Wright & Company became his company's financial representative in that city. These bankers were at the same time the agents of our state for the sale of its canal bonds. Besides Holbrook, there were in London Richard M. Young, then one of our United

D. B. Holbrook

Miles A Gilbert

States senators, and Ex-Governor John Reynolds, agents for the state and arranging with Wright & Company to take charge of the state's bond sales. Daniel Webster was also there, and while there gave his written opinion to Holbrook regarding his company's title to the lands it had mortgaged to the New York Life Insurance and Trust Company to secure the payment of its Cairo bonds.

Holbrook did everything, was everywhere, saw everybody, legislators and capitalists and other men of prominence and influence whom he supposed might aid him. He secured in London large sums of money and must have used, here in Cairo, more than a million of dollars. He paid large prices for the lands he bought from the Kaskaskia people or their heirs or grantees. The old record books "D" and "E," of 1836, 1837 and 1838, now at the court-house, show very large sums as the considerations for the various deeds taken by Holbrook. He and his company had great faith in their enterprise, and they determined to obtain titles to the land almost regardless of the price demanded.

We cannot go very fully into this matter here, but will hurry on to its close by saying that Holbrook worked on faithfully even after the failure of Wright & Company. He must have known, however, long before the end came that his attempt must meet a fate not wholly unlike that which came to the Kaskaskia people in 1818. The great London bankers had turned against Wright & Company and brought them to bankruptcy, and he knew that if he could not raise money on his Cairo bonds at the outstart in this country, he certainly could not do it now that the whole financial world was in a state of suspense as to what would be the outcome of the monetary depression almost the world over.

Holbrook, seeing that he could go no further, set about finding what entirely new arrangements might be made by which he and those associated with him might save something out of the failed enterprise.

A number of writers about Cairo have criticized him and some of them very severely. We do not know enough of the facts and circumstances, running through a number of years, to enable us to express a very satisfactory opinion as to those matters about which he was criticized. The work which he had undertaken was difficult in the extreme; but as we have before stated, he seems to have firmly believed that he could accomplish it. After the first two or three years he must have seen more clearly the difficulty of the situation. These called forth only greater efforts on his part; but when it became more and more evident that the situation was growing more and more doubtful, he may have resorted to measures which seemed more or less inconsistent with that straightforward kind of conduct about which all men speak well but which many of them find it exceedingly difficult to follow when overtaken by unexpected embarrassments. Observation shows that most men in times of severe financial trial and when failure seems impending, will turn aside here and there and do this or that and the other thing which they would have before severely criticized. Holbrook was determined that his enterprise should not fail, and it was a long time before he could see anything but success ahead of him. What he did at Washington and Springfield and New York, even as late as 1849, shows that his hope was not entirely gone, although his Cairo City and Canal Company had already sold out to the Cairo City Property Trust.

It may not be strictly accurate to speak of Holbrook as having begun the second attempt to start a city here. Breese, Gilbert and Swanwick seem to have first moved in the matter and to have sold to Holbrook, late in 1835 or early in 1836, an interest in their land entries here of August and September, 1835, and this seems to have been the first introduction of Holbrook to the proposed scheme. From that time forward, he became the leading spirit of the enterprise, long drawn out and beset with many difficulties.

Nothing shows more clearly Holbrook's influence than the closing months of Senator Douglas's efforts to obtain the land grant of September 20, 1850, for the Illinois Central Railroad. Douglas knew Holbrook well, and their interviews at Washington and elsewhere left no doubt upon his mind that Holbrook was all the while looking after the interests of Cairo and the railroad enterprise represented by the Great Western Railway charter of March 6, 1843. The legislature at Springfield, at the instance of Holbrook, amended the Great Western charter February 10, 1849, to the great disappointment of Douglas, who, fearing that his own plans might be seriously interfered with, left Washington for Springfield and there addressed the members of the legislature, whom he found more or less disinclined to accept his view of the situation; and there is no telling what shape the matter would have assumed had not Holbrook yielded his personal preferences. He seems to have done so only after obtaining an explicit promise that the act of the legislature incorporating the new central railroad company should contain a clause requiring it to start at and be built from Cairo. He remembered well the great effort made in 1838 to change the southern terminus of the state's central railroad from Cairo to a point near Grand Chain; and he put forth every effort to guard against another attempt of a like nature with the new road; and hence it is recited in the charter of February 10, 1851, that the road should run "from the southern terminus of the Illinois and Michigan canal to a point at the city of Cairo," and again, that it should "run from the city of Cairo to the southern terminus of the Illinois and Michigan canal."

We have elsewhere presented somewhat fully the early history of the Illinois Central Railroad, and have shown that it was originally a southern Illinois enterprise, if not in fact a Cairo enterprise. In considering Judge Breese's connection with the great undertaking, Holbrook must not be forgotten; nor should Jenkins, Gilbert and others, who assisted in the great work, although less prominently. As elsewhere stated, the New York and Chicago men did not care much whether the terminus should be at Cairo or fifteen or twenty miles up the Ohio River. It is probable that many of them preferred the Grand Chain location; but Holbrook stood in the way. He had many strong friends, and controlled two or three charters, which Senator Douglas felt should be gotten out of the way before he could rest easy regarding Holbrook and his fertility of expedients. Holbrook told him he would surrender his charters, but only upon condition that it should be plainly expressed in the act incorporating the railroad company that the southern terminus of the railroad should be at the city of Cairo.

From January 16, 1836, to February 10, 1851, we have the period of something over fifteen years, during all of which Holbrook never swerved an inch in his devotion to the city of Cairo. The very best years of his life he had put into his attempt to establish it; and if we follow along and note with some care the steps marked out plainly from 1836 to this time, we must readily agree that the Cairo of to-day owes its existence more to Darius Blake Holbrook than to any other man.

The following short sketch of her father was furnished me by his daughter, Baroness Caroline Holbrook Von Roques.

"Darius Blake Holbrook was born in Dorchester, Massachusetts. The Holbrooks were from Shropshire, England. His mother was a Ridgeway. Her family came to the United States in 1628. Richard Ridgeway was the brother of Sir Thomas Ridgeway, the first Earl of Londonderry, 1622, which title lapsed and passed to the Tempests, on failure of male heirs in England. The Ridgeways came to the United States on the ship Jacob and Mary in November, 1679. They landed in the Delaware River and settled in Springfield township, Burlington County, New Jersey.

"He was a prominent man in the city of New York for many years, and had great ability and large personal influence with all with whom he was associated. Besides his work in establishing the city of Cairo, Illinois, and in securing the great land grant for the Illinois Central Railroad, he was associated with Cyrus W. Field in laying the first Atlantic cable. He died in New York City, January 22, 1858. His wife was Elizabeth Thurston Ingraham; and their only child, now Baroness Caroline Holbrook Von Roques, married William Chandler, of the banking house of St. Johns, Powers & Company, of Mobile, Alabama. To them were born Holbrook St. John Chandler, who died in Paris unmarried, and Florence Elizabeth Chandler, who married James Maybrick in St. James, Picadilly, London, and whose children are James C. Maybrick and Gladys Maybrick."

Miles A. Gilbert.—Miles A. Gilbert was born in Hartford, Connecticut, January 1, 1810. After he had finished his education in 1829, he went into the wholesale store of Peas & Company in Middletown, Connecticut, where he remained two years. In the autumn of

1831, having an advantageous offer made him, he went to New Orleans as head salesman in a large wholesale dry goods establishment and remained there until May, 1832, when the weather becoming very hot and fearing yellow fever, he purchased a general assortment of goods suitable for the country trade and went to Kaskaskia, where he arrived June 8th, of that year, and where he engaged in merchandising for eleven years, having two stores in the country and one in town. He went east once a year to purchase dry goods and to New Orleans to purchase groceries. On the 17th day of November, 1836, he married Ann Eliza Baker, eldest daughter of the Hon. David J. Baker, senior. In the spring of 1843 he was appointed sole agent of the Cairo City and Canal Company and moved to Cairo in April of that year. During that year he had the cross levee built, which kept out the great flood of 1844. After remaining here for three years, he asked the Trustees to be relieved and some one else appointed in his place. This was promised but not fulfilled for several years. In the spring of 1847, having spent most of the previous fall and winter at Alton with his family, he moved to St. Mary's Landing on the Mississippi, where he owned about three thousand acres of land; and in the latter part of 1848, he had a portion of the same surveyed and laid out in town lots, and called the place "Ste. Mary, Mo." He continued to act as agent for the company, going to Cairo two or three times every month, until finally Samuel Staats Taylor, in April, 1851, was appointed to succeed him as agent.

He was an active union man and did much to keep the state of Missouri in the union. In 1866 he was elected county and probate judge of St. Genevieve County and was twice elected thereafter and held that office for the period of twelve years. He died at his home, Oakwood, Ste. Mary, January 21, 1901. In one of the obituary notices in the "Ste. Genevieve Herald" of January 26th, a few days after his death, it is said that Judge Gilbert was a man of clear judgment and of singular justness and fairness in all the relations of life, and was loved by his many friends and respected by all who knew him.

To show the relationship between the Gilberts, the Bakers and the Candees, it may be stated that Judge Gilbert's sister, Eunetia, married Stephen S. Candee. They were the parents of Mrs. Anna E. Safford and of Mr. Henry H. Candee, now deceased. We know of no families now in Cairo who have been so long and so prominently connected with our city and its varied interest as these I have just mentioned. I need not say they have ever been held in very high esteem. I have a number of times herein referred to Cairo as being in its origin largely a Kaskaskia town. Here is another illustration of the fact.

In the "History of Alexander, Union and Pulaski Counties," often referred to herein, is a somewhat lengthy biographical sketch of Judge Gilbert; and we take from the same an account of some of the events which took place in 1843, when he was placed in charge of the affairs of the Cairo City and Canal Company, which had then been forced to suspend all its work and operations of every kind. It gives us a clear view of the very unfortunate condition of things which followed the failure of that company. The account is dated May 11, 1883, and is as follows:

"The company having failed in the spring of 1843, I was selected as its agent to take charge of all of its property at Cairo. A large number of men were thrown out of employment and were in a wild, ungovernable state of confusion, clamoring for their pay. Many of them wanted me to sell the splendid machinery in the machine and carpenter shops, a building one hundred and fifty by two hundred feet, which was full of the most expensive machinery, most of which was attached to the building. I had no authority to remove the machinery and so told them, and thereupon they made all kinds of threats that they would break into the buildings and take out what they wanted. The leaders went off to gather up their mob forces and I at once secured four or five good laboring men on whom I could rely and barricaded the doors and windows and was ready for them when they returned. I had shot guns and pistols, all I wanted. They first tried the main front door, then the windows, but not successfully. Then they went for ladders, when I went to a window upstairs and told them I was put there to protect the property and protect it I would; and that if they got one piece of it it would be over my dead body; but that if they would wait until matters could be arranged in New York, where the president of the company was raising money to pay off all the laboring men, their interests would be fully protected. I further told them they had no lawful right, or right of any kind, to break in and take any of the property, and that if they injured me, or should kill me in my effort to protect the property, it would be murder. I plead with them to refrain from violence, the evil consequence of which would fall upon themselves, and that if they would go away and be peaceful and quiet they would receive their pay in due time. They went off about a hundred yards and held a consultation, and came back to the charge more furious than before. The building back of the levee was about ten feet above the ground, and in its center was a very large trap door for taking in machinery and lumber and putting out the same. The mob succeeded in breaking this trap door open, and then attempted to boost their men up into the building. I stood over the trap door with a pistol in one hand and a good effective club in the other, and called some of them by name and stated that I did not want to hurt them but that I would kill the first man that put his head above the floor. Several of them put their hands up over the floor and I gave them each a good blow with my club. Finally, after every imaginable way had been tried, they had one man who was somewhat intoxicated agree to get in. He tried it, I warned him, and when his hands came above the floor I hit them a good rap but he did not mind it. They kept pushing him up and I gave him another severe blow. They still kept on forcing him up into the room, when, I renewing my attack upon him with greater force and strength than ever, he called out to them to let him down and out and they did so. They could find no other to take his place, and I had the men with me block up the trap door and further barricade the windows. They came to the charge off and on that whole day. They smashed up the doors and windows but did not succeed in obtaining entrance, and finally after dark went away. I kept watch with my men all the night, and kept guard for many days until the better men of the mob, finding that they were likely to get into great trouble, influenced the others to desist from further attempts."

We have elsewhere referred to this incident and experience of the Cairo City and Canal Company, but here we have the account from first hand and from one of the company's leading representatives.

Samuel Staats Taylor came to Cairo as the agent of the Trustees of the Cairo City Property, April 15, 1851. He remained here until his death at his home in Cairo, May 14, 1896. He was here, therefore, forty-five years. On his arrival he took immediate charge and supervision of all the trust property and continued in its management under the directions of the Trustees until near the time of his death. There were a few changes in the personnel of the Trustees; and in the year 1876 the trust property was sold in proceedings in the United States court at Springfield to foreclose the Hiram Ketchum mortgages given in 1863 and in 1867, and a new trust formed under the name and style of the Cairo Trust Property, and he and Edwin Parsons became the Trustees of the new trust.

It is quite impossible to give an account, in any kind of detail, of Col. Taylor's long and hard work during the forty-five years of his stay here. I have called it hard work. It was such work, such care, such management, that had he known what the work would be, its long continuance and its disappointing results, he would not have consented to undertake it. But he and his Trustees and the shareholders, one and all, seemed to have had strong hopes that the third attempt to establish a city here would certainly prove successful. On no other theory can we account for their purchase of the Holbrook interests, and their subsequent endeavor to bring order out of disorder and confusion, and infuse into the public mind the trust and belief so remarkably disappointed twice before.

Their undertaking was more than the building of a city. The site it was to occupy was to be protected against the abrading currents of the great rivers and from their overflowing waters.

Their very first important contracts related directly to the construction of levees to keep out the high waters and to securing the banks upon which the levees stood. It does not now seem that they ever contemplated gradually filling the town to high-water mark instead of inclosing a large district of country with levees and protecting the same from the cutting of the rivers. They expected the town would grow rapidly and that all their lands would be needed to supply the demand for town lots. Hence they, from the very first, economized space, and made their lots 25 by 100 feet only, and their streets 50 and 60 feet in width, with a few exceptions, and dispensed with alleys altogether.

Very truly,
S. Staats Taylor
Trustee

W P Halliday

The Trustees and the stockholders must have looked upon Col. Taylor as the man for the place and the undertaking; and he must have known that his selection indicated what they expected of him. He came in the faith and belief that their and his work was reasonably practicable and promising of success, whatever else it had been in 1818 and in 1836. They and he well knew of the former failures and the causes thereof. These must have afforded no inconsiderable light in deciding in favor of the third attempt or venture. Their eyes were fully open to the geography and topography of the situation. One thing only was required, and that was money. Men to plan and manage the enterprise and use wisely the funds provided were within easy reach, comparatively. They could not have been blinded by the shining of the outlook. The experiences of their predecessors were sufficient to temper any exuberance of spirit and to indicate what errors and mistakes were to be avoided.

Col. Taylor came here as the representative of a new company. It was not a corporation but a land trust; but for all practical purposes it was a corporation, a foreign corporation. It owned or controlled almost every acre of land from the junction of the two rivers to an east and west line north of Cache River. These lands amounted to 9732 acres.

Eastern men, under the lead of Senator Douglas, had procured their charter of February 10, 1851, for their Illinois Central Railroad. This was but two months before the arrival of Col. Taylor at Cairo. The road was this time certainly to be built, and as in former cases, it was to be built *to a point at the city of Cairo.* This requirement of the charter, therefore, at once brought the railroad company and the Trustees together to negotiate as to the terms upon which the company might enter Cairo and establish its southern terminal facilities. Col. Taylor had been here less than three months when the contract of June 11, 1851, was entered into by the railroad company and the Trustees. A supplemental contract was made by the same parties May 31, 1855, to make clearer some of the provisions of the first contract, and to provide for other features of the situation not before considered.

We recite these matters and things here to show the importance of the situation with which Col. Taylor was expected to deal. He was on the ground and soon came to know more than any one else about the needs of the Trustees and of the land enterprise in which they had embarked. The Trustees needed their city site protected from floods; so also did the railroad company; but the latter needed lands and rights-of-way and could not build upon the natural surface but upon earth embankments only; and hence it was naturally provided that the embankment should extend around the city and be and become protective levees upon which the railroad company's tracks should be placed and its trains run. Wide embankments were not needed for railroad purposes but were for protection against the rivers; and hence the embankments were to be eighty feet wide on the top and sufficiently high to keep out the highest known waters in the rivers. *These con-*

tracts are not recorded, for what reason I do not know, but they have been printed in three or four editions of our city ordinance books, commencing with that of 1872.

Col. Taylor, time and time again, complained of the failure of the railroad company to observe the requirements of these contracts, and he carefully kept an account of its shortcomings and made a record of the moneys he had to spend to make good what it should have done. In the course of time, the Trustees sued the company in the United States Court at Springfield to recover what they claimed to be due from the company. Whether or not it was so intended, the suit, it seems, became much like a suit to obtain a proper construction of a contract. One important branch of the controversy related to the duty to protect the site of the city or the river banks, where the levees were, or were to be, from abrasion and destruction. The railroad company said its duty was to build the levees, but that under the contracts the Trustees were to maintain the site or foundations upon which the levees were, or were to be built. We cannot pursue this matter further than to say that July 18, 1872, the long pending suit was compromised by a release of the railroad company from the two contracts and its conveyance back to the Trustees of its 100-foot strip of ground around the city and the payment to the Trustees of $80,000.00. (See book No. 7, page 287, in the recorder's office.) With this exception and possibly one or two others, the Trustees and the railroad company have been in accord,—too much so, some have thought, for the good of the city. Col. Taylor's supervision here extended for many years to levee building and repairing, to river bank protection, to clearing off the dense woods which everywhere covered their extended acreage, to laying out, surveying and platting the town itself, a most difficult undertaking,—to fixing the prices of lots and lands and making sales thereof, to wharf construction and the collection of wharfage, to preparing as best he could, with the means at his command, for river floods, and to looking after the health of the city and largely to the general welfare and government of the people. The town or city was in large measure the town and city of the Trustees, and his duty extended almost to everything that in any way related to them or to the people of the community. To attend to and properly supervise all these divers matters and things and report them annually and fully to the Trustees and stockholders a thousand miles away, was, as we have already said, hard work and labor. Most men would have fled from such exacting duties, but Col. Taylor performed them very faithfully for forty years.

But Col. Taylor's faithful service extended, in one or two respects, beyond reasonable bounds. The alternative could have been loss of position only, which could never have been a very great loss to him. The Trustees seldom, if ever, required him to do anything which he personally thought he ought not to do. Let us explain:

It was to be expected that the Trustees would have litigation of greater or less importance. They were non-residents and citizens of New York and Philadelphia; and when they were sued they uniformly removed the case to the United States Circuit Court at Springfield. Col. Taylor was here and had charge generally of the situation, including the litigation, and when it became necessary to remove a case from a state to a Federal court, he generally made the requisite affidavits and executed the other necessary papers. Until 1888, if the suit involved as much as $500.00, a removal could be had. In that year the amount was increased to $2000.00. This uniform custom of the Trustees gained them no favor with the people of Cairo. But on the contrary, it removed the Trustees farther from the people of the town and separated the latter farther from Col. Taylor, although a resident and citizen with them. From 1851 to 1864, Col. Taylor had been a resident of Cairo and a citizen of the state and had been town Trustee for the two years' term of the town's existence and mayor of Cairo six several times; but in the year 1864 he changed his citizenship from Illinois to Missouri and took up his residence in St. Louis. Scarcely any one knew this. He and his family remained here at his residence on Washington Avenue and Sixth Street and afterwards on Washington Avenue and Twenty-Eighth Street. He had no home or residence in St. Louis, but claimed to have a room or rooms at the Southern Hotel. This change in citizenship was due, no doubt, to a desire to render better service to the trust in respect to litigation. Under the city acts of incorporation of 1857 and 1867, and the amendment of 1868, none of the higher officers of the city were required to be citizens or residents of Illinois. Col. Taylor no doubt supervised this feature of the enactments. No change came until the city became incorporated under the general act of April 10, 1872, for the incorporation of cities and villages, which was in January, 1873.

We refer to this here for the purpose of accounting in some degree for the increasing want of sympathy and co-operation between the people of the town and the Trustees and their representative. Something of this kind had no doubt come over from the Holbrook administration. It seems to have had a steady growth until there arose in the city two parties, the one the Taylor party and the other the anti-Taylor party. It made its appearance, in a small way, almost as far back as 1851, the year Col. Taylor came here. It arose chiefly from the first efforts of the Trustees to control the wharf and collect wharfage from all water craft of every description. There were all kinds of boats at the landing, flat boats, keel boats, trading boats and steamboats, and many of the Cairo people were largely interested in the business done on the rivers.

This state of feeling between the people and the Trustees is further seen in the charge Col. Taylor made against the four other town Trustees in 1856, which was that it was their custom to hold meetings and transact town business without letting him know anything about the meetings. And so the little breach widened more and more, until in the year 1864 the people put up David J. Baker for mayor against Col. Taylor, who had been elected mayor six several times, beginning with 1857. H. Watson Webb was elected mayor in 1863 without opposition. Judge Baker's father was David J. Baker, senior, who was a very able man, lawyer and judge and had long been a man of the Trustees' own right hand; and it was hardly to be supposed that David J. Baker, junior, also an able man and a lawyer, would yield to entreaties to make the race for mayor against Col. Taylor, who up to that time had been very successful in vanquishing his opponents. Judge Baker made the race, however, which he would not have done had he not known of the very strong feeling against the Trustees and their Cairo policies. It was a heated contest, such as never had occurred before in Cairo and probably not since. In a vote of 734, Judge Baker received a majority of 26 votes. Even at this time, you will find a few men in Cairo who can tell all about that city election. It was a kind of landmark, a fixed date from and to which many things were referred or calculated. It was at this time that Col. Taylor changed his citizenship from Illinois to Missouri.

There were no politics in this situation of things in the city. It was a Taylor party and an anti-Taylor party. Col. Taylor was on the ground and was regarded as representing, in the highest degree and in every sense, the Trustees and their management. There was something of a personal nature in it, arising from the belief that Col. Taylor entered heartily into the plans of the Trustees and had just as little sympathy for the people as the Trustees themselves, the one in Philadelphia and the other in New York.

Since that election there has never been another at which there was such a drawing of the Taylor and the anti-Taylor line; but the Trustees are still with us, with a change of name and some changes in interest. Many years ago the city began to pass out of their hands and to enter upon self-control. It is a better state of things, and it would no doubt have been better had it commenced earlier.

It may be thought that I have devoted too much space to these matters. But I reply that few towns or cities in the country have been so peculiarly situated as Cairo. About this I need only refer to the chapter on Cairo in "Servitude to Land Companies." It may be also very properly remarked that the Trustees, and Col. Taylor as their immediate and most important representative, became to the people of Cairo public men or officials whose acts and doings in very many respects affected the general public interests. The people were here and interested in the city and its growth and prosperity, and they believed the Trustees could do more than all others for the city which they had started out to build. Persons bearing such relations to public interests cannot reasonably expect the same exemption from comment and criticism as may one whose interests and duties are wholly personal or individual. The party spirit, so long existing in the city, was of such nature and extent that to omit reference to it in a history of the city could scarcely be justified. It was talked of and written about here at home and in other parts of the country, and the town was spoken of frequently as owned and controlled by a few persons, and they living at a distance. It was a custom of the people of the place to notice somewhat carefully whether the new arrivals in the city for residence here would ally themselves with the one or the other party. And as still further showing what the condition of things was in this respect it may be stated that an election of no kind could be held without this spirit openly making its appearance. In these more modern times we often hear it enjoined upon the business and leading men in the community *to get together;* but in Cairo for three or four decades such an expression was never heard. The one party generally felt too strong to talk about such a thing, and the other was never in a sufficiently good humor to mention the matter. It was not a feud,—no, not at all; but it is expressing the thing rather mildly to say that it was a constant state of strained relations.

Col. Taylor was never a man of the people. His birth, his training, his tastes, his life, were away from and in a sense above them. They looked upon him as without sympathy for them and as caring nothing for their interests. His life here seemed in keeping with his claim of citizenship elsewhere. There were exhibited all those appearances of foreign landlords; for such were the actual relations of the Trustees to the people. Col. Taylor's manner and carriage all indicated, perhaps too much but yet naturally, that he dwelt apart and not among the people, who thought he ought to be more of a servant to them and less of a lord over them. They would have welcomed his advances, but none seem ever to have been made. He did not seem to know this because he did not feel it. It was out of keeping with his strong nature, which did not appear to need those associations and that friendly social intercourse which most men desire and seek.

While the policies of the Trustees may not always have been what the interest of the city and the people at large required or needed or thought they needed, Col. Taylor himself was ever watchful of the interest of the town and its peculiar site and situation. Under his administration of the trust, for he seemed to administer it, no one ever tinkered with the levees. To him they were as the very life of the city. He had gone through all the trying experiences of river floods, beginning with 1858, and knew far better than any one else what the levees meant to the city; and no one could remove a shovel of earth from them or excavate an inch near these city life securities or dream of piercing through them with any kind of an opening, without the most formal permission, signed, sealed and delivered beforehand. And when any levee was to be pierced or cut anywhere or for any purpose, the engineers were examined, cross-examined and minutely instructed, and supplementing it all we would see him personally present to make sure all was going on just right. This is a fair illustration of the attention he gave to everything he had in hand which was of any consequence.

We have often heard of men who in a marked degree attracted the attention of others when appearing in public. Col. Taylor was such a man. No one could meet or see him without at once feeling that he was in the presence of a strong, not to say great, character. His stature, his mould, his brow, his eye, his steady look and expression, in a word, his commanding presence, told, plainer than words could tell, that here nature had been lavish of her splendid gifts. And is it strange that here in this small city one should be found so much above most men? Why not? Greatness such as that to which I have referred is not geographical.

Is it true that almost all men of great character and spirit at last find life a disappointment? Col. Taylor did. The hope that brought him here and kept him here so long and until it was too late to look or go elsewhere, failed him at last. He had spent many years in the service of the United States Bank at Philadelphia in times as stirring as any that have ever occurred in the history of the country, some years in New York, some years also in Chicago, and his coming here to take charge of almost a barren situation or site upon which to build a city must have arisen from a belief that there were great things before him. Some persons may disagree with me, but Col. Taylor was a great man and could never, in his maturer or later years, have felt that he had come into his own or had in a large measure made out of his life what he had hoped. He lived in some respects a far-off life, if we may be allowed such an expression. He may have been happier than he seemed; but it may well be doubted that, could the offer have been made, he would have chosen to live over again the same life. That, too, is not strange; for the number is not large that would so choose.

The following is from the biographical notices of officers and graduates of Rutgers College, deceased during the year ending June, 1896:

"Samuel Staats Taylor was born in New Brunswick, New Jersey, November 18, 1811, and died at his home in Cairo, Illinois, on May 14, 1896. His father's name was Augustus FitzRandolph Taylor, an eminent physician of that place. His grandfather, John Taylor, was Professor of Languages in Queen's College at the outbreak of the Revolutionary War and recruited a company from among the students, which he led to the field. The original ancestor of the family came to America from England with Sir George Cartwright in 1640, and settled the province of New Jersey. His mother's name was Catharine Schuyler Neilson, daughter of Colonel John Neilson, a native of New Brunswick.

"He graduated in 1829 with the second honor of his class. From an early period of his life he was designed by his parents for the legal profession, his own inclination tending in the same direction. He read law in the city of New York with an older brother, John N. Taylor, and was admitted to the bar as an attorney at the age of twenty-one, and three years later he was admitted to the higher degree of counselor, and was considered one of the most promising and brilliant lawyers of the period. His career at the bar, however, was short. In 1836 he accepted a confidential position as Secretary of the Board of Directors of the United States Bank of Philadelphia, a position of great responsibility, which he retained until the memorable failure of that corporation in 1841. He was then appointed by the trustees to assist in winding up the complicated affairs of the company. In this capacity he operated until 1851, having supreme control of the interests of his employers in the States of Ohio, Indiana, Illinois, Wisconsin, Missouri and Iowa, and transacting all the business incident to the most gigantic enterprise of the kind in the nation and requiring executive talent and ability of the very highest order. In April, 1851, he removed to Cairo, where he assumed charge of the Cairo city property, and in 1861 was made a Trustee of the property by the stockholders, which relation he sustained till his death. He was elected the first mayor under the charter of 1857, and was re-elected to this position for five consecutive terms. From 1865 till 1875 he was president of the Cairo and St. Louis Railroad Company, was a director of the City National Bank since 1865, and, in fact, was identified with every interest of the city after his arrival there."

William Parker Halliday.—Capt. Halliday was so long and so prominent a citizen of Cairo that I may very properly follow the sketches of Holbrook, Gilbert and Taylor with a short sketch of his life. One reason for this is that I have not found in any book or pamphlet any notice of him. I infer this want of reference to him was due to his own choice, insisted upon, no doubt, when solicited for information about himself. There are many men and not a few women, long well known in Cairo about whom I should like to leave here some fitting words of remembrance; but to select them from others, with or without their permission, and say just what the public would expect or desire me to say, would be so difficult an undertaking that I found I could not enter upon it. The few of whom I have spoken have been largely public characters, and concerning them I have felt at liberty to speak somewhat freely, though I hope always candidly, if not always justly.

Capt. Halliday was born in Meigs County, Ohio, July 21, 1827. He received such an education as was then generally given boys and young men in the community where the family lived. It was good enough, or supposed to be good enough, for all *practical* purposes. Wherein it may have been wanting his native talent largely supplied the want. At an early time in life, he sought employment on the Ohio River. He was clerk first and afterwards captain on steamboats navigating that stream. Possessing rare business talents, and the war coming on, he improved the opportunities it afforded to prosecute successful business enterprises, and as a result he became very prosperous. So uniformly were his business ventures successful that in a comparatively short time, his property and means had so accumulated as to greatly reinforce his naturally fine business abilities. Natural talents for business and the possession of means were as leverage to each other, and the increase in wealth was something in the nature of a geometrical progression.

To express the above in fewer words, it may be said, Capt. Halliday was first, last and always a business man. His life was devoted to business, that is to the acquisition of money, property, wealth. Naturally this absorbed almost all his time and thoughts. It could not have been otherwise. It was not different with him from others whose chief object and constant aim were the transaction of business. As in other cases and always, one becomes molded into a type, and life is lived on and out in the accomplishment of the same unvarying object or purpose. It is so in everything to which men turn attention. Success, marked success, comes only to those who set but one goal before them. Capt. Halliday may not have said so, may not have thought so, but he had beyond doubt determined early in life to acquire wealth; and to this everything else was made to tend. No mechanism could have worked with greater precision. He was a strong man, a gifted man, and everything in and about him focused upon this one thing, the acquisition of wealth. Just what he expected it to bring him, no one can tell. Perhaps he never thought much about what it would or could afford him. He cared nothing for office, not much for politics, not very much for religious matters, and not much for society. All these were subordinate, some of them very much so. How else could it be? Few men are able to fill many spheres of energy. In proportion as there are many, the success in any one is not often very great. Ordinarily life must be centered upon some one thing, in order to achieve high or great results. To be a statesman, one must study politics; to be a scientist, the most painstaking work for years must be entered upon and unremittingly pursued; to be a professional man of any kind, with hopes for success therein, almost everything else, outside of the chosen profession, must be laid aside. Captain Halliday had no doubt observed this and applied it strictly in the prosecution of his chosen work.

In these business times, Capt. Halliday was one of a thousand. His sphere of activity was by no means broad. The small city of his residence and life was not fruitful of opportunities; but he had laid hold of so many branches of business, that combining the same would have put him alongside of many of the great business men in the cities.

His whole life was one of practical education. He saw very early the importance of attention to details. He knew better than any one in his employment that if the apparently small things are neglected there will be no large results. He carried on no business about which he did not soon know more than any one else in his service. To him almost all the details of salt making, coal mining and transportation, cotton growing, banking, and many other branches of business were as familiar as are the ordinary details of the simplest business enterprises.

He had a few maxims about which he said little, but they were all of a practical and business-like nature. Having come to Cairo before the war, and the war having opened, opportunities multiplied. He improved them, and his success and prosperity were beyond his expectations. As he grew in wealth, he grew even faster in capabilities for management, and hence his spheres and branches of business multiplied and widened. There was little competition in his business enterprises anywhere. This was greatly to his advantage. The little opposition he met with in business did not have the best effect upon him; nor would it have had on any one. He was restive when unexpected obstacles appeared in his way. This was natural. Strong men often fire up when opposition appears. They regard it as useless and intended only to annoy; whereas, they should treat it as the exhibition of the same spirit and prowess they themselves possess and exercise freely. Capt. Halliday acquired large wealth, considering the size of his town and the amount of the business done here. His business, however, represented that of many places. Had he lived in some one of our great cities and taken hold of business as he did here, he would probably have acquired tens of millions, instead of a few here at home. This may be said to be very doubtful; but what he actually did here is a fair indication of what he could and would have done where business transactions of great magnitude were carried on.

Capt. Halliday had more than a fair degree of caution. It was not generally known that he ever ventured much, except in some of his earlier operations. If he ever made much or lost considerable in stock or other like transactions in the large cities, few persons were told of it. He always kept his own counsels; and if he seemed at times more ready to let matters get abroad, it was the better to conceal the actual matter in hand. Ambitious as he was to gain wealth and the prominence it is generally supposed to give, he had seen so many overtaken by calamity, that he seems to have set very definite boundaries to his ventures.

I might extend this description of this remarkable man; but however long it might be made, it would all be in further illustration only of those features of his character and life I have above endeavored to set forth.

I must be permitted to say here of Capt. Halliday something of what I have elsewhere said of Thomas Wilson. Wilson had fought Taylor and Halliday for many years; but after a long lapse of time, the fires of local election strife began to burn low, and William reached out his strong right hand and took hold of Tom's and the hatchet was buried. Each admired the other for the grit that was in him. Nature had made them giants,—local giants it may be, but nevertheless giants. They would have been that anywhere, I suppose. And so I say of Halliday as I have said of Wilson, that had he obtained or taken the education and training he might have had or taken in early life, the great business world of this great country would everywhere have stopped for a while to note the fact of his death. But it is said, had these two men been trained in college life or something equivalent thereto, if there is any equivalent, they might never have attained to what they did here. This is possible, probably probable. As heretofore stated, this view puts a discount on education of all kinds and everywhere. Had Lincoln, Douglas and Logan been college men, so called, it is altogether probable they never would have become the great public men they were. A very little thing often turns the current of one's life; but how superficial, how illogical, how flimsy is such a line of argument as this against the claims of higher education. Once, when Capt. Halliday returned from Chicago where he had attended a meeting of the board of directors of the Illinois Central Railroad Company, I had a talk with him in his office in the City National Bank. I noted his expression of countenance as he spoke of Stuyvesant Fish, the president of the company, and of his acts and management in their meeting. Especially did he speak of the fact that Fish was a Yale man; and it seemed to me that he thought Fish's college training had been of immense advantage to him. And may he not himself have felt that had he received the training Fish had, he would have felt himself possessed of a strength and confidence that were now beyond his reach.

A few years before Mr. Lincoln came very prominently before the country, he went to Cincinnati to assist in the trial of certain insurance cases, on his side of which Edwin M. Stanton was the leading counsel. Stanton's management and exhibition of learning and knowledge were a kind of revelation to the Springfield lawyer, who, when he returned home, spoke of his impressions of the great Pennsylvanian, and of the amazing advantage college life and training gave men, as it seemed to him. Lincoln saw in Stanton what Halliday saw in Fish.

But in emphasizing Capt. Halliday's talents and taste for business, I must not be understood as disallowing to him other excellent and great qualities, which often co-exist with close attachment to some one great moving purpose of life. He was, I think, on the right side in all the important moral and charitable questions and enterprises to which his attention was drawn. He did much for the poor of the community, but without ostentation or trumpet-blowing of any kind. Persons who knew him better than I did I am sure will say a great deal more to this effect than I have said. No one went to him for any worthy purpose who was turned away without aid. What he did for the public library, will, in its careful and wise management, live far into the distant future when all of us have gone and most of us have been forgotten. I have spoken of him as a remarkable man; and while his great abilities were devoted so exclusively to the acquisition of wealth, they would, in other conditions and times, have lifted him high above most men in whatever sphere of life they had been exercised. He, like and yet unlike Col. Taylor, was a great man, as little as the world may have known the fact. Greatness of another kind, to which he might have easily attained, would have carried his name far beyond the ordinary boundaries of wealth-giving fame. He seemingly possessed all the elements of a great general, whether in war or in the great business battles of the world. While he knew his limitations better than any one else, yet he could have been placed in few positions where he would not have risen fully to the exacting demands of the hour and achieved victories of lasting renown.

THE HALLIDAY BROTHERS.—There were five of them, a somewhat exceptional number: William P. Halliday, Samuel B. Halliday, Edwin W. Halliday, Henry L. Halliday, and Thomas W. Halliday. Of the eldest and the youngest I have elsewhere spoken at some length; of the former, because so prominent in the financial world, and of the latter, because so long in official life. Of them all, I may be permitted to say that while they differed from each other, they all exhibited features of character and conduct that would have given them prominence anywhere in the business world. No doubt in some one or two important respects, each one excelled the others. This was shown in those matters and things to which they gave their chief attention. Speaking of them and their families, so well represented here with us and elsewhere, it can be said that they have always stood for the better things, not with assumption or pharisaically, but openly and firmly. They pushed their business enterprises with diligence, and had there been more of such men it would have been better for the city and for them also, I have no doubt. It will not detract from them nor from old Scotland, to say they were and are Scotch people, although native Americans. Possibly, this may account somewhat for the solidity of character so uniformly exhibited by them. Of the five brothers, William and Samuel came here before the war; and in 1862, Henry and Thomas came. Major Edwin W. Halliday came here after the close of the war. He is the only brother of the five now living; and I regret to say that he seems to have found it best for the health of Mrs. Halliday to remove to San Diego, where relatives of the family have long resided. In the "Memoirs of the Lower Ohio Valley" are found interesting biographical sketches of Major Edwin W. Halliday and Mr. Henry L. Halliday. There are also therein biographical sketches of Henry E. and Douglas Halliday, sons of Henry L. Halliday, deceased, and of William R. Halliday, a son of Samuel B. Halliday, deceased. The one of Major Halliday contains perhaps more of family history than any of the others.

CHAPTER XXV

THE GROWTH OF "THE THREE STATES"

THE taking of the census every ten years by the general government has come to embrace so many things besides an enumeration of the inhabitants of the several states and territories that it seems there is now no telling to what it will not hereafter extend. It is to be hoped that it will not become so encumbered that its usefulness will be materially impaired. Whatever it was or has been, it ought now to be fairly reliable, at least as to the numbering of the people. Few of us know or appreciate what the work of its making has become. It is now one of the great administrative features of the government, and it is to be regretted that so few people care to know of the wonderful amount and variety of very useful information the census reports afford them.

We here give the population of the three adjacent states of Kentucky, Illinois and Missouri, beginning with the year 1810, when Illinois and Missouri were territories. We give this chiefly to show the comparative conditions of these great divisions of our country in 1810 and 1820. It will be seen that Kentucky had become quite a populous district of country when Illinois was almost uninhabited, and that the Ohio River was the outer and almost abrupt boundary of our civilization.

YEAR	KENTUCKY	ILLINOIS	MISSOURI
1775	300	———	———
1784	30,000	———	———
1790	73,679	———	———
1800	220,955	2,458	———
1810	406,511	12,282	20,845
1820	564,317	55,211	66,586
1830	687,917	157,445	140,455
1840	779,828	476,183	383,702
1850	982,405	851,470	682,044
1860	1,155,684	1,711,951	1,182,012
1870	1,321,011	2,539,891	1,721,295
1880	1,648,690	3,077,871	2,168,380
1890	1,858,635	3,826,351	2,679,184
1900	2,147,174	4,821,550	3,106,665
1910	———	———	———

POPULATION OF ALEXANDER COUNTY AND CAIRO

Year	County	Cairo	Year	County	Cairo
1820	626	——	1860	4,707	2,188
1830	1,300	——	1870	10,564	6,267
		(supposed)	1880	14,809	9,011
1840	3,313	2,000	1890	16,563	10,324
1850	2,484	242	1900	19,384	12,566
			1910	——	——

In 1890 and 1900, on the announcement of the city's population the people of the city were very much surprised and disappointed, and in both cases succeeded in having the census of the place retaken. In both instances four or five hundred were added to the number first found; but still the additional number was regarded as much too small. This of course, is a very common occurrence throughout the country; but as to the city of Cairo it is probable an unusually large number of residents are absent from the city on the rivers and in the railroad service.

About the close of the year 1864, the city council ordered a census of the city's population to be taken, and for that purpose appointed William J. Yost, whom many of us well remember as then and afterwards one of the city's best citizens and whose character and standing assured the people of the doing of the work with proper care.

On the 14th day of January, 1865, he filed his report which was sworn to by him and is now found on record in Journal C, pp. 503-505 of the city records. He says he did not himself go above 34th Street or along the levees because of the bad roads, but as to those places not actually visited, he had consulted others and made careful estimates. The following shows the result of his work.

	White	Colored	Total
1st ward	1552	447	1999
2nd ward	2328	567	2895
3rd ward	934	442	1376
4th ward	1672	627	2299
Totals	6486	2083	8569

WHITE AND COLORED POPULATION OF THE COUNTY IN 1850 AND SINCE

Year	White	Colored	Total
1850	2,464	20	2,484
1860	4,652	55	4,707
1870	8,268	2,296	10,564
1880	10,239	4,568	14,807
1890	11,672	4,891	16,563
1900	13,084	6,300	19,384
1910	——	——	——

These figures show the relative increase in the white and colored people since the year 1860.

By the Federal census the population in 1860 was 2,188. Yost's census January 14, 1865, made it 8,569, an increase of 6,381 in four years. It will be remembered, however, that our four years of war had added largely to our population; and that in 1870 the population had fallen from 8,569 in January, 1865, to 6,267, a decrease of 2,302.

CHAPTER XXVI

ALEXANDER COUNTY, ITS OTHER TOWNS, AND ITS EARLIEST SETTLERS

THE territory of the county was a part of St. Clair County, when that county was organized by Governor Arthur St. Clair March 27, 1790. It became a part of Randolph County, which was organized by him October 5, 1795. It became a part of Johnson County, when that county was organized by Governor Ninian Edwards September 12, 1812. It continued a part of Johnson County until January 2, 1818, when it became a part of Union County, then organized, but only by attachment thereto *until it should be formed into a separate county,* which was done March 4, 1819. It was, therefore, a part of or attached to Union County from January 2, 1818, to March 4, 1819. Its boundaries were the two rivers, and on the east, a north and south line between ranges one and two east, and, on the north, an east and west line between townships thirteen and fourteen, south range. These boundaries embrace about three hundred and seventy-eight square miles.

The first section of this act of March 4, 1819, fixed the boundaries of the county and gave it the name of Alexander County, for William M. Alexander, who lived at America, the county seat. I have not been able to obtain much information concerning Doctor Alexander. He was a practicing physician in America and its vicinity, and also something of a politician and public man. He represented the county in the lower house of the legislature in 1820 and 1822. He was also speaker of the house in 1822 and 1824. In the "Historical Encyclopedia of Illinois," of 1900, is a short sketch of him. He is there said to have gone from America to Kaskaskia and subsequently to some part of the south where he died, but the date and place of his death could not be given by the writer of the sketch. In Chapter I of that part of the "History of Alexander, Union and Pulaski Counties" which relates to Alexander County are found extracts from the diary of Col. Henry L. Webb, of Trinity, at the mouth of Cache River. Col. Webb speaks of Doctor Alexander and of his being in co-partnership with him in certain business enterprises. In Chapter II Doctor Alexander is again spoken of. I regret very much that I am not able to say more concerning this man whose name our county bears. The second section of the act appointed Levi Hughes, Aaron Atherton, Daniel Phillips, Allen McKenzey, and Nesbit Allen, commissioners to locate the permanent seat of justice or county seat. The third section required the courts, elections, etc., to be held "in the house of Wm. Alexander, in said county, until the public building should be erected."

His house was very probably at America on the Ohio River. The commissioners located the county seat at America, where it remained until it was removed to Unity by the act of January 18, 1833.

The county of Pulaski was organized March 2, 1843, and all of Alexander County east of the west bank of Cache River and east of Mill Creek was taken off and included in Pulaski County. This left no part of the river in Alexander County, and reduced the area of Alexander from three hundred and seventy-eight square miles to about two hundred. The county seat remained at Unity until February 4, 1845, when the legislature enacted a law removing and permanently locating it at Thebes, in the southeast quarter of section eight, township fifteen south, range three west, "commonly called Sparhawk's Landing" on the Mississippi River.

On the 18th day of February, 1859, the legislature passed a law providing for the holding of an election on the first Tuesday of November, 1859, to determine whether the people of the county desired to remove the county seat from Thebes to Cairo. The election was held on the 8th day of November and resulted in a vote of five hundred and seventy for removal and three hundred and ninety against removal. The polls were open at Cairo, Unity, Thebes, Santa Fe, Clear Creek, Dog Tooth, and Hazlewood. The judges of the election at Cairo were Daniel Hannon, John Ryan and Hugh Dolan; and the clerks were J. W. Timmons and John H. Robinson.

It will, therefore, be seen that America was the county seat of the county fourteen years; Unity twelve years; Thebes fourteen years, and Cairo now fifty years. The court-house at Thebes, a stone structure, still occupies the hillside just as it was built in 1845. The property now belongs to Isaac D. Dexter.

The courts of the county, after 1859, were held at different places in Cairo until the erection and completion of the present court-house on Washington Avenue and Twentieth Street. The contract for its erection was let March 2, 1863, to Mr. J. K. Frick, whom a few of our citizens will remember very well, for $28,000.00. It seems that Mr. Frick surrendered his contract after he had done a large part of the work. He was released, his sureties discharged, and the contract for the completion of the building let to John Major for $32,000.00. The building was not completed until the early part of 1865, and the first court held therein was the July term 1865 of the Court of Common Pleas, presided over by Judge John H. Mulkey, the judge of that court. (The writer was present at that term of court and obtained from the court the requisite certificate, which he subsequently presented with his New York license to the clerk of the supreme court at Mount Vernon and obtained an Illinois license. At that time he had not decided to locate in Cairo.) The lots now constituting the court-house grounds were conveyed by the Trustees of the Cairo City Property by deed of October 20, 1862, recorded in Book D, pp. 291, etc. The lots are 13 to 27, block 48, First Addition to the city. The deed is upon *condition* as to the use of the property; but no reversion is provided for, as in the case of lot 30, block 47, in the city, on which the first school-house was erected in 1853.

In the "History of Alexander, Union and Pulaski Counties," will be found interesting notices of America, the first county seat, and of Trinity on the Ohio at the mouth of Cache River. Besides these old towns, which no longer exist, there was the town of *Marseilles* laid out by Dr. Daniel Arter and Benjamin F. Echols, located on the east half of the northeast quarter of section three, township sixteen one west. The plat was acknowledged March 6, 1839, and recorded in Book D, pages 60, 61, and 62. The town embraced part of the immediate neighborhood of our present Villa Ridge. The Illinois Central Railroad of 1837 ran across the northeast corner of the town as platted.

There was also the town of *Alexandria* on the Mississippi River just below the present Sante Fe. It was laid out by Alexander M. Fountaine and Chas. M. Thurston, of Louisville. The plat was recorded in Book D, on pages 46, 47 and 48, March 23, 1838. It contained eighty-nine blocks or squares, and 1038 lots. It embraced part of those claims and surveys, of four hundred acres each, which, with other claims and surveys, will be found fully described hereafter.

The public and business men of those early days kept up with the times quite as well as our public and business men do now, perhaps even better. There was so much less going on and so much more leisure, that what was comparatively easy then would be quite impossible now. It was well known at Kaskaskia and all over the state, which was then what is southern Illinois now, that the Cairo enterprise (of 1818) had failed and the effect of this was to cause other men acquainted with this region to seek another and a better site for a city, near enough to the confluence of the two rivers to avail of all advantages the same afforded. The site chosen was America on the Ohio, about twelve miles from its mouth. Comegys and his associates were quite pretentious enough in choosing the name of a city in Africa for the name of their city at this point; but these other men who chose their site further up the Ohio were still more pretentious, it seems, and gave the name of a continent to their proposed town and called it America. Trinity became a rival of America and to a large extent supplanted it, so far as the river business was concerned. Both claimed to be the head of navigation. Trinity had the best harbor and was closer to the junction of the two rivers.

The earliest settlers in what is now Alexander County, of which we have any account, were the families of Joshua, Abraham and Thomas Flannary, John McElmurry and Joseph Standlee. Their settlements were on the Mississippi River just south of Sante Fe. They established there a "Station Fort," and the same was known far and near as McElmurry's Station. Governor John Reynolds, in his history of Illinois, speaks of this station fort; and in another place, he gives the names of the early settlers, in southern Illinois, whose claims to land had been investigated, allowed and confirmed. When these settlements were first made we have not been able to ascertain. All we know is that they were made prior to September 3, 1783, the date of our treaty of peace with Great Britain at the close of our war of the Revolution; and it may be that they were made prior to the treaty of February 10, 1763, when the French surrendered the Illinois country to Great Britain. In other words, these settlements may have been made under grants of some kind from the French prior to 1763, or under grants from England prior to 1783. Our government was required by the fifth clause of the treaty of 1783 to protect all settlers in districts of country surrendered by Great Britain to our government and which had not been in actual arms against it; and as early as 1788, it took steps to secure to such settlers their rights to lands occupied and cultivated by them. The acts of congress of March 3, 1791, and of March 26, 1804, prescribed the course to be pursued by claimants desiring to establish their rights to the lands occupied by them. These acts and certain prior resolutions of 1877, limited the quantity to be claimed by heads of families, their heirs or assigns, to four hundred acres, and claimants were required to show *actual occupancy and cultivation* as conditions to the allowance and confirmation of their claims. The act of March 26, 1804, established a land office at Kaskaskia, and the claimants were required to present their claims and the evidences thereof to the register and receiver of public moneys there, who were called commissioners, and who investigated each claim and allowed or disallowed the same, and reported all claims to congress for confirmation or for such modification of their action as congress might choose to make.

We do not know how many claims were presented to the commissioners for lands in what is now our county; but of those presented, six were allowed and confirmed, as follows:

To John McElmurry, Jr., Claims 680 and 681, Surveys 525 and 526; to Joseph Standlee, Claim 2564, Survey 684; to Abraham Flannary, or his heirs, Claim 531, Survey 529; to Joshua Flannary, or his heirs, Claim 530, Survey 528; to Thomas Flannary, or his heirs, Claim 529, Survey 527. These four hundred acre tracts of land will be found outlined on all of our county maps.

By the treaty of Paris of February 10, 1763, Spain acquired from France and from Great Britain all their claims to territory west of the Mississippi River, and she retained all that territory until October 1, 1800, when she ceded it to France, and the latter on the 30th day of April, 1803, ceded it to the United States. Under the French and Spanish a number of settlements had been made on the Mississippi River in what is now the state of Missouri; at New Madrid, at Cape Girardeau, at Ste. Genevieve and at some other points. As late as 1795, Gayoso de Lemos built a station fort at what is now Bird's Point. He had come there to meet a delegation from Kentucky and probably to confer with representatives of General James Wilkinson.

Stone Court House at Thebes, Erected in 1845

Court House at Cairo, 1864

He was the governor of Louisiana and was endeavoring to further Spanish interests in this part of the country. Houck's ("Missouri.") It will be remembered that during our war of the Revolution, General George Rogers Clark and many other public men of that time feared that Spain, being so near us on the west, might make some movement or other which would require strong measures to counteract or resist, as is shown by General Clark's letter of September 23, 1779, given elsewhere. We cite these historical facts to show that there were no doubt very early settlements on the easterly side of the Mississippi River from the mouth of the Ohio to Cahokia, besides those at or near Kaskaskia.

When we recall the fact that Kaskaskia was settled as early as 1700 and that John Laws' operations twenty years later extended up the river as far as Fort Chartres where he expended probably a million of dollars in the construction of the fort and other works and that hundreds of slaves were carried there and to other points to do the work required by their various enterprises, we cease to regard it as strange to find that settlements were made here and there on the river but of such small extent as to have well nigh escaped the searches of his torians. It is very interesting indeed to read of the extent and nature of the intercourse between the French settlements in upper and lower Louisiana, from the years 1700 to 1763, when the French relinquished to Great Britain well nigh everything they had in America. The Mississippi was the great bond or rather the artery between the Canadians and Louisiana French. All north of the Ohio was Canadian and all south Louisianaian.

This is quite a digression; but it is given here as evidence of the earliest settlements on our side of the Mississippi and near to the mouth of the Ohio, and also strengthening what has been said elsewhere about Juchereau's settlement here in 1702.

Returning to the Flannarys, we have only to add that the following letter from the General Land Office shows the source of our information regarding those four hundred acre tracts of land.

General Land Office,
Washington, D. C., April 5, 1909.

Miss Edna L. Stone,
Stoneleigh Court, Washington, D. C.
Madam:—

In response to your recent personal inquiry, I have to advise you that the claims Nos. 681, 680, 529, 530, 531 and 2564, mentioned in the letter of Mr. John M. Lansden to you, which letter is herewith returned to you, were confirmed by the act of Congress of May 1, 1810 (2 Stat., 607), to the persons whose names are shown on the surveys thereof on the plats of Tps. 16 S., Rgs. 2 and 3 W., photolithographic copies of which were secured by you. These claims are embraced in the statement of claims in virtue of improvements affirmed by Commissioners Michael Jones and E. Backus, register and receiver at Kaskaskia, said statement being dated December 31, 1809. This statement may be found in printed form in the American State Papers, Duff Green's Edition, Vol. 2, pages 132 to 134, inclusive. This statement does not contain a transcript of the evidence introduced in support of these claims, but in their general report, found on page 102, said Commissioners state:

There are four species of claims upon which, as commissioners for this district, we have had to act, . . . 3d. Those founded on the having actually improved and cultivated land in the country, under a supposed grant of the same by court or commandant. . . .

Relating to these claims, there have been passed by Congress the following laws, viz: . . . A law of the 3d of March, 1791, ordaining, thirdly, that where lands have been actually improved and cultivated, under a supposed grant of the same, by any commandant or court claiming authority to make such grant, the Governor of said territory be empowered to confirm to the person who made such improvements, their heirs and assigns, the land supposed to have been granted as aforesaid, or such parts as he may judge reasonable, not exceeding to any one person four hundred acres.

. . . .

III. Of Improvement Rights.

From the proclamation of Colonel Todd, the first commandant under Virginia after the conquest, and from the many proofs we have had of verbal permission having been given by him and succeeding commandants to individuals to settle on the public lands, we have raised the presumption, that in all cases where we have found an actual improvement and cultivation upon vacant lands, it was made under what the law of 1791 terms a "supposed grant;" as we fully believe every individual settling upon such lands thought himself authorized to do so by the then existing authority of the country.

In our own construction of the term "actual improvement and cultivation," we have supposed it to mean, not a mere marking or deadening of trees; but the actual raising of a crop or crops, it being in our opinion a necessary proof of an intention to make a permanent establishment; and we have allowed but one improvement claim to the same man, in which we are clearly warranted by the 4th section of the law of 1791.

For the authority of the said commissioners to make report on these claims, reference is had to the act of March 26, 1804 (2 Stat., 277), and the act of March 3, 1805 (2 Stat., 343). Very respectfully,

Fred Dennett,
Commissioner.

CHAPTER XXVII

HARRELL'S SHORT HISTORY AND "THE HISTORY OF ALEXANDER, UNION AND PULASKI COUNTIES"

IN the preface I have spoken of the short history of Cairo, written by Moses B. Harrell in 1864, and constituting the first fifty pages of a city directory of that year. It is an excellent history, condensed, of course, almost to the utmost limit.

Mr. Harrell was perhaps the only man in Cairo who could turn out such a piece of work in the short time he speaks of, and at the same time touch almost everything and that, too, in so connected a way as to impress one with the thought that the work of arrangement and condensation was his most difficult task. He had come to Cairo at a very early day, namely, July 8, 1848. He had been engaged almost all the time in newspaper work. His fine memory, his extensive knowledge of all local matters, his large store of general information, his easy use of his pen, and his fluent style, enabled him to do with ease what other men could do only with much effort and much time.

Let me introduce here a short account of the coming of the Harrells to Cairo, given me by Mr. Wm. Harrell a month or two before his death, which occurred here, August 11, 1909, in his eighty-ninth year. There were four brothers, Bailey S., born in 1809; William, in 1820; Isaac L., in 1826; and Moses B., in 1828. The family had come from Virginia to Boone County, Kentucky. They removed across the river to Cleves, Ohio. Bailey made a trip down the river in 1833. He did not stop here. There was nothing here then but one or two cabins. William passed Cairo about the 25th of December, 1837, on a flatboat, about 18x85 feet, loaded with apples, cider, flour and meats, and a great many other kinds of produce. There were five men abroad. The boat and cargo belonged to Nathan Sidwell, of Cincinnati. They stopped a few days at Caseyville on account of the ice. They did not stop at Cairo, but went on south to New Orleans, where they remained a week. He went back as far as Vicksburg on a steamboat and from thence coasted along the river for a considerable distance, when he took another steamboat and went on to Cleves, where he arrived about the first of April, 1838. The old log hotel at the point and some shanty houses were all that he saw here at that time. A few acres of ground were cleared in the vicinity of the hotel. The river was high enough so that he could get a pretty good view of the place. On his trip to New Orleans they met three or four steamboats, one the Diana, one the Shippen and another the Hutson, all of them sidewheel boats. Bailey and he made a trip to New Orleans in 1840, on the Steamer General Morgan, on which they shipped a large number of sheep. They sold out very soon and returned on the steamboat Southerner. In the same year he made another trip on a flatboat owned by Scott Harrison, the father of President Harrison. They did not go further than Natchez, where they sold their shipment.

In the fall of 1841, Bailey and he came here with two flatboats, cattle in one, and a general assortment of produce in the other. They sold all they had to Howard and Hylan, who built the first levees here. Their cargoes brought them about two thousand dollars. Six hundred of it was paid in the bills of the Cairo bank at Kaskaskia. On the way home, on a steamboat, they heard that the bank was "a little shaky," and a man told them if they would discount the bills at six per cent he would take them. They did so and had been home not more than a week or two when they heard that the bank had failed. This was the bank authorized by the act of January 9, 1818, entitled, "An Act to incorporate the City and Bank of Cairo," granted to John G. Comegys and others by the legislature of Illinois territory. At this time a frame addition had been built to the old hotel, and the building was full of people, who came to buy real estate. Straw beds had to be put down on the floor, so great was the number of people here. There were twelve or fifteen houses north of the hotel, up along the Ohio, and a few houses back of the levee. The company had put up a few good houses. There was a foundry and a machine shop, large buildings, and two saw-mills. There were three stores, one of which was occupied by Captain Falls. Howard & Hylan had built the Ohio levee, a small levee from the point up to Eighteenth or Nineteenth Street. They also built a cross levee, or part of one, extending from Seventeenth or Eighteenth Street out westward near the office building of the Trustees. He described somewhat fully the large warehouse, or stone foundation for a warehouse, built on or adjoining the levee near Fourth Street and extending back to or near Commercial Avenue. He said it seemed impossible to purchase real estate in Cairo then. He heard some men talking about the matter, and one said to the other that he had offered $20,000.00 for some property, *but the fools would not sell.* At that time the steamboats, or almost all of them, ran between the island and the Misissippi levee and came around close to the point. Lawyer Gass went over on the island and endeavored to make a settlement, that is, to acquire a pre-emption right, but the water came up so high around him that the calking came out of his boat and he had to leave the place. Bailey and he came again in 1844. They remained here after that time. There was little change in the town from 1841 to 1844. In 1841, Howard and Hylan were anxious to buy all they had. Their men, who were chiefly Irishmen, were almost starving and they needed supplies for them. Everything was going to wreck and people leaving the town, so much so that the population was reduced to two or three hundred. There was a strip of land cleared, extending back a quarter of a mile from the Ohio side, probably not so far around the saw-mills, the foundry and the machine shops. Beyond the cleared places, the timber was generally very heavy.

The other history spoken of in the preface is the "History of Alexander, Union, and Pulaski Counties," published in 1883. It is a large work, containing nine hundred and twenty-six double column pages. The three parts of it relating to Alexander County and Cairo, were written by Mr. H. C. Bradsby, also a resident of Cairo many years. Like Harrell, he was a newspaper man and a good writer. He was connected with the Cairo newspapers many years, and was a correspondent of a number of the newspapers in the large cities. His part of this large book was well done.

While it might be allowable to reproduce in this book almost all of what is contained in Harrell's short history, because of the very few copies in the city, the other one, in any view, would have to be left as an independent history up to the time of its publication, twenty-seven years ago. With this history in so many libraries and families in the city, I have felt it my duty to omit many matters and things which are set forth and often very fully presented in this large history of those three counties. One will find that it presents many matters not referred to by me at all, or only very briefly. I have omitted them or merely mentioned them, because found in the other book; and hence persons who may not find herein what they are searching for should refer to the other work. It is to be regretted that it has nothing that can properly be called an index. Its value is greatly impaired by this omission. It would be much more useful, at least for us here, were those parts of it relating to Cairo and Alexander County brought together and, with a good index, bound in a separate volume. Two hundred and ten pages of the book relate to Cairo, two hundred and thirteen to Union County, fifty-seven to Alexander County, eighty-six to Pulaski County, sixty to biographical sketches of Cairo men, and two hundred and seventy-eight to biographical sketches of men of Union and Pulaski Counties.

To facilitate reference to this large volume of 1883, I have given further on a list of the citizens of Cairo whose biographical sketches appear therein.

CHAPTER XXVIII

OTHER RAILROADS—ILLINOIS CENTRAL AND THEBES RAILROAD BRIDGES —THE CAIRO HARBOR AND BACON ROCK—FERRIES: CAIRO'S NEED OF

RAILROAD COMPANIES—Cairo has become quite a railroad center. The roads together with the rivers reaching southward and northeastward and northwestward give us transportation facilities equaled by very few other places in the country. The railroads centering here are of such importance to the city as to require a short account of each one of the same. Besides the Illinois Central Railroad, so fully spoken of elsewhere, we have now the Mobile & Ohio Railroad, the Cleveland, Cincinnati, Chicago & St. Louis Railway or Railroad, commonly called the Big Four, and across the river in Missouri, the St. Louis, Iron Mountain & Southern Railway and the St. Louis, Southwestern Railway. Besides these we have the Cairo & Thebes Railroad which will soon be completed and put in operation.

The Illinois Central Railroad Company was chartered February 10, 1851, and its construction extended through the years 1852 to 1855. There has been some little controversy as to when the Illinois Central Railroad was finished and first opened for operation. In the "Cairo City Times" (volume I number 17, edited by William A. Hacker and Len. G. Faxon) of September 20, 1854, is found a communication from William P. Burrall, the president of the railroad company, to the executive committee of the company, dated at Chicago, September 7, 1854, in which he says that

> Since the 1st instant I passed in company with our chief engineer, R. B. Mason, Esq., over the entire line between Cairo and La Salle, 308 miles, and find its condition to be as follows:—The track is laid and ready for operation from Cairo north 88 miles, with the exception of the bridge over the Big Muddy River, 60 miles north of Cairo. . . . From La Salle south the track is laid 134 miles, with the exception of a piece of 10 miles north of Decatur. . . . The limit work to complete the main line is, therefore, the track laying over the space between the point 88 miles north of Cairo and that of 134 miles north of La Salle, which is a distance of 86 miles, at the end of which is a strong party now employed in laying track and approaching each other. When they meet the entire main line will be ready for operation. . . . North of La Salle our track is laid 16 miles to the Aurora junction. From that junction to Freeport, 60 miles, the grading is now substantially ready for the track. . . . I think, therefore, that on the 1st day of January next we may expect the whole line, from Cairo to Galena to be ready for operation by regular trains, giving us by Chicago and Galena road, a line from Chicago to Galena, by Aurora extension road a line from Cairo to Chicago, and by the Ohio and Mississippi road a line from St. Louis to Cairo. . . . On the Chicago branch the track is laid from Chicago south 143 miles and the grading is complete, ready for the rails for a further distance of 33 miles. . . . We have, therefore, now actually laid 409 miles of track.

The first time-table of the Cairo trains appears in a number of issues of the said newspaper in which it is stated that on and after "Monday, January 8th (1855), passenger trains will leave Cairo at six o'clock A. M., connecting at Sandoval with the Ohio and Mississippi Railroad for St. Louis; at Decatur with the Great Western Railroad for Springfield, Jacksonville and Naples; at Bloomington with the Chicago and Mississippi Railroad; at La Salle with the Rock Island Railroad for Rock Island and Davenport; and at Mendota with the Chicago and Aurora Railroad for Chicago."

There are a number of other references in this newspaper to work on the Central, but I can find no statement as to the time when trains were first in operation over the whole line of about 710 miles of railroad. It must have been as late as the first of October, 1855, when the road was fully completed and in operation. As late as August 1, 1855, the travel to Chicago was still by the main line to Mendota and thence by what is now the C. B. & Q. See "Times" of August 8, 1855.

The Mobile & Ohio Railroad Company was chartered by the legislature of Alabama February 3, 1848, by the legislature of Mississippi February 17th, by the legislature of Tennessee February 28th, and admitted to the state of Kentucky on the terms of its Alabama charter by an act of the legislature of Kentucky of February 26th, of that year. The road was finished to Columbus, Kentucky, twenty miles south of Cairo, two or three or more years after the Central was finished to Cairo. The congressional land grant of September 20, 1850, was to aid in building a railroad from Chicago to Mobile, and these two railroad companies, the Central and the Mobile & Ohio, were to receive and did receive the benefits of that act; and there was, therefore, some two or three years before the Civil War a railroad from Chicago to Mobile, with the exception of the gap of twenty miles between Cairo and Columbus. These two companies for many years filled this gap, as it were, by the running of steamboats for transfer purposes between those two cities.

On the 28th day of February, 1870, the legislature of Kentucky incorporated the Kentucky & Tennessee Railroad Company, the incorporators of which were A. B. Safford, Rufus P. Robbins, George W. Eggleston, Jacob L. Martin and Thomas H. Corbett; and on the 5th day of June, 1872, this company agreed with the Mobile & Ohio Railroad Company to build the road and to lease the same in perpetuity to the latter company. The Kentucky company was authorized to build a road from a point opposite Cairo to some point on the Mobile & Ohio between Columbus and the Tennessee line, and was authorized by its charter to make a lease in perpetuity to any other railroad company. This arrangement having been made, the Mobile & Ohio Company, in the year 1880, constructed a road from what is now South Columbus, a mile or a mile and a half east of Columbus, up to what is now called East Cairo. From that time until 1886, it operated its road as a single line from Mobile to East Cairo.

A little before or after this, the Illinois Central acquired a road or two constituting a line from New Orleans to Jackson, Tennessee, and thereupon extended the line from Jackson to Fillmore, some two or three miles south of East Cairo and at the place where Fort Holt existed during the war. The company operated its car ferryboat between Fillmore and its railroad incline just south of its present elevator in Cairo until a few years afterwards, when the company extended the road to a point in Kentucky almost opposite the elevator and the ferriage was thereafter almost directly across the river. The Mobile & Ohio Railroad ferried its cars directly across the river to the incline of the Wabash Railway Company below the Halliday Hotel for a number of years.

THE CAIRO & ST. LOUIS RAILROAD COMPANY was chartered February 16, 1865, the incorporators of which were Samuel Staats Taylor, William P. Halliday, Isham N. Haynie, Sharon Tyndale, John Thomas, William H. Logan, and Tilman B. Cantrell. The company found it very difficult to arrange for the construction of its road, and when it did so it was only for a narrow gauge road or one of the width of three feet only. Its construction was not undertaken until 1871, and the road not finished and put in operation until early in 1875. It was operated with varying degrees of success until proceedings were instituted in the United States court at Springfield to foreclose the mortgage given to secure the bonds issued to obtain moneys to build the road. The property was sold under the decree entered in the suit and purchased on behalf of the bond-holders, and on the 1st day of June, 1881, a new company, called the St. Louis & Cairo Railroad Company, was organized, and to it all the property was conveyed. That company continued to operate the road up to the 1st day of February, 1886, when it leased its property to the Mobile & Ohio Railroad Company for the period of forty-five years from January 1, 1886, on the condition that the lessee would reconstruct the road and make it of the standard gauge and pay certain annual rentals. The lessee entered upon the work at once and completed it at a comparatively early day, and from that time to this, the latter company has operated the road, to the great advantage, it is said, of both the lessor and the lessee. It may be here remarked that in all the experiences of railroads the world over, few have gone through more trying or distressing times than those gone through by the Mobile & Ohio Railroad Company during the war. The road had been bonded, as were and are almost all roads, and consequently it came out of the war burdened with a very heavy indebtedness. It was like beginning existence over again but under the most trying circumstances. About this time, it was taken charge of by Mr. William Butler Duncan, of New York, whose very careful and wise management brought the road steadily up from its depressed condition to one of prosperity and assurances for the future. He has been with it continuously, and it is due largely to his judicious management that the road now occupies a position so favorable and so sharply in contrast with what it was when he took hold of it. His extension of the road from Cairo to St. Louis, by obtaining the lease upon the St. Louis & Cairo Railroad, has proven to have been one of the most fortunate things which could have been done for either company, and shows a foresight and judgment of a high order in railroad management. A number of years ago, the Hon. E. L. Russell, of Mobile, became the president of the company and among the many other things inaugurated and carried out by him, may be mentioned the discontinuance of the very expensive method of the transfer of the company's cars across the Ohio River by railroad ferryboats. One of the large boats used for such purposes was the railroad ferryboat the W. Butler Duncan. The company's ferriage contract was with the Big Four people or their predecessors, and the expense to the company was large. In place of this, Mr. Russell found it best to effect an arrangement with the Illinois Central Railroad Company by which the company's trains could have the use of the Illinois Central bridge; and it is now understood that this arrangement for the joint use of the bridge is to continue until the expiration of the lease of the St. Louis & Cairo Railroad to the Mobile & Ohio Railroad Company, which occurs January 1, 1931. It is said that this change in the method of transfer across the Ohio River has been of a very great advantage to the company, giving as it does an all rail line from Mobile to the great city of St. Louis. Mr. Russell seems to have had full faith in the propriety of making this change; and I am sure it has been a matter of great pleasure to him that the results have so clearly proven the wisdom of the new method. One cannot overestimate the importance in railroad building or management of lessening the cost of getting over or across a great river. It is said this particular railroad bridge has fully justified its construction. More than this might no doubt be said.

After the acquisition by the Illinois Central Railroad Company of the roads south of the Ohio River and extending to New Orleans, the connection of Chicago with Mobile changed to a connection of that city with New Orleans; and on the other hand, by the lease above mentioned, Mobile has become connected with St. Louis. These cross connections can hardly be said to have been in the contemplation of the great land grant of September 20, 1850, in aid of a railroad from Chicago to Mobile.

The Cairo & Vincennes Railroad Company was incorporated by our legislature March 6, 1867, the incorporators of which were, among others: D. Hurd, William P. Halliday, Isham N. Haynie, S. Staats Taylor, D. T. Linegar, N. R. Casey, Green B. Raum, A. J. Kuykendall, George Mertz, John M. Crebs, Walter L. Mayo, John W. Mitchell, William R. Wilkinson, Robert Mack, Samuel Hess, Aaron Shaw, James Fackney, Jesse B. Watts, W. W. McDowell and B. Rathbone. The work of constructing the road began in 1868, but after considerable grading had been done at different places along the line, the work was suspended and was not resumed until certain important county and city bond matters had been rearranged because of forfeitures. The road was completed and through trains began to be operated in January, 1873. For a number of years the company occupied Commercial Avenue, throughout its whole length, with its tracks, under an ordinance approved by John H. Oberly, April 16, 1869. This use of Commercial Avenue continued until a change was made by a city ordinance approved on the 23d day of March, 1886. This road and company followed about the same course as that shown above in the case of the Cairo & St. Louis Railroad. It led to the organization of the Cairo, Vincennes & Chicago Railroad Company, which leased the property to the Wabash Railway Company; and after a number of years the property came into the hands of the Big Four people, that is, the Cleveland, Cincinnati, Chicago & St. Louis Railway Company, which is now operating the road and its northern extensions from Vincennes or from St. Francisville just this side. This road, like the Cairo & St. Louis, was in the hands of receivers for a considerable time during foreclosure proceedings. For a part of the time the same was under the management of Mr. Samuel P. Wheeler, whom most of us well remember as having resided here very many years until his removal to Springfield. He had been the general solicitor of the company almost from its organization. He came from New York to Mound City in 1859, and from thence to Cairo in 1865. He was one of the ablest lawyers we have ever had, and was with all the members of his family very highly esteemed. About the same time, that is, in the earlier days of this railroad, there were also here Mr. Roswell Miller, who has long been one of the leading railroad men of the country, and Mr. Thomas W. Fitch, the auditor of the company, now doing business in New York City, and whose place of residence is Summit, New Jersey. The writer spent a week at his home a year or two ago, and can never forget the many kindnesses then shown him by Mr. and Mrs. Fitch.

I cannot say much concerning the roads across the river in Missouri, save that the Iron Mountain road is the somewhat distant successor of the old Cairo & Fulton Railroad, which away back in the early fifties received a land grant very similar to that of September 20, 1850. The road has quite a history, and there were many acts of congress passed in regard to the same. The Cotton Belt Railroad is now a well-known road constructed many years ago, running from Bird's Point down through the cities of Malden, Paragould, Pine Bluff to Texarkana in Arkansas on the Texas and Arkansas line. It now extends on into Texas and with its branches, reaches Sherman, Fort Worth, Gatesville and other points in that state. The Cairo & Fulton road was to extend from Bird's Point through Poplar Bluff and Little Rock on to Fulton, Hempstead County, Arkansas.

The Cairo & Thebes Railroad Company was organized on the 25th day of September, 1905. It seems to have arisen out of a desire to obtain better facilities for trade between Cairo and the southeastern part of Missouri. While the Illinois Central had a direct connection with Thebes, there was a pretty general feeling that it was very desirable to have another and a more direct connection with Thebes and the excellent means there afforded by the great bridge for crossing the Mississippi River. The company set out at once and vigorously to prosecute the work of constructing the road. It is said that many difficulties were encountered which were not expected. Then, too, the financial depression of 1907 seems to have almost arrested the work, which has now been resumed with a good prospect of its early completion. Just how, or by whom, or in what connection the road will be operated, has not been as yet made known; but those in charge of the enterprise will no doubt adopt such plans and measures as will make its operation of mutual advantage to both the company and the people it was intended to serve. It is to be regretted that the company desired and that the public authorities allowed the tracks to extend into the city as far as Washington Avenue, where the passenger and freight stations have been established. The advantage of reaching the avenue over that of stopping at Walnut Street is not apparent. Both are in the center of the city. Had they come no further than Walnut Street, every legitimate purpose of the company would have been fully served, and on the other hand other public interests would not have suffered. The city authorities seem to have forgotten they had valuable public property in that block. A railroad yard with its smoking engines and its noise close to a public library will certainly not suffer by the presence of the library; but that the library will escape detriment from the presence of the railroad yard is scarcely believable. It is greatly to be hoped that the effect will not be so bad as many of us fear. It was a great thing, of course, to have the block filled, but balancing the advantages and disadvantages, the library property will be found to be on the losing side.

The present officers of the company are: Egbert A. Smith, president; J. Bruce Magee, vice-president; Edward G. Pink, treasurer; and William S. Dewey, secretary and general attorney. President Smith has worked hard and faithfully to secure the construction of this road for the city, as he has for every other enterprise which seemed to be for its interests.

It is now less than eighty-five years since the first railroad was constructed in the United States or in America. How many have been built within that time and when and the mileage of each and the approximate cost thereof, might be ascertained, I suppose, by a very laborious search of books and records. A full and accurate account of the moneys expended, of bonds issued and sold, of municipal aid sought and obtained, of land grants made, of interest accrued and paid and not paid, of losses to persons at home and abroad, to municipalities, to corporations, to states and to nation, would require more volumes than President Eliot's five-foot bookshelf would hold.

Seventy-five years of the general business experience of our country would be interesting could it be condensed into a volume or two and proper space given to what has been lost and won in what the world persists in calling *gambling in railroad stocks.*

But over against the vast sums of money which have been expended and lost in railroad building and wrecking in the United States, we must place the wonderful development of the country which never could have come about but for the existence of the railroads. Whatever may be said the one way or the other, no chapter in our country's financial or business history will present so many features of wisdom and folly as will the chapter relating to our railroads since the first construction of the same began.

Illinois Central Railroad Bridge.—It is said that after the southern line of the Illinois Central Railroad Company had been extended up to the Ohio River, there arose and continued for a number of years something in the nature of a controversy in the company's board of directors as to whether they should undertake to build a bridge across the Ohio River. It is further said that on the Kentucky side, the company sought to ascertain whether a solid rock foundation for piers could be found at such depths as would justify the undertaking. Nothing was done, however, until engineering skill had assured the company that it was entirely practicable to rest the piers on the sand in the river bed. This view of the matter could hardly have been in the nature of an experiment; although in the case of the great Eads bridge at St. Louis, and we suppose of all bridges up to that time, solid rock foundations had always been sought and reached. Following the construction of the Cairo bridge, with its piers so supported, came next the construction of the great Memphis bridge across the Mississippi.

The company, on the 29th day of March, 1886, obtained from the Kentucky legislature a charter for the construction of a bridge across the Ohio River, either by the Illinois Central Railroad Company or by the Chicago, St. Louis & New Orleans Railroad Company, or by both. All of the bridge, except the Illinois approach was constructed by or in the name of the latter company, and the Illinois approach by the Illinois company. The first bill passed was vetoed by the governor because it permitted the bridge to be built from any point in Ballard County, Kentucky, to the Illinois shore. The act approved by him required its construction from the Kentucky side to the Illinois side at any point below the mouth of Cache River. The bridge was begun in 1886, and opened for traffic October 29, 1889. It is called a truss bridge and is of the length of a little less than a mile across the river proper; and each of the approaches is about one and a half miles in length. The whole length of the bridge is a little under four miles. The original cost of the bridge was three to four millions of dollars; but the filling of the approaches added largely to the cost of the structure, and at this time the outlay for the same as it now stands has probably been four to five millions. Bridges may be built across the Ohio

Illinois Central Bridge, Ohio River

OPENING
OF THE
THEBES BRIDGE
MAY 25TH 1905

River in conformity to the acts of congress of December 17, 1872, and February 14, 1883, but under the supervision of the secretary of war. For bridges across the Mississippi special acts must be obtained from congress. Owing to the great height to which the Ohio River rises at Cairo at certain times in the year, this bridge was required to be fifty-three feet above high-water mark, which is considerably above the level of the adjoining lands. This made necessary the very long approaches. The piers, therefore, of the bridge are of great height from the caissons to the floor of the bridge. The width of the first two river spans on the Illinois side is five hundred and eighteen feet each, and of the other seven spans four hundred feet each. From the bottom of the lowest foundation of any pier to the level of the steel work on the two longest spans is two hundred and fifty feet (or exactly 248.94 feet). From low-water mark to the floor of the bridge it is 104.42 feet. (See cut of river bed elsewhere.)

THE THEBES BRIDGE.—Mr. Charles S. Clarke, the vice-president and general manager of the Missouri Pacific Railway Company, very kindly furnished me with one of the beautiful souvenirs of the opening of this noted bridge, and from the same I have taken the first cut of the four of the bridge. The second one is of the whole bridge taken from the upper Illinois side; the third one of the east or Illinois approach, and the fourth is of the Missouri or west approach. Mr. Clarke is now one of the board of directors of the bridge company. Ground was broken on July 8, 1902, and the first train passed over the bridge, going, from east to west, April 18, 1905.

The Southern Illinois and Missouri Bridge Company was incorporated under the laws of the state of Illinois on the 6th day of December, 1900. On the 26th day of January, 1901, the act passed by congress, authorizing the construction of the bridge, was duly approved by the President.

The bridge is a steel, double-track structure, cantilever type, of five spans, the cantilever or channel span being 671 feet long, each of the other spans being 521 feet long.

The approaches to the bridge are of concrete. The western approach consists of six 65-foot arches and one of 100 feet. The eastern approach consists of five 65-foot arches.

The entire length of the bridge, including the concrete approaches on either side, is 3,910 feet.

Nine hundred and forty-five thousand cubic feet of concrete were used in the construction of the approaches, and twenty-seven million pounds of steel were required for the superstructure.

The spans are sixty-five feet in the clear above high water, 108 feet above low water.

The distance from extreme bottom of channel pier, which rests on bed rock, to the top of the cord, is 231 feet.

THE CAIRO HARBOR.—The Cairo harbor is one of the very best on either of the two rivers. It is never difficult for the largest vessels navigating the rivers to move about therein with comparative ease. The only collision of any consequence that has taken place in the harbor within the last thirty or forty years was that between the railroad ferryboat W. Butler Duncan and the steamboat The New South. The New South was backing out from the landing opposite Sixth Street and the Duncan was going down the river keeping well over to the Kentucky side, when The New South struck her a severe blow and caused her to sink. The matter was litigated a long time and The New South found to be at fault.

On the 1st day of November, 1909, the river gauge showed the stage of water to be eight and a half feet, a low stage, and at my request Mr. William McHale, now deceased, on that day ascertained for me the depths of the water in the river from Second to Thirty-eighth Streets. The depths were taken some little distance from the Illinois shore, then about the middle of the channel, and then considerably further over toward the Kentucky shore. The width of the river examined must have been a quarter of a mile, at least, and probably more. The depths, counting from the Illinois side toward Kentucky, were as follows:

Opposite 2d Street, 40, 36 and 24 feet; 6th Street, 43, 34 and 30 feet; 10th Street, 37, 32 and 24 feet; 14th Street, 34, 28 and 20 feet; 18th Street, 24, 32 and 18 feet; 22d Street, 32, 26 and 20 feet; 26th Street, 34, 26 and 18 feet; 30th Street, 37, 27 and 15 feet; 34th Street, 37, 32 and 15 feet; and 38th Street, 40, 25 and 12 feet.

It is observed that at every point, except one, 18th Street, the deepest water is on the Illinois side and that much the lowest water is on the Kentucky side, and yet deep enough at that low stage of water to serve all ordinary purposes. We have but to add to the above figures the readings on the gauge to get the depths at any stage of water. It will be seen that when the gauge reads 30 to 50 feet, the depths will range from 55 to 80 feet, on the Illinois side. The contour of the bed of the river, as seen in the cut of the railroad bridge elsewhere found, establishes the substantial correctness of the above figures.

Bacon Rock.—In July, 1874, Captain R. W. Dugan removed from the mouth of the Ohio River a dangerous obstruction to navigation, called up to that time *Bacon Rock*. The "Cairo Bulletin" of July 11th of that year states that the government had contracted with Captain Dugan for the removal of the obstruction. It was a conglomerate and was removed by blasting, which continued for some weeks. Many of our citizens will remember hearing the loud explosions that occurred during the progress of the work. It was out some little distance from the Illinois shore and but a short distance north of the strongly marked water-line between the waters of the two rivers. Divers were sent down to explore the base of the obstruction and to see its character and extent. They found it to be of the length of about seventy feet and of the width of thirty, and its general shape to be that of a whale's back. We have no account of the character or nature of the surrounding materials, nor how far in any direction the conglomerated material extended, nor of its connection, if any, with other or kindred formations. At that time the river was very low and a considerable portion of the rock exposed. This occurred very seldom. To persons standing on the Ohio levee, the appearance of the rock rising out of the water was quite a sight. This is due somewhat to the fact of the apparent absence in our vicinity of anything like rock formations. It was a dangerous obstruction, but only in low-water times. It is a little remarkable that the government did not take hold of the matter long before that time. Large pieces of the blasted materials were brought up to Cairo and the "Cairo Bulletin" of August 2, 1874, noted the fact that Mr. Jewett Wilcox, of the St. Charles Hotel, now the Halliday, forwarded some large pieces to the Southern Normal School at Carbondale.

In the "Cairo City Times" of Wednesday, February 21, 1855, we find the following:

> Last Sunday, the H. D. Bacon, from St. Louis to New Orleans, struck *"that rock"* a few yards from the wreck of the Grand Tower and sunk within three or four minutes. After her boiler deck was under water she floated down about a mile and is now lying on the Kentucky side. A number of yawls, skiffs, etc., started immediately for her, and as soon as the steamer Graham could get up steam she went down and took off the passengers, who numbered some twenty-five or thirty. No lives were lost. She was heavily laden with whiskey, flour, cattle, etc. She went down so suddenly that there was no time to cut the cattle loose and they were all drowned. Her cargo consisted of freight taken from the James Robb, which sunk near Cape Girardeau last Friday. The Bacon was insured in three different offices in St. Louis, for $15,000. We could learn nothing in relation to the insurance on her freight.

In the same column of the "Times" the arrival and departure of steamboats are given, and it seems that the Bacon arrived from St. Louis on Sunday, the 18th of February, and departed the same day for New Orleans, but did not get further than the obstruction to which it gave its name.

FERRIES: CAIRO'S NEED OF.—By the act of February 21, 1845, Bryan Shannessy and Patrick Smith were authorized to establish and maintain a ferry across the Ohio River, "and land passengers, baggage and stock at the depot at Cairo." The fourth and last section of this act repealed the act to incorporate the Great Western Railway Company, approved March 6, 1843. Why this repealing act was placed in the ferry act, I do not know. By the act of February 14, 1861, the ferry act of 1845 was amended. We know very little as to what was done under the act.

The Cairo City Ferry Company was chartered February 13, 1857, the incorporators of which were Samuel Staats Taylor, Ninian W. Edwards, John A. McClernand, John A. Logan, Bryan Shannessy and Calvin Dishon. The charter authorized the company to establish and maintain a ferry over the Ohio River to Kentucky and over the Mississippi River to Missouri within three miles of the junction of the two rivers; and the right was made exclusive for ten years. The legislature retained the right to alter, amend or repeal the act as the public good might require, after twenty years. This company, or those persons representing it, have for forty to fifty years done almost all the ferrying we have had.

By an act of March 6, 1867, the Valley Ferry Company was chartered, the incorporators of which were David T. Linegar, Patrick H. Pope, James S. Morris, J. Reed, John Hodges, Alexander H. Irvin and H. Watson Webb. The ferry was to be across the Ohio and Mississippi Rivers to Kentucky and Missouri and within three miles of the junction of the rivers. This company soon after its incorporation began the operation of a ferry here between the three states. Capt. John Hodges seems to have been in charge of their ferryboat, the Rockford, which was brought by him from Metropolis to Cairo in April, 1867. Controversies arose between the two companies concerning exclusive rights of ferriage, and there not being business enough for the two, the Valley Company discontinued its ferry.

A person seeing Cairo so nearly surrounded by the two great wide rivers, would very naturally expect the city to have reasonably good ferries for passage to and from the city and to and from the outlying country districts. As for bridges for other than railroad purposes, that is not to be thought of. So far from our having good ferrying facilities, the rivers have seemed as walls or barriers across which passage could be made only in the most primitive way. We have here within the city eight to ten miles of river frontage, entirely surrounding the city, excepting the rather narrow neck of Illinois land of the width only of something over a mile. We have never had anything like good ferriage facilities. This is due to the difficulties of the situation, that is, to the extreme distance of the rise and the fall of the rivers, and the unstable river shores, especially on the Mississippi. It seems impossible to construct permanent landing-places. Those we have had have been shifted from place to place so that they have never been anything but of the poorest kind. I cannot dwell upon this matter, but desire to say that the absence of good ferrying facilities has been a great and ever-continuing drawback to the prosperity of the city. Perhaps the time has gone by for regaining the ground that might have been gotten and held, had the city been strong enough to do so. Towns of a more or less prosperous growth have grown up near us and have well supplied the people who might have come to Cairo had they been able to get here easily. The city, it seems, has never been able to offer free ferriage; but were it able to do so and to make the approaches reasonably easy and free from danger, our people would be astonished at the local trade which could still be drawn to the city. I have elsewhere referred to local trade as the main support of many of the best cities of the state. The now less useful rivers are the same effective barriers to local trade they have always been. I do not know what the city could now do; but at the earliest practicable time it should, with the hearty co-operation of the people, arrange in some way to reduce to the minimum the expense of reaching the city from across the two rivers. If it could be made free, it would be far better.

CHAPTER XXIX

CAIRO BANKS—BUILDING AND LOAN ASSOCIATIONS—THE CUSTOM HOUSE—THE HALLIDAY HOTEL—THE SPRINGFIELD BLOCK—THE COURT OF COMMON PLEAS—ALEXANDER M. JENKINS

CAIRO BANKS.—On the 2d day of March, 1839, the legislature granted to the Cairo City & Canal Company the right to use the banking privileges granted by the Territorial Act of January 9, 1818, to the City and Bank of Cairo, the tenth section of which required the banking business of the corporation to be transacted at Kaskaskia; hence, the reason why the bank bills represented on the opposite page were issued at Kaskaskia. Bills were issued from time to time and to such an extent that the legislature thought best to interfere; and on March 4, 1843, it repealed the act of January 9, 1818, so far as it related to banking.

The City Bank of Cairo was organized in the year 1858 under the general banking law of the state, by Mr. Lotus Niles, of Springfield. Of this bank Mr. James C. Smith was president and Mr. Alfred B. Safford was the cashier. It carried on its business in Cairo up to the time of the organization of the City National Bank.

The Planters Bank of Cairo was organized under the same general banking act in the same year and by a Mr. Trimble, of McCracken County, Kentucky. It did business here for a few years and seems to have been succeeded by the First National Bank of Cairo.

The First National Bank of Cairo was organized on the 24th day of July, 1863, under the National Banking Act of February 25, 1863. The first board of directors were John W. Trover, Daniel Hurd, Robert W. Miller, and the president, cashier and teller were John W. Trover, Daniel Hurd and William H. Morris. The bank continued to do business for many years; but its experience was somewhat varied, and its stock depreciating, Capt. William P. Halliday acquired the controlling interest in the stock, and after having carried on the business of the bank for a year or two, found it best to discontinue the institution.

The City National Bank of Cairo was organized February 7, 1865, under the same National Banking Act. The first board of directors were William P. Halliday, Samuel B. Halliday, A. B. Safford, S. Staats Taylor, and G. D. Williamson. The first of these became its president, the second its vice-president, and the third its cashier. They continued in these positions up to the times of their respective deaths. This bank continued to transact a large business in Cairo for over forty years, and until merged into the present First Bank & Trust Company.

The Enterprise (Savings) Bank of Cairo was chartered March 3, 1869, the incorporators of which were William P. Halliday, William H. Green, and Alfred B. Safford. It was conducted chiefly as a savings bank and did a large business until its merger, with the City National, into the First Bank & Trust Company.

The First Bank & Trust Company was organized on the 2d day of January, 1907, and is the successor of the City National Bank and the Enterprise (Savings) Bank above mentioned. The present officers and board of directors of the bank are as follows: John S. Aisthorpe, president; Henry S. Candee, Walter H. Wood, and William P. Halliday, vice-presidents; H. R. Aisthorpe, cashier and secretary; Thomas P. Cotter, Reed Green, H. E. Halliday, Andrew Lohr, Peter Saup, Paul G. Schuh and Thomas J. Smyth.

There was no other bank in Cairo besides the two National Banks from the year 1865 until the year 1875, when Thomas Lewis, long a resident of Cairo, organized the Alexander County Bank under the state banking law of February 15, 1851, and only a short time before that act was repealed by the adoption of the state constitution of 1870. The officers of that bank were P. C. Canady, president; Henry Wells, vice-president; Thomas Lewis, cashier; and Thomas J. Kerth, assistant cashier. About one year later, the bank was reorganized, with Judge Fredolin Bross as president; Peter Neff as vice-president; Henry Wells, cashier; and Thomas J. Kerth, assistant cashier. It continued its banking business until July 1, 1887, when it was changed to a national bank, and called the Alexander County National Bank. Its present board of directors and officers are as follows: Edward A. Buder, president; Charles Feuchter, vice-president; James H. Galligan, cashier; Charles O. Patier, Calvin V. Neff, William Kluge, N. B. Thistlewood, David S. Lansden, George Parsons, and Thomas Boyd. In the year 1889, the Alexander County Savings Bank was organized. Its officers and directors are those of the Alexander County National Bank.

The Cairo National Bank was organized in August, 1903, under the same national banking act. It has done a prosperous business and seems to have fully justified its establishment. The present board of directors and the officers are as follows: Egbert A. Smith, president; W. F. Grinstead, vice-president; E. E. Cox, cashier; and Q. E. Beckwith, assistant cashier; Daniel Hartman, M. J. Howley, E. J. Pink, T. J. Kerth, P. I. Nassauer, Oscar L. Herbert, and F. Teichman.

Building and Loan Associations.—These associations might properly be called institutions of the city. That would be saying a great deal for them, but not more than they deserve. The evil of waste and prodigality is all prevailing. Anything that tends to teach frugality, economy, saving, thrift, should stand in great favor. Anything that tends to afford means or methods by which homes may be procured is certainly a very great thing in any civilized community. By means of these associations hundreds of homes have been secured in

Cairo-Kaskaskia Bank Bills

Custom House and Postoffice

our city; and besides this, the invaluable lesson of economy has been widely and strikingly taught.

The Cairo Building and Loan Association was established in the year 1880. Esq. Alfred Comings has been at its head all the time, and to him, more than to any other man, its success has been due. It is the pioneer society and should have the credit accorded all pioneers. I would be glad to give some statistics here, all of which would be strongly confirmatory of what I have said of the above associations. The present officers and directors of this association are: Henry Hasenjager, president; Wm. Schatz, vice-president; A. Comings, secretary; J. H. Galligan, treasurer; P. A. Conant, L. H. Myers, W. P. Greaney, John C. Gholson, Charles F. Miller, and Paul G. Schuh.

The Citizens' Building and Loan Association was established in the year 1887. Its present officers and directors are: E. A. Buder, president; M. J. Howley, vice-president; J. C. Crowley, secretary; E. E. Cox, treasurer; John W. C. Fry, E. G. Pink, G. T. Carnes, Charles Feuchter, and G. P. Crabtree.

The Home Building and Loan Association was established in 1890. Its present officers and directors are: Alexander Wilson, president; C. R. Stuart, vice-president; E. C. Halliday, secretary; George T. Carnes, treasurer; Miles Fred'k Gilbert, attorney; E. J. Stuart, G. P. Crabtree, C. B. Dewey, and T. L. Pulley.

The Central Building and Loan Association was established in 1899. Its present officers and directors are: J. B. Magee, president; C. S. Carey, vice-president; Edward L. Gilbert, secretary; Thomas J. Kerth, treasurer; William S. Dewey, attorney; Frank Thomas, H. S. Antrim, T. J. Pryor, A. T. DeBaun, A. J. Rees, W. P. June, and Ira Hastings.

The Greater Cairo Building and Loan Association was established in the year 1905. Its present officers and directors are: Paul G. Schuh, president; Bernard McManus, Jr., vice-president; Matt C. Metzger, secretary; Wm. P. Greaney, treasurer; Frank Ferguson, Walter Denzel, Reed Green, Ed. Hall, and Peter Day.

The capital stock allowed to each of the above five associations is $1,000,000.

The Custom House.—Cairo was made a port of delivery by the act of congress of August 3, 1854. It was discontinued August 31, 1885, and re-established September 4, 1890. The following named persons were surveyors of the port in the order named:

Col. John S. Hacker, 1854 to 1858; Levi L. Lightner, 1858 to 1861; Col. James C. Sloo, in 1861; Daniel Arter, 1861 to 1869; George Fisher, 1869 to 1885; John F. Rector, 1890 to 1894; Frank

Cassiday, 1894 to 1898; Thomas C. Elliott, 1899, to the present time. Cairo was never a port of entry. We suppose no place or point in southern Illinois was made a port of *entry* since the old act of February 28, 1799, the 14th section of which created a collection district, called the District of Massac. The territory embraced in the district included the lands "relinquished and ceded to the United States by the Indian nations at the treaty of Greenville, August 3, 1795, lying near the confluence of the Ohio and Mississippi Rivers, and on the north side thereof and from the mouth of the Ohio to the eastern side of the river Wabash." Fort Massac, or such other place as the President might designate, was made the *sole port of entry* for the district, and a collector was to be appointed who should reside thereat. Ports of entry are those ports established by law at which imported goods are fully described, that is, entered in and according to the form prescribed therefor. The entries are made by the owner of the vessel, a consignee of the goods, or other properly authorized person. Ports of delivery are those at which goods may be delivered and unloaded after having passed ports of entry.

On the 18th day of February, 1859, the legislature ceded to the United States jurisdiction over block thirty-nine in the city for the construction of a building for a United States court, a post-office and a custom house. The Trustees of the Cairo City Property, on the 28th day of April, 1866, conveyed to the United States the said block, bounded by Washington Avenue, Poplar Street and Fourteenth and Fifteenth Streets; and in the years 1868 to 1871, various appropriations, amounting to one hundred and eighty-four thousand dollars, were made by congress for the erection of the present building on the block. The entire cost of the property is said to have been as much as two hundred and twenty-five thousand dollars. The government began the erection of the building in the year 1869, and the same was completed in the year 1872. The building was planned by the supervising architect at Washington, Mr. A. B. Mullett, who, when he came here and saw that the main floor of the structure was to be on a level with the then existing levees, ordered so much of the stone courses of the walls removed as would bring it down to the present grade. This recalls the fact that long before that time, it was the desire of a great many persons to have all the buildings of a permanent character erected to the grade of the levees; and I believe the city established such a grade. Winter's block building on the corner of Seventh Street and Commercial Avenue, now the property of Mr. Edward A. Buder, was built to this high grade; but it appearing that a lower grade was likely to come into general use, especially as the city government favored the lower grade, the owners of the building at very great expense lowered the same to the present grade. The beginning of the construction of the custom house building to the high grade was about the last important attempt made in the city to build to that grade. The fine property of the Trustees on the east side of Washington Avenue, between Eighteenth and Nineteenth Streets, is another example of high-grade construction. It is a matter of great regret that this high-grade method of building and street filling could not have been carried out. I do not suppose the city will ever return to it. Too much has been done and too much money expended to allow of the change. As heretofore stated a number of times, it was a question of money, but Supervising Architect Mullett could not have regarded the matter of expense as important in the case of the Cairo custom house. As elsewhere remarked, the government could not accept the transfer of the block above mentioned and erect thereon an expensive building without the strongest assurances as to the title of the Trustees. This was perhaps the most important instance in which the Trustees undertook to show a title back to the government itself, or as we generally say, a perfect title. Mr. James C. Rankin was for a time superintendent of the construction of the custom house. He was succeeded by Mr. George Sease. Although forty years ago many of our citizens will remember those gentlemen.

THE HALLIDAY HOTEL.—The "Commercial Gazetteer of the Ohio River," with a map of the river from Pittsburg to Cairo, and published at Indianapolis in 1861, by G. W. Hawes, contains quite a long list of Cairo advertisers, a few of whom only can be mentioned. There is not a word in any of its four hundred and forty-six pages to indicate that the war had then opened. The following are some of the advertising cards in the book: I. & W. Adler, clothing; John Antrim, wholesale and retail dealer in clothing, hats, caps, etc.; Atlantic Hotel, F. E. Wilson, 15 Ohio Levee; Blelock & Co., booksellers; H. H. Candee and M. S. Gilbert, wholesale grocers, forwarding and commission merchants, No. 1 Springfield Block; John Cheek, hay, corn, oats, etc.; The City Bank of Cairo, A. B. Safford, cashier; Charles Galigher & Co., Cairo City Mills, Premium Eagle Flour; Graham, Halliday & Co., forwarding merchants and wharfboat proprietors; Hamilton & Riley, dry goods; Planters Bank, Bank Building, Ohio Levee, Walter Hyslop, cashier; G. F. Rasor, International Saloon, Ohio Levee; A. B. Safford, general insurance agent and cashier of City Bank of Cairo; Smyth & Brother, wholesale and retail grocers; J. Q. Stancil, butcher and meat market, Commercial Avenue; A. F. & J. B. Taylor, wholesale grocers, commission and forwarding merchants, No. 9 Springfield Block; Trover & Miller, forwarding commission and grocery merchants, No. 11 Ohio Levee; F. Vincent, wholesale and retail dealer in produce, provisions, etc., 18 Ohio Levee; I. Walder & Co., wholesale and retail dealers in clothing; Williamson, Haynes & Co., commission and forwarding merchants on their new wharfboat; Wilson & Co., forwarding and commission merchants, No. 4 Springfield Block; William Winter, hardware, Commercial Avenue, and restaurant, Ohio Levee.

Among the numerous hotels named are the St. Charles, the Lamothe House, the Louisiana House, the Virginia Hotel and the Central House. The St. Charles Hotel twenty years afterwards became the Halliday Hotel.

I may speak of the Halliday Hotel as one doing and having long done great credit to our city. Were almost everything else in the city made to correspond with it, we would have a fine city of fifty to one hundred thousand people. If we could "grow twenty feet high and swell out in proportion," in the language of Dickens, so as to correspond with the hotel, the Illinois Central Railroad bridge would be at the center of the city instead of being on its north boundary line.

On the 9th day of February, 1857, the legislature of the state incorporated the Cairo City Hotel Company. The incorporators were Ninian W. Edwards, John T. Smith, John E. Ousley, Hiram Walker, William Butler, Daniel Hannon, Thomas Ragsdale, James C. Conkling, John Cook, Philip Wineman, Thomas H. Campbell, Benjamin F. Edwards, W. J. Stephens and Abraham Williams. The hotel was in the course of construction when the inundation of June 12, 1858, occurred; and the water coming in all around the foundation and reaching a large storage of lime, the effect was such as to cause a part of one of the walls to fall. The work went on at once after the subsidence of the water, and the hotel was finished and named the St. Charles and opened about the first of January, 1859. It was conducted by different persons from time to time, under leases from its owners; and like almost everything else in Cairo, had a somewhat varied experience, especially after the war closed. During the war its business was up to its full capacity all the time. Afterwards it shared largely in the general shrinkage which took place. The ownership of the hotel changed but two or three times, and in the year 1880, Halliday Brothers acquired the property, and so improved it as to make it almost a new building. Its name was changed to "The Halliday" and opened under the new management July 1, 1881. New improvements were made from time to time, until in 1908, the very large addition was made on the south side, greatly enlarging its capacity and rendering it in every respect a first-class modern hotel. The property now belongs to the estate of Capt. Halliday, and with the Gayoso Hotel, of Memphis, has been under the management of Mr. L. P. Parker for a number of years. Mr. Parker has long stood in the front rank of hotel managers. If the reader will turn to Chapter XXX and read the account there given by a Frenchman he will see what the Frenchman said of the hotel about the time it was first opened. The Frenchman's language is extravagantly commendatory; but the fact is that this hotel from the day it was first opened to the present time has been far above the character and standing of almost any hotel anywhere in the country in a city not larger than ours.

THE SPRINGFIELD BLOCK.—This block when it first received its name extended from 6th to 8th Streets and fronted on what is now Ohio Street. The buildings were erected by Springfield men, including Governor Joel A. Matteson, and almost all of the hotel men above mentioned. Governor Matteson erected the City National Bank building, changed considerably in the last few years and now the property of the First Bank & Trust Company. The rooms on the second and third floors of this building were occupied during the war by many distinguished army men. General Grant, while here in 1861, occupied the second-floor rooms on the north side of the building, rooms now constituting the law offices of the Hon. Miles Frederick Gilbert. In that pamphlet of 105 pages, entitled "Past, Present and Future of Cairo," frequently referred to herein, those Springfield men set forth the fact that they had invested three to four hundred thousand dollars in Cairo in the purchase of lots and in the making of improvements thereon, and claiming that for the damages done them by the inundation of June 12, 1858, the Trustees, or the Illinois Central Railroad Company, or both together, should reimburse them.

THE COURT OF COMMON PLEAS.—This court was established by our legislature for the city by the act of February 6, 1855. It was amended in many important particulars by the act of February 14, 1859. It had jurisdiction to the amount of fifty thousand dollars and of all crimes except those of treason and murder. Its first judge, the Hon. Isham N. Haynie, was appointed by Governor Joel A. Matteson February 13, 1856, and again January 8, 1857. The law provided that in 1861, and every six years thereafter, the judge of the court should be elected by the people of the city. Judge John H. Mulkey was elected judge of the court June 12, 1861, and again June 27, 1867. He held the office until it was abolished by the act of February 19, 1869. H. Watson Webb was appointed prosecuting attorney of the court April 24, 1856, and served in that capacity until June 26, 1867, when Fountain E. Albright was elected to succeed him.

Judge Haynie was born at Dover, Tennessee, November 18, 1824. He worked on a farm to obtain means to study law and was licensed in 1846. He was a lieutenant in the 6th Illinois volunteers in the Mexican War. On his return, he resumed the practice in 1849, and in 1850, was elected to the legislature from Marion County. He graduated from the Kentucky law school at Louisville, in 1852. In 1860 he was presidential elector on the Douglas ticket for this congressional district. In 1861 he became colonel of the 48th regiment Illinois volunteers. He was at the battles of Fort Donelson and Shiloh, and was severely wounded in the latter battle. In 1862, he was defeated for congress by the Hon. William J. Allen, and the same year he was made brigadier general in the Union army. He resumed the practice of the law at Cairo in 1864, and in 1865 was appointed by Governor Oglesby, adjutant general of the state. He died while holding that office at Springfield in November, 1868. He was the senior member of the firm of Haynie, Marshall & Gilbert for a while before his removal to Springfield, the junior member having been the Hon. William B. Gilbert, who has been somewhat longer than the writer a member of the Cairo bar. Most of the above facts regarding General Haynie are taken from the "Historical Encyclopedia of Illinois."

Judge Mulkey lived many years in Cairo and was well known,

not only here in southern Illinois, but all over the state. He stood very high as a lawyer and jurist, and few such men have a better established reputation with the bar and the judges of our courts throughout Illinois. Quite a full biographical sketch of Judge Mulkey is found in volume eleven of the publications of the Illinois Historical Society, now in our public library and owned by a number of our citizens. There was more of politics in the repeal of the act creating the court of common pleas than there was of good to the city. It may be here stated that many real-estate titles in the city are based on judgments of this court.

Alexander M. Jenkins.—I have delayed speaking of Judge Alexander M. Jenkins, in the hope of obtaining answers to my letters to a number of persons for information concerning him, but for some reason the letters seem to have been neglected, and hence the appearance here of what I have relating to this somewhat noted man, who held our circuit court here during the years 1859-1863. The following very brief account of him I have taken from the "Historical Encyclopedia of Illinois":

> Alexander M. Jenkins, Lieutenant Governor (1834-36), came to Illinois in his youth and located in Jackson County, being for a time a resident of Brownsville, the first county seat of Jackson County, where he was engaged in trade. Later he studied law and became eminent in his profession in southern Illinois. In 1830, Mr. Jenkins was elected representative in the seventh general assembly; was re-elected in 1832, serving during his second term as speaker of the house; and took part the latter year in the Black Hawk War as captain of a company. In 1834, Mr. Jenkins was elected lieutenant governor at the same time with Governor Duncan, though on an opposing ticket, but resigned, in 1836, to become President of the first Illinois Central Railroad Company, which was chartered that year. The charter of the road was surrendered in 1837, when the state had in contemplation the policy of building a system of roads at its own expense. For a time he was Receiver of Public Moneys in the Land Office at Edwardsville, and in 1847, was elected to the State Constitutional Convention of that year. Other positions held by him include that of Justice of the circut court for the third judicial circuit, to which he was elected in 1859, and re-elected in 1861, but died in office February 13, 1864. Mr. Jenkins was the uncle of General John A. Logan, who read law with him after his return from the Mexican War.

I may here say that it has been stated a number of times that Judge Jenkins, as far back as 1832 or 1833, when in our state legislature, proposed the survey of a line for a railroad from the mouth of the Ohio River to Peru on the Illinois River. I have tried very hard to verify this statement or claim but have been unable to do so. It is said that the records of the proceedings of the legislature of that early day are so incomplete or so lack fullness that the mere absence of anything therein relating to such action on his part would not at all justify the conclusion that no such action had been taken.

We have already seen how Jenkins and Holbrook were associated together in 1836 and subsequent years in efforts to build a city here and an Illinois Central Railroad. We know very little of their mutual dealings either as individuals or as representatives of their companies;

A. M. Jenkins.

U. S. Battleship Concord, Cairo Harbor

but our circuit court records here show that Joel Manning, as assignee of Jenkins, on the 15th day of November, 1845, sued Darius B. Holbrook on a promissory note under seal and in the words and figures following:

"Alton, Ill., May 26, 1837.

For value received, I promise to pay to the order of Alexander M. Jenkins the sum of Twenty Thousand Dollars in three years from date, at the Branch of the State Bank of Illinois at Alton.

$20,000. D. B. Holbrook (Seal)"

On the back of the note is the following: "Received city of N. York June, 1839, one hundred and fifty dollars ($150) on the within note;" and also the following endorsement: "For value received of him I hereby make over and assign and transfer the within note to Joel Manning, May 20th, 1840. A. M. Jenkins." On the back of the summons is the following return: "Served by reading the same to D. B. Holbrook on the 23rd day of November, 1845. A. W. Anderson, Sheriff, Alex., Ill."

Judgment was recovered on this note for the amount due thereon; and it seems there was also a foreclosure suit based on a mortgage given to secure the note, and the mortgaged property sold and the proceeds of the sale credited on the note. This entry of credit consists of four or five lines and seems to be in the handwriting of Col. S. Staats Taylor; but he was not here at that early day, and the entry seems to have been made a long time ago.

When the writer came to Cairo many years ago he frequently heard Judge Jenkins spoken of as a very able man. The Hon. Monroe C. Crawford, of Jonesboro, I am sure, would speak in the highest terms of Judge Jenkins, both as to his excellency as a man and his great ability as a judge.

Besides Judge Jenkins, there were a number of other men of strong character who were associated with Jenkins, Holbrook, Breese, Gilbert and others, of whom I have not been able to say more than a word. There were David J. Baker, senior, Thomas Swanwick, Anthony Olney, Kenneth McKenzie, John M. Krum, who became and was for a long time a very prominent lawyer and citizen of St. Louis, and a number of others whom I would like to mention more or less fully. Joel Manning, above mentioned, was long a resident of Brownsville, quite a celebrated old town of Jackson County, Illinois, the site of which is now in a cornfield. Manning was secretary of the Illinois & Michigan Canal Board and was in public life many years. With reference to the Holbrook-Jenkins note above described, we may say that the promoters of the Cairo of 1836 were active business men and took hold of their enterprise with great energy; and it is no wonder that some of them became heavily involved. The outlook was so bright and promising that they ventured quite too much in many cases.

CHAPTER XXX

EXTRACTS FROM BOOKS, PAMPHLETS AND LETTERS

THERE has never been, in all probability, a time since the year 1750 when there was not a small settlement of some kind here, a house or cabin or two or three of them and now and then more of them. They were erected, of course, on timbers high enough to be above the spring floods. Trees of all kinds and suitable for every purpose were near by, and to the hardy woodsmen it was easy enough to construct suitable cabins to shelter their families and the few strangers who called at the point on their voyages up and down the rivers. There were no doubt small cleared patches of ground where were grown a few vegetables for their use; and it is not quite out of the question to suppose that some of them threw up small embankments to protect their possessions from the usual high water which they well knew must be expected at almost any time in the early part of the year. We must not forget that in those very early days there were adventurers enough, considering the state of the country. We must not suppose that there were none except those who kept accounts or journals of their travels. For every one who kept a diary or journal and preserved it for the use of himself and others, there were five or ten who scarcely thought of posterity or how they might hand their names down to coming generations. Even some of the voyagers of high degree and standing seem to have noted very few of the wonders they saw. We read their very meager accounts, and get just enough to cause us to want more. But it was the new world and everything was wild and strange, and there were few and slight chances to examine carefully and write fully about what they saw or heard in the ever changing scenes the rivers afforded. We may speak of a single instance:

General Clark's letter, found elsewhere, of September 23, 1778, tells of his having to keep an armed boat at the point to watch both the English and the Spanish. His men were no doubt encamped on the point, and near by them were very probably woodsmen, hunters and others, although Clark said the ground was too low for the establishment of a secure and permanent fort.

The travelers were almost always voyagers, and most of them were upon the Ohio, in the later times. The river reached into the Alleganies and near the regions of settled habitations. The landing on the Ohio side here was always good. There was no trouble with low water and seldom with high water, except for a month or two in the spring time. The current was always near to this shore, and whatever kind of boat or vessel was used, it naturally came closer to the landing on the Ohio side bewteen the two rivers. The little cutting of the banks here has always been on our side, and for a hundred years or more none at all has been known on the Kentucky shore just opposite our city.

Can we in any better way use a reasonable number of pages than by giving a page or two from the travelers and writers who passed along the rivers as well before as after there was a settlement here?

From Fortesque Coming's "Sketches of a Tour of the Western Country"; 1807-1809.—Of this Englishman, Thwaites speaks in his preface as follows in "Early Western Travels," Vol. IV, pages 9-10: "In plain dispassionate style he has given us a picture of American life in the west, at the beginning of the nineteenth century, that for clear-cut outlines and fidelity of representation has the effect of a series of photographic representations. In this consists the value of the book for students of American history. We miss entirely those evidences of amused tolerance and superficial criticisms that characterize so many English books of his day, recounting travels in the United States—a state of mind sometimes developing into strong prejudice and evident distaste, which has made Dickens' 'American Notes' a caricature of conditions in the new country."

He and a friend left Pittsburg July 18, 1807, in a "battau or flat bottomed skiff, twenty feet long, very light, and the stern sheets roofted with very thin boards, high enough to sit under with ease and long enough to shelter them when extended on the benches for repose, should they be benighted occasionally on the river, with a side curtain of tow cloth as a screen for either the sun or the night air." They spent many months at different points along the river and did not reach this part of the country until the month of May, 1808. The following is from pages 226-278 of Vol. IV:

"May 22nd, at day break we gladly cast off, and at a mile below Wilkinsonville, turned to the left into a long reach in a S. W. and S. direction, where in nine miles farther, the river gradually narrows to a half a mile wide, and the current is one fourth stronger than above. Three miles lower we saw a cabin and small clearing on the right shore, apparently abandoned, five miles below which we landed in the skiff, and purchased some fowls, eggs, and milk, at a solitary but pleasant settlement on the right just below Cash Island. It is occupied by one Petit with his family, who stopped here to make a crop or two previous to his descending the Mississippi, according to his intentions on some future day.

"Two miles and a half from hence, we left Cash River, a fine harbor for boats, about thirty yards wide at its mouth, on the right, and from hence we had a pleasant and cheerful view down the river, and a S. S. E. direction five miles to the Mississippi.

"First on the right just below the mouth of Cash River, M'Mullin's pleasant settlement, and a little lower a cabin occupied by a tenant who labored for him. A ship at anchor close to the right shore, three miles lower down, enlivened the view, which was closed below by Colonel Bird's flourishing settlement on the south bank of the Mississippi.

"We soon passed and spoke the ship, which was the Rufus King, Captain Clarke, receiving a cargo of tobacco, &c., by boats down the river from Kentucky, and intended to proceed in about a week, on a voyage to Baltimore. It was now a year since she was built at Marietta, and she had got no further yet.

" At noon we entered the Mississippi flowing from east above, to east by south below the conflux of the Ohio, which differs considerably from its general course of from north to south.

"We had thought the water very turbid, but it was clear in comparison of the Mississippi, and the two rivers being distinctly marked three or four miles after their junction. The Ohio carried us out almost into the middle of the Mississippi, so that I was almost deceived into thinking that the latter river ran to the westward instead of to the eastward; by the time, however, that we were near mid-channel the Mississippi had gained the ascendancy, and we were forced to eastward with increased velocity, its current being more rapid than that of the Ohio. We soon lost sight of the labyrinth of waters formed by the conflux of the two rivers, and quickly got into a single channel, assuming gradually its usual southerly direction. We now began to look for Fort Jefferson, marked in Mr. Cramer's Navigator as just above Mayfield Creek on the left, but not seeing either we supposed they were concealed by island No. 1 acting as a screen to them."

In the "Recollections of the Last Ten Years in the Valley of the Mississippi," by the Rev. Thomas Flint, which is a collection of letters by the author to the Rev. James Flint, we find in letter twelve, pp. 85 and 86, the following:

" The 28th of April, 1816, we came in sight of what had long been the subject of our conversation, our inquiries and curiosity, the far-famed Mississippi . . . turning the point, and your eye catches the vast Mississippi rolling down her mass of turbid waters, which seem, compared with the limpid and greenish colored waters of the Ohio, to be almost a milky whiteness. . . . A speculation was gotten up to form a great city at the Delta, and in fact they raised a few houses upon piles of wood. The houses were inundated and when we were there, ' they kept the town,' as the boatmen phrase it, in a vast flat boat, a hundred feet in length, in which there were families, liquor shops, drunken men and women and all the miserable appendages to such a place. To render the solitude of the pathless forest on the opposite shore more dismal, there is one gloomy looking house there."

Long's Expedition to the Rocky Mountains; 1819.—This expedition was sent out by the Hon. John C. Calhoun, the Secretary of War under President Andrew Jackson. The men who went were Major S. H.

Long, of the United States Corps of Topographical Engineers, John Riddle and William Baldwin, both of Pennsylvania, Thomas Say, Augustus E. Jessup, Titian Ramsey Beale, James D. Graham, of Virginia, and William H. Swift, of Massachusetts. They were well equipped and had delayed their start somewhat for better preparation. In this respect, they were in better condition than were Lewis and Clark, fourteen years before. Calhoun's instructions to them showed he had in mind the honor and success which came to Jefferson in sending out the expedition he did to the Oregon coast.

They left Pittsburg on the steamboat Western Engineer, May 3, 1819, and reached the mouth of the Ohio River the afternoon of May 30. Edwin James, botanist and geologist of the expedition, wrote the account of the journey and of the work accomplished, and the same makes four volumes of Thwaites' "Early Western Travels," beginning with Vol. XIV.

Major Stephen Harriman Long, whose name was given to one of the high peaks of the Rocky Mountains, Long's Peak, 14,000 feet high, was the father of Henry C. Long, who was for many years the chief engineer of the Cairo City Property management and also an engineer here for the Illinois Central Railroad Company. He prepared the very valuable topographical map of Cairo, dated July 2, 1850, which shows the whole face of the point as it existed when the Holbrook people turned over the abandoned city to the Trustees of the Cairo City Property. This was almost a year before Col. Samuel Staats Taylor came here, which was April 15, 1851. A photograph copy of Long's topographical map, made from the original now on file in the War Department at Washington, is found on another page.

Major S. H. Long had become Col. Long before the year 1850, and we find that in that year he caused a very full and complete survey to be made of this place and its immediate vicinity. The work was done under his direction and supervision but by his son, Henry C. Long, who addressed his report to "Col. Long, U. S. Top'l Engineer, Supt. Western R. Improvements, &c, Louisville, Kentucky." The report is dated at Louisville, September 2, 1850, and Col. Long submitted the same to Messrs. Davis and Taylor, Trustees of the Cairo City Property, City of New York, by a letter dated at Louisville, September 4, 1850. A part of the report is found in Chapter VIII.

James describes fully their journey down the Ohio. Nearly every city, town, village and hamlet comes in for its proper share of attention, getting just about what every one would suppose it ought to have. On pages 84 and 85, we read as follows:

"On the 30th, we arrived at a point a little above the mouth of Cash river, where a town has been laid out, called *America*. It is on the north bank of the Ohio, about eleven miles from the Mississippi, and occupies the first heights on the former, secure from an inundation of both rivers, (If we except a small area three and a half miles below, where there are three Indian mounds, situated on a tract containing about half an acre above high-water mark.) The land on both sides of the Ohio, below this place, is subject to be overflowed to various depth, from six to fourteen feet in time of floods; and on the south side, the flat lands extend four or five miles above. The aspect of the country, in and about the town, is rolling or moderately hilly, being the commencement of the high lands between the two rivers; but below it, however, the land is flat, having the character of the low bottoms of the Ohio. The growth is principally cottonwood, sycamore, walnut, hickory, maple, oak, &c. The soil is first-rate, and well suited to cultivation. Here follows quite an account of America and the adjacent country, in which it is said, 'This position may be considered as the head of constant navigation for the Mississippi.')" . . . "In the afternoon of the 30th (May, 1819), we arrived at the mouth of the Ohio river.

"This beautiful river has a course of one thousand and thirty-three miles, through a country surpassed in fertility of soil by none in the United States. Except in high floods, its water is transparent, its current gentle and nearly uniform. For more than half of its course, its banks are high and its bed gravelly.

"The confluence of the Ohio and Mississippi is in latitude 37° 22′ 9″ north, according to the observations of Mr. Ellicott, and in longitude 88° 50′ 42″ west, from Greenwich. The lands about the junction of these two great rivers are low, consisting of recent alluvion, and covered with dense forests. At the time of our journey, the spring floods having subsided in the Ohio, this quiet and gentle river seemed to be at once swallowed up, and lost in the rapid and turbulent current of the Mississippi. Floods of the Mississippi, happening when the Ohio is low, occasion a reflux of the waters of the latter, perceptible at Fort Massac, more than thirty miles above. It is also asserted, that the floods in the Ohio occasion a retardation in the current of the Mississippi, as far up as the Little Chain, ten miles below Cape Girardeau. The navigation of the Mississippi above the mouth of the Ohio, also that of the Ohio, is usually obstructed for a part of the winter by large masses of floating ice. The boatmen observe that soon after the ice from the Ohio enters the Mississippi, it becomes so much heavier by arresting the sands, always mixed with the waters of that river, that it soon sinks to the bottom. After ascending the Mississippi about two miles, we came to an anchor, and went on shore on the eastern side. The forests here are deep and gloomy, swarming with innumerable mosquitoes, and the ground overgrown with enormous nettles. There is no point near the confluence of the Ohio and Mississippi from which a distant prospect can be had. Standing in view of the junction of these magnificent rivers, meeting almost from opposite extremities of the continent, and each impressed with the peculiar character of the regions from which it descends, we seem to imagine ourselves capable of comprehending at one view all that vast region between the summits of the Alleghanies and of the Rocky Mountains, and feel a degree of impatience at finding all our prospects limited by an inconsiderable extent of low muddy bottom lands, and the unrelieved, unvaried gloom of the forest.

"Finding it necessary to renew the packing of the piston in the steam-engine, which operation would require some time, most of the gentlemen of the party were dispersed on shore in pursuit of their respective objects, or engaged in hunting. Deer, turkeys, and beaver are still found in plenty in the low grounds, along both sides of the Mississippi; but the annoyance of the mosquitoes and nettles preventing the necessary caution and silence in approaching the haunts of these animals, our hunting was without success.

"We were gratified to observe many interesting plants, and among them several of the beautiful family of the orchidae, particularly the orchis spectabile, so common in the mountainous parts of New England.

"The progress of our boat against the heavy current of the Mississippi, was of necessity somewhat slow. Steam-boats in ascending are kept as near the shore as the depth of water will admit; and ours often approached so closely as to give such of the party as wished, an opportunity to jump on shore. On the first of June, several gentlemen of the party went on shore, six miles below the settlement of Tyawapatia bottom, and walked up to that place through the woods. They passed several Indian encampments, which appeared to have been recently tenanted. Under one of the wigwams they saw pieces of honeycomb, and several sharpened sticks that had been used to roast meat upon; on a small tree near by was suspended the lower jaw-bone of a bear. Soon after leaving these they came to another similar camp, where they found a Shawanee Indian and his squaw, with four children, the youngest lashed to a piece of board, and leaned against a tree.

"The Indian had recently killed a deer, which they purchased of him for one dollar and fifty cents—one-third more than is usually paid to white hunters. They afterwards met with another encampment, where were several families. These Indians have very little acquaintance with the English language, and appeared reluctant to use the few words they knew. The squaws wore great numbers of trinkets, such as silver arm-bands and large ear-rings. Some of the boys had pieces of lead tied in various parts of the hair. They were encamped near the Mississippi, for the purpose of hunting on the islands. Their village is on Apple Creek, ten miles from Cape Girardeau.

"June 2d. As it was only ten miles to Cape Girardeau, and the progress of the boat extremely tedious, several of the party, taking a small supply of provisions, went on shore, intending to walk to that place.

"About the settlement of Tyawapatia, and near Cape à la Bruche, is a ledge of rocks, stretching across the Mississippi, in a direct line, and in low water forming a serious obstacle to the navigation. These rocks are of limestone, and mark the commencement of the hilly country on the Mississippi. Here the landscape begins to have something of the charm of distant perspective. We seem released from the imprisonment of the deep monotonous forest, and can occasionally overlook the broad hills of Apple Creek, and the Au Vaise, or Muddy river of Illinois, diversified with a few scattered plantations, and some small natural meadows.

"About five miles above Cape Girardeau we found the steam-boat Jefferson, destined for the Missouri. She had been detained some time waiting for castings which were on board the Western Engineer. Several other steam-boats, with stores for the troops about to ascend the Missouri, had entered that river, and were waiting to be overtaken by the Jefferson and the Calhoun, which last we had left at the rapids of the Ohio. On the 3d of June we passed that insular rock in the middle of the Mississippi, called the Grand Tower. It is about one hundred and fifty feet high, and two hundred and fifty in diameter. Between it and the right shore is a channel of about one hundred and fifty yards in width, with a deep and rapid current."

. . . .

"The Grand Tower, from its form and situation, strongly suggests the idea of a work of art. It is not impossible that a bridge may be constructed here, for which this rock shall serve as a pier. The shores, on both sides, are of substantial and permanent rocks, which undoubtedly extend across, forming the bed of the river. It is probable, however, that the ledge of rocks called the Two Chains, extending down to Cape à la Bruche, presents greater facilities for the construction of a bridge than this point, as the high lands there approach nearer the river, and are less broken than in the neighborhood of the Grand Tower. The Ohio would also admit of a bridge at the Chains, which appear to be a continuation of the range of rocks here mentioned, crossing that river fifteen miles above its confluence with the Mississippi. We look forward to the time when these great works will be completed."

Alexander Phillip Maximilian, prince of Wied-Neuwied, made a journey down the Ohio from Pittsburg in the years 1831 and 1832. The following is what he says of his trip from Smithland at the mouth of the Cumberland to the mouth of the Ohio, which he reached March 20, 1832. (Thwaites' "Early Western Travels," Vol. XXII, pp. 200-204.)

"At this place the Paragon took in wood and provisions. Not far from Smithland is the mouth of the Tennessee River, which is said to be more considerable than the Cumberland, and to have a course of 1,200 miles. The little village, Paduca, on the left bank of the Ohio, appeared to have much traffic, and a number of new shops had been built. The Western Pilot of the year 1829 does not mention this place—a proof of its recent origin. From hence we came to the spot where Fort Massac formerly stood, stones of which are still found. We lay to some hundred paces below to take in wood, of which our vessel consumed twelve cords daily. The grass on the banks was already of a bright green colour, and a race of large, long-legged sheep were grazing on it. We lay to for the night.

"Early in the morning of the 20th of March we approached the mouth of the Ohio, where it falls into the Mississippi, 959 miles from Pittsburg, and 129 3-4 miles from St. Louis. The tongue of land on the right, which separates the two rivers, was, like the whole of the country, covered with rich woods, which were partly cleared, and a few houses erected, with an inn and store, and the dwelling of a planter, where we took in wood. In this store we saw, among heaps of skins, that of a black bear, lately killed, of which one of the three cubs, a very comical little beast, had been kept alive. This young bear had on his breast a semicircle of white hair. The settlement, at which we were now, has no other name than Mouth of the Ohio. We now entered the Mississippi, and ascended it, keeping to the left or eastern bank."

The following is from the diary of Mr. Caleb B. Crumb, furnished me by his son, Mr. D. S. Crumb, of St. Louis, through Mr. Robert P. Bates, of Chicago. It is one of the most interesting papers to be found anywhere relating to the early history of this locality. In a letter of October 15, 1909, to Mr. Bates, accompanying the extract, Mr. Crumb says of his father, " That on the trip spoken of, he met, by accident, a Mr. Sanford, the recorder of deeds and the clerk of the Circuit Court at Jackson, the county seat of Cape Girardeau County, Missouri, who became interested in the young fellow, evidently in rather rough company on the raft, and offered him, off hand, a position in his office, and that on his return up the river he stopped over and did some work in his office, and that he then returned home, but that twenty-two years later, after some reverses at Morris and Chicago, he went to Jackson on the invitation of Mr. Sanford; and from that time dates the establishment of the Crumb family in Missouri."

" Mouth of the Ohio River, May 29, 1836.

"I am a raftsman now and can much more skillfully wield the oar than the pen. At this time I ardently desire language to suitably describe this neglected place, which evidently awaits a high destiny.

" While I stand in this southwest corner of the State of Illinois on a beautiful point of land commanding a full view of the majestic ' Father of Waters ' on the right and the limpid Ohio on the left, I seem to see in the place of the two houses which at present constitute this un-named village, a noble and flourishing city, containing thousands of inhabitants, enjoying the unparalleled advantages of an unbounded expanse of fertile country around it and a water communication alike uninterrupted by the parching heat of summer or the fettering cold of winter. I confidently believe that this almost desert point of land is susceptible of greater improvement than any other equal portion of land in America.

" Mr. Bird's is the only family residing here at present. The Union Hotel is a fine building as also the store which is set up about ten feet above the ground on wooden piles. Both buildings are of wood."

From "Eight Months in Illinois," by William Oliver, Newcastle upon Tyne, 1843:

"Before arriving at the mouth, we looked out anxiously for the Father of Waters; but could not, even after we were told he was in sight, distinguish him, until we came very near, and then it was more from the quantity of ice floating on his surface than from any local feature, that we became aware of his presence. This results from the Ohio gradually bending, particularly on the left shore, in the direction of the course of the Mississippi. One might readily suppose it only a bend in the river. The place of junction has the appearance of a large lake; and from the landing-place, at Bird's Point (Cairo), there is a view of seven or eight miles down the Mississippi, and of nearly as much up the Ohio. The Mississippi is here one mile and the Ohio one mile and three quarters, wide.

"As the boat was bound for New Orleans, and I intended to ascend the Mississippi, I was set ashore to wait for some boat which should pass for St. Louis. The appearance of the rivers was grand, but the adjuncts were anything but agreeable. The place had a bad name, and certainly did not seem very captivating or safe, from the number of idle, vagabond-looking boatmen who were strolling about its desolate shores. These were some of the crews of a great number of flat boats or scows, which lined the shores of the Ohio, and who durst not, with such unwieldy things, venture into the ice on the Mississippi. Fortunately, there were five of us travelling the same route, and as we had become in some measure acquainted during our voyage down the Ohio, we felt the more confident. Whilst one watched the luggage, the rest went about to see if they could procure accommodation at any place besides the inn, as it had anything but a good character. We might have saved ourselves the trouble, however, as there was no other dwelling, except a log hut, full of the choppers of wood for the steamers. We walked about the bank till near dark, in the expectation of a boat for St. Louis, or some other town up the Mississippi; but night approached without any boat appearing, and we reluctantly had our things carried to the house, which aspired to the distinction of hotel. Two of our party, however, found one of the owners of a flat boat whom they knew, and got themselves huddled into his boat, amongst a cargo of horses, fowls, Yankee bedposts, &c. I looked down into their den, and how they contrived to stow themselves away at night along with four or five people belonging to the boat, I do not pretend to guess. On going into the bar-room of the inn, I was somewhat surprised to find it very much like the bars of other inns; there were, to be sure, two or three strange outlandish-looking gentry sitting around the stove; but such visions are very frequently met with in all the taverns and boats on those rivers.

. . . .

"The prospect had now become rather dreary. The ice on the Mississippi was so dense, that it was very doubtful if any boat would venture into it; it was certain that no boat, except one of the strongest and most powerful, would make the attempt, and equally certain that there would be some danger and risk of losing the boat.

There was no road from the point in any direction; no such thing dreamed of as a stage, nor so much as a wagon for love or money. Taking it on foot, with the chance of bivouacking in the woods for two or three nights, was the only chance of getting away. To be sure, the landlord had a horse, which he very politely offered us for three times its value, but when he 'obnoxiously made his approaches,' we declined the proffered favour.

"All went on very well till a short time after supper, when, as we were sitting in the bar-room, two men, Kentucks, came in; one of them desiring to write a letter, the other, as ugly a looking fellow as I ever saw, standing by. The scribe had scarcely commenced, when the landlord went up to him, and enquired if he was not the person who had lately insulted him at the wood-yard. The Kentuck denied that he had done anything to insult him. 'Do you not reckon it an insult, sir,' said the landlord, a tall, thin fellow, with an agueish look, and a dreadful cough, 'to moor your flat boat at my wood-yard, where you have no right to bring it, and when I merely mentioned it to you, and cautioned you that you might get your boat staved by some of the steamers which came to the yard for firewood, do you call it no insult to threaten to put a bullet through me? If it had not been that I was alone, sir, I would have pitched you into the river.' 'Well, sir—now, sir,' edged in the little Kentuck, 'hear me, sir, will you, sir, give us the usage of a gentleman, sir—speak to us as one gentleman ought to speak to another, sir.' 'Yes, sir, treat us like gentlemen, sir—treat us genteelly, &c., &c.,' said the tall, ugly Kentuck. After an immense deal of palaver, and the most horrible swearing on both sides, for about a quarter of an hour, the writer tore his letter to pieces, saying he found this was no place for gentlemen, that he would disdain to stay in it any longer, and that he would report the landlord's behaviour, and do all in his power to injure his custom. The brawl had now come to such a height, and there was so much gesticulation, that I looked every moment for the long knives, which are very generally carried, and had serious apprehensions that the fray would end in bloodshed. The Kentucks had been gradually retreating towards the door, on attaining which, they said somewhat I did not hear, but which so enraged our landlord that he rushed after them in the dark, and such a shrieking and shouting arose, that I thought some of them had got stabbed, particularly when one cried murder. There had been no harm done, however, but the affair did not look much better when the landlord came into the bar-room, took up his rifle and carefully examined the priming, and the bar-keeper and he began hastily to load two or three other guns and some pistols. The Kentucks, having been joined by their companions at the boat, now commenced shouting and firing guns in bravado, to see, as I understood, if they could induce their opponents to come out and have a regular battle; our landlord, however, merely went to the door and fired off a pistol, to let them know that he was prepared for them. Nothing more took place, and in a short time all was quiet.

"Next morning (it was Sunday) when I awoke, the sun was just rising over the forest of Kentucky, and through two windows on opposite sides of the room I could lie in my bed and look out on the two mighty rivers, the Ohio glittering in the rays of the sun, and studded with immense quantities of driftwood, and the Father of Waters covered with an almost entire mass of ice, moving steadily along with a sort of mysterious hurtling noise, the dense, dark forest lining the distant shore of each. There was the stillness of death, save that sound proceeding from the ice-clad river, and now and then the report of a gun, rolling on till lost in the woods.

"The boatmen of the numerous flat boats were mostly provided with guns, and shot ducks on the river, or went to the woods to shoot deer, which were in great abundance, particularly on the Kentucky side of the Ohio. After breakfast, the whole forest far and near seemed to be alive with men, cracking and shooting in all directions; its being Sunday, not seeming to influence in the slightest degree these almost lawless denizens of the western wilderness.

"There was, on this day, an occurrence at Bird's Point (Cairo), which I was inclined to suspect would not be frequent. A priest, of what persuasion I know not, happened to be amongst us, who, having intimated a desire to preach, was permitted by the landlord to occupy a room in the hotel. A considerable number, I think about thirty, attended, and it was strange to look round on the rough, weather beaten, and, in some instances, savage-looking faces of the hearers. The preacher delivered a very appropriate and sensible discourse.

"Another day passed in tedious expectation. The frost having become less intense, and the influence of the sun being very considerable, so much so, indeed, that some of the people walked about through the day with their coats off, the ice had grown somewhat thinner. It takes a severe frost to preserve the ice from being thawed before it reaches this latitude, 37° north. This day two boats came down the Mississippi from St. Louis, and their report of the difficulty and danger of coming down made our case almost hopeless. The boats had come in company all the way, the one in the wake of the other, and that which had sailed foremost had not a board left on her paddle wheels. When there was such difficulty in getting down, it may easily be conceived that there would be still greater difficulty in ascending against a current of five or six miles an hour.

"A boat came up the river from New Orleans, for Cincinnati, whose report rather revived us again, as she had been able, though with considerable difficulty, to make way against the ice, which, however, was thinner below than above the junction of the rivers. There was no ice on the Ohio. This boat told us of one which we might expect in a few hours, on her way to St. Louis; but night came and no boat.

"This must be a very unhealthy place, as it lies so low, that when the Mississippi rises in June, from the melting of the snow on the Rocky Mountains, it overflows almost every foot of land, all around far into the forest, and on the Mississippi, at frequent intervals, for about 30 miles up the river. The inn is set upon posts of seven or eight feet high, and is placed on the highest point of ground in the neighborhood, and a sort of gangway, also raised on posts, and cross logs, connects the house and store, at which is the landing place for passengers and goods, when the water is high. The landing is on the Ohio, the Mississippi being nearly a quarter of a mile from the inn.

"To those who do not know the locality, it may appear singular that there is no town on this point—a fact, however, of itself sufficient to indicate the impracticability of such an undertaking. No doubt a town might be built, but the whole point is composed of an alluvion so very friable, that if the Mississippi, in one of his ordinary freaks, were to change his course, the whole affair might be swept away in a few days. Some may think of embankments, but that is a dream, the baseless fabric of a vision. For a long way up the river there is no shore, but a perpendicular mud bank, which is constantly being undermined and tumbled into the river; besides, the whole point is liable to periodical inundation.

"On the afternoon of next day (Christmas) the long-looked-for boat arrived, and we were gratified to hear her captain say he was determined to proceed. So much time, however, was put off in fixing some trees to the bows of the boat, to ward off the ice, that night approached, and the captain thought proper not to venture into the ice till next morning.

"Early next morning we started. A considerable number of people had collected on the extreme point to witness the attempt. It certainly was with some anxiety that we saw the bows of the boat enter the ice, and the shaking and agitation caused by the striking of the paddles on the large pieces, were very considerable; we found, however, that the boat could make way, though slowly, and in a short time nobody seemed to care much about it."

In January, 1849, *Col. Henry L. Webb, of Trinity,* at the mouth of Cache River, or possibly at that time of Cairo, was making up a company for a trip to California by way of New Orleans, Brownsville, Mexico and Arizona, and John Woodhouse Audubon, a son of John James Audubon, the great ornithologist, arranged to join Col. Webb with a large number of men and to proceed from Cairo on their journey. They came down the Ohio from Pittsburg and reached Cairo about February 12th, and New Orleans February 18th. He speaks of Col. Webb and his wife and son, the latter of whom was H. Watson Webb, we suppose. Here is an account of his arrival and short stay at Cairo:

"Large flocks of geese and ducks were seen by us as we made the mouth of the Ohio, and the numbers increased about Cairo. The ice in the Mississippi was running so thick that the 'J. Q. Adams' returned after a fruitless effort to ascend the river. All Cairo was under water, the wharf boat we were put on, an old steamer, could only accommodate thirty-five of our party, so that the other thirty had to be sent to another boat of the same class; the weather was extremely cold, with squalls of snow from the north with a keen wind. There was no plank from our boat to the levee of Cairo, the only part of the city out of water. Will it be wondered at that a slight depression of spirits should for an instant assail me? But when a man has said he will do a thing it must be done if life permits, and in an hour we found ourselves by a red hot stove, the men provided with good berths for the place, cheerfulness restored, and after an hour's chat, while listening to the ever increasing gale outside, we parted for the night to wake cold, but with good appetities even for the horrible fare we had, and as young Kearney Rodgers said, as we looked at the continents of coffee stains, and islands of grease here and there, with lumps of tallow and peaks of frozen butter on our once white table cloth, 'Is it not wonderful what hunger will bring us to?'

"Here we found Col. Webb with his wife and son. I was much pleased with the dignified and ladylike appearance of Mrs. Webb; once she had been very beautiful, now she was greatly worn, and had a melancholy expression, under the circumstances more appropriate than any other, for her husband and only son were about to leave her for certainly eighteen months, and perhaps she was parting with them for the last time. We chatted together in rather a forced conversation, until the 'General Scott' for New Orleans came by, and then went on board, paying eight dollars for each man and five dollars each for Col. Webb's three horses. So much for Cairo; I don't care ever to see it again."

The flood of which Audubon here speaks was the same one written about by Editor Sanders in his "Cairo Delta," of March 20, 1849. It was the same flood that broke through the Mississippi levees, the crevasse in which is seen on the large map of July, 1850.

Lieutenant-Colonel Arthur Cunynghame, in his "Glimpse of the Great Western Republic," London, 1851, says, on pp. 2 and 3:

"My absence from Montreal was to be seven weeks, and I proposed, in the first instance, to travel about a thousand miles west, and to strike the Mississippi well to the northward, in the State of Iowa, to enjoy a few days' grouse shooting; thence to travel about fifteen hundred miles down the Mississippi to New Orleans, visiting any places worthy of attention on the way; passing through the Southern States, to Savannah, Charleston, and returning to Montreal through the most flourishing cities of the Union—Washington, Baltimore, Philadelphia, New York and Boston.

. . . .

"On the evening of the 26th, (October, 1850) we at length arrived at Cairo. Here I found several steamboats, bound both up and down the river, waiting for cargo, and for passengers. I was particularly struck with the neat and cleanly appearance of the 'Lexington,' and as she was advertised to sail on the following day for New Orleans, and her draught of water was considerably less than that of the 'Atlantic,' of which I was by this time heartily tired, I determined to engage a berth on board her. The owner of the 'Atlantic' was exceedingly unwilling that I should do so, assuring me that the 'Lexington' would not leave Cairo for some days, whereas the clerk of that vessel stated that she would certainly depart the following morning. Amongst all these contradictory assertions I was somewhat puzzled, but determined to abandon the 'Altantic'; I therefore sacrificed a few dollars, and obtained an exceedingly good stateroom in my new boat.

"The site of the town of Cairo was purchased many years since by an English company, of which, I understand, the Rothschilds were to be the principal shareholders. Geographically speaking, there is perhaps no position in the whole of the United States which would promise better for the site of a large city than that of Cairo. It is situated at the fork of the Ohio and Mississippi. The navigation for large boats during a low state of water commences here. The mid-winter navigation when the upper waters of both these rivers are choked with ice, is free to this point; from its position, it would naturally be the spot where the great railroads from north to south of the western parts of the United States would traverse. These advantages have, however, been as yet paralyzed by the fearful floods which annually lay all this country under water, frequently rising much above an embankment, here called a 'levee,' which some years since has been thrown around the site of the intended city. The enterprise of the west, however, has now grown to such a pitch, as to overcome all natural obstacles where any chance of gain exists; and this winter the whole site of Cairo city is to be placed in the market, the company having determined, as an inducement to purchasers, to build a dike around it that will bid defiance even to this mighty stream. No doubt, on the subsiding of the waters, that is, during the summer, an unhealthy miasma will invade its precincts. Yet this will not deter thousands from occupying this position, nor will there be any want of persons to supply the places of those who may succumb to its effects; for a species of Californian *yellow fever,* which rages in parts of the United States, never abates in consequence of the innovations of any other; and thus Cairo, though now insignificant, may in a few years excel, both in wealth and in size, as it speedily will in intelligence, its older namesake, Cairo on the Nile, whose propensities to overflow her banks are the same as the Mississippi. Another cause, I was informed, which has retarded Cairo, was that the company, following the English custom, declined to sell the lots, and were only willing to let them on long leases. When so much land and city lots are in the market, property under these restrictions will rarely attract purchasers; but now that they are to be for *bona fide* sale, no doubt they will find purchasers."

From "Guide Americain," by Jules Rouby, Paris, 1859.—There is some error in the date, but the reference is to the Halliday Hotel. The Illinois Central, however, was completed about three or four years before the hotel. The translation is sufficiently literal to show its French origin.

" Cairo, five and a half miles below, in the State of Illinois, is the site of Eden, according to the celebrated English novelist, Charles Dickens. This insignificant village, which comprises as yet only two hundred and fifty to three hundred inhabitants, and whose beginning goes back several years, occupies from the commercial point of view, a situation almost unrivaled in the entire world; thus no mediocre ambition is there cherished. Seated at the confluence of the Ohio and Mississippi, at the apex of the delta formed by those two powerful water-courses, it aspires to become some day an eminent city, a colossal center of progress and of business; in a word, to become the key of all the commerce of the south, west, and northwest of the United States. It is true that this enterprise presents unimaginable difficulties for its realization, and that up to the present time, the town of Cairo has marked its ambitious pretensions only by superhuman efforts to arise from a small estate and to defend its alluvial flats against the two streams which constantly threaten it with inundation and unhealthfulness. These two streams are not, however, invincible, and it is entirely probable that American ability will in the end triumph over them by means of perseverance, labor, and expenditure of money. The results, howsoever obtained by this intrepid ability, permit one to dream for Cairo the brilliant destiny that its incomparable geographical situation promises, and that the indefatigable activity of its populace is preparing. Let us note, in passing, that this tiny village gives itself, as much as possible, anticipatory airs of a great city. Already there are to be seen several buildings for business purposes of a monumental aspect, and an hotel which would honor the finest city of both worlds.

"Cairo will soon become the terminus of the Illinois Central Railway, now in course of construction, and at this point must occur some future day the welding of a continuous transportation route on the perimeter of the great federal republic."

CHAPTER XXXI

FORT JEFFERSON—BIRD'S POINT AND THE BIRDS

TO the people of Cairo, Fort Jefferson has so long been one of their very few places for outings that we are justified in giving a short sketch of it here.

It seems that the matter of the establishment of a fort at or near the mouth of the Ohio River was taken up by General George Rogers Clark and Col. John Todd with Governor Patrick Henry and then with Governor Thomas Jefferson, in 1778 and 1779, and that the fort and block-houses were constructed early in 1780. In the Virginia State Papers, Vol. I, will be found the correspondence relating to the matter. Among the letters are the following: Lieutenant Governor John Page to Col. Todd, at Kaskaskia, Aug. 16, 1779; General Clark to Governor Jefferson, Sept. 23, 1779; General Clark to Capt. Silas Martin, Sept. 30, 1779; General Clark to Col. Todd, March, 1780; and Col. Todd to Governor Jefferson, June 2, 1780.

The other letters, not above referred to, show the low state to which the post had become reduced; the starving condition of the troops and the settlers assembled there; the constantly threatened dangers from the Indians; the frequent request for aid and its tardy arrival; the attacks upon the fort by the Indians under the lead of James Colbert, a Scotchman; the repulses and the final abandonment of the place as a post and settlement, probably in 1781. Some of the settlers returned eastward and others removed to Kaskaskia.

The following is the letter from General Clark to Governor Jefferson above referred to:

LOUISVILLE, September 23, 1779.

DEAR SIR:—I am happy to find that your sentiments respecting a Fortification at or near the mouth of the Ohio is so agreeable to the Ideas of every man of any judgment in this Department. It is the spot that ought to be strong and Fortified, and all the Garrisons in the Western Country Dependent on it, if the ground would admit it, but the misfortune is, there's not an acre of ground nearer the Point than four miles rise the Ohio, but what is often Ten feet under water. About twelve miles below the Point there is a beautiful situation, as if by nature designed for a Fortification by every observation that has been taken, which lays a quarter of a degree within the State of Virginia. Its elevation is such that a small expense would render it very strong and of greater advantage than one four miles up the Ohio. In case you have one built, a few years will prove the propriety of it. It would immediately become the Key of the whole Trade of the Western Country and well situated for the Indian Department in General. Besides many Salutary Effects it would render During the War, by awing our Enemies, the Chickesaws, and the English Posts on the Mississippi. The strength of the Garrison ought not to be less than Two Hundred men, when built. A Hundred families that might easily be Got to Settle in a Town would be a great advantage in promoting the place. I am sensible that the Spaniards would be fond to settle a Post of Correspondence opposite to it, if the ground would admit. But the country on their side is so subject to inundations, that it is impossible. For the want of such a Post I find it absolutely necessary to station an armed boat at the Point so as to command the navigation of both rivers, to defend our Trading Boats and stop the great concourse of Tories and Deserters that pass down the River to our Enemies. The Illinois, under the present circumstances, is by no means able to supply the Troops that you Expect in this department with provisions, as the crops at Vincennes was so exceedingly bad that upwards of Five Hundred Souls have to depend on their Neighbors for Bread. I should be exceedingly glad that you would commission some Person to furnish the Troops in this Quarter with provisions, as the greater Part must come from the Frontiers for the ensuing year, as I can't depend on the Illinois for supplies more than will be sufficient for two hundred and fifty men. There is an easy conveyance down the Tennessee River and Provisions more plenty on Holsten than in the neighborhood of F. P. H. [Fort Patrick Henry]. Colonel John Campbell, who promised to deliver this letter to Your Excellency I believe would undertake the task at a moderate salary, and a gentleman of undoubted veracity. But pray, sir, order as much Provisions Down as will serve the Troops you intend sending out, at least six months.

I am, Sir, with the greatest respect, your humble servant,

GEO. CLARK.

It will be observed that General Clark desired to establish the fort here at the point, but the low ground and the frequent inundations forbade it. It will also be noticed that he speaks of maintaining an armed boat at the point. At that time the whole country west of the Mississippi was owned by Spain. Our Revolutionary War was then going on; and it was not expected that the Spanish government would be very friendly to the cause of the colonies, and hence Clark's desire to keep his eye on the Spanish territory lying just across the river.

In the letter of Clark to Martin of Sept. 30, 1779, Clark suggests the granting of forty or fifty thousand acres of land to persons who would come and settle in the vicinity of the fort; and Todd in his letter to Jefferson of June 2, 1780, says: "I therefore granted to a certain number of families 400 acres, to each family, at a price to be settled by the general assembly." These two letters throw considerable light upon the origin of such land claims as those of the Flannerys, the McElmurrays, and of Standlee in this county of ours.

I am indebted to Col. Emmet W. Bagby, of Paducah, for the following account of the fort, taken chiefly, it seems, from Vol. II, pages 39 and 40, of Collins' "History of Kentucky," ed. of 1882.

FORT JEFFERSON.—"Under intimations from Governor Patrick Henry, dated January 2, 1778, that 'it was in contemplation to establish a post near the mouth of the Ohio, with cannon to fortify it,' coupled with express instructions from Thos. Jefferson, next Governor of Virginia, dated June 28, 1778, and repeated in January and April, 1780, Gen. Geo. Rogers Clark, with about 200 soldiers, left Louisville early in the summer of 1780, and proceeding down the river to a point on the Mississippi called the Iron Banks, five miles below the mouth of the Ohio, then in the State of Virginia, there erected a fort with several block-houses, which he called Fort Jefferson. One object was to fortify the claim of the United States to the Mississippi River as its western boundary, south of the Ohio. Governor Jefferson had engaged a scientific corps, with Dr. Thomas Walker at its head, to ascertain by celestial observations the boundary line between Virginia and North Carolina, or the point on the Mississippi River intersected by the latitude of 36° 30′, the southern limit of Virginia. Gen. Clark was instructed 'to select a strong position near the point, and there establish a fort and garrison; thence to extend his conquests northward to the lakes, erecting forts at different points, which might serve as monuments of actual possession, besides affording protection to that portion of the country.' The result of Clark's bold operations, thus authorized, was the addition to the chartered limits of Virginia, and so recognized by the treaty of peace with Great Britain in 1783, of that immense region—afterwards called the 'North Western Territory,' and ceded by Virginia to the United States—which now comprises the five great states of Ohio, Indiana, Illinois, Michigan and Wisconsin.

"The Chickasaw Indians were in 1770 the undisputed owners of the territory on the west of the Tennessee River, including the ground at the mouth of Mayfield Creek, where Fort Jefferson was built. By some unexplained oversight or neglect of positive instructions, or inability to comply with them, this site had not been purchased of the Indians, nor their consent obtained to the erection of the fort, thus arousing their most bitter resentment. After awhile they began marauding and then murdering individuals of the isolated families who had settled around the fort, thus driving them into the fort, and butchering many, including the whole family of Mr. Music, except himself. In their skirmishes, they captured a white man whom they compelled, at the risk of his life, to reveal the true condition of the garrison and families, already reduced, by sickness and absences, to about thirty men, of whom two-thirds were sick with fever and ague. These were commanded by Capt. George, according to Mann Butler, and others, and according to Gov. John Reynolds, by Capt. James Pigott. The Indians, who now came a thousand or twelve hundred strong to the work of bloody extermination, were led by Colbert, a Scotchman, who had gained great control over them. The siege lasted five or six days, the inmates of the fort being reduced to terrible extremities by famine, sickness, scarcity of water, watching and fighting. Their principal food was pumpkins with the blossoms yet on them. They had sent for succor, but the distance was great. They refused a demand for a surrender within an hour, although notified that a strong force had been sent to intercept the small assistance expected. A desperate night assault was made, but as they crowded on, Capt. Geo. Owen, commander of a block-house, raked them with great slaughter, with a swivel loaded with rifle and musket balls. Other efforts to storm the fort, and to set fire to it, were bravely resisted. At last Gen. Clark arrived from Kaskaskia, with provisions and reinforcements, and the baffled savages sullenly withdrew, still threatening vengeance The fort was abandoned shortly after, from the difficulty of supplying it because so remote.

"During the late civil war, a long six-pounder iron cannon buried beneath the fort was partially exposed by the caving in of the Mississippi River. Jos. Dupoyster, who owns the site of the fort, dug it out, but was robbed of it by Federal soldiers then stationed at Cairo.

"Among the soldiers of Gen. Clark at Fort Jefferson, were Wm. Biggs, James Curry, Levi Teel, David Pagon, John Vallis, Pickett, Seybold, Groots and many others."—(See also English's "Conquest of the Northwest," Vol. II.)

The following is the commission given James Colbert, Nov. 23, 1780, by Major General John Campbell, commanding his Majesty's forces in the Province of West Florida.

"Reposing especial trust and confidence in your loyalty, zeal and attachment to his Majesty's Person and Government, and by virtue of the powers and authorities in me vested, I do hereby constitute and appoint you a leader and conductor of such volunteer inhabitants and Chickasaw, Choctaw, Creek or other Indians as shall join you, for the purpose of annoying, distressing, attacking or repelling the King's enemies, when, where and as often as you

shall judge proper for the good of his Majesty's service, subject always to such further orders and instructions as you shall from time to time receive from me or any other person or persons duly authorized for the purpose."
—Virginia State Papers, Vol. I.

BIRD'S POINT AND THE BIRDS.—This point or place, now Cairo, for some considerable time, and probably at different times, bore the name of Bird's Point. The family of the Birds were originally Virginians. One or more of them, it is said, came west as early as 1779 and 1780, when those families or settlers came to the vicinity of Fort Jefferson at the solicitation of Governor Jefferson and General George Rogers Clark. Clark had impressed upon Jefferson that as a part of the plan of establishing the fort, an attempt should be made to get a hundred families or more to come and settle on the lands adjacent to it. It was supposed that a permanent post could be thus established which would greatly aid in protecting the frontier country. One or more of the Birds were here on this point between the rivers as early as 1795. There were then few settlers anywhere in this region of the country. All of the Fort Jefferson people had dispersed, as it were, after the abandonment of the fort. Many of them had gone back eastward. They were too far from their old homes and had gotten too near the borders of what seemed to them the exclusive domain of the Indians. The Birds could make no entries of land at that time, and it seems they went on to the Cape Girardeau settlement, where many of their relatives named *Byrd* were. The change in the spelling of the name was no doubt comparatively recent. Many of our citizens remember George W. Henricks, the contractor and builder. His sons, the lawyers Wm. E. and George W., insisted that there should be a letter "d" in the name, and they put it there for themselves and their families, but their father never adopted the new spelling.

Abram Bird purchased land on the Missouri side as early as 1798; and their operations there and here resulted in the use of the same name for each place at different times; but so far as the *point* goes it was more applicable to the Illinois than to the Missouri side.

The large tract of land, about 800 acres, just south of town and now owned by Mr. Egbert A. Smith, owes its origin to a small island up where the river turns eastward and towards the present Bird's Point and Kentucky shore. It was far out in the river, and its growth was chiefly eastward and toward the Illinois shore. In 1850 it had reached half the distance to the Ohio, and within a few years it threw out a sand bar which extended so far toward the Kentucky shore that boats which did not come out of the Illinois channel, but passed down the Missouri channel, had to run close to the Kentucky shore and then turn around the sand bar and come on up to the Cairo landing. This island was put down on the old river guides as Bird's Island. Afterward it took and held for a long time the name "Cairo Island." This point was also once called Willow Point. An early English traveler making a trip down the Ohio and writing about the place, said it had no other name beside Willow Point. Bird's Point, and Ohio City near by, once seemed to be very hopeful of a prosperous growth. This was chiefly in the years of the Cairo and Fulton Railroad, 1855 up to 1861.

In Houck's recent and valuable "History of Missouri," Vol. II, p. 164, where the prairie on which Charleston now stands is spoken of, it is said:

"This prairie was known during the Spanish occupancy as 'Prairie Carlos,' but afterwards among the American settlers became known as 'Mathews' Prairie.' It was a favorite pasture of buffalo and in 1781, when Fort Jefferson was besieged by the Indians, Joseph Hunter, crossing the river, hunted and killed buffalo here, and carrying the meat to the river thus supplied the starving garrison. The first pioneer settler was Charles Finley, in 1800. He sold his claim to Abram Bird, senior. Edward Mathews came to this prairie in the same year; so also Edward, junior, Joseph and Charles Mathews. Abram Bird in 1798 received a grant from De Lassus on the Mississippi, opposite the mouth of the Ohio and which thus became known as "Bird's Point." He and his brother Thompson were related to the 'Byrds' of the Cape Girardeau district, although spelling their names differently. The original grant has long since been carried away by the Mississippi and much other land belonging to the family."

It was not until 1817 that William and Thompson Bird made a trip to Kaskaskia, the seat of the land office, and entered the lands they desired and which they had long known and no doubt lived upon. Thompson Bird, in the name of Thompson Bird & Company, on the 26th day of July, 1817, entered the *southwest quarter of section* 25, containing 160 acres, and on the same day William Bird entered the *southeast fractional quarter* of the same section containing 112.29 acres and on July 28, 1817, William Bird entered *fractional section* 36, containing 46.47 acres. This shows that at that time there was no island adjoining or near to the Illinois shore; otherwise it would have been embraced in William Bird's purchase of *fractional section* 36. Nor does the government survey of 1807 show anything south of the main land or shore. This small strip of land of 46.47 acres lay just south of an east and west line running through block 56 in the city. William and Thompson Bird together paid for these lands $637.52, which was at the rate of $2.00 an acre, the price then required to be paid. These lands embraced what is now the whole of the southern part of the city, lying south of an east and west line just south of the stone depot at 14th and Ohio Streets, and east of a north and south line running just east of the Safford school building in block 80, in the First Addition to the city. It embraced all of the city as first platted, all of the second and third additions and part of the first addition.

Some of us have often heard Kentuckians speak of the *Jackson Purchase,* reference always being had to western Kentucky, between the Tennessee and Mississippi Rivers. This descriptive phrase arose in this way: President Monroe appointed Isaac Shelby and Andrew Jackson to make a treaty with the Chickasaw Indians for all that part of the country lying north of the south line of Tennessee and between the Tennessee, Mississippi and Ohio Rivers. The treaty was concluded October 19, 1818, and was signed by Shelby and Jackson and a number of the Indian chiefs of that nation, among them Major General William Colbert, Col. George Colbert, Levi Colbert and James Colbert, half-breeds, and descendants of the James Colbert mentioned above. This treaty seems to have been somewhat supplemental to the treaty of September 20, 1816, signed by Andrew Jackson, D. Meriwether and J. Franklin for the United States and the Colberts and other Indians for the said tribe. In the treaty of October 19th, and among the amounts of money the government was to pay the tribe was "the sum of ten hundred and eighty-nine dollars to Major James Colbert, interpreter, for that amount of money taken from his pocket in the month of June, 1816, at the theatre in Baltimore."

Concerning Fort Jefferson much additional information is contained in vol. V, Illinois Historical Collections "Kaskaskia Records," Alvord.

CHAPTER XXXII

MISCELLANEOUS PAPERS—JUDGES OF THE SUPREME, CIRCUIT AND COUNTY COURTS—MEMBERS OF THE LEGISLATURE AND OTHER BODIES—COUNTY, CITY AND OTHER OFFICERS—LISTS OF EARLY RESIDENTS OF THE CITY, ETC.

FIRE OF DECEMBER 8, 1858.—On the 8th day of December, 1858, about six months after the disastrous inundation of 1858, the city hall or court-room and the office of the register of deeds on Ohio Street, between Sixth and Eighth Streets, was destroyed by fire; and on the 18th day of the February following, the legislature passed an act for the restoration of the records as far as possible, the preamble of which is in these words:

"Whereas the city hall, court-room and office of the register of deeds, at, in and for the city of Cairo, was, on the eighth day of December, A. D. 1858, consumed by fire, with all the records and proceedings of the corporate authorities of said city, the records of judgments, decrees and files of the court of common pleas of said city, and the records of deeds registered and recorded by the said register of deeds therefor, together with all other documents relating to the offices aforesaid or contained in the archives thereof; therefore, Section 1, be it enacted, etc."

This fire accounts largely for the absence of early city records, such as ordinances and proceedings of the Trustees of the town of Cairo from March, 1855, to March, 1857. No doubt this fire made way with very much that would have possessed great historic interest.

THE CEMETERY OF THE LOTUS.—On the 3d day of February, 1853, the legislature incorporated the Cairo Cemetery Association. The incorporators were Samuel Staats Taylor, Henry Clay Long, George D. Gordon, Patrick Corcoran, Thomas S. Taylor and Charles Davis. It was authorized to purchase and hold not exceeding fifteen acres of land for cemetery purposes.

A tract of land five hundred feet in width and thirteen hundred and seven feet in length and amounting to fifteen acres, situated about a quarter of a mile, more or less, east of the Mobile & Ohio Railroad and about two miles, or a little less, above the Illinois Central bridge was surveyed and platted into blocks, lots and avenues, on the 29th day of November, A. D. 1855, for a cemetery, for the use of the people of the city of Cairo. The tract of land is a part of the northwest quarter and the southwest quarter of section ten and a part of section nine, in our township. The cemetery was used for a number of years; and among Col. Taylor's papers are quite a number relating to it. A very interesting one is the original certificate of survey made under the hand and seal of Mr. John Newell, "Deputy County Surveyor in and for Alexander County, State of Illinois." Mr. Newell afterwards became and was for a number of years the president of the Illinois Central Railroad Company and was still later the president of the Lake Shore & Michigan Railway Company. He was one of the very noted railway officials of the country, long after his residence here in this county.

"THE ORPHAN ASYLUM OF SOUTHERN ILLINOIS AT CAIRO."—On the 18th day of August, 1866, the Trustees of the Cairo City Property, Taylor and Parsons, conveyed to Captain Daniel Hurd, trustee for the Protestant Orphan Asylum of Cairo, Illinois, for the consideration of one thousand dollars ($1000), lots 14, 32, 33, 34 and 35, in block 42, in the First Addition to the City of Cairo; and about that time those persons who were associated with him arranged for the erection of a building upon the lots and the incorporation of the society; and on the 25th day of February, 1867, the same was incorporated by an act of our legislature and the above name given to the society. The names of the incorporators are the following: Mrs. D. Hurd, Mrs. H. W. Wardner, Mrs. A. B. Fenton, Mrs. G. D. Williamson, Miss Jennie Sloo, Mrs. J. C. Rankin, Mrs. D. T. Parker, Mrs. A. B. Safford, Mrs. William Stratton, Mrs. Rachel Slack, Mrs. H. W. Webb, Mrs. J. M. Morrow, James C. Sloo, Daniel Hurd, Henry W. Webb, Henry H. Candee, Charles Galigher, A. B. Fenton, Samuel R. Hay, Alfred Comings, William J. Yost, John Olney, and Charles Latimer.

Some time during the war, the Christian Commission people erected on the south side of Fourth Street, between Ohio Street and Commercial Avenue, a building for the prosecution of their army work. This building was purchased by the Orphan Asylum people and removed to the lots above described, and the structure stands there now just about as it was placed forty-three years ago. On the 29th day of January, 1883, they purchased from the Trustees, for the consideration of four hundred and fifty dollars, lots 15, 16 and 17, immediately west of said lot 14. The first deed is recorded in Book O on page 360; and the second deed in the same book, on page 412½. For many years the society was conducted as originally established; but after a time it was deemed best to close the institution and rent the property. This was done for quite a length of time. A few years ago, however, it was thought best to make an effort to open and conduct the same as was originally intended by the act of incorporation. I remember very well Mrs. Louise R. Wardner coming here from La Porte many years ago and severely criticizing many of us for leaving the institution shut up so long; but those in charge of its interests did not for a year or two, or more, see their way clear to open it. It is believed that since it has been again opened it has been fairly well maintained; but the credit thereof is largely due to the earnest and faithful women of the organization and to a few men.

THE CAIRO DRAINAGE DISTRICT.—The Cairo Drainage District was established in 1889. It is inclosed by what we may call levee embankments of fourteen or fifteen miles in length; that is, by the city's cross levee on the south, by the levee embankment of the Cleveland, Cincinnati, Chicago & St. Louis Railway Company on the east or Ohio side, by the levee embankment of the St. Louis & Cairo Railroad Company, or its lessee, the Mobile & Ohio Railroad Company, on the west or Mississippi side; and by a levee or embankment along Cache River on the north. It contains about 4,000 acres of very fertile and valuable land, quite a portion of which still belongs to the Trustees of the Cairo Trust Property. For the reclamation of this extensive track of land from the annual invasions of the rivers we are indebted chiefly to Col. Samuel Staats Taylor.

I have before spoken of our great need of local trade. Here is indeed the creation of a large district which will for all time to come add largely to the trade and business of the city. It is as a monument to Col. Taylor; for none could have seen more clearly than he the city's need of adjacent supporting territory.

STEAMBOAT "TENNESSEE VALLEY"

Bureau of Navigation,
Washington, February 3, 1910.

Mr. John M. Lansden,
614 Commercial Ave., Cairo, Ill.

SIR:

This office has received your letter of the 31st ultimo relative to the steamboat 'Tennessee Valley.' P. E. 61, granted at New Orleans April 23, 1842, shows that at that time M. W. Irwin was her master and part owner; that Samuel G. Patton of Florance was part owner; that she was built at Cairo, Ill., in 1841; that she was measured by Seth W. Nye, Surveyor; that her length was 204 feet and 2 inches; that her breadth was 33 feet and 4 inches; that her depth was 7 feet and 8 inches; that she measured 495 and 41-95 tons, and that she had a square stern with cabin above. No record is found of the surrender of the enrolment and the Bureau is unable to state whether she was 'burned or otherwise destroyed.' The name of her builder is not specified on the record here. It may be that you will be able to obtain further information regarding her from the Custom House at New Orleans.

Respectfully,
E. G. CHAMBERLAIN, Commissioner.

Memorandum of Information Obtained at Coast and Geodetic Survey, in Regard to Cairo.

The magnetic declination decreases at rate of one minute per annum at Cairo. At date 1910 4-10, it stands East 4° 35′.

In regard to the station of the Geodetic Survey at Cairo:

The station is on the new city levee, between the Illinois Central and the Mobile and Ohio Rairoad tracks, west of the west end of West 33d Street. This levee extends northeast from an iron post which was set by the levelling survey as a bench mark, and which is 250 feet southeast of the Mobile and Ohio signal station. The magnetic station is about 705 feet northeast along the city levee from this bench mark and 12 feet north of the center of the levee on the slope. The station is marked by a Bedford limestone post 5 x 5 x 30 inches, projecting six inches above the ground and lettered, U. S. C. and G. S. 1908. The following true bearings were determined:

Steeple of St. Joseph's Catholic Church..........64° 25′ .8 east of south
A cupola ....65° 06′ .8 east of south
Base of flagstaff of Redman & Magee Co. elevator 15° 09′ .1 east of north
Bench mark of river survey.......................52° 30′ .7 west of south

The following are magnetic observations made June 11 and 12, 1908:

Lat.	Long.	Declination[1] East	Dip[2]
37° 00.8′	89° 11.6′	4° 47.2′	67° 49.6″

Commercial Bodies, Clubs, Fraternal Orders and Other Organizations.—I have not had the time to speak of these organizations in detail, and it is quite impossible to say much of them in any other way. They are as numerous, and I have no doubt quite as efficient and successful, as are the like societies and organizations of other cities of the size of Cairo. I have not the means at hand and am not able to give anything like a satisfactory account of them; and a partial account would be so unsatisfactory to the members of the various bodies that they would not excuse me for the errors and omissions which would probably appear in the several accounts. The commercial bodies, with which so many of our business men are identified, have been working hard and faithfully for many years for the advancement of the interests of the city. Every one recognizes their great usefulness. I would like to say here a few words in regard to a number of the business men who have taken leading parts in the good work of upbuilding the city; but every one will recognize the difficulty of making just the right selections and of saying just the right things concerning particular individuals. I would be glad to have it understood that it is from no oversight or forgetfulness on my part that this omission occurs. The work I have bestowed upon this book has been much more than I expected; and more recently I have found it absolutely necessary to bring it to an end, whatever errors or omissions may appear therein.

It would require no little time and work to go over all these matters with any degree of fullness, and to add thereto accounts of our water works, established in 1885, and furnishing us an abundant supply of good water, our gas and electric lighting, our street car and interurban railroad service, our extensive manufacturing interests and other large and important business enterprises, our shipping facilities by river and rail, our extensive and fine street improvements, and our great advancement in the matter of the erection of better buildings of all kinds, public and private;—all these matters, and many others, have been so fully set forth from time to time by our commercial bodies in illustrated pamphlets and descriptive circulars, that it is quite unnecessary to present them in a book like this which reaches the hands of comparatively few persons, and they chiefly residents of the city.

[1]The angle between the magnetic meridian shown by the compass, and the geographical meridian.

[2]The angle the needle makes with the plane of the horizon.

Besides this, our city directories contain so much relating to very many of these matters that to give them here would be almost a useless repetition. Our last city directory, the one for 1908-1909, by Mr. George B. Walker, is a very useful city book indeed. Besides the general information it contains about our societies, fraternities, commercial and other organizations, etc., it contains so many names of persons now resident in the city that it will likely increase in value the further we get away from the time of its publication. I know of no one having Harrell's directory of 1864, and all subsequent directories. A complete set of them would be exceedingly valuable, chiefly for the names of the people of Cairo resident here about the dates of the respective publications of the books.

HISTORICAL PLACES IN THE CITY; SOME DISTINGUISHED PERSONAGES.—I might cut the first one of these subjects very short by saying there are no historical places in the city, and give as a reason that Cairo is but a few years old, not over *fifty-seven.* It was started in 1818, but only on paper. It was started again in 1836, but lived out scarcely ten years. At best, it was in a state of suspended animation from 1843 to 1853, when in December of the latter year the first opportunity was given for the purchase of lots or other real estate. The federal census of 1850 gave the place two hundred and forty-two inhabitants. It was without any kind of town, village or city government. It was little more than what Maximilian, Prince of Wied-Neuwied, said it was in March, 1832. He said it had no other name than the *"Mouth of the Ohio."* On the 1st day of October, 1853, the Trustees published their first notice that they were ready to offer lots for sale; but they offered none until December 23d of that year; and the first lot sold was lot eight, block twenty, in the city, at the southwest corner of Third Street and Commercial Avenue. It was sold to Peter Stapleton, whose family is still well represented here in Cairo.

This may be said to be the time of the starting of the present city of Cairo. It will be *fifty-seven* years ago, December 23, 1910. We have here nothing now which came over to us from the decade of 1836 to 1846, the Holbrook regime; nor have we here now any building or structure that was here in December, 1853, save the little school house building on Eleventh Street. There are a few old houses now claiming existence along with the Springfield block, the stone depot and one or two other places, but they have been moved about and so repaired as to be now past recognition. About all we have are a few sites of old but long since perished buildings, a few of which merit brief notices. I have elsewhere spoken of the Halliday Hotel. Let me here mention two or three others. The Rev. Timothy Flint, who passed here in the year 1816 (1818), recorded the fact that the hotel then here was kept in a large boat one hundred feet long. I need not repeat what is elsewhere said by him in Chapter XXX. The old hotel, built and maintained so long at the point, and a little outside of the point of junction of our present levees, must have been built as far back as 1830, probably earlier. Before that time one or two or more houses had been erected in that immediate vicinity. Mr. Crumb, quoted in the same chapter, gives us an account of what he called the fine hotel there on the 29th of May, 1836. The same hotel was there during the whole of the Holbrook administration. Mr. William Harrell speaks of it and tells how it was crowded with guests in the early forties, and of a large addition having been built to accommodate the greatly increased custom. The Englishman, William Oliver, who stopped there three or four days in 1841, tells us of his experience while here and at the hotel, waiting for the arrival of a steamboat to take him up the Mississippi. We cannot realize the extent of the travel down the Ohio and down the Mississippi from here, and up the Mississippi to St. Louis and other points at that early day. They, the two rivers, were then the great highways of travel, and it was not until much later times that other courses and means of travel took the place of the rivers.

About the last official reference we have to that old hostelry is found in ordinance No. 65, adopted March 7, 1858, wherein a license was granted for the erection and operation of a distillery for ten years upon two or more acres of ground in the southern part of the city outside of the levees and including the "Old Cairo Hotel site." The old distillery building, seen in the picture of the point, gave way in 1861 to the construction of Fort Defiance, the successor, after one hundred and sixty-nine years, of the fort of Sieur Charles Juchereau de St. Denis. Fort Defiance lived out the war of four years. It defied the Confederates successfully for that length of time, but had to yield to the demands of peace and trade and was supplanted by the first station buildings of the Cairo & St. Louis Railroad Company. These disappeared in a few years, and there now stands, only a few rods north of the old site, Mr. Henry E. Halliday's grain elevator, like some tall sentinel guarding faithfully the oldest of the historic sites our city affords. But older than them all, and adding to their interest, is the foot of the Third Principal Meridian, planted almost on that very spot more than a hundred years ago.

Next to that old hotel was the Taylor House, on four or five lots, at the southwest corner of Fourth Street and Commercial Avenue, where Mr. Henry Hasenjaeger now resides. It was completed early in the year 1855, and opened on the 9th day of May of that year. It was a large building and no doubt took its name from Col. Samuel Staats Taylor, who at that time owned the lots. A Mr. Grimes, of Paducah, seems to have been the first proprietor of the hotel; and the "Cairo City Times" of September 12, 1855, notes the sale of the hotel business by him to a Mr. Swinney, formerly of the Walnut Street

House, of Cincinnati. About the time of the opening of the hotel, a large number of the members of the state legislature and other guests of the Illinois Central Railroad Company, probably three hundred persons, visited Cairo, and most of them were entertained at the Taylor House. Among them were Governor Joel A. Matteson, Ex-Governor John Reynolds, Judge Lyman Trumbull, and many other persons of note. With the mention of these somewhat noted men visiting Cairo in the bright dawn of its third attempt to become a city, I may here also mention a number of persons who were here before and since that year, 1855, and all of them very distinguished indeed. It may be going back somewhat too far, but it is history, and that is what we are endeavoring to write. As I have already stated, General Andrew Jackson was here with fifteen hundred soldiers, two or three days, in January, 1813. Abraham Lincoln no doubt landed his well ladened flatboat here on his two trips down the Sangamon, the Illinois and Mississippi Rivers to New Orleans, in 1831. Zachary Taylor was here in February, 1849, after his election to the presidency, but before his inauguration. Vice-President John C. Breckinridge was here in April, 1858. James A. Garfield was here in October, 1868. Ulysses Grant was here in 1861 and 1880. Jefferson Davis was here June 8, 1881. Theodore Roosevelt was here in October, 1907, and William H. Taft was here in October, 1909. It is to be hoped that some one will prepare a suitable account of these two last occasions, in which most of the others just mentioned might also be given their proper places. I have said nothing as to the distinguished persons here during the Holbrook administration in which so many Englishmen were interested; nor have I undertaken to refer to the great number of distinguished persons who were here during the war.

THE CHAMBER OF COMMERCE OF 1865.—The hopes of the people of Cairo were perhaps quite high enough when the war began, but they rose much higher during its continuance. Every one seemed assured of a bright future for the city. One of the evidences of this is found in the incorporation, February 16, 1865, two months *before* the close of the war, of the Cairo Chamber of Commerce, the incorporators of which were George D. Williamson, D. Hurd, Henry Winter, James W. Musson, John N. Patton, John M. Cyrus, William P. Halliday, Cornelius O'Callahan, A. B. Safford, James McKenzie, Ward L. Smith, John Clancy, Dyas T. Parker, H. H. Johnson, Thomas Wilson, and James S. Rearden.

Further along will be found a list of the officers and members of the body, taken from a pamphlet of twenty-five pages, printed early in that year by the Cairo Democrat Company. The pamphlet contains the charter of the company, approved by Richard J. Oglesby, governor, and the somewhat extensive rules and regulations of the association. I have given the list of officers and other members chiefly because it will recall to many persons now in Cairo so many of the more prominent men of Cairo of forty-five years ago.

OFFICERS OF THE CAIRO CHAMBER OF COMMERCE

From March, 1865, to March, 1866.

President,
Wm. P. Halliday.

Vice President,
Jno. M. Cyrus.

Secretary,
F. G. Chapman.

Treasurer,
A. B. Safford.

Directors

S. N. Fullinwider,
D. T. Parker,
A. B. Safford,
J. W. Musson,
C. R. Woodward,
D. Hurd,
E. D. Trover,
Joseph McKenzie,
G. D. Williamson,
S. S. Homans,
Jno. N. Patton.

Committee of Appeals.

D. Hurd,
J. B. Reed,
S. N. Fullinwider,
P. T. Mitchell,
J. K. Frost,
D. T. Parker,
E. Maxwell,
J. W. Musson,
C. Schultz.

Committee of Arbitration, from March to September, 1865

Samuel Payne,
A. H. Powers,
Ward L. Smith,
C. R. Woodward,
S. S. Homans.

Committee of Arbitration from September, 1865, to March, 1866

A. B. Safford,
J. Cushing,
A. Comings,
P. Chapman,
G. D. Williamson.

Names of the Other Members

C. M. Osterloh, D. H. Philips, William Lonergan, E. Hodge, John C. White, J. B. Humphreys, John Walters, L. T. Bonaceua, Isaac Mooney, J. McDonald, J. D. Huntington, P. G. Schuh, F. Bross, J. S. Rearden, C. C. Davidson, J. F. Noyes, H. M. Evans, William Stratton, James Kooken, Andreas Doll, F. M. C. DeVassa, C. Close, A. J. Harrison, A. A. Arrick, Thomas Lewis, T. G. Lansden, Jewett Wilcox, Wm. G. Priest, R. I. Condiff, O. P. Lyon, Jno. Wilson, J. G. Haydock, R. G. Furguson, Dan Able, J. P. Prather, J. S. Byington, James S. Swayne, A. Nuernberger, P. Grossmuck, Peter Neff, Wm. Simpson, A. Williams, I. Williams, M. D. Picard, B. Smyth, Chas. Galigher, Al. Amiss, S. P. McGuire, A. R. Whitaker, Thos. Winter, Chas. Scudder, Henry Johnson, David J. Baker, Sol. A. Silver, Fred. Foster, W. N. Swayne, H. W. Hubbard, Wm. Truesdail.—See the "Daily War Eagle" of April 17, 1865, for the names of Irwin Maxwell, William H. Schutter and others.

THE JUDGES OF THE SUPREME, CIRCUIT AND COUNTY COURTS, AND MEMBERS OF THE LEGISLATURE AND OF OTHER BODIES.—Alexander County was part of the third judicial circuit until 1857, when other circuits were established and the county included in the nineteenth circuit. In 1873, it became part of the first judicial circuit, where it still remains. The judges who have held our circuit court since the organization of the county in 1819, are as follows: Richard M. Young, Henry Eddy, Alexander F. Grant, Jeptha Hardin, Walter B. Scates, William A. Denning, William K. Parrish, John H. Mulkey, William H. Green, Monroe C. Crawford, Wesley Sloan, John Olney, David J. Baker, John Dougherty, Oliver A. Harker, Daniel M. Browning, Robert W. McCartney, George W. Young, Joseph P. Robarts, Alonzo K. Vickers, Warren W. Duncan, William N. Butler and A. W. Lewis. The following are the names of Cairo citizens who have been judges of our courts here and elsewhere: William A. Denning, judge of the supreme court from January 19, 1847, to December 4, 1848; David J. Baker, judge of the supreme court from June, 1878, to June, 1879, by appointment of Governor Shelby M. Cullom, to fill the vacancy occasioned by the death of Judge Breese, which occurred June 28, 1878; John H. Mulkey, judge of the supreme court from June, 1879, to June, 1888; David J. Baker, from June, 1888, to June, 1897; John H. Mulkey, William H. Green, John Olney, David J. Baker, Joseph P. Robarts and William N. Butler, judges of our circuit court; Levi L. Lightner, Alexander C. Hodges, Fredolin Bross, Reuben S. Yocum, John H. Robinson, and William S. Dewey, judges of our county court.

Our county has had but one member of Congress and that is our present member, the Hon. N. B. Thistlewood. The following are the names of the members of the legislature from our county in the order given: Daniel W. Munn, Reed Green and Walter Warder, members of the senate; William M. Alexander, Henry L. Webb, Wilson Able, William A. Denning, John Hodges, F. M. Rawlins, Henry W. Webb, John H. Oberly, Claiborne Winston, Alexander H. Irvin, Thomas W. Halliday, Harmon H. Black, D. T. Linegar, Reuben S. Yocum, Charles F. Nellis, Reed Green, Walter Warder, William Q. McGee, S. B. Miller and Richard E. Powers, members of the house. Members of the Constitutional Convention of 1862, William A. Hacker. Member of the Constitutional Convention of 1870, William J. Allen. Member of the State Board of Equalization, 1868 to 1872, Thomas Wilson. Presidential elector on the Republican ticket, 1868, Daniel W. Munn; on that ticket, 1872, David T. Linegar.

The names of the present city and county officers are as follows: George Parsons, mayor; Robert A. Hatcher, city clerk; Frank B. Armstrong, city treasurer; Hunter Bird, city attorney; Angus Leek, special city counsel; Ernest Nordman, city comptroller; Andrew Whitcamp, police magistrate; J. G. Cowell, chief of police or city marshal.

City aldermen: First Ward, Patrick C. Scullin and Calvin V. Neff; Second Ward, George G. Koehler and Tom L. Faudree; Third

Ward, Thomas W. Williams and Edward A. Burke; Fourth Ward, Leo McDaniel and Frank Ferguson; Fifth Ward, Fred D. Nellis and Dr. John T. Walsh; Sixth Ward, Daniel E. Kelly and Frank E. Cannon; Seventh Ward, William M. Magner and William P. Greaney.

County officers. Board of County Commissioners: Dr. John J. Jennelle, chairman; Dr. Edwin Gause and Calvin V. Neff; Jesse E. Miller, county clerk; Alfred Brown, circuit clerk; Fred D. Nellis, sheriff; Alexander Wilson, state's attorney; Professor S. E. Gott, county superintendent of schools; William D. Lippitt, assessor and treasurer; Dr. James McManus, coroner.

The present judges of the first judicial circuit are William N. Butler, Cairo; Warren W. Duncan, Marion; and Albert W. Lewis, Harrisburg. The present judge of our county court is William S. Dewey.

Postmasters of the "Mouth of the Ohio" and of the City of Cairo.—The records of the postoffice department at Washington show the following named persons to have been postmasters here at this place, with the dates of their appointments: Thomas I. Jones, "Mouth of the Ohio," November 8, 1837; James D. Allen, "Mouth of the Ohio," February 9, 1839; James M. Ingraham, "Cairo, late Mouth of the Ohio," June 11, 1839; John D. Marsh, November 27, 1839; Thomas L. Mackoy, November 30, 1841; Bryan Shannessey, April 14, 1842; Addison H. Sanders, July 10, 1847; Moses B. Harrell, September 26, 1849; Bailey S. Harrell, March 14, 1850; Henry Simmons, February 18, 1852; Bryan Shannessey, June 16, 1853; Samuel S. Brooks, August 23, 1853; Leonard G. Faxon, June 14, 1858; Alexander G. Holden, January 10, 1860; David T. Linegar, March 27, 1861; James C. Sloo, November 7, 1863; William A. Looney, June 6, 1865; John M. Graham, July 23, 1866; George W. McKeaig, July 9, 1870, held until February 12, 1883, when William M. Murphy was appointed; Thomas Wilson, August 9, 1885; Alexander H. Irvin, January 7, 1889; John Wood, June 27, 1889; Michael J. Howley, December 12, 1893; John F. Rector, January 21, 1898, and Sidney B. Miller, the present postmaster, December 12, 1901.

Although this list was said to be complete, yet it seems that Walter Falls was postmaster here at a very early day.

The following are the names of the lawyers, physicians, and dentists now resident in the city:

Lawyers: Hunter Bird, Wm. N. Butler, Wm. S. Dewey, Miles Frederick Gilbert, William B. Gilbert, Miles S. Gilbert, Reed Green, Harry Hood, John M. Lansden, David S. Lansden, Angus Leek, Frank Moore, Michael J. O'Shea, Walter Warder, Walter B. Warder, and Alexander Wilson.

Physicians: A. A. Bondurant, S. B. Carey, R. E. Clancy, W. C. Clarke, H. A. Davis, Samuel Dodds, James W. Dunn, E. E. Gordon, W. F. Grinstead, J. B. Hibbitts, James McManus, G. H. McNemer, J. J. Rendleman, D. A. Stevens, J. E. Strong, John T. Walsh, Charles Weber and J. E. Woelfle.

Doctors E. S. Dickerson and W. H. Fields are worthy representatives of the colored people of the city.

Dentists: N. W. Cox, J. H. Davis, F. M. Harrell, Bert Harris, J. J. Jennelle, T. D. Morrison, and E. D. Morrow.

The Arab Fire Company of Cairo was incorporated by a special act of the legislature February 16, 1865, and the names of the incorporators were as follows: Henry Winter, H. Watson Webb, George Cushing, James Capritz, A. G. Holden, John H. Robinson, George W. Weldon, David J. Baker, Jr., George Winter, Wm. Smith, D. Webster Baumgard, Charles D. Arter, Wm. Sandusky, Joseph Meigler, Henry Lattner, C. H. Wentz, John Hayward, Van R. Hall, Edward Mansford, John H. Gossman, Wm. Tell, John Major, Wm. J. Yost, John Myers, Casper Hock, Fred Keiler, Henry Franken, Henry Messner, John Hodges, Jr., E. F. Davis, A. H. Irvin, Wood Rittenhouse, John Jaquish, David T. Linegar, Henry Harris, Wm. B. Miller, James Gordon, George Stormer, Jerry Cantrell, Wm. Alba, Philip Theobold, John C. White, George W. Burrows, L. D. Jones, August Kramer, Chas. W. Henderson, Jacob G. Lynch, Charles Bromback, Edward Koblatz, Fred Whitcamp, Joseph K. Frick, Charles Pfifferling, Joseph Kosminski, W. W. Villito, A. Wittig, Edward Wittig, George Van Brocklin, Frederick Theobold, Cornelius Cafferty, and J. Parker Timmony.

The Rough and Ready Fire Company was incorporated by a special act of the legislature March 7, 1867, and the names of the incorporators were as follows: B. M. Munn, Fredolin Bross, William T. Beerwort, John Scheel, Joseph B. Taylor, Ferdinand Amon, Henry Sigfried, Charles Eble, John Harst, Charles Frank, Henry F. Goodyear, Joseph Helen, Sr., August Bieland, James Kinnear, John Maxey, Philip Schmitt, R. G. Jameson, Andrew Dentinger, Michael Ruggaber, John Ritter, John Schmitt, Martin Strauhal, Hiram Walker, Peter Zimmerman, James S. Swayne, Niles Swayne, Peter Ehs, William Seifried, John Sackberger, Adam Neff, August Veirun, Joseph Farquar, John Royaker, Christian Orth, Peter Kuhn, Sr., J. G. Steinhouse, Joseph Lehmes, Charles Mehner, Joseph M. Veirun, James Axley, Charles Feuchter, F. M. Stockfleth, Henry Brown, John Koag, Fred Sheeler, George G. Smith, Frank Swoboda, Philip Howard, Louis Blattau, Joseph Steagala, Alexander Wittig, August Homann, and John Goetgen.

The Hibernian Fire Company No. 4 was incorporated January 5, 1877, under the general act for the incorporation of such companies, approved April 18, 1872, and the names of the incorporators were as follows: Henry Stout, Patrick O'Loughlin, Smith Torrence, Michael J. Howley, William McHale, James F. Miller, Albert Susanka, Harmon Able, Patrick Fitzgerald, Frank Gazzola, Patrick H. Corcoran, Thomas R. Shook, Martin Gannon, James Greaney, James Garland, Thomas Stack, Richard Murphy, Benj. F. Blue, James Powers, Phil K. Howard, Stephen T. McBride, Phillip J. Thistlewood, Wm. M. Williams, Jesse Mahaffie, Michael Stapleton, Robert Smyth, Patrick Burke, James Ross, Richard Fitzgerald, John A. Powers, Martin Coffey, Thomas Boyle, John M. Hogan, Felix Cross, and Richard R. Hurd.

After these there were one or two other fire companies but all of them were practically discontinued when, under the lead of Mayor Charles O. Patier, the council established the paid fire department of the city. All of the three companies above named were in existence for some considerable time before their incorporation. Before their time there was a fire company called the Relief Fire Co. No. One (1), whose engine house was on the north side of Seventh Street between the two avenues. It was the first fire company of the city.

We have given the names of the incorporators of these companies for the reason that among them are so many names which many of the present residents of Cairo will be glad to recognize. Of the Arab Fire Company, Mr. Henry Winter was from the beginning to the end the leading spirit. Of the Rough and Ready Company, Mr. William

Beerwort was in many respects the most prominent member. Of the Hibernian Fire Company, almost every one would speak of Mr. William McHale as probably its chief and most prominent representative. It is indeed interesting to look over the names of these members of the old but no longer existing companies, and recall their lives in our community. Those companies were favorites of our citizens, much above, I am inclined to think, what was generally noticed elsewhere. They were well supported during their entire existence, and nothing they asked at the hands of the public was probably ever denied to them.

THE OLD CAIRO VETERAN CLUB WAS ORGANIZED FEBRUARY 13, 1891.—We quote from its small pamphlet containing a statement of its object, together with its by-laws, list of members, etc.:

"The Old Cairo Veteran Club, citizens of Cairo, in the year 1857, was organized at the hall of the Arab Fire Company, in the City of Cairo, Ill., on the night of February 13, 1891, by the following named gentlemen to wit: Hon. David J. Baker, Judge F. Bross, John Howley, John McNulty, John Antrim, Joseph Brankle, R. H. Baird, Captain William M. Williams, F. Vincent, Henry Winter, Jacob Lehning, John Clancy, Hank Goodyear, John O'Shea, William Lonergan, James Summerwell, Nat Prouty, John Sackberger, William M. Downs, Andrew Lohr, James Quinn, William Garren, Richard Murphy, Martin O'Shea, John Barry, Edward Jones, Pat Cahill, Martin Driscoll, Thomas Mehan, C. Osterloh, R. H. Cunningham, Charles Thrupp, Michael Glynn, August Marqued, Joseph McKenzie, Isaac Farnbaker, Charles Frank, Albert Susanka, Henry Loflin, Dennis Stapelton, H. H. Candee, W. F. Raefesnider and James Mehan.

"There are forty-three in number, the object being for a yearly fraternal gathering of not only the present resident citizens of Cairo, who were here in 1857, but all those *non-residents,* who were here then and who are living now, to meet and mingle with us at our yearly banquets and talk over old times, one with another, and drink a toast to the departed ones, and a toast to the living ones, for soon we all must go; the main object being to keep up the memories of by-gone days."

"Officers: President, Robert H. Baird; vice-president, John Howley; treasurer, F. Bross; secretary, Henry Winter; sentinel, James Summerwell.

"CAIRO CITIZENS ELIGIBLE FOR MEMBERSHIP.—S. S. Taylor, John Kelly, George Zeller, Matt Walsh, Bat Cashman, Henry Drake, Doct. Wm. Wood, John Sullivan, Con Sheehan, Michael Horrigan, Michael Galvin, John Pollock, J. Y. Turner, F. Malinski, Peter Neff, C. W. Henderson, Thomas Sullivan, Peter Ehs, John Dillon, M. Kobler, Pat Coladine, Charles Gayer, Frank Cocheran, Nicholas Williams, Peter Donnelly, L. S. Marshall, Dennis Coleman, and Geo. Staedtler.

"NON-RESIDENTS ELIGIBLE FOR MEMBERSHIP.—Christopher Ledwidge, Hickman, Ky.; Capt. Wm. H. Sandusky, Central City, Ky.; Capt. W. J. Stephens, Springfield, Mass.; Isaac Clarke, Nashville, Ill.; Henry Rudolph, Evansville, Ind.; Paul W. Allen, Chicago, Ill.; Joseph Fellenbaugh, Beech Ridge, Ill.; Prest. Ex. Norton, L. & N. R. R., Brooklyn, N. Y.; E. F. Davis, Birmingham, Ala.; David Wright, DuQuoin, Ill.; H. Watson Webb, San Diego, Cal.; Solomon Fairinbach, Unity, Ill.; Bailey S. Harrell, Cleves, O.; Moses B. Harrell, Chicago, Ill.; N. W. Graham, Carbondale, Ill.; Moses Foss, Los Angeles, Cal.; Thomas Leary, Kansas City, Mo.; George W. Kendrick, Charleston, Mo.; James Morris, Ullin, Ill.; George McKenzie, Dyersburg, Tenn.; Julius Shessler, Niagara Falls, N. Y.; L. G. Faxon, Paducah, Ky.; Isaac Adler, Cincinnati, O.; Thomas Wilson, Villa Ridge, Ill.; John O'Neil, Odin, Ill.; John H. Mulkey, Metropolis, Ill.; John W. Trover, Birmingham, Ala.; J. B. Humphreys, Chicago, Ill.; Wm. Lyerley, America, Ill.; Geo. W. Reardon, Denver, Col.; John Myers, Birds Point, Mo.; James Ross, Kansas City, Mo.; Edward Gray, Cape Girardeau, Mo.; W. P. Timmons, Springfield, Mo.; Isaac W. Timmons, Winona, Minn.; Wm. Thomas, Chicago, Ill.; Gid. Phillips, Louisville, Ky.; Henry To. Aspin, Champaign, Ill.; Wm. Hunt, St. Paul, Tex.; Samuel Tilden, Kinmundy, Ill.; Harry Ketchum, New York City; Robert J. Hunt, Louisville, Ky.; Henry Brown, St. Louis, Mo.; James Powers, Villa Ridge, Ill.; Joseph Lufkin, Villa Ridge, Ill.; Richard Noyes, San Francisco, Cal.; Capt. Ned Kearney, Natchez, Miss.; George Bellows, Olmstead, Ill.; John Henry, Topeka, Kan.; John Moley, Kansas City, Mo.; J. H. Knickerbocker, Springfield, Ill.; W. S. Lane, Mounds, Ill.; B. F. Parker, Chicago, Ill.; Mat P. Tilden, Centralia, Ill.; Gotlieb Kobler, Grand Tower, Ill.; Andrew Dole, Grand Tower, Ill.; Andrew Ritter, Murphysboro, Ill.; Fred Koehler, Murphysboro, Ill.; Peter Zimmerman, Kansas City, Mo.; Charles Clarke, St. Louis, Mo.; Frank Bedard, St. Louis, Mo.; John Devine, Chester, Ill.; John Newell, Pres't N. Y. Central; Cornelius Willett, Washington, D. C.; and Capt. P. S. Drown, St. Louis, Mo.

POLL BOOK OF THE FIRST CITY ELECTION, HELD MARCH 7, 1857

Poll List City Election

F. B. Dicken
James Martin
Richard Ives
P. Smith
Patrick Green
T. N. Gaffney
Pat Calahan
Jno. Mitton
Thos. Sullivan
N. C. Bridges
Andrew Gary
John Conner
James Riley
D. Mahanny
Mike Fitzpatrick
James Mahony
Thos. Roach
Mike Gallaghan
Wm. H. Scott
Andr. Gray
John Foley
M. O'Brien
Thos. Handy
Levi Stancill
B. Shannessy
Henry Devlin
Thos. Smith
Martin Egan
Pat Conner
James Degear
Mike Gary
James O'Conner
Richard Dugan
George Sloan
R. H. Cunningham
Mike Fitzgerald
F. C. Huber
John Stewart
Pat Burke

John O'Calahan
James Garland
R. Garland
David Warner
T. Hibbard
William Brown
John Lance
Chas. Dotton
Rich'd Nann
David Wright
John McDonald
Moses Foss
James Summerwell
E. Wood
Thos. Mehan
C. Buckley
James Dinan
Robt. Fisher
E. Hay
F. Cowhan
John Ryan
T. Calahan
Mike Gannon
Mike Sullivan
Pat Galvin
T. Roach
J. Sullivan
I. Walls
W. Crownan
Geo. Maguire
Ed. Conner
C. Manly
Grundy Bryant
John McGhee
Thos. Ryan
Dan Connelly
Thos. Devin
John Fitzpatrick
Thomas Green

B. Golden
D. Lahanahan
W. Clavin
I. A. Kooken
W. I. Morgan
Jos. Brankel
Pat. Fitzsimmons
L. G. Faxon
E. Willett
S. Guthrie
James Quinn
M. Fitzgerald
I. M. Moore
James Todd
H. Walker
Wm. Lee
John Powell
J. Twohig
James Crowley
B. Mooney
C. Brice
John Cahil
W. B. Clark
R. Murphy
N. Devore
G. W. McKenzie
C. Morningstar
E. Burns
J. Hogan
John Kelly
J. Johnson
Thos. Lane
I. Callett
James Egan
W. Banks
P. McMannanry
W. Cashman
R. Motherway
W. Newell

P. Fay
C. Boyle
P. Clevin
J. Dunseith
P. Griffin
J. Cain
P. H. Wheeler
W. R. Burke
J. Connell
R. Pyburn
P. C. Cossey
J. Haden
B. Cashman
J. B. Dean
J. Cothnie
M. Norris
J. Sullivan
D. McKinney
John Lane
P. Egan
T. Calahan
John Dailey
H. Derick
T. Mulroy
John Cullen
P. Doud
P. Dolan
J. Sullivan
P. Sweney
W. M. Williams
Charles Johnson
T. J. Wood
John Kahler
A. W. McKay
J. G. Cormick
James Handlin
F. Seavery
John Broderick
Wm. Hank

P. Cope
A. McTigue
Con Conners
Wm. Hunt
Wm. Elliott
T. Manley
C. Shunhge
T. Murphy
Jos. Smith
M. Long
Wm. Shea
D. Roach
J. Calleghan
James Caton
J. Lyons
John Sullivan
John Whaley
I. L. Harrell
Wm. Lonergan
J. W. O'Neal
I. Adler
P. W. Allen
M. McKay
P. Neff
P. Doud
Pat O'Brien
Mike Welsh
Thos. Flynn
A. Krawinkel
S. F. Rand
Jonathan Peck
H. Barringer
J. D. Plause
Peter Stapleton
W. Farnnur
C. Egeny
J. D. G. Pettijohn
M. Ryan
R. B. Rollf
P. McCabe
D. Burke
I. H. Viney
C. Petras
C. Knitz
I. Farnbaker
Wm. Carroll
P. McIlvay
P. Egan
Chas. Coons
C. D. Finch
M. Dignan
M. Thornton
D. Cochoran
James Moore
D. Manahan
B. Leifler
Thos. White
D. Stapleton
M. Fitzgerald

G. W. Rearden
Wm. Simpson
Thos. McDeviney
Henry Riccord
D. McMurtry
I. L. Smith
John McNulty
C. Schmitzdorff
F. Osterloh
J. Farrell
M. Welsh
S. Crow
James Welsh
H. Bourgraff
A. Mulcott
J. E. Lynch
John Cotter
Thos. Mulroney
M. Towers
J. White
M. Mahanny
C. C. Willitt
F. Whitcamp
J. Wilkins
J. Antrim
J. W. Strawhaul
M. Shea
A. Towers
Jno. T. O'Shea
W. Crum
G. L. Rattlemiller
M. P. Tilden
M. Griffie
F. Eble
J. White
S. J. Littlefield
Wm. Garen
W. A. Jonte
S. Fahrenbach
M. R. Hopper
J. Kennedy
Jno. Q. Harmon
W. T. Finch
J. J. Miles
Jno. Myers
L. W. Young
Thos. M. Keagny
C. M. Osteloh
M. Reagen
P. Smidt
G. D. Gorden
L. Lockeryear
W. Stratton
D. Hurd
M. Leftcovitch
F. Malinski
T. McCarthy
R. J. Yost
Jno. Potts

Arthur James
Benj. Smith
John Greenwood
M. Kobbler
Peter Mayo
J. Manahan
M. Galvin
E. Burrows
J. W. Green
John Gill
V. R. Hall
M. W. Parker
H. Gilo
John Maxey
D. C. Stewart
J. H. Kitchill
J. W. Henry
Frank Wall
G. Cable
T. Standing
A. Kelly
A. Phelps
M. C. Learey
John Rady
M. McCarty
M. Hunt
H. H. M. Butts
Jos. Lattinker
W. D. Finch
James Mullitt
Jacob Witchett
I. Maxwell
Dan McLaughlin
Chas. Gayer
D. B. Powers
Robert Miller
M. Ruggaber
Fiddle Fry
John Petercumber
M. G. Stokes
A. H. Fletcher
H. Doyle
K. Brophey
Julius Schusler
Henry Myers
Jacob Fry
J. H. Lufkin
C. F. Watson
C. Steigler
Jno. Howley
Jno. Reed
Jno. Costin
A. Pickman
T. Radigan
C. A. Whaley
T. Smith
W. C. Lewis
A. Ritter
E. Babbs

G. R. Hunt
Roger Finn
J. W. Ritter
H. Rodoff
N. Yocum
M. Hogan
H. H. Davis
W. Pinkston
F. Knowles
O. P. Carnahan
I. Lee
J. C. White
John King
A. Slick
R. J. Billington
R. D. Campbell
John Cannon
James Eightman
D. Divine
M. Phillips
R. C. Kieley
W. C. Sanders
A. T. Smith
G. A. Phillips
W. Drumer
Mike Quinn
I. Lehning
John Hendricks
H. Whitcamp
C. Benjamin
O. Sullivan
S. Rhino
A. Mann
A. Williams
Henry Harris
Fred Tobener
J. F. Aubry
J. Wehn
Wm. Little
G. Gattin
P. Broderick
John Billings
Jno. W. Stewart
Jno. Scheel
J. Rigney
R. T. Napoleon
W. J. Stephens
F. Bross
C. Kobler
S. O'Conner
Geo. Poor
C. Henderson
A. D. Finch
Jacob Grunder
P. Corcoran
S. Tilden
Thos Wilson
H. H. Candee

At an election held in the City of Cairo, in the County of Alexander and State of Illinois, on the Seventh day of March, in the year one thousand eight hundred and fifty-seven the following named persons received the number of votes annexed to their respective names, for the following described offices to-wit: For mayor S. S. Taylor received 211 votes, W. J. Stephens 159 votes, and I. N. Haynie 1 vote. For alderman for first ward, John Howley received 121 votes, P. Stapleton 75 votes, P. Burke 65 votes, C. M. Osterloh 64 votes, T. Wilson 63 votes, J. Cotter 61 votes, G. W. McKenzie 50 votes, J. Greenwood 31 votes, H. H. Candee 70 votes, J. Littlefield 9 votes, W. D. Finch 3 votes, A. Williams 2 votes, D. Burke 1 vote, W. M. Williams 1 vote, S. S. Taylor 1 vote, H. F. Aspen 1 vote, H. Barringer 1 vote, Jas. Stewart 1 vote, and Pat. Smith 1 vote. For alderman for second ward H. Whitcamp received 49 votes, P. Neff 51 votes, H. H. Cunningham 44 votes, R. Frim 44 votes, J. Antrim 41 votes, and G. W. Rearden 39 votes. For alderman for third ward C. A. Whaley received 65 votes, C. Manley 43 votes, M. Egan 43 votes, L. G. Faxon 31 votes, Jas. Summerwell 27 votes, and M. Foss 18 votes. For alderman for fourth ward Wm. Standing received 47 votes, T. N. Gaffney 44 votes, and L. B. Perkins 3 votes.

Certified by P. Corcoran, Thos. Wilson and Samuel Tilden, Judges of the Election. Attested by H. H. Candee and Geo. Killogg, Clerks of the Election.

CITIZENS OF CAIRO, BIOGRAPHICAL SKETCHES OF WHOM ARE CONTAINED IN THE FOLLOWING BOOKS:

In "Biographical Encyclopedia of Illinois," 1875.—Judge William J. Allen, Judge David J. Baker, Judge Fredolin Bross, George Fisher, Judge William H. Green, David T. Linegar, Daniel W. Munn, Alfred B. Safford and Horace Wardner.

In the "United States Biographical Dictionary for Illinois," 1876.—Judge David J. Baker, Judge Fredolin Bross, Robert H. Cunningham, George Fisher, Charles Galigher, Judge William H. Green, William B. Gilbert, Miles F. Gilbert, John D. Gillham, James Johnson, George E. Lounsbury, John H. Oberly, Charles O. Patier, Joe M. Phillips, Horace Wardner, Samuel P. Wheeler and Henry Winter.

In General John M. Palmer's "Bench and Bar of Illinois," 1899.—Judge William N. Butler, Judge William S. Dewey, Miles F. Gilbert, Judge William H. Green, John M. Lansden, Judge John H. Mulkey and Judge Joseph P. Robarts.

In "Historical Encyclopedia of Illinois," 1900.—Judge William J. Allen, Judge William H. Green, Judge Isham N. Haynie and Daniel W. Munn.

In "Memoirs of the Lower Ohio Valley," 1905.—Belfield B. Bradley, George J. Becker, Edward A. Buder, Eberhard Bucher, Christopher Beck, Judge William N. Butler, Lee B. Davis, Edmund S. Dewey, Anthony P. Ehs, Charles Feuchter, Mrs. M. E. Feith, James H. Galligan, William B. Gilbert, Miles F. Gilbert, Miles S. Gilbert, William C. Gilbert, Barry Gilbert, Reed Green, William P. Greaney, John B. Greaney, Charles E. Gregory, Major Edwin W. Halliday, Henry L. Halliday, Henry E. Halliday, Douglas Halliday, John Hodges, Samuel Hastings, John J. Jennelle, William Kluge, John M. Lansden, John A. Miller, L. P. Parker, George H. Pendleton, Joseph B. Reed, John T. Rennie, Ernest H. Riggle, James S. Roach, H. T. Stephens, Elmer Smith, Joseph Steagala, Joseph W. Wenger and Benjamin F. Woodward.

NAMES OF CITIZENS OF CAIRO, BIOGRAPHICAL SKETCHES OF WHOM ARE FOUND IN THE LARGE COUNTY HISTORY. A FEW OF THEM ARE IN PART I, AND THE REMAINDER IN PART V, IN ALPHABETICAL ORDER AS GIVEN THEREIN:

Willliam Alba, Conrad Alba, George M. Alden, Judge William J. Allen, John Antrim, Dr. Daniel Arter, Robert H. Baird, Sanford P. Bennett, Adolph Black, Byron F. Blake, Henry Block, Herman Bloms, Walter L. Bristol, Edward

A. Buder, Henry Hinsdale Candee, Andrew J. Carle, William G. Cary, Benjamin E. Clark, Jefferson M. Clark, Albert C. Coleman, William M. Davidson, Gideon Desrocher, Charles W. Dunning, William Eichhoff, Eugene E. Ellis, Isaac Farnbaker, George Fisher, Nicholas Feith, Judge Miles A. Gilbert, Hon. William B. Gilbert, Hon. Miles F. Gilbert, Jacob A. Goldstine, J. J. Gordon, Judge Wiliam H. Green, Horace A. Hannon, A. Halley, Edgar C. Harrell, George W. Henricks, Jesse Hinkle, John Hodges, John Howley, Cicero N. Hughes, Jacob Klein, Francis Kline, William Kluge, Michael Kobler, Christian Koch, John Koehler, John A. Koehler, Frederick Korsmeyer, Frank Kratky, Charles Lame, Charles Lancaster, Thomas Lewis, Hon. David T. Linegar, Andrew Lohr, William Lonergan, William Ludwig, Jacob Martin, James S. McGahey, James W. McKinney, Herman Meyers, Judge John A. Mulkey, William M. Murphy, Peter Neff, Judge H. K. S. O'Melveny, George F. Ort, Christopher M. Osterloh, Miles W. Parker, Charles O. Patier, Alamanzer O. Phelps, George B. Poor, Thomas Porter, Nathaniel Prouty, John T. Rennie, Wood Rittenhouse, Joseph H. Rittenhouse, John H. Robinson, Samuel Rosenwater, James Ross, Alfred Boardman Safford, Herman Sander, William G. Sandusky, Peter Saup, Sol. A. Silver, Paul G. Schuh, James R. Smith, Robert Smyth, George W. Strode, Frank W. Stophlet, Simpson H. Taber, James M. Totten, Francis Vincent, Harry Walker, Judge George W. Wall, Jacob Walter, Henry Wells, Samuel P. Wheeler, Charles W. Wheeler, Scott White, Dr. E. W. Whitlock, William M. Williams, George D. Williamson, Thomas Wilson, Henry Winter, Maj. William Wolfe, William Wood, John Wood, C. R. Woodward, Judge Reuben S. Yocum.

Persons Resident in Cairo January First, 1910, Who Were Residents Prior to 1861

Mrs. Mary Axley, Mrs. Elizabeth Arter, Charles F. Arter, John M. Antrim, Mrs. Marie Bouchet, Jean Bouchet, Mrs. Mary A. Byrne, Mrs. Fransina Baird, Henry Baird, Mrs. Mary Barry, Herman F. Brinkmeyer, Frank Bemis, Chris Bemis, Mrs. George Clark, Mrs. Mary Cannon, Mrs. Mary Cuhl, Mrs. M. Cahill, Pat Cahill, Mrs. Lizzie Collins, Dan. Callahan, John Clancy, John C. Crowley, Frank Carle, Mrs. Julia Davis, Mrs. Peter Donnelly, Michael Driscoll, Mrs. Mary Ehlman, Charles Eichhoff, Mrs. Angeline Fry, Frank Fry, George M. Fry, John W. C. Fry, Mrs. Anna Feuchter, Mrs. Wilhelmina Frank, Maurice J. Farnbaker, Sol. Farnbaker, Mrs. Annie M. Guion, Mrs. John Glade, Mrs. Anastasia Gayer, Mrs. Josephine Gilhofer, Mrs. Ann Gorman, Charles Galigher, John P. Glynn, William B. Gilbert, Mrs. Henry Hixon, Henry Hixon, Mrs. Mary A. Howley, Mrs. A. Halley, Mrs. Fred Hofheinz, Mrs. Lizzie Hubbard, Horace A. Hannon, Charles W. Henderson, Daniel Hartman, John Hogan, John P. Hogan, John S. Hacker, James Higlen, John Haffley, Mrs. A. M. Koch, Mrs. Louisa Kleb, Mrs. Mary Kline, William Kluge, George G. Koehler, Louis H. Kaha, Mrs. Catherine Lincoln, Mrs. Margaret Lampert, Mrs. Mary A. Loflin, Mrs. Georgia Lippitt, Phil Lehning, Sr., Jacob Lehning, Andrew Lohr, Mrs. Xavier Martin, Miss Anna Malinski, Mrs. Susan Malinski, Mrs. Isabel Marston, Thomas Meehan, Patrick Mahoney, A. McTigue, Calvin V. Neff, A. William Neff, Mrs. John O'Shea, Mrs. Catherine Osterloh, Charles Osterloh, Samuel Orr, Mrs. Henry C. Partee, Henry C. Partee, Patrick J. Purcell, Nathaniel Prouty, James Quinn, Mrs. Katherine Smith, Mrs. Frances Stewart, Mrs. Hannah Sullivan, Mrs. Anna E. Safford, Mrs. Hulda Steagala, Mrs. M. Summerwell, Mrs. Kate Stapleton, Mrs. Hermine Schulze, Mrs. Margaret Smith, John Sullivan, John Sheehan, William H. Sexton, Con Sheehan, Peter Saup, Thomas J. Sloo, Egbert A. Smith, Cyrus Smith, Julius Serbian, Mrs. James Tuttle, Mrs. Kate Thomas, John Y. Turner, Mrs. Virginia Vincent, Henry Vincent, Minnie Vincent, Mrs. Felitza Walder, Mrs. Elizabeth Walsh, Miss Josie Winter, Gus Winter, Claude Winter, William Winter, Mrs. L. E. Williamson, Mrs. Kate Wentworth, Mrs. Nick Williams, Gus Williams, William M. Williams, George Wilson, William White, Isaac Walder, George Yocum. Mrs. Elizabeth (Smith) Walsh has the distinction of having resided in Cairo longer than any other person now here. According to the records of St. Patrick's Church, she was born July 14, 1843.

THE LYNCHINGS OF WILLIAM JAMES, A COLORED MAN, AND OF HENRY SALZNER, A WHITE MAN, ON THE NIGHT OF NOVEMBER 11, 1909, James for assaulting and then murdering Anna Pelly, a young white woman, on the night of November 8, 1909, and Salzner for the alleged murder of Mary Salzner, his wife, on the 18th day of August, 1909. This occurrence so revived in the minds of the public everywhere the fact that Cairo had long borne a hard name that it seems proper for me to speak of it in this chapter, much as I would like to pass it by. Such an event, adding to the notoriety of the city and followed so soon by its very natural results, could not be left unnoticed by any one pretending to write a history of the city. I cannot do more, however, than to give a very condensed statement of the facts. James had lived in Cairo a number of years and was at the time engaged in driving a team for one of the business houses of the city. He was an unusually muscular and strong man, and above the average in intelligence for one of his race. He seems to have lain in wait for his victim and to have seized her within a rod or two of her home and carried her into an unfrequented alley, two or three hundred feet distant, and there choked her to death by the use of pieces of a flour sack. She was employed as a saleswoman in a dry-goods store in the city, and was last seen as she alighted from a street car two or three blocks from her home. It was early in the evening, but dark and raining. The family supposed she had gone to spend the night with one of her young lady friends and the crime was not discovered until the next morning. I cannot give the details of the search with the aid of blood-hounds nor of the arrest of James and of the two colored women at whose houses he spent parts of Monday night, nor of the statements of one of them respecting pieces of flour sacks similar to those found at the place of the crime and at the undertaker's. For very full information, see the "Cairo Bulletin" and the "Evening Citizen" of November 9th, 10th, 11th and 12th, 1909. He and the colored women denied knowledge of the crime. He was held by the police the remainder of Tuesday and until the evening of Wednesday, when they delivered him into the custody of Sheriff Frank E. Davis, who, fearing mob violence, at once took him from the city on an Illinois Central train. He left the train at Dongola, twenty-seven miles north of Cairo, fearing violence from assemblying people at Anna, where Miss Pelly had formerly lived. He went eastward with the intention of reaching and taking a train on the Cleveland, Cincinnati, Chicago & St. Louis Railway; but before he could do so, he was intercepted by a mob from Cairo, which had seized a train of the railroad company and gone up the road to the place they were told he was approaching. They found the sheriff, his deputy, Thomas A. Fuller, and the prisoner in the woods near the railroad, and taking the prisoner from them brought him to Cairo and to the intersection of Commercial Avenue and Eighth Street, and there, after trying to hang him to the steel arches spanning the intersection of those streets and finding it slow and difficult work, they shot him to death, and then dragged the body to the place of the crime, a mile distant, and there burned it. Proceeding thence to the court-house, on Twentieth Street, where Salzner was confined on an indictment charging him with the murder of Mrs. Salzner, they broke down his cell and took him a square or two distant and there hung him to a telegraph pole, and then after shooting the body many times, they dispersed. It may be stated here, but of course for no purpose of extenuation, that no one else was molested, nor was any property injured, save the injury and damage at the court-house.

The news of the crime and the search for the criminal spread rapidly over the adjacent country and brought to Cairo large numbers of people, too many of whom were quite ready to join the Cairo contingent for purposes of vengeance. The numbers increased during the long three days, but little was done to counteract the constantly growing feeling that the severest punishment should be dealt out to the criminal and in the most summary way. The number of the leaders and active members of the mob was very large and probably about equally composed of men of Illinois, Kentucky and Missouri.

James seems to have confessed to no one but members of the mob, and not fully to any of them. The most he said seems to have been that he was not the only guilty person. He may have named Alexander as a partner in his crime. No large number of people in the city regretted the mob's disposition of James. A like, but a somewhat modified statement, may be made relative to Salzner. The horror of James' crime seemed to touch every home in the city. What processes of reasoning hurried through the minds of the people it is useless to conjecture. What they thought about the law taking its course, or about the thwarting of the law, or the slow and uncertain proceedings of the courts and the failures of justice therein, or of the dangers white women were in from the debased negroes of the town, is also conjectural. To their one question, what would you do had she been your daughter they wanted no reply nor did they often get any. Many persons think themselves able to state the one single cause of an event, when in fact there may have been many. In this case, there were probably many causes tending to produce the mob-like feeling in the minds of many people; but the fact that the victim was a young white woman and the assailant and murderer a black brute of the city would have put a strain upon any community not altogether congealed in its own complaisant self-sufficiency.

After a calamity, it is always easy to tell what should have been done to prevent it. Had the persons criticized been given the opportunity of viewing the matter just as their critics had, there would have been little or no room for criticism. This was the first occurrence of the kind in the city of Cairo. The Joe Spencer affair of 1855, detailed in Moses B. Harrell's history and the "History of Alexander, Union and Pulaski Counties," could not be called a lynching in any sense of the word.

All that can be justly said in criticism of the city and county officers is that they should have expected a mob almost from the outstart. They were intent on finding the criminal but seem to have overlooked the matter of his protection when found. This should have gone along with every step of their search. They should have known better than others the state of feeling in the city. James could not have been gotten away too soon. His arrest and detention here three days and then his taking from the city convinced the gathering mob that the officers regarded him as the criminal. The crime was so horrid, so fiendish, so like the crime of Seay J. Miller, the Springfield negro, who killed the two Ray daughters down in Kentucky just north of Bardwell July 7, 1893, that they should have known the impossibility of their protecting James when it became known that he was probably the guilty person. Governor Deneen, it may also be remarked, might have been called upon much sooner.

We need not comment upon the evil that comes to communities which tolerate or connive at mob violence. Salzner, who had been in jail for a long time and whose crime, whatever it was, was generally and fully known, would not have been lynched had not the mob lynched James; nor would the attempted lynching of the negro John Pratt have taken place in February, 1910, and the consequent loss of life in the attempt, had not the lynchings in November occurred. These occurrences of November and February, and the divers and sundry results growing out of them, together with the opprobrium cast upon our city, set before us in the clearest light the evil that flows from a community taking or allowing others to take the law into their own hands. The solecism of attempting to enforce the law by its most flagrant violation is too obvious for comment.

CHAPTER XXXIII

CAIRO AS A BUSINESS PLACE OR POINT—THE FUTURE OF THE CITY

THE geographical position of Cairo is certainly as favorable for business purposes as nature has anywhere afforded the people of the country, at least so far as inland points are concerned. The low site and the abrading rivers have been great drawbacks. As to these features of our situation, it has always been a question of money, much money, to put us on an equality with other places. They have no doubt turned away men and capital, which would have sought the place time and time again, had these deterrent causes not existed. They have always been with us and will so continue, until we attain such strength in population and wealth as will make the burden to counteract them comparatively light. They are great disadvantages, clearly seen to be such, when we consider what the situation would be, had there been a higher and an unyielding point of land here. This was the reason given by General George Rogers Clark in 1779 for establishing Fort Jefferson on the Kentucky side just below us instead of at this place. But after all, the advantages of the location will always outweigh its disadvantages, although the same have long seemed to be about equally balanced.

A sufficient time has elapsed to show that Cairo is a good business point. Its trade has been and is chiefly with the south. It is largely a southern city. Its local trade has never been large. What the prosperous and strong cities of other parts of the state have had as their chief and sometimes their sole reliance, we have had here in the minimum. The rivers have their advantages. They make Cairo what it is; but they have been as walls encompassing the city and shutting out local trade, which would otherwise have been a constant source of growth and prosperity. Every stranger remarks upon the fine, not to say the wonderful geographical position, and ask why there isn't a large, even a great city here. Cairo business men express different views about the matter. They concede that the question is a very pertinent one, but their answers are sometimes far from satisfactory. Let me give here a few lines from a man who was here during the war, and who a few years since wrote a fine book in which Cairo is often mentioned. General Clark E. Carr, in "The Illini," heretofore quoted from, writes as follows, on pages 19, 20 and 418:

" 'So you think, General, that Chicago will be the great city of Illinois,' my father asked. 'Not at all, sir, not at all. Chicago will be a great city, but Cairo will be *the* great city. Look at her position, on the great Father of Waters, at its confluence with the Ohio! Think of the trade and commerce that is already coming up the Mississippi from New Orleans and all the parts of the south. Think of all that comes down the Ohio from Pittsburg, Cincinnati, and Louisville, and the other cities, besides what comes from the Tennessee and Cumberland. Think of all that will come down from the upper Mississippi and the Missouri;—and all this to meet at Cairo! It will be the largest city on this continent; and the time is sure to come when Cairo will be the largest city in the world.' "

. . . .

"As we rounded the point at Cairo into the Ohio River, I asked the General if he remembered prophesying, on our boat trip around the lakes, that Cairo would be a great city. 'That was before the days of railways,' he replied. 'Had there been no railways, my prophesy would have proven correct. Cairo possesses more natural advantages for inland water transportation than any other of the west; but the railways have taken the business elsewhere. There is another thing in which I was mistaken. I thought the great prairies could never be settled, and if they were, the prairie land would be worth far less than the timber land. It now seems that we were all mistaken, and that the prairies could all be brought under cultivation, and that the best lands are the prairie lands.' "

How much of General Carr's book is matter of fact and how much is matter of fiction I do not know. I give the above simply as another strong evidence of what the expectations of the public were regarding our city of Cairo, which has proved such a disappointment to so many people and for so long a time. The time has probably passed for making Cairo a great or a relatively large city. Time and opportunities for cities, like time and opportunities for individuals, pass by. Large cities absorb, not to say exhaust, the population of large districts of country and therefore large cities are found only at considerable distances apart. There are too many large cities, comparatively, near us now to justify any hope that Cairo will ever attain to anything like what was expected of it half a century ago. All that can be hoped for now is a wholesome steady growth, which will assure a population and business that can give it something of a commanding place among the more important cities of the valley of the Mississippi.

Further than as just stated, we cannot venture an opinion about the future of the city, except only to point to the picture of the Concord facing the beginning of this chapter. That war vessel in the harbor means only one thing to us, and that is, that if the Mississippi River were deepened or otherwise improved, as the interests of this great valley seem to require, instead of one sea-going vessel seen in our harbor here, there would be a score of them. The river should be what it is not now, a great commercial highway, worthy of the twenty-five states whose waters it carries to the sea.

There is now no probability that the site of the city will ever be raised to or near to the level of the surrounding levees, as was urged by Judge Miles A. Gilbert and was for a while intended fifty to sixty years ago; and hence the imperative need of their maintenance to a grade above any and all floods. What these may be, or how high they may rise, no one can tell. There are many contingencies. For the maintenance of the levees we may regard ourselves as amply able; but there is another matter of much greater importance; and that is, the safe maintenance of the site of the city against abrasion by the rivers. I have spoken of this once or twice elsewhere. It should be kept constantly in mind as the first of all things concerning our city. While we will be able to bear, from time to time, a certain part of the expense incident to the preservation to the river banks or shores, the erosion may at times become so great as to require government aid. We hardly know what we would have done or how we would have escaped, had not the government come to our aid thirty to thirty-five years ago, and at later times. We can in most cases depend, I suppose, upon such aid; but that we should need it at all or at any time is not a very pleasant contemplation. Our interests may now and then be regarded by the government authorities as differing from the interests of navigation or river improvement. Our stone wall fronting the Ohio reminds us that our whole attention must not be given to the Mississippi; but the latter river is by far the chief source of concern. Its long straight stretch toward us, for miles above the city, presents a kind of threatening aspect that we would be glad to see changed. It has moved backward and forward, now away from us and again toward us, but its general tendency, for seventy-five years, has been to the eastward. Pushed over to the west or prevented from moving eastward, the great river has turned somewhat aside and to the south and has been for years devouring the Missouri shore and uniting with the Ohio further down. I do not know that it is so; but it would seem that there is a tendency of uniting rivers to move their point of junction further in the direction of the united streams. If this is true, and there are no other intervening causes, the Mississippi will continue to draw the junction point further to the southward, leaving the Egbert A. Smith possessions entirely undisturbed This may somewhat relieve the pressure upon our western and most threatened border. But it is very conjectural, indeed. When one takes a map or chart of the Mississippi River, he will see both above and below us that there is no discoverable *rule* of movement in that great river. Bend after bend, of varying lengths, everywhere appear, defying all reasons for their existence.

There are, however, so many interests represented here now that we can safely hope that all the needed aid will be forthcoming in ample time. The large interests of the government and those of the great railroad companies, not to mention any other sources of power and influence, ought to forbid any serious apprehension of danger. And yet our location or situation is highly peculiar, and requires from us an attention and care, from which almost all other places in the country are free.

If we discharge faithfully our duty in respect to our levees and river banks, we can safely depend upon the general movement of things elsewhere and quite beyond us for our much greater growth, if such we are to have. River improvement on a large scale is seemingly growing in favor, and should it materialize in proportion to its importance, Cairo may well hope to share more largely in its benefits than almost any other city in the great valley. It is not, however, very clear, at this time, that a depth of fourteen feet, or anything close thereto, can be had and maintained to points north of us, or even to this place, to the satisfaction of the country at large, whose means are to be devoted to the enterprise. It will be a great valley movement in which our own interests here will be regarded as merely incidental—incidental, it is true, but great, nevertheless. It will not be long until the valley of the Mississippi contains a population as large as the present population of the whole country—a hundred millions and Illinois ten millions thereof. This may be too far hence to be made much of now; but we hope this for the future of our city.

It would be wrong for me to omit saying that Cairo's future depends, in one important sense at least, upon the people of the city themselves. They cannot change its geographical features, nor its topographical features very much; but they can and should make it a place from which good and desirable people will not turn away except for business reasons or supposed business disadvantages.

I have desired to keep the size of this book down to very moderate proportions, but have not been able to do so. It seems large for the size of the city; but it must be remembered that while a small city it has had quite a remarkable history. Few cities of the state have been the objects of more legislation or of more documentary transactions of almost every kind. It is the history of three several attempts to start a city, one in 1818, one in 1836, and one in 1846, out of the latter of which the present city has grown. Had I used all the materials collected and which might well have found a place in the book it would have been very much larger. I may also add that I have probably, here and there, devoted too much space to certain matters and too little or perhaps none at all to others of greater importance. Whether this be so or not, I can truly say that there are very many matters of more or less importance which have had to remain unnoticed in order to keep the book within the desired limits.

TABLE OF TEMPERATURES, ANNUAL PRECIPITATIONS, AND HIGHEST AND LOWEST WATER IN THE RIVERS

	Maximum Temperature	Date of Maximum Temperature	Minimum Temperature	Date of Minimum Temperature	Annual Precipitation	Greatest Amount of Precipitation in 24 Hours	Date of Greatest Amount of Precipitation in 24 Hours	Highest Water	Date of Highest Water	Lowest Water	Date of Lowest Water
1871	...	....	..	....	.....	....	....	....	....	1.0	Dec. 24
1872	99	Aug. 25, 26	-7	Dec. 24	26.52	2.50	Apr. 8	....	....	0.5	Dec. 22
1873	96	July 15	-8	Jan. 29	50.86	2.53	Jan. 15, 16	42.6	Feb. 26	3.7	Oct. 16, 17
1874	101	Aug. 10–13	6	Jan. 15	47.63	2.83	Feb. 20, 21 Mar. 5, 6	47.3	Apr. 26–27	3.0	Nov. 10, 13
1875	96	July 16	-11	Jan. 9	52.93	2.74	Nov. 22, 23	45.2	Aug. 7	5.3	Jan. 25
1876	97	July 19	0	Dec. 9, 30	55.60	5.17	Jan. 17, 18	46.4	Apr. 6	0.3	Dec. 30
1877	94	July 5	-4	Jan. 9	39.47	2.10	July 29	40.6	Apr. 14	1.1	Jan. 1
1878	96	July 9	4	Dec. 25	41.76	2.21	Apr. 19, 20	37.1	Apr. 29	6.0	Oct. 18, 22
1879	96	July 10, 11	-6	Jan. 4	45.41	4.97	June 27, 28	36.5	Dec. 31	2.6	Oct. 9, 10
1880	94	July 14, 15	-3	Dec. 29	49.56	2.35	May 20, 21	44.6	Mar. 21–23	5.7	Nov. 29
1881	103	Aug. 12	0	Jan. 14	32.13	2.01	Dec. 13	45.8	Apr. 19, 20	5.3	Sept. 7–9
1882	94	June 25	4	Dec. 7	61.58	4.24	May 9	51.8	Feb. 25, 26	7.3	Dec. 18, 19
1883	92	Aug. 22	7	Jan. 21	52.58	3.07	Oct. 18	52.2	Feb. 26, 27	4.7	Sept. 30
1884	92	June 23 July 3	-16	Jan. 5	51.66	2.90	Sept. 29	51.8	Feb. 21, 22, 24	7.1	Sept. 23
1885	96	July 30	-4	Jan. 22	31.99	1.70	Dec. 8, 9	39.0	Jan. 25, 26	8.4	Oct. 20
1886	97	Aug. 17	-9	Jan 9	37.98	1.97	Nov. 16, 17	51.0	Apr. 18, 19	3.8	Nov. 11, 12
1887	98	July 30	-1	Jan. 2	26.75	1.81	Dec. 31	48.6	Mar. 9, 10	2.0	Dec. 31
1888	97	Aug. 2	0	Jan. 16	41.90	2.04	July 17	45.3	Apr. 3–6	1.8	Jan. 1
1889	91	July 13	6	Feb. 23	37.74	2.96	Nov. 7, 8	34.5	June 24	2.5	Oct. 22, 23
1890	96	June 30	11	Mar. 1	50.53	2.47	Feb. 24, 25	48.8	Mar. 12, 13	8.7	Dec. 25
1891	93	June 3	14	Nov. 29	39.56	2.43	Nov. 16	46.2	Mar. 4–6	2.0	Oct. 10–13
1892	94	July 25	0	Jan. 20	38.71	2.80	Aug. 11, 12	48.3	Apr. 28	3.9	Oct. 27–30
1893	94	July 28	0	Jan. 15	48.79	3.03	June 2, 3	49.3	May 9–13	4.7	Sept. 5 Oct. 31
1894	100	Aug. 13	-4	Jan. 25	30.51	1.69	Feb. 7, 8	37.0	Feb. 16	2.9	Nov. 1, 2, 3, 5
1895	95	June 3	-9	Feb. 8	33.57	2.09	June 15	33.1	Jan. 22	1.1	Nov. 5, 6
1896	98	July 30	8	Jan. 4	39.36	3.16	May 16, 17	39.2	Apr. 13	5.6	Sept. 16
1897	98	July 31	4	Jan. 26	44.10	4.59	June 22, 23	51.7	Mar. 25–28	2.5	Oct. 20–29
1898	94	July 2	7	Dec. 14	48.66	4.42	Sept. 20 Oct. 1	49.8	Apr. 6	7.6	Oct. 10
1899	97	Sept. 6	-14	Feb. 13	42.42	3.46	June 13	46.2	Mar. 30 Apr. 4	3.0	Oct. 15, 16, 27
1900	97	Aug. 21	0	Feb. 17	36.89	2.88	June 7, 8	39.2	Mar. 17	5.8	Sept. 21, 22
1901	106	July 23	-4	Dec. 20	31.68	3.36	July 29, 30	43.2	May 2	2.9	Nov. 21-2-7-9
1902	98	Aug. 3	7	Jan. 27	33.07	2.47	Dec. 14, 15	42.2	Mar. 17	7.3	Sept. 26
1903	95	July 11	-1	Feb. 17	32.91	1.64	Feb. 14, 15	50.6	Mar. 15–17	2.9	Dec. 20
1904	93	Aug. 25	1	Jan. 26	32.00	2.61	Jan. 21, 22	49.1	Apr. 5	3.2	Dec. 25, 26
1905	94	June 18	-7	Feb. 13	39.48	3.96	June 28	38.6	May 24	8.2	Feb. 4
1906	92	June 29	3	Feb. 6	46.92	3.70	Nov. 17	46.9	Apr. 9	12.0	Nov. 12–5–7
1907	97	July 25	10	Jan. 26	45.58	2.68	Feb. 23, 24	50.4	Jan. 27	9.5	Nov. 1
1908	96	Aug. 17	10	Feb. 2	38.47	2.83	Feb. 13, 14	45.6	Mar. 18	4.3	Oct. 17–19
1909	99	Aug. 28	4	Dec. 30	43.05	3.20	Feb. 22, 23	47.3	Mar. 17	7.0	Oct. 15, 16

ACKNOWLEDGMENTS

IN almost all cases I have given the names of the authors from whom I have quoted. Where they are not given, it will be observed that the matters stated are of such a general historic nature as to require no reference to authors. Hence it is, there are no footnotes nor anything in the nature of a bibliography.

I am indebted to many persons for favors shown me in the prosecution of my work. Mayor George Parsons gave me every opportunity to examine the books and records of the Trustees of the Cairo City Property and of the Trustees of the Cairo Trust Property, the former extending back as far as the year 1846, and embracing some papers and records coming over from the Holbrook administration of 1836 to 1846. The Hon. William B. Gilbert, whose father, Judge Miles A. Gilbert, knew all about Cairo from 1836 to 1851, furnished me the photograph of his father from which the picture herein was made; also the map of Cairo, of 1838, showing the line of the proposed canal from Cache River down to the point, and also the blank certificate of stock, such as was issued by the old Cairo City & Canal Company. Mr. Michael J. Howley has rendered me invaluable services in a great many matters and ways. His work has so aided me that but for it I would have had much more to do or the work would probably have been left undone. I am indebted to the following named persons for pictures of the persons named from which their photogravures were made: To Mrs. Joseph W. Wenger, for the photograph of her grandfather, Col. Samuel Staats Taylor; to Mrs. John S. Aisthorpe, for the photograph of Captain William P. Halliday, taken probably in the year 1874, when Mr. William Winter, whom so many of us remember, had his art rooms on Sixth Street between the two avenues; to Dr. B. N. Bond, of Bellingham, Washington, for a photograph copy of the oil painting of his father, Governor Bond, painted by Gilbert Stuart, of Washington, D. C., in 1812; to Dr. W. W. Kane, of Pinckneyville, for the picture of Senator Elias Kent Kane, his grandfather; to Mrs. General John A. Logan, of Washington, for the portrait from which the picture of Judge Alexander M. Jenkins was taken; to Mr. Sidney S. Breese, of Springfield, for the photograph from which the picture of Judge Sidney Breese, his grandfather, was taken. Baroness Caroline Von Roques, who, in the month of September, 1909, was residing temporarily at Stamford, Connecticut, and who is now deceased, sent me a beautiful small picture of her father, Darius Blake Holbrook, and it was from that picture that the fine picture herein of him was taken. The pictures of the two old gunboats are copies from old photographs kindly furnished me by Mr. E. C. Halliday; and the pictures of the Cairo-Kaskaskia bank bills are from the original bills, now the property of Mr. James H. Galligan.

I hope it will not be regarded as out of place for me to speak of the collection of books, maps, papers, documents, clippings, etc., now in Mayor Parsons' offices as the representative of the Trustees. Though given every opportunity for examination, I found the work entirely too hard to admit of very extensive or thorough searches. It would take two persons a month or two or more to go over them and select and catalogue all that they might find deserving of preservation. Many of us knew what Col. Taylor's custom or habit was in this respect, but no one would suppose that the collections were so extensive and all in such a good state of preservation. I do not know what Mayor Parsons or the Trustees will be able to do with them. I only know that when he or any one else undertakes the work of assortment it will be found an exceedingly laborious one.

In the course of my work I have collected a large number of interesting documents which I had hoped to include in an appendix; but I found that to do so would enlarge the book to twice its present size, and hence their omission. Among them are a number of maps and plats. Could the city or the public library management take charge of them and have the same printed and bound in some comparatively cheap form, it would well justify the work and expense. At all events, those I have and the large number belonging to the Trustees ought to be preserved in our public library in some suitable shape or manner. I am sure Mr. Parsons would heartily favor such a course. Such matters can be postponed only at the risk of partial or entire loss of interesting historical information. Mr. Michael J. Howley, who has for a long time done so much in the way of gathering and printing in our city papers interesting matters of local history, could perhaps do more than any one else in furthering such an undertaking as this.

INDEX

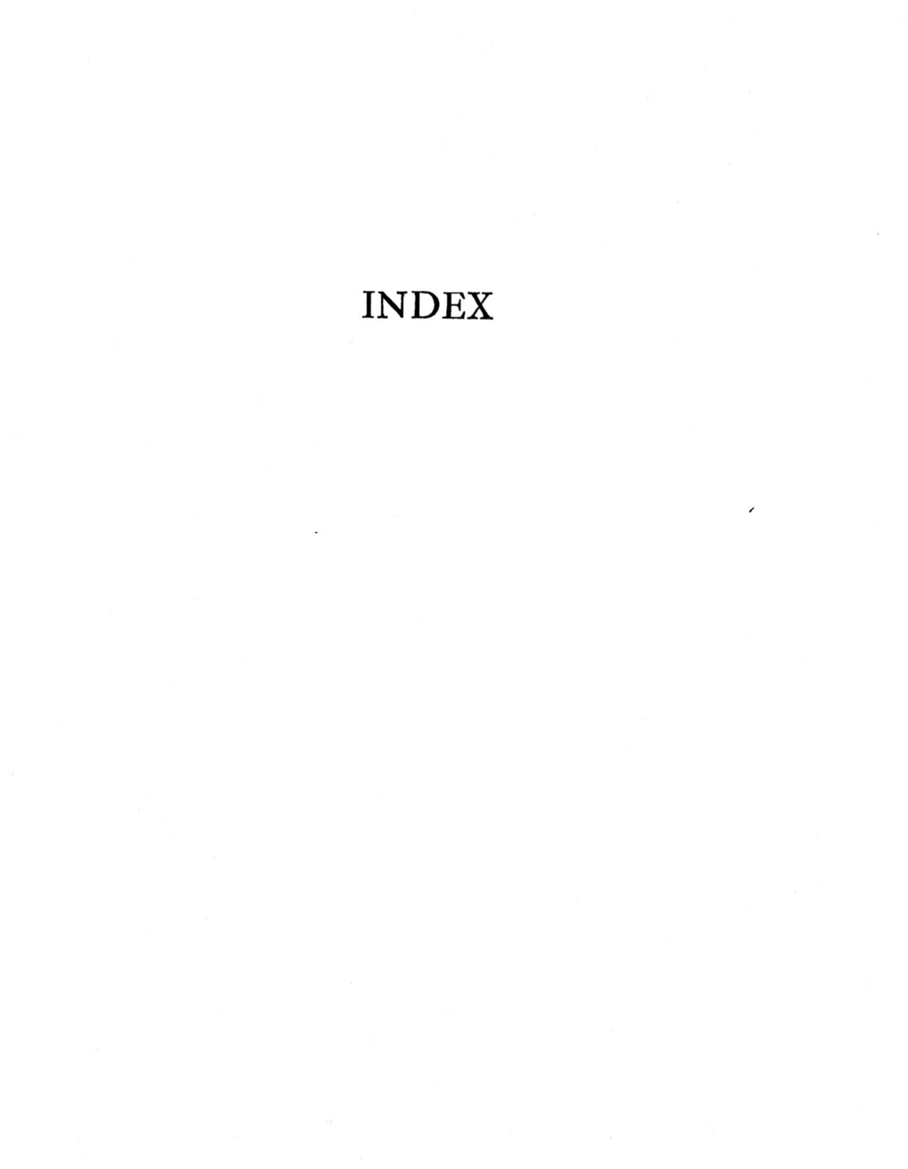

INDEX

B

C

H

I

S

T

NOTE: Pages 268 and 271 to 276 contain lists of names of several hundred other residents of Cairo, most of them of many years ago. To have given them in the Index would have been but a repetition of the same.

LIST OF SPONSORS

OF THIS EDITION

Alexander-Pulaski U.S. Bicentennial Commission

Wolffe Berbling
Del Black
Mr. & Mrs. Miles Bonner
Mr. & Mrs. O. T. Booker
Boyd Butler
Lynn Byrd
Bill Cammack
Edna Capoot
Brenda Cobbs
Laura Maude Connell
Janet Currier
M. C. Currier
Mr. & Mrs. James Dale
Mrs. Odie Dale
Mr. & Mrs. Danny Dean
William P. Egan
Martha Evers
Mr. & Mrs. Owen Evers
Donald Gertis
Lucille Gertis
Ethel Hartman
Mr. & Mrs. Miles Hartman
Rita Helen Hartmann
Mrs. Charles Hood
Mrs. Mickie Jones
Howard E. Keller
Jed Keller
Phyllis Ledford
Fred Ent Lehning
Amanda Lutz
Carole Magnuson
Jo K. Marchildon
Edna Moreland
Guyla Moreland
Michael Moss
Grace Moyers
Ralph Myers
Mr. & Mrs. Russell Ogg
Mr. & Mrs. Solomon Parker
Mr. & Mrs. Edward Pawlisch
Marilyn Phillips
Jack Pomeroy
Curtis Profilet
Delores Raub
Dr. A. L. Robinson, M.D.
Booker T. Robinson
Henry Schnaare
M. R. Simpson
Martha Smith
Timothy R. Sowers
Mr. & Mrs. Ed Spatz
Mrs. Don Taylor
Halley N. Thistlewood
Gloria Thurston
Cathryn Vick
Hon. & Mrs. James Walder
Karen Wallace
Mary Pat Whitis
James Dean Williams
Hon. & Mrs. Fred Winkler
Mrs. J. Mercer Woodward

Southern Illinois University Bicentennial Committee

Richard Bradley
Pete Brown
Tom Busch
Boyd Butler
Charles Daugherty
Michael Dingerson
Joe Goodman
Clifford Harper
Doris Hofer
Robert House
Stephen Jackson
Rex Karnes

Ralph McCoy
James McKeown
Archibald McLeod
T. Richard Mager
Herb Meyer
A. B. Mifflin
Thomas Mitchell
Malvin Moore
Emmet Pearson
Frank Rackerby
Carroll Riley
David Rochelle
Connie Rosenlieb
John Y. Simon
Vernon Sternberg
Charles Tenney
Tom Watson

Board of County Commissioners of Alexander County

Norman R. Hughes, *Chairman*
Chris Eugene Farris
James Wissinger

And

Robert L. Lansden